FIGHTING WORDS

FIGHTING WORDS

COMPETING VOICES FROM THE PACIFIC WAR

Sean Brawley, Chris Dixon and Beatrice Trefalt

GREENWOOD PRESS
An Imprint of ABC-CLIO, LLC

A B C 🦅 C L I O

Santa Barbara, California • Denver, Colorado • Oxford, England

First published in 2009 by Greenwood Press

1 2 3 4 5 6 7 8 9 10

Introduction and Compilation © Dr. Sean Brawley, Dr. Chris Dixon,
Dr. Beatrice Trefalt 2009

ABC-CLIO, LLC
130 Cremona Drive, P.O. Box 1911
Santa Barbara, California 93116-1911

British Library Cataloguing-in-Publication Data: a catalogue record for this book
is available from the British Library

Library of Congress Cataloguing-in-Publication Data

Competing voices from the Pacific War : fighting words / edited by Sean Brawley,
Chris Dixon and Beatrice Trefalt.
    p. cm.—(Fighting words)
    Includes bibliographical references and index.
    ISBN 978-1-84645-010-5
    1. World War, 1939-1945–Campaigns–Pacific Area.   2. World War, 1939-1945–
Personal narratives.   3. World War, 1939-1945–Japan.   I. Dixon, C. J. (Chris J.).
II. Brawley, Sean, 1966-.   III. Trefalt, Beatrice.

    D767.C615 2009
    940.54–dc22
                                                                    2008039320
    ISBN 978-1-84645-010-5 (hardback)

Designed by Fraser Muggeridge studio
Typeset by TexTech International

To

Gloria and Reg Pritchard
Tom Davin
Ngaio Trefalt

CONTENTS

SERIES FOREWORD

Fighting Words is a unique new series aimed at a broad audience, from college-level professors and undergraduates to high-school teachers, students and the general reader. Each volume in this series focuses on a unique historical controversy, told through first-hand accounts from the diverse perspectives of both the victors and the vanquished. The series is designed to introduce readers to a broad range of competing narratives about the past, giving voices to those often left silent in the secondary literature.

Each volume offers competing perspectives through relatively short primary documents, such as newspaper articles, contemporary chronicles, excerpts from participants' letters or memoirs, as well as other carefully selected sources; brief introductions provide the necessary background information and context to help guide readers through the disparate accounts. Where necessary, key documents are reproduced in their entirety. However, most of the documents are brief in nature, and sharp in content, which will help to promote general classroom discussion and debate. The inclusion of vivid and colourful accounts from the participants themselves, combined with other primary sources from all sides, gives the series an exciting and engaging flavour.

The *Fighting Words* series is designed to promote meaningful discussion and debate about the past. Furthermore, the volumes in this series encourage readers to think critically about the evidence that historians use, or ignore, to reconstruct an understanding of that past. Each volume will challenge accepted assumptions about the topics covered, and readers will question the nature of primary sources, the motivations, agendas and perspectives of the authors, and the silences inherent in all of the sources. Ultimately, readers will be left to ponder the question, whose history is this?

J. Michael Francis

ABOUT THE SERIES EDITOR

Dr J. Michael Francis received his PhD in 1998 from the University of Cambridge, where he specialised in colonial Latin American history. Since then, he has taught at the University of North Florida, where he is an associate professor of history. He has written numerous articles on the history of early-colonial New Granada (Colombia). In 2006, he edited a three-volume reference work called *Iberia and the Americas: Culture, Politics, and History* (ABC-CLIO). His most recent book, *Invading Colombia: Spanish Accounts of the Gonzalo Jiménez de Quesada Expedition of Conquest*, was published in 2007 by Penn State University Press.

Dr Francis serves as book review editor for the journal *Ethnohistory*, and series co-editor for *Latin American Originals* (Penn State University Press). He also sits on the advisory board of the University Press of Florida. In 2007, Dr Francis was appointed as a research associate at the American Museum of Natural History in New York. At present, he is completing a new manuscript entitled *Politics, Murder, and Martyrdom in Spanish Florida: Don Juan and the Guale Uprising of 1597*, which will be published in 2009 by the American Museum of Natural History Press.

ABOUT THE AUTHORS

Sean Brawley is an Associate Professor of History and Teaching and Learning Fellow at the University of New South Wales, Australia. His previous publications have covered a diverse range of fields including race, immigration and military conflict in the Asia-Pacific in the twentieth century, terrorism studies and sports history.

Chris Dixon is an Associate Professor of History and Coordinator of the Cultural History Project at the University of Queensland, Australia. His first two books explored the social and cultural dimensions of racial and gender reform in pre–Civil War America. He has also co-authored textbooks dealing with the Pacific and Vietnam Wars, and has written on the cultural and social aspects of the United States at war during the twentieth century.

Beatrice Trefalt is a Senior Lecturer in the Japanese Studies programme in the School of Languages, Cultures and Linguistics at Monash University, Australia. Her field of research is modern Japanese history, especially the legacies of the Asia-Pacific war. Her current research project focuses on the post-war repatriation and reintegration of citizens from Japan's wartime empire.

PREFACE

This book explores the dramatic and bloody struggle that raged across the Asia-Pacific region during the 1930s and 1940s. The sources included here highlight the ways in which the war was experienced, understood and remembered by those caught up in one of the twentieth century's most bitter conflicts. By providing first-hand accounts, from ordinary 'foot soldiers' as well as generals, from Japanese as well as Allied participants and from civilians as well as combatants, the authors enable readers to assess the conflict from a range of perspectives. Although the intention is not to provide a day-by-day account of the course of the war, the book covers the major turns of the conflict, from the lead-up to the attack at Pearl Harbor in December 1941, to the Japanese surrender in September 1945. And whilst the constraints of space preclude a close examination of the clash between China and Japan, some consideration is given to the experiences of those involved in what was one of the war's most brutal theatres. Throughout, the authors not only explain the *context* in which the various 'competing voices' were written, but also explore the different *forms* of 'fighting words' that comprise this volume.

ACKNOWLEDGEMENTS

Sean would like to thank his co-authors for the stimulating conversations and collegial approach to the project. Colleagues in the School of History and Philosophy at the University of New South Wales and the staff of the various libraries and archives in Australia, the United States and the Netherlands involved in the project have all played their part. I offer my gratitude to them. I have also received enthusiastic support from members of the 'Staunch Flight' of 22 Squadron Royal Australian Air Force and the Opfor and Instructors at Leadership in Action. Thanks guys and 'Fix Bayonets'! Finally, my immeasurable thanks and love to my family, especially Susan, Nathaniel, Caitlin and Alexander. Tom, Elizabeth, Sam and Jacob also deserve to be mentioned in dispatches. My dedication for this book is to my grandparents, who heard as well as read the 'Fighting Words' of World War II.

Chris says a big 'thank you' to Sean and Bea, whose enthusiasm and sense of humour make collaborative work a pleasure. Thanks are also due to the members of the School of Humanities and Social Sciences at the University of Newcastle. In particular, the regulars in the Curry Club – Roger 'The Dodger' Markwick, 'Big Al' Rolls, Troy Duncan, John Germov and Owen Jackson – were fine colleagues and are good mates. I'm grateful for the support offered by the members of the Cultural History Project at the University of Queensland and my colleagues in the School of History, Philosophy, Religion and Classics. With good cheer and efficiency, librarians at both the University of Newcastle and the University of Queensland helped identify and procure sources. Thanks also to Bob Wischnia, for his hospitality during a visit to Austin, Texas, and a series of marathon conversations regarding the relative merits of 'war films' and 'combat films'. My dedication is to the late Tom Davin. Born in Ireland; captured by the Japanese in Java in 1942, while serving with the Royal Air Force; a survivor of the horrors of the Burma Railway; and then, in 1962, at a point in life when few people would contemplate even more change, Tom was part of the post-war migration to Australia, in part because he liked the Australians he had encountered during the War. Amongst Tom's many achievements, none was more significant than the seventh of his nine children – Lorna – who for the last twenty-five years has been my companion and partner through thick and thin. Finally, my thanks go to our son, Sam, the light of our lives.

Beatrice would like to thank, first of all, Sean Brawley and Chris Dixon for their collaboration, support and patience during this project. Special thanks also to Sandra Wilson for advice and encouragement, and to Iwane Shibuya, for her help in reading and checking my translations.

Thanks to all around me – too many to mention by name – for friendship, support and the occasional 'reality check'. You know who you are. Most of all, I am grateful to young Ngaio Trefalt, whose patience with her mother's various projects makes everything possible.

We would also like to thank Michael Francis, at the University of North Florida, for his enthusiastic support of this project. Simon Mason and Liane Escorza, of Greenwood World Publishing, demonstrated remarkable patience, and were thoroughly professional and efficient during the publication process. Our thanks also go to Linda Ellis-Stiewing and Maheswari PonSaravanan for helping see the project through to completion.

NOTES ON TRANSLATIONS BY BEATRICE TREFALT

All readers will be aware of the difficulty and the creative nature of translation. There are many reasons why simple transliteration is not desirable, not least because English translated too closely from the Japanese quickly runs into semantic issues and becomes incomprehensible without a knowledge of Japanese grammar. Here, I also wanted to make the English as 'natural' as possible because we often already approach Japanese material – especially wartime material – with certain assumptions about 'otherness'. As a historian and as a translator, it is important to me that the translation itself does not become part of what supports such assumptions. I would like readers to be aware of these 'agendas' when reading my translations. My efforts to write clear English and to understand and transmit the meaning of the Japanese authors in language that is familiar rather than foreign ultimately make the readers reliant on my understanding of the sources. While readers can take me and other translators on trust, the most reliable thing to do, ultimately, would be to read the original. Whilst this is not possible for every language, it is possible for at least one or two per person. I take this opportunity to remind readers generally, and students specifically, about the importance of learning other languages, and encourage everybody to be part of the project of making other cultures and other histories readable and understandable – in each other's languages.

INTRODUCTION

The momentous conflict that raged across the Asia-Pacific region during the 1930s and 1940s touched the lives of millions of people. The war was waged with a savagery that shocked participants at the time, and has horrified generations since. It extended across a battlefield that stretched thousands of kilometres from the eastern Pacific to India, and from the oceans south of Australia to the Aleutian Islands in the north Pacific. The war was fought on and below the sea, in the skies and on territories ranging from the steamy, almost impenetrable, jungles of the South Pacific and Southeast Asia to the villages and cities in China, Vietnam and a score of other nations. The war pitted Japanese against Americans, Australians and British, and saw Indians, Vietnamese, Russians, and others, take up arms. Often, the war was fought at close quarters, in circumstances little different from battles waged centuries earlier, but it ended with a demonstration of devastating Allied technological superiority that heralded changes to the conduct of warfare and international relations that few could have foreseen during the 1930s. When the war began, large tracts of the Asia-Pacific region were colonies, ruled from afar with scant regard for the well-being and aspirations of the colonised. By 1945, the assumptions that had underpinned the colonial venture had been challenged and repudiated, and succeeding decades witnessed the dismantling of the colonial empires. At the front lines, battles continued to be fought by men. But the Pacific War was a 'total war', which involved women and children, often thousands of kilometres from the front lines where their husbands, fathers, brothers and sons lived, fought and died in their hundreds of thousands.

For Americans World War II began with the Japanese attack at Pearl Harbor in December 1941. But for others in the Asia-Pacific region, the war had been raging since 1937, when Japan invaded China after several years of sporadic clashes with Chinese forces in and around Manchuria, which Japan had invaded and occupied in 1931. During the early stages of their Pacific War, Americans, Australians and others were horrified by the brutality displayed by their Japanese foes. But the Japanese had been waging war in that fashion since the 1930s, against civilian as well as military 'targets'. By August 1945, when the war ended, an estimated 20 million Chinese had died, a wartime loss of life exceeded only by the Soviet Union. During the decades since 1945, the Japanese government's reticence to admit to its wartime excesses has caused continuing resentment amongst its former adversaries. This issue is played out across many fields. One issue that attracts intense international coverage focuses on Japanese school textbooks. The Japanese government's registration of a famous atrocity-denying textbook

on the list of possible choices for school curricula understandably leads
to acrimonious exchanges between China and Japan, and Korea and Japan,
and condemnation across the world, even if the textbook is actually
favoured only by a tiny minority of Japanese schools. Long after the
war's end, the politics of history continue to connect the past to the
present in a very direct, contentious manner.

Reasons for the long reach of wartime animosities – years beyond
the end of war itself – are many. In war, and especially in the Pacific
War, the enemy (whichever side he or she is on) is brutal, venal, diseased,
to be eradicated and not fit to share the company of humankind. The
enemy knows no friendship, no loyalty, no love, no honour, no forgiveness, no feelings and no humanity.[1] Few fail to be mobilised by indignation,
by a sense of injustice, by the appeal to moral duty or by wartime opportunities to feel indignant and morally superior. And just as these animosities
were encouraged initially by the fighting words of propaganda – appeals
to justice or to duty, accusations of injustices or moral failures, or appeals
to national survival or altruistic duties – so the end of the war often added
new layers to these fighting words. Animosities are not quelled by victory
or defeat: initial aims remain out of reach; settlements are unfair; justice
is unfulfilled; and punishments are too harsh, or not harsh enough. The
echoes of wartime propaganda can still be heard in many of the historical
controversies that pit the former enemy nations against each other, and in
those that pit veterans and others against each other in the same nation.

The sources presented here were, for the most part, created during the
war, or are based on the memory of the experience of the war. Many of
them are fuelled by the hatred of the enemy and the sense of indignation
at the enormity of what the enemy is attempting to do. Many aim to
mobilise, to convince or to stir the spirit. Others were created to sustain
people through pain, loss, horror, hopelessness, incredulity, discovery,
excitement, despair and fear. Some were created as a testimonial, an
attempt to ensure that what was happening, or what had happened,
would not be forgotten. Some are laconic; others wildly emotional. Some
make grandiose pronouncements; others merely inform. Some quip and
joke; others lead us to the depth of horror. All of them illustrate how the
war was portrayed, experienced, read about, thought about and felt by
a generation that will in a few years have disappeared. These sources are
a tangible link to the variety of ways in which the war was experienced, a
link to the time when the echo of wartime hatreds was created, an echo
that still shapes many debates in the Asia-Pacific region.

Importantly, this book allows for a reading of sources across enemy
lines, which critically distances the reader from the action. While there
are undoubtedly cultural differences in the many backgrounds of the
authors of these sources, what also becomes obvious is that the sources

read, ultimately, the same. Whether they express the emotions of battle, the justification for war or the deep disgust at inhuman behaviour, the sources may as well have been written in the same language originally. This is not to say that experiences can be generalised. It is to say exactly the opposite; that is, that they cannot be generalised even across one supposedly distinct culture. The sources in this book provide ample evidence of this.

In welcoming the development of the 'New Literacy Studies' of the mid-1990s, David Barton, Mary Hamilton and Roz Ivanič have emphasised one of the most important aspects of this new academic field: 'Literacies are situated. All uses of written language can be seen as located in particular times and places. Equally, all literate activity is indicative of broader social practices.'[2] Greater insights into the Pacific War can be achieved when the primary sources under analysis are explored for not only what they say about given events and themes but how the very words 'reflect social structures in which they are embedded and which they help shape'.[3] In this respect, this study reflects the notion that it is important to explore 'the relationship between writing and effect'.[4] In examining all the sources present in this study, readers are encouraged to consider how such fighting words were received by their audiences – whether that audience was a nation or an individual.

To assist the reader, each form of writing that appears in this study is contextualised when it first occurs, and is often placed within the broader history of the specific genre. The authors also consider how these 'fighting words' may have been shaped or transformed by the war itself. Finally, we also give some attention to how historians approach and use such sources.

The 'competing voices' – the authors of the 'fighting words' – in this study are ranged across a number of divides. The first and most obvious is the divide between combatants. The forms of writing examined provide insights into the Japanese and Allied ways of war. The translation of pertinent Japanese sources (and some other non-English-language sources) has been an important aspect of this enterprise. Some have been translated by third parties and have previously appeared in a variety of forms. Others have been translated specifically for this study and therefore appear in English for the first time. American, Japanese and Australian voices predominate, but others are also heard: a British sailor, a Hungarian physicist, a Malayan Chinese schoolgirl, a New Zealand housewife, an Indian prisoner of war, a Canadian journalist, a Vietnamese nationalist and a Dutch colonial official, amongst others.

A second divide – which informs the first – relates to cultural difference and its impact on ways of writing. The main protagonists in the Pacific War were the products of diverse cultural traditions.

Paul S. Dull has contended that to understand the Japanese navy at war, one must understand the impact of language on thought:

Japanese military and political thought is heavily influenced by the Japanese language. Language is not merely a tool for human communication; language is itself a means by which the realities of the world are divided and viewed ... the fact the written language uses ideographic symbols also heavily influences the form and content of Japanese thought.[5]

Despite the significant Westernisation that came with modernisation after the mid-nineteenth century, Japanese language and culture continued to inform distinct literary and literacy traditions. These combined to produce ways of writing that differed from similar genres in the English-speaking world. Where possible, the contextualisation of sources in this study highlights existing scholarly work in cognate fields and provides signposts of understanding for an English-speaking readership. How far such cultural differences can (or should) be taken (or explained), however, can be contentious. Even among the authors, there is a range of views on this subject. If the impact of Westernisation on Japanese reading practices was as significant as some scholars have claimed, then to what degree were ways of writing transformed?[6] Alas, the degree to which an individual might have been so influenced is simply outside the research practicalities of this study, but readers are encouraged to reflect on these issues.

The third and final divide is the distinction between forms of public and private writing. Ways of writing produced for public consumption, government decision making and military records have been the 'traditional' sources used to examine the Pacific War in its political and military contexts. Private ways of writing have played a role but have usually been confined to prominent politicians and military commanders.

Most of these 'public' documents were in fact not 'public' at their time of generation. Newspapers, however, were an exception, and these remain a valuable public primary source for historians. Literacy rates dramatically improved in the early twentieth century, and newspapers were a key source of information for many people. Even in those parts of the Asia-Pacific with lower literacy rates, newspapers were a key means through which opinions were formed, articulated and disseminated. In some combatant nations – particularly the United States, but also in Australia, New Zealand and Britain – weekly 'news magazines' such as *Time* or *The Bulletin* were also important resources for a public hungry for news from the front lines.

During the 1930s and 1940s, radio began to supplement newspapers and magazines as one of the most important forms of media. Millions of Americans, as well as British Prime Minister Winston Churchill, for example, first learned of the attack at Pearl Harbor via radio. And political leaders – including Presidents Franklin D. Roosevelt and Harry S Truman, along with Japan's Emperor Hirohito – also understood the power of radio as a means of shaping public opinion. Yet, whilst the press and radio were significant amongst all the nations at war in the Asia-Pacific, they faced varying degrees of government control. The strictures that were placed on the Allied media were far less restrictive than those faced by Japanese journalists and editors, but they were significant nonetheless, and in each case governments were keen to harness the press and media to build and sustain popular support for an increasingly costly war.

Contrasting and problematising these public sources (which were often given 'official' status, then or later) are the more personal or private writings, usually written in the first person singular.[7] These are generally private or semi-private documents, such as diaries or letters, but they can also be publicly available sources, such as published memoirs. Into the 1960s many historians were sceptical of such sources, particularly when the social status of the writer in question was low. Their subjectivity made them unreliable. The 'new social history', however, transformed the lived experience of ordinary citizens into subjects worthy of historical pursuit. Within this context private or personal documents were often the only viable source, and the background of the author mattered little. Later, this was augmented by the growth of interest in oral history. Mary Lindemann has noted that for today's historians, these personal, private documents are central because they endow 'ordinary lives with agency, dignity, and texture'. Furthermore, such sources can be analysed from new perspectives that are not first and foremost preoccupied with the reconstruction of a reality. They can, for example, be 'valuable testimonies to the kind of self-image current in a particular milieu'.[8] Martha Howell and Walter Prevenier have noted that diaries 'can almost never' be 'treated as reliable reports about an event, but must be read in terms of the very individual perspective from which they were written, as an index of what the author ... considers his truth'.[9]

Even memoirs, a genre that grew dramatically after World War II, but which continued to be viewed sceptically have proved rich resources for historians.[10] Partly because they are by their very nature highly subjective, partly because they are such closely edited accounts of the life being chronicled, and partly because they are often teleological (meaning they explain the outcome rather than the process of the life in focus), memoirs were long regarded as dubious historical sources. But these highly selective and edited 'retrospective narratives' are now valued as sources that can reveal 'a great deal about the writer's political intentions and his tactics, as well as his ideology and the culture of the age'.[11] Indeed, some historians have contended that memoirs have a value beyond that of more immediate forms such as diaries. Jeremy D. Popkin has suggested that 'hindsight may allow a clearer view of what was really important about past experiences than the author had at the time'.[12]

After a long time in the historiographical shadows, sources based on private writing have achieved a prominent place in the study of military history. Whilst some historians contend this is not 'military history' but rather the study of 'war and society', such sources are increasingly being exploited to enhance 'operational' military history. With reference to Napoleon's army, Allan Forrest has acknowledged the power of personal, private writings for the military historian. Such documents are 'personal testimonies that provide explanations of military motivation and routes into men's minds and souls'.[13]

The range and diversity of personal sources pertaining to the Pacific War are due largely to earlier developments in the universalisation of education. This is not to suggest that all combatants were authors or diarists or even letter writers. The exigencies of total war, for example, compelled the warring nations to lower their educational standards to put more men into uniform. This occurred at a time when the technological developments of war were seeking an increasing intellectual commitment from service personnel. In Japan, for example, the recruitment of less-educated citizens had consequences for military training. Training booklets had to be re-written in simplified form because many soldiers did not know all of the Japanese characters describing aspects of their training, which resulted in accidents.[14]

There remains one important consideration that must be taken into account when considering the sources, both public and private. Censorship was a fact of life during the Pacific War, and the consequent restrictions must be borne in mind when considering many of the public and private documents produced. The correspondence of service personnel, whether they were serving on the front lines or elsewhere, was subject to varying degrees of censorship. Fearing that the correspondence of military personnel might somehow fall into enemy hands, or that loved ones at home might inadvertently betray information about deployments or morale, the armed forces of all combatant nations regarded censorship as an important task. Some wartime correspondence includes blank spaces, where the censors have excised sections of a letter. Wartime correspondence was further complicated by the difficulties of transmitting mail. In general, the Allied armies and navies did a better job of this than their Japanese counterparts, who found it increasingly difficult to travel between their homeland and the remaining vestiges of the contracting empire. Yet, for all those caveats, letters and other forms of correspondence are amongst the most useful and insightful forms of fighting words from the Pacific War.

Censorship is also a consideration in the examination of those most private of writings – diaries. In theory, many servicemen and servicewomen were prohibited from keeping diaries. As with correspondence, it was feared that vital military information was at stake if diaries fell into enemy hands. But, fortunately for the historian, soldiers, sailors and airmen kept diaries, which provide us with telling insights into their experiences, fears, attitudes and hopes. For some servicemen and servicewomen, maintaining a diary was one means of coping with the trauma of total war. The very act of recording one's experiences and emotions could be cathartic, and could help one to make sense of what in ordinary, civilian life would have been unimaginable and intolerable. There were, inevitably, other coping mechanisms. As some of the fighting words recorded in this collection reveal, humour, much of it distasteful to those far removed from the front lines (and to subsequent, more politically correct generations), was part of every serviceman's repertoire for coping with trauma, far removed from the experiences of their civilian lives. Even for those facing the greatest adversity – Allied prisoners of war, for instance, or Japanese troops confronting almost certain death as the tide of war turned in the Allies' favour – the words they recorded in their diaries betray an often humbling amalgam of humility, hope, despair and defiance. At the same time, because many diarists continued to have an audience in mind when writing, they engaged in various acts of self-censorship.

A number of factors determined the selection of sources for this study. First and foremost was their ability to speak to the broad themes mentioned in the chronological and thematic essays that commence each chapter. Second was their representativeness as an example of a way of writing that was popular or important during this conflict. Third was the desire to present as diverse a range of ways of writing as possible. This study showcases an eclectic mix of public and private primary sources relating to the Pacific War. They reflect the variety of mediums and styles that were used in both the public and private spheres to record the conflict. And they are contextualised within their genre and as sources historians use when examining the conflict.

Sources range from political speeches to V-Mail letters home, from court martial transcripts to private diaries and from newspaper reports to ships' logs. The range is deliberately expansive, but not exhaustive. Some important ways of writing associated with the Pacific War remain to be explored. Tattoos, for example, gained a renewed currency during the Pacific War, and thanks to master tattooists such as Honolulu's 'Sailor Jerry' Collins, the written word played its part *on* the bodies of service personnel, alongside images, with a range of phrases from lessons learned ('My Ruin') to desires ('Homeward Bound') to commemoration ('in memory of my father') to the patriotic pledge tattoo ('Death before Dishonour').[15] Another example was cinema. During the pre-war period, Hollywood had played an important role in constructing perceptions of the Pacific as the 'South Seas'. During the war Hollywood continued to produce such films alongside a new cinematic genre – the Pacific War film.[16] Films such as *Bataan* and *Wake Island* were produced just a few months after the battles they depicted and so their images and scripts, and the public receptions they generated, constitute another collection of fighting words.

This study focuses on that aspect of World War II in the Asia-Pacific usually referred to as the 'Pacific War'. Whilst the Sino-Japanese War and the war fought between the Allies and Japan in Burma were of central significance to the course of World War II more generally, they are of tangential importance to this study and are only discussed within the context of the Pacific War. The major protagonists were Japan and the United States, with supporting roles from Australia, New Zealand, Great Britain and the Netherlands, along with European and American colonial possessions in Southeast Asia.

The chapters that follow commence with introductory essays. These essays are both chronological and thematic, tracing the course of the Pacific War and introducing some of the major historiographical arguments and trends. The book commences with an evaluation of the background to the Pacific War. Since the late nineteenth century, Japan and the Allied nations – particularly the United States – were on a long-term collision course in the Asia-Pacific. Underpinning the growing strategic, political and economic tensions were deeply rooted cultural differences, which rendered compromise more difficult, and complicated the task of diplomats seeking a peaceful resolution. During the late 1930s, although many people in the West were concerned by Japan's increasingly assertive nationalism and bellicose rhetoric, and were appalled by the behaviour of Japanese forces in China, there was little inclination to use force to thwart Japanese expansionism. Notwithstanding their long-standing colonial possessions in the Asia-Pacific region, in the period after the September 1939 invasion of Poland by Germany, few Europeans were in a position to do anything more than merely observe events in the faraway Asia-Pacific regions. Similarly, whilst the United States had a long-standing interest in Chinese affairs, and had its own colonial presence in the Asia-Pacific, the continuing public revulsion toward the slaughter of World War I, coupled with deep-seated doubts about the process of American entry into that conflict, fuelled isolationist sentiment.

Chapter Two examines the Japanese attack at Pearl Harbor. In the immediate wake of that attack, 7 December 1941 was indelibly etched into American political and popular consciousness, and became a reference point for United States relations with the rest of the world: that date not only signified the end of American isolationism but became a moment laden with historical significance and resonance, as the comparison between the attack on Pearl Harbor and the attacks of 11 September 2001 attest.

Subsequent chapters explore the experiences of those involved in the front-line conflict between Allied and Japanese forces. As Japan attacked the United States at Pearl Harbor, it launched simultaneous assaults on American, British and Dutch territories in Southeast Asia. In rapid succession, Japanese forces occupied Hong Kong, then Malaya and Singapore, before attacking the Dutch East Indies. By early May, Japan had also ousted the Americans from the Philippines. Japan also attacked Allied possessions and bases throughout the Pacific, including Guam, the Gilbert Islands and Wake Island. During early 1942, as Japanese forces occupied the Solomon Islands and advanced southwards through New Guinea, they seemed almost unstoppable. It was widely feared that Japan intended to invade Australia. Within six months, however, the Japanese had reached the limits of their triumph. In mid-1942, with two major naval battles – first in the Coral Sea and then at Midway – Allied forces turned the tables on the Imperial Japanese Navy. On land, too, the Allies thwarted the Japanese, first in New Guinea, and then at Guadalcanal. From late 1942, until 1945, at terrible cost, the Allies gradually pushed the Japanese back toward their home islands. Chapters Three, Five and Six trace the shifting fortunes of the war on land, while Chapter Four highlights the experiences of those fighting the war at sea and the significance of naval encounters such as the Battles of the Coral Sea and Midway.

During 1941 and 1942 the mass surrenders of Allied armies exposed the colonial powers' limitations, and many Japanese believed they were involved in a struggle to liberate Asia and the Pacific from the tyranny of European and American colonialism. The experience of occupation, however, challenged notions of Japanese benevolence. Chapter Seven explores the complex array of experiences and emotions of the occupied, and the occupiers, throughout the Asia-Pacific.

No less ambiguous were the experiences of Japanese and Allied civilians on the home fronts. If the millions of servicemen who fought on the front lines experienced the worst horrors of twentieth-century warfare, they were not the only victims of total war in the age of industrialised, technological warfare. The boundary between front line and home front was often indistinct. It is perilous to generalise about home-front experiences. Americans' memories of World War II as the 'the last good war' are based not only on the moral and political certainties of that conflict when contrasted to the scarring divisions resulting from subsequent wars in Indochina and the Middle East, but also on the fact that World War II signalled an end to the social and economic hardship associated with the Great Depression. For Australians the war years – which began in 1939 with the commencement of war in Europe – were a time of stoic hardship, material privation and a fear of Japanese invasion. For the British, and others in Europe, the war in the Asia-Pacific could seem remote, almost a sideshow to the more immediate conflict raging in Europe. For the Japanese, living in a society caught between tradition and change, there was nothing remote about the war. By 1945 Japan was being subjected to the fullest measure of total war. Having launched the conflict against the United States with a surprise attack, and having prosecuted the war with a savagery that initially seemed unthinkable to the Allies, Japan received little sympathy from its foes. Despite these differing contexts, as Chapter Eight reveals, there were common elements to life on the Japanese and Allied home fronts. In each case, civil liberties were tested, the boundary between 'public' and 'private' life was challenged, especially for women, and people were forced to deal with shortages of essential goods and services. Above all, the absences and loss of loved ones showed the universality of human grief. Yet, despite the brutalities and hardships, people coped. Nothing better demonstrated the capacity of human beings to cope with adversity than the experiences of those who were captured during the Pacific War. As the conflict became ever-more brutal, fewer prisoners were taken, but in the first months of the war, tens of thousands of Allied troops, in particular, were taken prisoner. The stories of this group constitute one of the darkest chapters of the conflict, and Chapter Nine explores the experiences and memories of Allied POWs, along with the smaller number of Japanese who fell into Allied hands.

Nothing better exposed the brutality and desperation of the Pacific War than the Japanese deployment of *kamikaze* suicide weapons late in the war, and the detonation of the atomic bombs over Hiroshima and Nagasaki in August 1945. If the notion of *kamikaze* was almost incomprehensible to the Allies, it did appear to provide further evidence that the Japanese as a people placed a lower value on human life. The deployment of *kamikaze*, moreover, confirmed what the Allies had already learned in the bloody fighting for Iwo Jima and Okinawa: Japan would fight to the bitter end. That conviction, in conjunction with an enthusiastic campaign to present the Japanese as sub-human – a task made easier by Japanese mistreatment of Allied prisoners of war – made the use of atomic weapons relatively straightforward. Ever since, however, controversy has raged surrounding the use of these new weapons. Was the use of the atomic weapons necessary to end the war, or was it the first stage in the Cold War? And would the Allies have used atomic weapons against Germany? But for the Allied soldiers who faced the prospect of a long and bloody battle for Japan, there was no uncertainty: the bombs hastened the end of the war and saved not only hundreds of thousands of Allied lives but also the lives of millions of Japanese who would have resisted to the end, rather than surrender. Chapter Ten includes explanations from leaders who decided to use the atomic bombs, the words of victims who survived atomic warfare and the sometimes speculative words of newspaper writers – Japanese and Allied – who struggled to describe the significance and aftermath of this new and devastating weapon.

Chapter Eleven explores the process by which Japan surrendered to the Allies. In a culture in which surrender constituted a profound form of humiliation, the notion of national defeat at the hands of an adversary who had been presented as little more than barbaric was difficult to accept. Put simply, many Japanese considered death preferable to surrender. Despite the strength of that conviction, however, many Japanese looked forward to the end of the war, and there was considerable frustration – muted in public during 1944 and 1945, but evident in many post-war writings and memoirs – at their leaders' apparent determination to fight on until Armageddon descended upon the nation. That dichotomy between a determination to fight on and an acknowledgement that there was little to be gained by continuing to fight against increasingly overwhelming odds was evident in the upper levels of the Japanese government and military establishment. For the Allies, August 1945 signified victory over a determined and at times fanatical adversary. In Japan, the physical and emotional legacies of defeat, revealed most starkly by the atomic bombing of Hiroshima and Nagasaki, led to national humiliation, despair and uncertainty. But neither the Allies' euphoria nor Japan's despair was absolute: in both cases, whilst there was widespread relief that the worst was over and a sense that people could begin planning for the future, rather than merely surviving in the present, millions of people had to set about rebuilding shattered lives and coping with loss.

Fighting in the Pacific War ended in August 1945, but the war's legacies were profound. As the final chapter highlights, the massive physical and human destruction bequeathed a heavy burden for generations to come. Yet the war also precipitated a profound shift in international power relations, as the European nations realised – at different times, and at varying costs – that they could not reclaim that which they had lost in 1941 and 1942. From India, through Indochina and Southeast Asia, into China, and across the Pacific, the 'winds of change' blew away the remnants of European colonial power.[17] At the same time as the United States – which had never imagined itself as a colonial power, but which was increasingly regarded as such by anti-colonial movements – jousted with the Soviet Union for supremacy across much of the area that had been fought over during the late 1930s and 1940s, Japan set about repeating the economic miracle that it had performed in the late nineteenth and early twentieth centuries, albeit with a society and a political system completely transformed by the war, where democracy, human rights and a commitment to peace remain enshrined in the Constitution.

CHAPTER ONE
THE PATH TO WAR

The present reign of terror and international lawlessness began a few years ago. … It began through unjustified interference in the internal affairs of other nations or the invasion of alien territory in violation of treaties. It has now reached the stage where the very foundations of civilization are seriously threatened.

President Franklin D. Roosevelt, 1937

The long rivalry between Japan and the United States in the Asia-Pacific region, culminating in their bitter 1941–1945 war, had its origins in the second half of the nineteenth century. During this period both nations experienced dramatic industrial, political and cultural transformations – all of which had crucial consequences for their international aspirations. Following the tumult of the Civil War, Americans' energies were directed to economic and industrial growth, and westward expansion. By century's end, the United States had emerged as a leading industrial and economic power. Japan, too, experienced remarkable change during the latter decades of the nineteenth century. In the wake of the West's forced ending of Japan's self-imposed isolation in the 1850s, and following the Meiji Restoration of 1868, Japan developed a modern, industrial economy. Whilst Japan and the United States shared certain aspects of economic development from the mid-nineteenth century, their situations were not directly analogous: whereas the United States was blessed with an abundance of raw materials, Japanese economic growth and prosperity were dependent upon the importation of raw materials from abroad.[1]

Japan and the United States had long pursued relatively introspective foreign policies. Although American 'isolationism' had always pertained primarily to its dealings with Europe, during the latter decades of the nineteenth century, the nation began exercising a foreign policy commensurate with its economic power. Similarly, while Japan had traditionally sought to remain aloof from the vagaries of international politics, during the late nineteenth century, the nation looked outward, determined to avoid the fate of China and to establish itself as the pre-eminent power in the Asia-Pacific region. Japanese expansion was premised on a strident nationalism and reflected a dynamic, modern economic system.

China was an important focus for both Japan and the United States. Whereas Japan responded to the European challenge by appropriating aspects of Western models of political and economic development, China appeared to almost fragment in the face of Western and then Japanese expansion. In 1894–1895, a dispute about Korea led Japan to declare war on, then defeat China. In 1899, the United States proclaimed an 'Open Door Policy' for China, which sought to expand American influence in China, as well as limit European and Japanese expansionism in the region. By the end of the nineteenth century, after a victorious war against Spain, the United States had acquired the former Spanish colony of the Philippines, as well as the former Portuguese colony of Guam, situated in the Pacific region of Micronesia. After considerable equivocation, the United States also annexed Hawaii. America's 'Manifest Destiny', long used to justify and explain westward expansion across the United States, now appeared to extend across the Pacific.

After triumphing in the Sino-Japanese War, Japan's leaders were confident they could further extend the nation's prestige and power – or, at least, continue to limit Russian interference in Korea and north China. Besides the United States, Japan's principal rival was Russia. In January 1904, after a surprise attack on Russian forces, Japan achieved a series of decisive victories over their adversaries. Under the terms of the 1905 Treaty of Portsmouth, Japan gained control over large sections of Manchuria. With the connivance of the United States, which hoped to direct Japanese energies towards northern Asia, rather than southward towards the Philippines, Japan also became the 'protector' of Korea – which it formally annexed in 1910.[2]

Having defeated a major European nation, and having acquired a significant colonial empire, Japan had established itself as a major power on the regional – and world – stage. Siding with the Western Allies during World War I, Japan claimed Germany's Pacific colonies north of the equator (including the Marshall, Mariana and Carolina islands) and the German territorial and economic concessions in China – notably the Shandong province. The territorial aggrandisement in China fuelled Japanese ambitions on the Asian mainland and led, in 1915, to Japan presenting China with the notorious 'Twenty-One Demands'.[3] Had those demands been accepted, China would have been rendered little more than a Japanese colony. The United States and the European powers, however, were unwilling to cede their influence in China, and although China was compelled to accept a revised list of Thirteen Demands, those revised demands did not extend Japan's influence in China.

The Japanese were frustrated by the European powers' determination to preserve their imperial status in Asia, and their bitterness was compounded by the decisions of the Versailles Peace Conference (1919). Whilst Japan's emerging international status was acknowledged by its position as one of the 'Big Five' powers at Versailles, the Japanese government – and public – was angered by the Conference's failure to recognise a declaration of racial equality and the limitation of its influence in China to Shandong. Moreover, the former German colonies in the Pacific were to be governed under the terms of a League of Nations mandate.[4]

World War I also brought frustration and disappointment for the United States. After declaring its neutrality in 1914, the United States was nonetheless drawn towards the Western Allies, and in 1917 joined the war. President Woodrow Wilson explained intervention in terms of America's mission to extend democratic principles. But after the carnage of the war, Americans repudiated the role of protector of international democracy and refused to join the League of Nations.[5] It was impossible, however, for the United States to retreat from the international stage. The increasingly interconnected economies of the 1920s meant the United States – the world's largest economic power – was involved in trading relationships that were crucial to American prosperity. During the 1920s, moreover, America's involvement in naval limitation, its role in undermining the Anglo-Japanese alliance, its racial policies at home and its role in forcing Japan to withdraw troops from Shandong, further antagonised Japan.

In 1921 and 1922, the United States hosted the Washington Armaments Conference, which led to a series of treaties setting limits on the size of the major powers' navies, recognising Chinese sovereignty and confirming the Open Door Policy. To the chagrin of many Japanese – who interpreted these treaties as attempts to stifle Japan's legitimate desire to consolidate its power and extend its sphere of influence – representatives at the Conference also agreed to respect each other's Pacific colonies. Japanese–American relations were further strained by American racial policies. In 1924 the US government legislated to curtail the immigration of Japanese (and other Asians) into the United States. Japanese politicians and opinion makers contended that the legislation reflected an underlying American racism and resentment towards Japan.

At home, Japan's experiment in liberal-democratic government and institutions was progressively undermined by ultra-nationalist and militarist groups, which exploited the worldwide economic crisis of the late 1920s and early 1930s for their own political gain. With the United States, the British Empire and prominent European nations withdrawing behind tariff walls, it was argued that if Japan was to survive the Great Depression, it had to expand its sphere of influence in Asia and the Pacific. This argument provided retrospective justification for the expansionist tendencies of the Japanese military which, in 1927, had dispatched an expeditionary force to northern China to protect Japan's economic interests. In 1931 Japanese forces deliberately destroyed a section of the Japanese-owned South Manchurian Railroad. This 'Manchurian Incident' (sometimes referred to as the 'Mukden Incident') was the pretext for a Japanese invasion of Manchuria, and signalled the beginning of a more assertive Japanese expansionism. For some Japanese, and for some historians in Japan and elsewhere, all conflict after the Manchurian Incident, until the surrender in August 1945, were parts of a single war, although others have contended otherwise.[6]

The United States, and other powers, did little to resist Japanese aggression. Partly because of the economic pressures associated with the Great Depression, many Western commentators and politicians sympathised with an over-populated Japan, unable to absorb its population through industrialisation. Territorial expansion appeared the only solution, and so better that expansion was into north Asia rather than towards American and European interests in Southeast Asia. Japanese expansion was also seen to have the added advantage

of reducing Japanese pressure on the United States and Australia
to end their restrictive immigration policies.[7] Japan ignored a series
of diplomatic protests, and paid no attention to a League of Nations
resolution calling for a withdrawal from Manchuria. In March 1933
Japan withdrew from the League of Nations.

Despite widespread apprehension within the United States regarding
Japanese expansionism and militarism, a majority of Americans
continued to believe the nation should avoid becoming entangled
in conflicts overseas.[8] During the mid-1930s, this isolationist sentiment
was reflected in a series of 'Neutrality Acts', designed to prevent
the nation from being misled into war by political miscalculation,
or by business leaders motivated by their own commercial interests,
as many Americans believed had happened in 1917.

Not all Americans, however, believed their nation could isolate
itself from the deteriorating international situation. And while the
greatest threat to world peace appeared to come from fascist aggression
in Europe, Americans were worried by Japanese expansionism,
particularly in China, a nation that continued to excite Americans'
commercial interests and for which there was a good deal of sympathy.[9]
Japan, emboldened by the League of Nations' ineffectual response
to the occupation of Manchuria, continued its advance into China.
By late 1936 Japanese forces had occupied important parts of Northern
China and areas around the commercial capital Shanghai.

The conflict in China deteriorated further in July 1937, after Japanese
and Chinese forces clashed at the Marco Polo Bridge, west of Beijing.
Who fired the first shot there remains a matter of debate. But attempts
to secure a conciliated resolution failed, and Japan launched a major
military campaign in northern China. Presaging what would become
almost commonplace throughout much of the Asia-Pacific region and
Europe during the 1940s, Japan subjected Chinese civilians as well as
soldiers to the horrors of 'total war'. The Japanese bombing of Shanghai,
and the publication of H. S. Wong's photograph of a distressed child
victim of the bombing, strengthened American ill-will towards Japan.
Even isolationists began to doubt the United States could remain aloof
from the deteriorating situation. Because Japan had not formally declared
war against China, American president Franklin D. Roosevelt was
not required to invoke the Neutrality Acts. This enabled China to buy
weapons and supplies from the United States. In October 1937, calling
for a 'quarantine' to control the 'epidemic of world lawlessness',
Roosevelt denounced Japanese aggression. Yet isolationism remained
strong within the United States and, confronted by criticism of his
'Quarantine Speech', President Roosevelt stepped back.

Many Japanese deeply resented what they regarded as American
hypocrisy. Referring to America's history of westward expansion,

Japanese leaders contended it was duplicitous for the United States to criticise Japan for using military conquest to expand its sphere of influence. Continuing their advance into China, in December 1937, Japanese forces occupied Nanjing. Thus began one of the most notorious episodes in twentieth-century history. For the next six weeks, Japanese forces subjected the defeated Chinese soldiers, and then the city's civilian population, to a frenzy of terror that led to the death of between 200,000 and 300,000 Chinese, and the rape of tens of thousands of women.[10]

At the same time as Japanese forces were inflicting their horrors in Nanjing, another episode further highlighted the crisis in Asia. On 12 December 1937, Japanese aircraft sank the American gunboat *Panay*, which had been escorting Standard Oil Company tankers on China's Yangtze River. Two American sailors died, in what nobody doubted was an intentional attack. Despite considerable public resentment towards Japan, however, and notwithstanding the outrage at the Rape of Nanjing, when Japan claimed the bombing of the *Panay* had been an accident, isolationist sentiment in the United States encouraged Roosevelt to accept a Japanese apology, along with two million dollars in compensation.

In December 1938, Japan declared a 'New Order in East Asia'. Claims that this new order was 'based on genuine international justice throughout East Asia' were widely dismissed. Put simply, Japan was declaring itself the dominant power in East Asia. Increasingly alarmed, the Roosevelt administration continued to support China, and Secretary of State Cordell Hull declared a 'moral embargo' on the shipment of aircraft to Japan. In July 1939, Hull announced that a 1911 Japanese–American trade treaty would not be renewed. Many Americans remained fearful that such sanctions might spark a war. Exports of cotton, machinery and oil to Japan continued.

In September 1939, when Germany invaded Poland, Americans' attention focused on Europe. At the same time as Americans feared becoming involved in another European bloodbath, there was also a growing realisation that a German victory would threaten America's economic and strategic interests – and, indeed, its very survival. These conflicting views forced Franklin Roosevelt to tread warily. Roosevelt was an internationalist, but he was a skilful politician, ever mindful of public opinion. Consequently, even as the international situation deteriorated during the late 1930s and into 1940, he refused to move American policy 'too far ahead' of the popular isolationist sentiment. He warned Americans, however, that they could not remain isolated from international events.

Having won the 1940 presidential election partly on the basis of his ability to position himself as neither an extreme isolationist nor an avid interventionist, Roosevelt moved to build American support for Britain and her Allies. Undeterred by the objections of isolationists, he bypassed the Neutrality Acts, and directed the US Navy to assume a greater responsibility for patrolling the Atlantic Ocean. In August 1941, Roosevelt and British Prime Minister Winston Churchill signed the 'Atlantic Charter', bringing the United States closer to the Allied cause and articulating a series of principles that Roosevelt hoped would underpin international relations in the post-war world. Both men, moreover, hoped an image of unity between their nations would deter Japanese aggression. Britain, anxious to preserve its Asian colonies, shared American anxieties about Japanese expansionism. These closer links between the United States and Britain, and other Allied nations, exacerbated Japanese concerns that their international aspirations were being stifled, and made it easier for the Japanese military to assume the ascendancy in political life.[11]

Through the 1930s the Japanese Army had dominated strategic policy and championed a doctrine known as 'Northern Advance/Southern Defense'. Following the path of assumed least resistance, Japan would extend its power into Manchuria and China while maintaining a defensive posture to the south that would not antagonise the United States, France and Great Britain. In 1939, however, three events compelled the Japanese to change their strategy. First, the path of least resistance had encountered many obstacles and was not securing the results expected. Second, Japan's actions in north Asia were increasing tensions with the Soviet Union. This tension became more problematic after Japan's nominal ally Germany signed a non-aggression pact with the Soviet Union in August 1939. Third, the German–Soviet agreement came into force at a time when the Japanese and the Soviets were engaged in the so-called 'Nomonhan Incident' – an armed conflict set around a border dispute between the two north Asian powers. The incident highlighted the Soviet resolve to resist the Japanese and caused several Japanese reversals. The lack of success in northern Asia and the changing international diplomatic situation gave the Imperial Japanese Navy the opportunity to advocate an alternative strategy of 'Northern Defense/Southern Advance'.

In autumn 1940, Japan negotiated with Vichy France to station troops in the north of French Indochina; by August 1941 Japan had occupied the entire French colony. In response, the United States extended its economic embargo against Japan. The two nations were now firmly on a path to war. The Japanese government could retreat from its expansionist policies, remove its troops from China where it had been fighting since 1937, and strive to restore relations with the United States, or it would have to secure new supplies of essential raw materials to fight the war in China – particularly oil.[12] With oil in short supply, Japanese leaders believed they had to act promptly.

THE SOURCES

A Japanese Newspaper Denounces America's Restrictive Immigration Legislation of 1924

In 1924 the Johnson Act – restricting the immigration of Japanese, and other Asians, into the United States – was passed into law. This legislation provoked deep resentment within Japan. Prior to the passage of the Johnson Act, the Japanese ambassador to the United States, Hanihara Masanao, had warned of 'grave consequences' if the American Congress voted to discriminate against Japanese immigrants. In the extract reprinted below, the editors of the *Japan Times and Mail* respond to suggestions that the Act was a reaction to Hanihara's statement. Although they were careful to distinguish the Senators' legislation from the views of other Americans, the editors' grievances against the Johnson Act were explicit and emphatic. Note, too, their reference to the treaties that were signed after the Washington naval conferences of the early 1920s. As always with media sources, we need to consider the extent to which the views expressed *reflected,* or *shaped,* public opinion:

The adoption by the American Senate of the exclusion amendment to the Immigration Bill has given a shock to the whole Japanese race such as has never before been felt and which will undoubtedly be remembered for a long time to come. The wonder is, rather, that the shock has not found expression in a louder outburst of indignation than is the case. The knowledge that Senators Johnson, Shortridge and company do not necessarily represent the entire American nation in offering an unnecessary affront, is largely responsible for the spirit of forbearance which seems to be generally ruling the mind of the nation for the present....

[T]he Senate has passed, with an overwhelming majority, an amendment which they know is a most humiliating one to the Japanese race, and the event cuts the Japanese minds deep, a wound that will hurt and rankle for generations and generations.

How came it to pass that the Senate should have chosen to act in so extraordinary a manner? The exclusion Senators themselves would have it believed that their ire was roused by Ambassador Hanihara's 'grave consequences' threat. They contend that the 'veiled menace' was an insult that no Power so great as the United States could bear, and its injured dignity could be vindicated only by a retaliation in kind, as by insulting Japan by way of return. Yet it is inconceivable that they did not know that in view of the distortion of facts and misrepresentation of figures, so freely resorted to by the exclusionists, the Ambassador could pen his note of protest in no other tone, and that read in a rational spirit there was nothing in it to constitute an international offense.

The whole thing cannot but lend itself to theory that the Senators were looking for some excuse to get angry, and insinuations and falsifications were so engineered as to entrap Ambassador Hanihara into committing himself with words such as could be turned into a most effective weapon by them.

Even if this is going too far behind the show, it may not be gainsaid that the Senate has been most unfortunate in the choice of time for taking its action. While professing to be jubilant over the increased prospects of permanency of peace in consequence of the Washington Conference, all Japanese have ever since felt in the secret recesses of their heart that their country has been considerably weakened in its naval strength. ... It has been said openly more than once in different quarters abroad that Japan is as good as crushed to a naval and economic helplessness, from which there will be no recovering for a generation or two. Mark, then, it is at such a time that the Senate of the United States has said practically this: 'We deliberately offer you this insult, knowing that you can do no more than make a wry face.'

No Japanese takes any stock in the excuse that Ambassador Hanihara's 'uncalled for words' provoked the Senators to resentment to teach Japan manners. All the leading American newspapers themselves, with the exception of course of those of Hearst interests, state that there was no occasion whatever for the Senators to get offended. The impression is not unnatural, therefore, on the Japanese side, that the American Senators took advantage of the adverse plight of Japan in developing and carrying into effect their scheme of making Japan and the Japanese victims of their political maneuvering.

This is extremely unfortunate. For a friendly turn in the hour of need will be remembered permanently, but an unfriendly act that takes advantage of one's helpless condition makes nothing of all the past and darkens the long future.

We are most deeply aggrieved that the American Senate has made itself an object of distrust and suspicion in the Japanese mind through an act which is characterized as unnecessary and ill-judged by the American organs of public opinion themselves.

The United States Neutrality Act of 1935

The Neutrality Acts passed by the US government during the mid-1930s were a response to public disillusionment with American involvement in World War I and to the growing international crises in both Europe and the Asia-Pacific. By preventing Americans from engaging in commercial relations with nations at war, and by preventing the government – specifically the Executive branch of government – from becoming embroiled in international disputes, the American Congress hoped the Neutrality Acts would ensure the United States did not become embroiled in another global conflict.

Legislative documents, such as the Neutrality Acts, were usually drafted by politicians with the assistance of public servants. The written words of documents produced by legislators and public servants are generally formal, with syntax and semantics reflecting their status as rule-making and legally binding documents. This often resulted in passive, jargonistic documents, which were inaccessible to most members of the general public. Nonetheless, despite the dense language in the Neutrality Acts, the Senators' sentiments were clear. And, as the previous document demonstrated, when the American Congress – or, indeed, any legislature – expressed itself on contentious matters, the international implications could be profound:

United States Neutrality Act, 31 August 1935, JOINT RESOLUTION 49 stat. 1081; 22 USC 441 note

Providing for the prohibition of the export of arms, ammunition, and implements of war to belligerent countries; the prohibition of the transportation of arms, ammunition, and implements of war by vessels of the United States for the use of belligerent states; for the registration and licensing of persons engaged in the business of manufacturing, exporting, or importing arms, ammunition, or implements of war; and restricting travel by American citizens on belligerent ships during the war.

Resolved by the Senate and House of Representatives of the United States of America in Congress assembled, that upon the outbreak or during the progress of war between, or among, two or more foreign states, the President shall proclaim such fact, and it shall thereafter be unlawful to export arms, ammunition, or implements of war from any place in the United States, or possessions of the United States, to any port of such belligerent states, or to any neutral port for transshipment to, or for the use of, a belligerent country.

The President, by proclamation, shall definitely enumerate the arms, ammunition, or implements of war, the export of which is prohibited by this Act.

The President may, from time to time, by proclamation, extend such embargo upon the export of arms, ammunition, or implements of war to other states as and when they may become involved in such war....

Except with respect to prosecutions committed or forfeitures incurred prior to March 1, 1936, this section and all proclamations issued thereunder shall not be effective after February 29, 1936....

SEC. 3. Whenever the President shall issue the proclamation provided for in section 1 of this Act, thereafter it shall be unlawful for any American vessel to carry any arms, ammunition, or implements of war to any port of the belligerent countries named in such proclamation as being at war, or to any neutral port for transshipment to, or for the use of, a belligerent country....

SEC. 6. Whenever, during any war in which the United States is neutral, the President shall find that the maintenance of peace between the United

States and foreign nations, or the protection of the lives of citizens of the United States, or the protection of the commercial interests of the United States and its citizens, or the security of the United States requires that the American citizens should refrain from traveling as passengers on the vessels of any belligerent nation, he shall so proclaim, and thereafter no citizen of the United States shall travel on any vessel of any belligerent nation except at his own risk, unless in accordance with such rules and regulations as the President shall prescribe....

Approved, August 31, 1935

Konoye Fumimaro's Plans for a 'New Order' in Asia (1938)

Justification for Japanese expansionism during the inter-war years was often predicated around a determination to curtail the influence of European and American colonial power, and provide stability in a troubled region. Because it was purportedly acting in the best interests of *all* Asians, Japan's leadership was presented as a positive and necessary consequence. Even after Japanese aggression in China challenged such benign motivations, Prime Minister Prince Konoye Fumimaro continued to argue that Japan's motivations were selfless and designed to unite rather than divide Asia. Konoye had held grave reservations about the Manchurian intervention and was seen as the Japanese politician best able to avert war and control the army. His ability to do so, however, was undermined by the policies already adopted by the Japanese government and military. American ambassador Joseph Grew suggested Konoye was a 'prisoner, willing or unwilling, of the terms precisely prescribed in conferences over which he presided'.[13] Konoye was not a particularly gifted public speaker and his speeches were usually read without the improvisation or emotion that often accompanied Roosevelt's public speaking. One observer suggested that he appeared a 'robot'.[14]

Konoye was no more able than his peers to avert war or control the military, and his claims for Japanese motivations in Asia ultimately proved illusory:

What Japan seeks is the establishment of a new order which will insure the permanent stability of East Asia. In this lies the ultimate purpose of our present military campaign.

This new order has for its foundations a tripartite relationship of mutual aid and co-ordination between Japan, Manchoukuo, and China in political, economic, cultural and other fields. Its object is to secure international justice, to perfect the joint defense against communism, and to create a new culture and realize a close economic cohesion throughout East Asia. This indeed is the way to contribute toward the stabilization of East Asia and the progress of the world.

What Japan desires of China is that the country will share in the task of bringing about this new order in East Asia. She confidently expects that the people of China will fully comprehend her true intentions and that they will respond to the call of Japan for their co-operation....

Japan is confident that other Powers will on their part correctly appreciate her aims and policy and adapt their attitude to the new conditions prevailing in East Asia....

The establishment of a new order in East Asia is in complete conformity with the very spirit in which the Empire was founded; to achieve such a task is the exalted responsibility with which our present generation is entrusted....

Franklin D. Roosevelt's 'Quarantine Speech', 5 October 1937

For much of the 1930s, President Franklin D. Roosevelt was torn between the isolationism that was so popular amongst Americans and his recognition that the United States could not stay aloof from the growing international crisis. Soon after the sinking of the *USS Panay* in December 1937, Roosevelt condemned the current 'reign of terror and international lawlessness', and urged the peace-loving nations of the world to work cooperatively to thwart the breakdown of international law and order. In the extract below, Roosevelt addressed two audiences: at the same time as he hoped to deter further Japanese aggression, he was conscious of the need to persuade the American public that isolationism was an unrealistic and perhaps naïve policy, that would not protect American interests:

The present reign of terror and international lawlessness began a few years ago.

It began through unjustified interference in the internal affairs of other nations or the invasion of alien territory in violation of treaties. It has now reached the stage where the very foundations of civilization are seriously threatened. The landmarks, the traditions which have marked the progress of civilization toward a condition of law and order and justice are being wiped away.

Without a declaration of war and without warning or justification of any kind, civilians, including vast numbers of women and children, are being ruthlessly murdered with bombs from the air. In times of so-called peace, ships are being attacked and sunk by submarines without cause or notice....

Innocent peoples, innocent nations are being cruelly sacrificed to a greed for power and supremacy which is devoid of all sense of justice and humane considerations....

Those who cherish their freedom and recognize and respect the equal right of their neighbors to be free and live in peace, must work together for the triumph of law and moral principles in order that peace, justice, and confidence may prevail throughout the world. There must be a return to a belief in the pledged word, in the value of a signed treaty. There must be recognition of the fact that national morality is as vital as private morality....

There is a solidarity and interdependence about the modern world, both technically and morally, which makes it impossible for any nation completely to isolate itself from economic and political upheavals in the rest of the world, especially when such upheavals appear to be spreading and not declining. There can be no stability or peace either within nations or between nations except under laws and moral standards adhered to by all. International anarchy destroys every foundation for peace. It jeopardizes either the immediate or the future security of every nation, large or small. It is, therefore, a matter of vital interest and concern to the people of the United States that the sanctity of international treaties and the maintenance of international morality be restored....

It seems to be unfortunately true that the epidemic of world lawlessness is spreading....

It is my determination to pursue a policy of peace and to adopt every practicable measure to avoid involvement in war. It ought to be inconceivable that in this modern era, and in the face of experience, any nation could be so foolish and ruthless as to run the risk of plunging the whole world into war by invading and violating, in contravention of solemn treaties, the territory of other nations that have done them no real harm and are too weak to protect themselves adequately. Yet the peace of the world and the welfare and security of every nation are today being threatened by that very thing....

War is a contagion, whether it be declared or undeclared. It can engulf states and peoples remote from the original scene of hostilities. We are determined to keep out of war, yet we cannot insure ourselves against the disastrous effects of war and the dangers of involvement. We are adopting such measures as will minimize our risk of involvement, but we cannot have complete protection in a world of disorder in which confidence and security have broken down.

If civilization is to survive, the principles of the Prince of Peace must be restored. Shattered trust between nations must be revived.

Stanley K. Hornbeck Discusses American Options to Curtail Japanese Aggression (1938)

Whilst Japanese leaders spoke of their nation's rights and responsibilities in Asia, during the late 1930s increasing numbers of Americans perceived Japan as an expansionist power, which threatened regional stability in the Asia-Pacific regions and posed a direct threat to American interests. Stanley K. Hornbeck served as special advisor to Secretary of State Cordell Hull during the late 1930s and early 1940s. Having lived and taught in China before commencing his career in public service, Hornbeck exemplified the sympathy many Americans held for China. Many of the state papers and the actions initiated by the United States during this period 'bore his strong imprint'.[15] He warned American politicians and diplomats that the United States had to stand up to Japanese expansionism. His language, and the policies he advocated, were regarded and derided by some of his contemporaries as alarmist and provocative. In the document below, reflecting the growing concern and frustration that many Asia-literate Americans felt in the wake of unfettered Japanese expansion into China, Hornbeck raised a number of possible American responses to Japan's policies. Written for a private rather than public audience, his plain-speaking, unambiguous document contrasted to the passive formal language found in the Neutrality Acts. Crossing the line between the public servant as advisor and the public servant as advocate, Hornbeck's words made a diplomatic resolution of the growing crisis less likely:

It is an important interest of the United States that Japan not gain control of China. It therefore would be our interest that Chinese resistance to Japan's effort to gain that control continue. The Japanese nation is today animated by concepts and is pursuing objectives which are in conflict with the concepts and the legitimate objectives of the United States. The Japanese are embarked upon a program of predatory imperialism. Unless the Japanese march is halted by the Chinese or by some other nation, the time will come when Japan and the United States will be face to face and definitely opposed to each other in the international political arena....

The American Government should formulate and adopt a program of action (a diplomatic "war plan") toward averting an armed conflict between the United States and Japan. In the conducting of our relations with Japan and with China we should not take haphazard and unrelated steps. Such action as we may take in the realm of the use of words should be related to action which we may plan to take in the realm of material pressure (positive or negative, or both). It should be our objective to have Japan's predatory march halted. ... That march will be halted only by the power of resistance of material obstacles and material pressures. Any nation which definitely opposes that march should be prepared in [the] the last analysis to use, if it proves necessary, armed force. ... [The United States], in formulating its course of action should make it its business to be prepared if necessary to use armed force.

The more we talk and the longer we refrain from resort to some substantial measures of positive (material) pressure toward preventing the Japanese from taking or destroying our rights, titles and interests in the Far East, the more likely will it be that resort by us to such measures at some future time – if and when – will be replied to by the Japanese with resort to armed force against us, which would, in turn, compel us to respond with armed force....

The most practicable course for us to follow would be that of giving assistance to the Chinese and withholding those things which are of assistance to the Japanese. ... If and when, however, we commit ourselves to that line of action, we should do so wholeheartedly and with determination. We should not take some one step without expecting, intending and being able to take further steps, many further steps, in the same direction. Such steps should include a combination of diplomatic, economic and potential military pressures. If this Government wishes to embark upon such a course, it should be prepared to consider seriously the taking of such steps as denunciation of the U.S-Japan Commercial Treaty of 1911, repeal of the Neutrality Act, retaliatory tariff measures against Japan, placing of embargoes upon trade and shipping between Japan and the United States, [and] disposal of our naval resources in which manner as to indicate to the Japanese Government and nation that we "mean business."

Japanese and American Newspaper Reports on the Fall of Nanjing

One of the most dramatic aspects of World War II was the manner in which 'total war' – war waged against civilians as well as combatants – became almost the norm. By 1945, the world had almost grown accustomed to slaughter and brutality that only a decade earlier seemed unimaginable. During the mid-1930s, the revelation that Japanese forces had massacred and raped tens of thousands of Chinese in the city of Nanjing (Nanking) sparked horror in the United States, and elsewhere. From the escalation of the 'China Incident' in July 1937, news about the war in China was daily front-page material for all Japanese newspapers, especially during the advance and the fall of the capital in Nanjing, which would – so far as it was understood in Japan – end the war against China with the defeat of Chiang Kai-shek. The Japanese conquest of Nanjing was therefore the object of great celebration in Japan, celebration tempered with the sober business of reporting Japanese war deaths. Needless to say, the horrors that were witnessed by those in Nanjing – now-infamous mass rapes and murders on an unprecedented scale – were not reported in Japan, although they were publicised in the West, thanks to the presence of Western journalists such as *New York Times* reporter F. Tillman Durdin. The *New York Times* was the best-known newspaper in the United States, widely trusted by Americans for its accuracy, and its fair-minded perspective on events. In the first excerpt below, Nakamura Seigo, special correspondent in Nanjing for the Japanese mass-circulation daily *Asahi Shinbun*, not only provided Japanese readers with his description of the city after its fall, but also conveyed the impressions of Tillman Durdin himself, whom Nakamura happened to meet on a street corner on 15 December. The juxtaposition of the *Asahi*'s description with that of the *Chicago Tribune* speaks for itself.

Asahi Shinbun, 16 December 1937

The Eerie Calm of a Subjugated 'Dead City'
Eyewitness report: the last day of Nanking, 'The scariest thing was the artillery', as reported by a *New York Times* journalist.
By Special Correspondent Nakamura in Nanking, dispatched 15 December 1937.

The dead city of Nanjing has started breathing again around Zhongshanlu. It is like the face of a man near death, whose recovery is signaled by a gradual return of colour. In the temporary office of the Asahi China Branch at Zhongshanlu, we can no longer hear the sound of guns and artillery. From the morning of the 14th, we've been hearing the sound of car horns and of car traffic, and it gives the illusion that Nanjing has returned to normal, forgetting the war completely. The centre of Nanjing, which had been said to be empty of all living people, but where there are in fact roughly 100,000, is also regaining its breath. Japanese soldiers are coming and going and chatting cheerfully.

I was standing at the corner of Zhongshanlu and Zhongzhengjiao Xinjiekou streets, when car with an American flag, headed south, stopped suddenly. Two Americans came out, and one of them said: 'you must be a Japanese reporter. I'm with the *New York Times* and this is a cameraman from Paramount'. They shook hands with me, and when I introduced myself as an *Asahi* correspondent, he said appreciatively 'oh, the *Asahi*!' The taller one was a cameraman with Paramount, Arthur Menken, and the shorter one was the *New York Times*'s Tillman Durdin. I asked them what they thought of the last days before the fall of Nanjing. Both of them said it had been terrifying and reported the following.

'The water supply was cut on the 9th and the electricity on the 10th, and from that time we could hear the echoes of gunfire and artillery from Jizinshan getting more and more intense, and at the same time, many of the soldiers of the central army in the city got quite anxious. The civilian population fled to the newly established international safety zone on the 9th. We felt that the fall of Nanjing would come soon. We don't know when Chiang Kaishek fled from Nanjing, but we suppose that he may have stuck it out at the military academy until the fifth or sixth. By the 11th, it was too dangerous to go outside because of the Japanese bombardment and artillery, and the Chinese army started to retreat. It was really a tragic retreat, avoiding the city centre and marching along the wall towards Hsiakwan gate. They probably wanted to use boats from Hsiakwan to retreat to the other side of the Yangtze. By the 12th, there were not many retreating soldiers left, so probably most of the troops had withdrawn by the 11th. On the 12th, the sound of battle was weakening, but that made the noise of the Japanese artillery on Zijinshan meteorological station and Fuguishan even louder, going over our heads towards the north of Nanjing. The most frightening was the artillery. It looks like the Chinese army suffered most from the Japanese artillery. On the 12th, all that was left was a small number of Chinese police. It's at that time especially that the city turned into a dead town, and became eerily quiet. At that time, we also thought that that was the end of Nanjing. It was a tragic moment, we felt like we were witnessing one of the world's tragedies'. So the reporter recalled.

As we were chatting, another car stopped, with reporters from Associated Press and the *Chicago Tribune*, who had been sticking it out here for one or two months to witness the end of Nanjing. Mark Daniel from AP said cheerfully, looking around, 'well, isn't this a historical press room!'

With few ways to communicate his story to the United States, F. Tillman Durdin had to wait until he had returned to Shanghai, from where he sent the story by telegraph. His colleague, *Chicago Daily News* reporter Archibald T. Steele, dispatched his story back to the United States in hours because he was able to convince the captain of the *USS Oahu* to transmit his story by the ship's radio transmitter. Residents of Chicago therefore read of the atrocities three days before their fellow citizens in New York City:[16]

The killing of civilians was widespread ... Some of the victims were aged men, women and children ... Many victims were bayoneted and some of the wounds were barbarously cruel.

The mass executions of war prisoners added to the horrors....

[T]he writer watched the execution of 200 men on the Bund. The killings took ten minutes. The men were lined against a wall and shot. Then a number of Japanese ... trod nonchalantly around the crumpled bodies, pumping bullets into any that were still kicking.

A large group of [Japanese] military spectators apparently greatly enjoyed the spectacle....

A favourite method of execution was to herd groups of a dozen men at entrances of dugouts and to shoot them so the bodies toppled inside....

Civilian casualties also were heavy, amounting to thousands....

The capture of Hsiakwan Gate by the Japanese was accompanied by the mass killing of the defenders, who were piled up among the sandbags, forming a mound six feet high. Late Wednesday the Japanese had not removed the dead, and two days of heavy military traffic had been passing through, grinding over the remains of men, dogs and horses.

The Japanese appear to want the horrors to remain as long as possible, to impress on the Chinese the terrible results of resisting Japan.

American Journalist and Essayist Otto Tolischus Writes from Tokyo, February 1941

In February 1941, Otto Tolischus, a Lithuanian-born journalist working in the United States, was sent to Japan by the *New York Times* to replace

Hugh Byas as the newspaper's Tokyo Bureau chief. Having earlier reported from Nazi Germany, the Pulitzer Prize winner was well placed to comment on the mood amongst the Japanese people, and on the nation's preparations for war. When war finally came, Tolischus was arrested along with other American correspondents and imprisoned. He endured solitary confinement, torture and beatings until his repatriation in a prisoner exchange in 1942. He went on to write three books on his wartime experiences.[17]

In comparison to other journalists, essayists were afforded the luxury of time in the preparation of their stories. Essayists fleshed out the stories that captured the front-page headlines and offered the first detailed attempts at examining and explaining what was making news.

Three days of looking and listening in Japan brought two things home to me. The first – and I was surprised at my own surprise at this – was the discovery that Japan was a country already at war. I knew that, of course – at war with China. But I learned what tricks juggling with words can play, and what a difference there is between knowing a thing and realizing its significance. Japan called her war in China the 'China Incident,' and we too, to save ourselves embarrassment under our Neutrality Laws, had refused to call the China war a war. As a result I, for one, had somehow detached Japan from the 'China Incident,' and I began to suspect that America as a whole, and even foreigners in Japan, labored under the same optical illusion. Whenever there was talk of war, it was not the 'China Incident' that was meant, but a war between Japan, America, and Great Britain.

The subconscious corollary drawn from this was that Japan was still at peace, and could make decisions as a country still at peace. But I knew from my own experience in Europe that the psychology and dynamics of a country at war are quite different from those of a country at peace, and create quite different reactions and compulsions. Japan, I realized, not only was at war, but felt herself at war and I began to wonder how far the rest of the world took this into account in dealing with Japan.

Having seen Germany at war, I recognized the symptoms. The material symptoms were obvious. Tokyo already had a dimout, and the bright lights which, I was told, once rivaled those of Broadway were gone. There were the same complaints about growing restrictions and declining standards of living – about shortages of all sorts of things, especially imported goods, about queues before food shops and the scarcity of taxicabs, about the price of ersatz materials and native whiskey – that I had heard in Germany. A still peaceful and well-supplied American public took them as a possible indication of Axis collapse, but I had learned to evaluate them as tokens of Axis determination to carry on according to the terms of 'guns before butter.'

CHAPTER TWO
PEARL HARBOR

As we receive the Imperial Edict of the declaration of war,
we cannot help but be dumbstruck with awe, and overwhelmed
by emotion. We must prepare ourselves, in order to be able later
to look back without shame at this crucial moment in history,
to sacrifice to the nation, according to the Emperor's wish,
our bodies and souls, joined together as one hundred million
brothers.

Asahi Shinbun, 9 December 1941

The war that broke out in Europe in September 1939 further exacerbated tensions between the United States and Japan regarding Japanese aggression in China. In September 1940, Japan signed the Tripartite Alliance with Nazi Germany and Italy, and negotiated the stationing of Japanese troops in Indochina, ostensibly to aid its military effort against the resisting Chinese nationalist government in Chongqing. From mid-1941, there were growing tensions throughout the Asia-Pacific region, as negotiations to resolve the deepening rift between Japan and the United States (and its allies) proved fruitless.[1] In August 1941, after the US government's sanction policy had the unintended consequence of blocking Japanese access to all sources of oil, the Japanese government proposed that Prince Konoye (recently returned to the Prime Ministership in yet another vain attempt to control the Army) meet with President Roosevelt. US Secretary of State Cordell Hull advised against such a meeting, arguing that Konoye lacked sufficient authority within his own government to enforce any agreement that might be reached. Instead, Roosevelt told the Japanese that negotiations could begin only *after* Japan agreed to respect the Open Door Policy and China's territorial integrity. In effect, the United States was demanding that Japan withdraw from China entirely. Konoye could provide no such assurance and negotiations ended.

While the war in Europe remained the priority, Roosevelt concurred with Hull that the United States had to thwart Japanese expansion. Hull now added to American demands by calling for a Japanese withdrawal from Indochina. Some historians have suggested that a more flexible American policy might have encouraged moderate elements, including Konoye, within the Japanese government. But the moderates' position was weakened by the failure of negotiations, and while Emperor Hirohito among others expressed concern about the risks of an attack on the United States, there was considerable support amongst Japanese military leaders for a military solution to the growing crisis with the United States. On 6 September 1941, a Japanese Imperial Conference decided that Konoye had just six weeks to resolve the crisis with the United States. The Conference also approved preparation for a surprise attack on Hawaii.

Konoye was in an invidious position. The Japanese military refused to countenance a withdrawal from China, and without that withdrawal there could be no compromise with the United States. In October, Konoye asked War Minister General Tōjō Hideki to consider a withdrawal of troops, while maintaining credibility by keeping some troops in the northern part of China. Tōjō's response did little to ease the situation: his 'maximum concession' was that Japanese troops would remain no longer than twenty-five years in China – provided the United States ceased aiding the Chinese. Rebuffed, and confronted with a threat from Tōjō to resign and bring down the entire Cabinet, on 15 October Konoye resigned as Prime Minister. His replacement, Tōjō, favoured a military solution to the crisis with the United States. This transition in power remains the subject of historical debate, particularly as it extends into still unresolved debates concerning the nature and extent of the Japanese Emperor's political power, his ability to influence decisions regarding the start of the war and whether one can credit later claims that he had been opposed to war.[2]

Further negotiations proved fruitless, despite various attempts to find a compromise. At the same time as a pro-war faction had assumed effective control of the Japanese government, Japanese envoy Kurusu Saburō conferred with Roosevelt and Hull. Japan's final proposal, delivered on 20 November, was emphatic: Japan would conquer no more territory if the United States agreed to restore trade with Japan, end aid to China and assist Japan to procure supplies (including oil) from the Netherlands (Dutch) East Indies. If the United States agreed to those terms, Japan would withdraw immediately from southern Indochina, and then, after a peace settlement – presumably on Japanese terms – had been reached with China, retreat from the rest of Indochina. Tōjō expected the US Administration to reject this proposal. But Roosevelt, hoping to buy time to improve America's military preparedness, and determined to avoid precipitating a crisis, ordered that negotiations continue. Nonetheless, Roosevelt considered Japan's proposal as unacceptable, and anticipated that Japan was increasingly likely to use military force to break the diplomatic impasse. Indeed, while negotiations were continuing the Japanese Navy stepped up its preparations for war. If all else failed, a military seizure of oil and resource-rich areas of Southeast Asia would at least allow Japan to negotiate from a position of strength.

American policymakers had clear information regarding Japanese plans, thanks to the work of American cryptanalyst Colonel William J. Friedman, who had broken the Japanese diplomatic code. Intercepted Japanese transmissions revealed that Tokyo expected negotiations to fail. On 26 November Hull reiterated the American demand for a Japanese withdrawal from China.

As the United States was rejecting Tōjō's demands, Japanese naval forces began moving secretly toward Pearl Harbor, the main American base in the Pacific and home to the US Pacific Fleet which had been recently relocated from San Diego. On 3 December American intelligence deciphered a message from Tokyo to the Japanese Embassy in Washington, instructing officials there to burn code books and destroy cipher machines. This was a sure sign that war was imminent. Yet although the signs pointed to war, and whilst it appeared Japan would fire the first shot, officials in Washington could not predict *where* an attack would take place. American officials believed a Japanese attack against British or Dutch possessions (an important source of raw materials) was the most likely scenario. On 25 November, after intelligence officers noted the departure of a Japanese task force heading in the general direction of Hawaii, a routine warning was sent to Pearl Harbor. American attention, however, was focused primarily on the movement of a large Japanese convoy southward, through the China Sea.

On 6 December the Japanese Embassy in Washington received the first thirteen parts of Tokyo's fourteen-part reply to Hull's message of 26 November. After reading the decoded messages, Roosevelt stated, 'This means war'.[3] Early on the morning of 7 December, the Americans decoded the final part of the Japanese message, wherein Japan rejected the American position, and severed negotiations. Ambassador Nomura Kichisaburō was told to deliver that message at 1 p.m. Washington time (7.30 a.m. in Hawaii), approximately half an hour before the Japanese attack was scheduled to begin. But delays meant the message was delivered over an hour late, by which time the attack had commenced.

In the early hours of Sunday, 7 December, 370 kilometres northwest of Pearl Harbor, the Japanese carriers launched their aircraft. Despite a dawn attack on a Japanese submarine at the entrance to the harbour, and despite US radar operators detecting the approaching aircraft, Japanese forces achieved complete surprise. At 7.55 a.m. the first wave of Japanese planes began dropping their bombs and torpedoes on American ships and air bases at Hawaii. During the two-hour attack, eight battleships were sunk or damaged, as well as numerous smaller vessels. In addition, 188 American planes were destroyed, and more than 2,400 Americans killed. The Japanese lost fewer than thirty aircraft. Although the attack on Pearl Harbor is generally understood to be the first strike by Japan, the Japanese attack at Kota Bharu on the Malay peninsula occurred about an hour earlier (because of the position of the international date line, it is recorded as 8 December 1941).

The US War Department had issued a warning message at noon (Washington time). But because radio contacts had been disrupted, that message was sent by commercial telegraph. Consequently, the message did not reach Hawaii for over eight hours – long after the attack. Even if that message had reached Hawaii more promptly, however, it is unlikely that officials there would have taken effective defensive measures, since few American analysts believed Japan could attack Pearl Harbor. Indeed, most American analyses of the debacle at Pearl Harbor are couched in terms of American diplomatic and military failures: 'how could we have let this happen?' In the short term, however, the events of December 1941 can be viewed as a triumph of Japanese audacity, planning and military skill. Maintaining radio silence to avoid detection, the Japanese fleet had made its way undetected 5,000 kilometres across the Pacific. Few

Americans had considered the Japanese capable of such a feat, just as few British or Australians expected the rapidity and effectiveness of the Japanese forces' approach and conquest of Singapore a few weeks later.

Few events in modern history have impacted so dramatically upon Americans as the Japanese surprise attack on Pearl Harbor. In an immediate sense, the Japanese raid unified Americans, bringing them together in a great patriotic endeavour to seek revenge and defeat their adversaries. Yet whilst the attack led to immediate and almost unanimous support for American entry into World War II, bewildered and angry Americans wondered how the Japanese been able to achieve such surprise.

Questions were raised about the official explanation of the events preceding the Japanese strike, and the attack has been the subject of persistent debate over American responsibility for the 'date that will live in infamy'. Since American intelligence analysts had cracked the Japanese diplomatic code, some writers have suggested those analysts should also have predicted the precise time and location of the Japanese attack. But while the intercepted messages revealed the Japanese were planning war, they did not yield precise military details, and made no reference to Pearl Harbor. Some writers have suggested that Roosevelt deliberately left the Pacific Fleet exposed at Pearl Harbor, where it would be vulnerable to Japanese attack.[4] Reasoning that Roosevelt wanted to involve the United States in the war in Europe but was prevented from doing so by American public opinion, proponents of this theory contend that the President deliberately provoked Japan into attacking American forces. But that theory rests on a series of unproved assertions regarding Roosevelt's motives and methods, and is also illogical: Even if the President somehow conspired to expose American forces, why did he expose so many ships to a Japanese attack?

Another group of writers have wondered why American commanders at Pearl Harbor were not warned more expeditiously about a possible Japanese attack. Proponents of this thesis have pointed to the tardiness with which a warning message was dispatched from Washington on the morning of 7 December.[5] However, the delay in transmitting the warning was a consequence of the casual approach on the part of those delegated to transmit the warning, rather than a result of a conspiracy on the part of American leaders to expose their fleet at Pearl Harbor. And American commanders believed the Japanese would be unable to approach Hawaii undetected. Pearl Harbor, they assumed, was too far from Japan to be the target of a major Japanese attack. The common American assumption was that Japan might attack in Southeast Asia. The disaster at Pearl Harbor was a consequence of incompetence and a lack of information, rather than a conspiracy to provoke Japan into war.

The sources that follow consist of several documents from the days preceding the attack at Pearl Harbor, along with several accounts of the Japanese attack and its aftermath. Considered together, they cast light on the priorities and actions of the Japanese and American governments, and convey the mixture of emotions experienced by the men and women caught up in the event that brought the United States into World War II. Although some of these recollections were not recorded until long after December 1941, raising questions about the accuracy of those memories, there can be no mistaking the chaos and confusion – as well as the courage and resolute determination – amongst the Americans caught so unaware on that fateful morning. And, as the penultimate document reveals, for the families of those American victims at Pearl Harbor – as for the families of the smaller number of Japanese casualties of the battle – the aftermath of 7 December brought continued suffering and anguish.

THE SOURCES

Prime Minister Tōjō Hideki Sums Up Japanese Sentiments, 1 December 1941

Speaking at an Imperial Conference a week before the attack on Pearl Harbor, Tōjō Hideki discussed the mood amongst the Japanese people. Although Japan's fledgling democratic traditions and institutions had been trampled in the 1930s, unlike his allies Hitler and Mussolini, Tōjō was not a dictator. A further distinction between Tōjō and Hitler and Mussolini was that while Tōjō was a popular prime minister, particularly during the early years, he was not a particularly charismatic leader. It was the task ahead, rather than Tōjō's words, that energised his audience.[6] And although the Japanese military was effectively running the country on a day-to-day basis by late 1941, Tōjō's comments suggest that Japanese leaders were mindful of popular opinion. The population was generally supportive of the military and largely convinced both of the legitimacy of Japan's interests in northeast China and of the need to protect them. They understood that waging war against the United States would require national unity and commitment that could not be taken for granted. Note, too, that Tōjō was under no illusion about the prospect of a last-minute diplomatic solution to the crisis with the United States:

When we take an overall view of popular opinion relating to Japanese-American problems, we conclude that the people in general are aware that our nation, in view of the present world situation, stands at a crossroads, one road leading to glory and the other to decline. They have shown an extraordinary interest in the diplomatic negotiations being carried out by the Government. Even though the Americans have given no indication that they would reconsider, and even though this has led to a rupture in diplomatic negotiations and [will lead] to the outbreak of war, they are prepared to accept this as an inevitable development. They are displaying the spirit characteristic of the Japanese people; and they are truly determined to undergo all manner of hardships, and to overcome adversity by united action.

The so-called nationalistic organizations have advocated a strong foreign policy; and once diplomatic negotiations end in failure, they will very likely demand that we move southward at once. Even the owners of small and medium-sized enterprises, whose livelihood has been much affected by the recent strengthening of economic controls – to say nothing of the laboring and peasant classes – are clearly aware of the position in which our country finds itself, and their spirits are high. It appears that they tend to want the Government to take an unambiguous position in executing a strong policy. There are, however, some within our large nation who would like to avoid war as much as possible at this time; but even these people have made up their minds that as long as the United States refuses to acknowledge our legitimate position, does not remove the economic blockade, and refuses to abandon her policy of oppressing Japan, our moving southward is inevitable, and if this action leads to a clash between Japan and the United States, this also cannot be helped.

To ensure that we will be able to maintain internal security in case an emergency situation arises following the rupture of Japanese-American negotiations, we have begun to make detailed plans for the more stringent measures that will be taken....

[W]e have especially strengthened our controls over those who are antiwar and antimilitary, such as Communists, rebellious Koreans, certain religious leaders, and others who we fear might be a threat to the public order. We believe that in some cases we might have to subject some of them to preventative arrest....

[T]here are the nationalistic organizations. Some of these tend to be very excitable; they are rash, and they may resort to violence. We believe they should be kept under observation and control; it may be necessary to temporarily detain those who would disturb the public peace....

[T]here is the control of rumors. We must be prepared for many rumors, given the serious nature of the situation. To stabilize the views held by the people, it will be necessary to guide public opinion, and at the same time to exercise strict controls over it....

[W]ith respect to various crimes that will arise in the confusion of war, we have finished conferring with the Ministry of Justice. We have given thought to various measures, especially making penalties more stringent, simplifying criminal trial procedures, and so on....

[W]e can anticipate that in a period of emergency the people are bound to be uneasy for a time because of food and monetary problems. We are paying particular attention to trends in attitudes among the people....

Franklin D. Roosevelt Appeals to Japanese Emperor Hirohito, 6 December 1941

On the afternoon of 6 December 1941, President Roosevelt wrote directly to Emperor Hirohito, hoping to ensure the maintenance of peace between the two nations. Referring to the Japanese occupation of Indochina, Roosevelt explained that Japan's southward advance had made many Asians, and Americans, anxious. Roosevelt's message, sent just hours before the Japanese attacked Pearl Harbor, raises interesting questions about his faith, or at least his hope, that a personal appeal to his counterpart might resolve the crisis between their two nations, even at that late hour. Given that Roosevelt's appeal was made public in the United States, it raises questions about the extent to which he assumed that war with Japan was likely, and shows he was determined to be seen by Americans as having made every effort to resolve the crisis peacefully. Finally, the message needs to be viewed in the context of the Japanese political system: the message was addressed to the Emperor because he was the sovereign ruler of Japan and its head of state, even if there are now debates about the extent of his authority:

The following message from the President to the Emperor of Japan was dispatched Saturday afternoon, December 6, and public announcement was made at that time that this message to the Emperor had been sent by the President:

Almost a century ago the President of the United States addressed to the Emperor of Japan a message extending an offer of friendship of the people of the United States to the people of Japan. That offer was accepted, and in the long period of unbroken peace and friendship which has followed, our respective nations, through the virtues of their peoples and the wisdom of their rulers have prospered and have substantially helped humanity.

Only in situations of extraordinary importance to our two countries need I address to Your Majesty messages on matters of state. I feel I should now so address you because of the deep and far-reaching emergency which appears to be in formation.

Developments are occurring in the Pacific area which threaten to deprive each of our nations and all humanity of the beneficial influence of the long peace between our two countries. Those developments contain tragic possibilities.

The people of the United States, believing in peace and in the right of nations to live and let live, have eagerly watched the conversations between our two Governments during these past months. We have hoped for a termination of the present conflict between Japan and China. We have hoped that a peace of the Pacific could be consummated in such a way that nationalities of many diverse peoples could exist side by side without fear of invasion; that unbearable burdens of armaments could be lifted for them all; and that all peoples would resume commerce without discrimination against or in favor of any nation.

I am certain that it will be clear to Your Majesty, as it is to me, that in seeking these great objectives both Japan and the United States should agree to eliminate any form of military threat. This seemed essential to the attainment of the high objectives.

More than a year ago Your Majesty's Government concluded an agreement with the Vichy Government by which five or six thousand Japanese troops were permitted to enter into Northern French Indo-China for the protection of Japanese troops which were operating against China further north. And this Spring and Summer the Vichy Government permitted further Japanese military forces to enter into Southern French Indo-China for the common defense of French Indo-China. I think I am correct in saying that no attack has been made upon Indo-China, nor that any has been contemplated.

During the past few weeks it has become clear to the world that Japanese military, naval and air forces have been sent to Southern Indo-China in such large numbers as to create a reasonable doubt on the part of other nations that this continuing concentration in Indo-China is not defensive in its character.

Because these continuing concentrations in Indo-China have reached such large proportions and because they extend now to the southeast and the southwest corners of that Peninsula, it is only reasonable that the people of the Philippines, of the hundreds of Islands of the East Indies, of Malaya and of Thailand itself are asking themselves whether these forces of Japan are preparing or intending to make attack in one or more of these many directions.

I am sure that Your Majesty will understand that the fear of all these peoples is a legitimate fear inasmuch as it involves their peace and their national existence. I am sure that Your Majesty will understand why the people of the United States in such large numbers look askance at the establishment of military, naval and air bases manned and equipped so greatly as to constitute armed forces capable of measures of offense.

It is clear that a continuance of such a situation is unthinkable.

None of the peoples whom I have spoken of above can sit either indefinitely or permanently on a keg of dynamite.

There is absolutely no thought on the part of the United States of invading Indo-China if every Japanese soldier or sailor were to be withdrawn therefrom.

I think that we can obtain the same assurance from the Governments of the East Indies, the Governments of Malaya and the Government of Thailand. I would even undertake to ask for the same assurance on the part of the Government of China. Thus a withdrawal of the Japanese forces from Indo-China would result in the assurance of peace throughout the whole of the South Pacific area.

I address myself to Your Majesty at this moment in the fervent hope that Your Majesty may, as I am doing, give thought in this definite emergency to way of dispelling the dark clouds. I am confident that both of us, for the sake of the peoples not only of our own great countries but for the sake of humanity in neighboring territories, have a sacred duty to restore traditional amity and prevent further death and destruction in the world.

Recalling the Attack on Pearl Harbor:
A Japanese Memoir

Because of the general dearth of translated primary materials on Japan's experience of the Pacific War, military and political memoirs are a genre much trawled by Western historians. Noting the growing number of memoirs being published in Japan during the 1950s, Nobutake Ike observed they were 'of great value' because 'they often contain material about personalities and events that are unobtainable elsewhere'. He also acknowledged, however, that memoirs were 'rarely models of objective writing'.[7] And whilst modern scholars are now more sympathetic to the historical value of memoirs, it remains important to distinguish a document produced at the time of an event being chronicled – such as a diary – from a memoir recalling that event. Understanding the chronology between such documents might also provide hitherto unconsidered insights.[8]

Japanese memoirs of World War II were influenced by two literary traditions within Japanese society. During the 1920s *seikatsu tsuzurikata* – life-experience composition – became an important subject in the Japanese classroom. This educational practice was strongly influenced by developments in Japanese literature, including the increasing popularity of the *shishosetsu* – 'I-novel' – as a literary genre. In contrast to approaches popular in the English-speaking world, Japanese students were instructed not to manipulate their experience to produce drama or closure (thus not engaging in the teleological as occurred in Western examples). Authors were seen to be writing for themselves, not for a reader. Students were instructed to tell their story 'as it really was' (*jijitsu*) and to consider the sensations the experience provoked. When these principles were extended to the 'I-novel', it meant that a Japanese reader applied critical judgment not to the written work itself but to the author's life.[9] Such judgments meant fictionalised dimensions of a work would be considered true in the midst of the evaluation of the life in focus.

Fuchida Mitsuo commanded the first wave of the air attack on Pearl Harbor. In 1951 his recollections were published in Japan; four years later, they were translated and published in English. Western stylistic approaches did find their way into the texts, and drama and closure were apparent in Fuchida's account. In these excerpts, Fuchida's delight that the American battleships were in port was tempered by his disappointment that no aircraft carriers were in Pearl Harbor when the Japanese attacked:

One hour and forty minutes after leaving the carriers I knew that we should be nearing our goal. Small openings in the thick cloud cover afforded occasional glimpses of the ocean, as I strained my eyes for the first sight of land. Suddenly a long white line of breaking surf appeared directly beneath my plane. It was the northern shore of Oahu.

Veering right toward the west coast of the island, we could see that the sky over Pearl Harbor was clear. Presently the harbor itself became visible across the central Oahu plain, a film of morning mist hovering over it. I peered intently through my binoculars at the ships riding peacefully at anchor. One by one I counted them. Yes, the battleships were there all right, eight of them! But our last lingering hope of finding any carriers present was now gone. Not one was to be seen.

It was 0749 when I ordered my radioman to send the command, 'Attack!' He immediately began tapping out the pre-arranged code signal: 'TO, TO, TO...'

Leading the whole group, Lieutenant Commander Murata's torpedo bombers headed downward to launch their torpedoes, while Lieutenant Commander Itaya's fighters raced forward to sweep enemy fighters from the air. Takahashi's dive-bomber group had climbed for altitude and was out of sight. My bombers, meanwhile, made a circuit toward Barbers Point to keep pace with the attack schedule. No enemy fighters were in the air, nor were there any gun flashes from the ground.

The effectiveness of our attack was now certain, and a message, 'Surprise attack successful!' was accordingly sent to *Akagi* [Flagship of the Japanese attack fleet] at 0753. The message was received by the carrier and duly relayed to the homeland....

The attack was opened with the first bomb falling on Wheeler Field, followed shortly by dive-bombing attacks upon Hickam Field and the bases at Ford Island. Fearful that smoke from these attacks might obscure his targets, Lieutenant Commander Murata cut short his group's approach toward the battleships anchored east of Ford Island and released torpedoes. A series of white waterspouts soon rose in the harbor.

Lieutenant Commander Itaya's fighters, meanwhile, had full command of the air over Pearl Harbor. About four enemy fighters which took off were promptly shot down. By 0800 there were no enemy planes in the air, and our fighters began strafing the airfields.

My level-bombing group had entered on its bombing run toward the battleships moored to the cast of Ford Island. On reaching an altitude of 3,000 meters, I had the sighting bomber take position in front of my plane.

As we closed in, enemy antiaircraft fire began to concentrate on us. Dark gray puffs burst all around. Most of them came from ships' batteries, but land batteries were also active. Suddenly my plane bounced as if struck by a club. When I looked back to see what had happened, the radioman said: 'The fuselage is holed and the rudder wire damaged.' We were fortunate that the plane was still under control, for it was imperative to fly a steady course as we approached the target. Now it was nearly time for 'Ready to release,' and I concentrated my attention on the lead plane to note the instant his bomb was dropped. Suddenly a cloud came between the bombsight and the target, and just as I was thinking that we had already overshot, the lead plane banked slightly and turned right toward Honolulu. We had missed the release point because of the cloud and would have to try again.

While my group circled for another attempt, others made their runs, some trying as many as three before succeeding. We were about to begin our second bombing run when there was a colossal explosion in battleship row.

A huge column of dark red smoke rose to 1000 meters. It must have been the explosion of a ship's powder magazine. The shock wave was felt even in my plane, several miles away from the harbor.

We began our run and met with fierce antiaircraft concentrations. This time the lead bomber was successful, and the other planes of the group followed suit promptly upon seeing the leader's bombs fall. I immediately lay flat on the cockpit floor and slid open a peephole cover in order to observe the fall of the bombs. I watched four bombs plummet toward the earth. The target – two battleships moored side by side – lay ahead. The bombs became smaller and smaller and finally disappeared. I held my breath until two tiny puffs of smoke flashed suddenly on the ship to the left, and I shouted, 'Two hits!'

When an armor-piercing bomb with a time fuse hits the target, the result is almost unnoticeable from a great altitude. On the other hand, those which miss are quite obvious because they leave concentric waves to ripple out from the point of contact, and I saw two of these below. I presumed that it was battleship *Maryland* we had hit.

As the bombers completed their runs they headed north to return to the carriers. Pearl Harbor and the air bases had been pretty well wrecked by the fierce strafings and bombings. The imposing naval array of an hour before was gone. Antiaircraft fire had become greatly intensified, but in my continued observations I saw no enemy fighter planes. Our command of the air was unchallenged.

Recalling the Attack on Pearl Harbor: An American Eyewitness

With the American aircraft carriers away from Pearl Harbor, the major targets of the Japanese attack were the battleships at anchor along 'Battleship Row'. A few minutes after the attack commenced, a Japanese bomb crashed through the decks of the *Arizona*; the ensuing fire spread rapidly, and the ship sank quickly. Over 1,300 Americans died as the *Arizona* went down. One of the survivors was Marine Corporal Earl C. Nightingale. In the wake of the attack, survivors such as Nightingale were called on to provide eyewitness accounts to help explain and understand the chain of events of that day. Many of these accounts were recorded and then included in action reports of those ships in the harbour on that fateful Sunday.

Eyewitness accounts are often assumed to be the 'fountainhead of all history'. But such accounts are no less problematic than memoirs, and those which describe battle environments are usually 'deficient': 'They only see a fraction of what was happening and often through screens of smoke'.[10] Despite the advantage of immediacy, an eyewitness has time to process their experiences; in converting those experiences into an account, eyewitnesses often construct a narrative, and a coherence, that did not exist at the time. Like memoirs, therefore, the validity of 'after-action' eyewitness accounts is open to question if they are being used to provide information. At the same time, however, the apparent weakness of eyewitness accounts can also be their strength: they are confined to small areas and can provide a spontaneous and visceral account that contextualises the big picture.

At approximately eight o'clock on the morning of December 7, 1941, I was leaving the breakfast table when the ship's siren for air defense sounded. Having no anti-aircraft battle station, I paid little attention to it. Suddenly I heard an explosion. I ran to the port door leading to the quarterdeck and saw a bomb strike a barge of some sort alongside the *Nevada*, or in that vicinity. The marine color guard came in at this point saying we were being attacked. I could distinctly hear machine gun fire. I believe at this point our anti-aircraft battery opened up.

We stood around awaiting orders of some kind. General Quarters sounded and I started for my battle station in secondary aft. As I passed through casement nine I noted the gun was manned and being trained out. The men seemed extremely calm and collected. I reached the boat deck and our anti-aircraft guns were in full action, firing very rapidly. I was about three quarters of the way to the first platform on the mast when it seemed as though a bomb struck our quarterdeck. I could hear shrapnel or fragments whistling past me. As soon as I reached the first platform, I saw Second Lieutenant Simonson lying on his back with blood on his shirt front. I bent over him and taking him by the shoulders asked if there was anything I could do. He was dead, or so nearly so that speech was impossible. Seeing there was nothing I could do for the Lieutenant, I continued to my battle station.

When I arrived in secondary aft I reported to Major Shapley that Mr. Simonson had been hit and there was nothing to be done for him. There was a lot of talking going on and I shouted for silence which came immediately. I had only been there a short time when a terrible explosion caused the ship to shake violently. I looked at the boat deck and everything seemed aflame forward of the mainmast. I reported to the Major that the ship was aflame, which was rather needless, and after looking about, the Major ordered us to leave.

I was the last man to leave secondary aft because I looked around and there was no one left. I followed the Major down the port side of the tripod mast. The railings, as we ascended, were very hot and as we reached the boat deck I noted that it was torn up and burned. The bodies of the dead were thick, and badly burned men were heading for the quarterdeck, only to fall apparently dead or badly wounded. The Major and I went between No. 3 and No. 4 turret to the starboard side and found Lieutenant Commander Fuqua ordering the men over the side and assisting the wounded. He seemed exceptionally calm and the Major stopped and they talked for a moment. Charred bodies were everywhere.

I made my way to the quay and started to remove my shoes when I suddenly found myself in the water. I think the concussion of a bomb threw me in. I started swimming for the pipe line which was about one hundred and fifty feet away. I was about half way when my strength gave out entirely. My clothes and shocked condition sapped my strength, and I was about to go under when Major Shapley started to swim by, and seeing my distress, grasped my shirt and told me to hang to his shoulders while he swam in.

We were perhaps twenty-five feet from the pipe line when the Major's strength gave out and I saw he was floundering, so I loosened my grip on him and told him to make it alone. He stopped and grabbed me by the shirt and refused to let go. I would have drowned but for the Major. We finally reached the beach where a marine directed us to a bomb shelter, where I was given dry clothes and a place to rest.

Remembering Pearl Harbor: A Nurse's Perspective

By convention, the battlefield was considered largely a male space; in practice, the total wars of the twentieth century meant women were often exposed to the same horrors as men. In the following extract, Lieutenant Ruth Erickson – a nurse at Naval Hospital, Pearl Harbor – recalls the events of 7 December 1941. In discussing the horror and chaos of that momentous day, she also said something about the way in which adrenaline and a sense of duty kept her fears at bay – at least initially.

Erickson's words are transcribed oral testimony – recollections provided fifty-eight years after the event. 'Oral history', such as Erickson's, is informed by memory. The unreliability of memory has seen many historians question the usefulness of oral history for historical research: it can be 'a slippery medium for preserving facts'.[11] Like memoirs, however, oral history can be the only available source for historians because of the paucity of surviving sources. Oral history touches the past directly in ways that other forms of historical evidence do not.[12] As war was generally considered men's business, women's experiences were devalued or ignored. Finally, further developments in historical methodology, critiquing the efficacy of more traditional forms of historical evidence, have given greater value to the role and usefulness of memory in history.[13] Like memoirs, what and how an individual remembers an event in their past provides historians with useful material for analysis.

Two or three of us were sitting in the dining room Sunday morning having a late breakfast and talking over coffee. Suddenly we heard planes roaring overhead and we said, 'The "fly boys" are really busy at Ford Island this morning.' The island was directly across the channel from the hospital. We didn't think too much about it since the reserves were often there for weekend training. We no sooner got those words out when we started to hear noises that were foreign to us.

I leaped out of my chair and dashed to the nearest window in the corridor. Right then there was a plane flying directly over the top of our quarters, a one-story structure. The rising sun under the wing of the plane denoted the enemy. Had I known the pilot, one could almost see his features around his goggles. He was obviously saving his ammunition for the ships. Just down the row, all the ships were sitting there....

My heart was racing, the telephone was ringing, the chief nurse, Gertrude Arnest, was saying, 'Girls, get into your uniforms at once. This is the real thing!'

I was in my room by that time changing into uniform. It was getting dusky, almost like evening. Smoke was rising from burning ships.

I dashed across the street, through a shrapnel shower, got into the lanai and just stood still for a second as were a couple of doctors. I felt like I were frozen to the ground, but it was only a split second. I ran to the orthopedic dressing room but it was locked. A corpsmen ran to the OD's [Officer-of-the-Day's] desk for the keys. It seemed like an eternity before he returned and the room was opened. We drew water into every container we could find and set up the instrument boiler. Fortunately, we still had electricity and water. Dr. Brunson, the chief of medicine was making sick call when the bombing started. When he was finished, he was to play golf ... a phrase never to be uttered again.

The first patient came into our dressing room at 8:25 a.m. with a large opening in his abdomen and bleeding profusely. They started an intravenous and transfusion. I can still see the tremor of Dr. Brunson's hand as he picked up the needle. Everyone was terrified. The patient died within the hour.

Then the burned patients streamed in. The USS Nevada had managed some steam and attempted to get out of the channel. They were unable to make it and went aground on Hospital Point right near the hospital. There was heavy oil on the water and the men dived off the ship and swam through these waters to Hospital Point, not too great a distance, but when one is burned. How they ever managed, I'll never know.

The tropical dress at the time was white t-shirts and shorts. The burns began where the pants ended. Bared arms and faces were plentiful.

Personnel retrieved a supply of flit guns from stock. We filled these with tannic acid to spray burned bodies. Then we gave these gravely injured patients sedatives for their intense pain.

Orthopedic patients were eased out of their beds with no time for linen changes as an unending stream of burn patients continued until mid afternoon.

A doctor, who several days before had renal surgery and was still convalescing, got out of his bed and began to assist the other doctors.

I was relieved around 4 p.m. and went over to the nurses' quarters where everything was intact. I freshened up, had something to eat, and went back on duty at 8 p.m. I was scheduled to report to a surgical unit. By now it was dark and we worked with flashlights. The maintenance people and anyone else who could manage a hammer and nails were putting up black drapes or black paper to seal the crevices against any light that might stream to the outside.

About 10 or 11 o'clock, there were planes overhead. I really hadn't felt frightened until this particular time. My knees were knocking together and the patients were calling, 'Nurse, nurse!' The other nurse and I went to them, held their hands a few moments, and then went onto others.

The priest was a very busy man. The noise ended very quickly and the word got around that these were our own planes.

18 August 1999

President Franklin D. Roosevelt Labels 7 December 1941 as a 'Date Which Will Live in Infamy'

Late in the afternoon of 7 December 1941, President Roosevelt summoned his secretary to the Oval Office. A state of war existed between Japan and the United States but Congress still had to make a formal declaration of war to give the President the requisite powers as Commander-in-Chief to prosecute the war. Off the top of his head, Roosevelt dictated the speech he would make to Congress the following day. While there was little time to redraft the speech, Roosevelt used the evening of that fateful day to refine the typed copy provided by his secretary. The most famous line of the speech had originally been dictated as a 'date which will live in world history'. Roosevelt replaced 'world history' with 'infamy', the term that became the central rhetorical theme of the speech.[14]

Roosevelt's speech rested comfortably within a long-held American tradition whereby, in an emotion-charged speech, the president asserts his leadership of the nation at a time of national crisis: 'through rhetorical conventions, presidents assume extraordinary powers as the commander in chief'.[15] Roosevelt's speech was broadcast to the nation via radio. He informed his fellow countrymen and women that the surprise Japanese attack would serve only to unite Americans in their determination to avenge the events of the day of 'infamy'. The Senate responded by voting unanimously in support of war. In the House of Representatives, the vote was 388 to 1. (Jeanette Rankin of Montana, who had also voted against war in 1917, was the lone dissenter.)

Yesterday, December 7, 1941 – a date which will live in infamy – the United States of America was suddenly and deliberately attacked by naval and air forces of the Empire of Japan.

The United States was at peace with that nation and, at the solicitation of Japan, was still in conversation with its Government and its Emperor looking toward the maintenance of peace in the Pacific. Indeed, one hour after Japanese air squadrons had commenced bombing in Oahu, the Japanese Ambassador to the United States and his colleague delivered to the Secretary of State a formal reply to a recent American message. While this reply stated that it seemed useless to continue the existing diplomatic negotiations, it contained no threat or hint of war or armed attack.

It will be recorded that the distance of Hawaii from Japan makes it obvious that the attack was deliberately planned many days or even weeks ago. During the intervening time the Japanese Government has deliberately sought to deceive the United States by false statements and expressions of hope for continued peace.

The attack yesterday on the Hawaiian Islands has caused severe damage to American naval and military forces. Very many American lives have been lost. In addition American ships have been reported torpedoed on the high seas between San Francisco and Honolulu.

Yesterday the Japanese Government also launched an attack against Malaya. Last night Japanese forces attacked Hong Kong. Last night Japanese forces attacked Guam. Last night Japanese forces attacked the Philippine Islands. Last night the Japanese attacked Wake Island. This morning the Japanese attacked Midway Island.

Japan has, therefore, undertaken a surprise offensive extending throughout the Pacific area. The facts of yesterday speak for themselves. The people of the United States have already formed their opinions and well understand the implications to the very life and safety of our nation.

As Commander-in-Chief of the Army and Navy, I have directed that all measures be taken for our defense.

Always will we remember the character of the onslaught against us. No matter how long it may take us to overcome this premeditated invasion, the American people in their righteous might will win through to absolute victory.

I believe I interpret the will of the Congress and of the people when I assert that we will not only defend ourselves to the uttermost but will make very certain that this form of treachery shall never endanger us again.

Hostilities exist. There is no blinking at the fact that our people, our territory and our interests are in grave danger.

With confidence in our armed forces – with the unbounded determination of our people – we will gain the inevitable triumph – so help us God.

I ask that the Congress declare that since the unprovoked and dastardly attack by Japan on Sunday, December seventh, a state of war has existed between the United States and the Japanese Empire.

The Japanese Population Is Told of the Attack

On the morning after the attack on Pearl Harbor and Malaya, Japanese newspapers announced to their readers the new state of war against the United States and its Allies. The front page of Japan's largest mass-circulation daily, the *Asahi Shinbun*, contained amongst extra-large headlines the Imperial Edict proclaiming war. The adjoining editorial, shifted for the occasion to the front page, provided a justification of the situation. For most Japanese, the editorial would have been more easily understood than the stilted language of the proclamation itself, although of course it did not deviate from, or provide critical appraisal of the proclamation. The editorial clearly suggests the momentous nature of the attack on United States and British interests for Japan, even for a nation that had been at war for several years already. For the population, accustomed to news of war on the China front and the sacrifices that entailed, the new state of affairs, including the exhortations for new and larger sacrifices, was both exhilarating and worrisome. The constant references to one hundred million Japanese is less a demographic truth (the population was not quite as large unless one included Japanese colonial subjects) as a commonly used rhetorical device suggesting unity and strength.

The imperial edict declaring war has been proclaimed and shall be adhered to strictly by the one-hundred million people of this nation. The elite of our Army and Navy have already acted in high spirits: in one short moment, they changed the face of the Pacific.

Despite our Empire's efforts to find a path of peaceful cooperation between the United States and Japan, and its desperate attempts to find a solution and seek reconsideration of the situation by the United States, the United States has stubbornly stuck to its mistaken principles and has been deaf to our justified claims.

On the contrary, not only has the US insisted on various unrealistic conditions, such as the full withdrawal of Imperial troops from China, the non-recognition of the Nanking government [the collaborationist government of Wang Chingwei] and the annulment of the Tripartite Alliance with Germany and Italy, but it has also strengthened its military preparations for the isolation of Japan, at the head of its satellite nations of England, Holland and Chongqing China. Thus all our efforts to reach a peaceful settlement have come to naught. In other words, unless we eliminate once and for all the US-led group of anti-Japanese nations from East Asia, we will be unable to reach our ultimate and most important national aims: the conclusion of the China incident and the establishment of the Greater East Asia Co-Prosperity Sphere. We have reached the stage, as Prime Minister Tōjō has said, when 'we will not only have to submit to their authority, lose the sovereignty of our Empire, and fail to reach conclusion on the China incident, but in the end we will put in great danger the very existence of the Empire'.

Having come to this, we must make a stand in order to protect the existence of the Empire itself, and one hundred million people as one must make unstinting efforts to fight to the ultimate end for victory.

As we receive the Imperial Edict of the declaration of war, we cannot help but be dumbstruck with awe, and overwhelmed by emotion. We must prepare ourselves, in order to be able later to look back without shame at this crucial moment in history, to sacrifice to the nation, according to the Emperor's wish, our bodies and souls, joined together as one hundred million brothers, whether it be on the war front or on the home front.

The enemy has superior resources. Not only that, but what the enemy stands for is his will for world conquest, with complete disregard of law. Consequently, we must break the enemy and consolidate the Empire. In order to construct a new order in East Asia, the people must overcome every hardship and break though every trial brought by Heaven even if the war should last a long time. We must establish solid foundations for a strong and everlasting Asia.

At the same time as the declaration of war, we are receiving one after the other momentous reports on our victories. These are extremely satisfying. Under the Emperor's grace, the will of Heaven always protects the Imperial nation when we fight armoured with an unstinting faith in loyalty for the nation.

At this decisive time for the fate of our nation, the day has come when we must give everything to this nation of one hundred million.

British Prime Minister Winston Churchill Reacts to the Japanese Attack at Pearl Harbor

By December 1941, Britain had been at war with Germany for over two years. After the fall of France in June 1940, Britain – and its empire – had stood alone against the Axis powers of Germany and Italy. During 1940 and 1941, the United States provided increasing aid to Britain, and after the German invasion of the Soviet Union in June 1941, Britain not only had a new ally in the European war but also knew that with the German Army preoccupied with the war on the Eastern Front, that there was little chance of a German invasion of the British Isles. Nonetheless, as German submarines wreaked havoc on British shipping in the Atlantic, Britain was far from secure. Prime Minister Winston Churchill knew his country's best chance of securing victory would come through American entry into the war. In his memoirs, penned soon after the end of the war, Churchill recalled his reaction upon hearing the news of the Japanese attack on Pearl Harbor, and reflected on his impressions of the United States and its people. Unlike many important political figures of the time, Churchill did not keep a private diary that might serve as a rough draft or memory jogger for his future recollections.

It was Sunday evening, December 7, 1941. ... I turned on my small wireless set shortly after the nine o'clock news had started. There were a number of items about the fighting on the Russian front and on the British front in Libya, at the end of which some few sentences were spoken regarding an attack by the Japanese on American shipping at Hawaii, and also Japanese attacks on British vessels in the Dutch East Indies. ... [O]n November 11 I had said that if Japan attacked the United States a British declaration of war would follow "within the hour". ... I asked for a call to the President....

In two or three minutes Mr. Roosevelt came through. "Mr. President, what's this about Japan?" "It's quite true," he replied. "They have attacked us at Pearl Harbour. We are all in the same boat now." I ... said "This certainly simplifies things. God be with you."...

No American will think it wrong of me if I proclaim that to have the United States at our side was to me the greatest joy. I could not foretell the course of events. I did not pretend to have measured accurately the martial spirit of Japan, but now at this very minute I knew the United States was in the war, up to the neck and in to the death. ... We had won the war. England would live; Britain would live; the Commonwealth of Nations and the Empire would live. How long the war would last or in what fashion it would end no man could tell, nor did I at that moment care. Once again in our long island history we should emerge, however mauled or mutilated, safe and victorious. We should not be wiped out. Our history would not come to an end. We might not even have to die as individuals. Hitler's fate was sealed. Mussolini's fate was sealed. As for the Japanese, they would be ground to powder. All the rest was merely the proper application of overwhelming force. ... No doubt it would take a long time. I expected terrible forfeits in the East, but all this would merely be a passing phase. United we could subdue everybody else in the world. Many disasters, immeasurable cost and tribulation lay ahead, but there was no more doubt about the end.

Silly people, and there were many, not only in enemy countries, might discount the force of the United States. Some said they were soft, others that they would never be united. They would fool around at a distance. They would never come to grips. They would never stand blood-letting. Their democracy and system of recurrent elections would paralyse the war effort. They might just be a vague blur on the horizon to friend or foe. Now we should see the weaknesses of this numerous but remote, wealthy, and talkative people. But I had studied the American Civil War, fought out to the last desperate inch. American blood flowed in my veins. I thought of a remark which Edward Grey had made to me more than thirty years before – that the United States is like "a gigantic boiler. Once the fire is lighted under it there is no limit to the power it can generate". Being saturated and satiated with emotion and sensation, I went to bed and slept the sleep of the saved and thankful.

A Case of Mistaken Identity: Reporting Casualties

Wars bring injury and death. Informing relatives of the status of their loved ones was an important task for the bureaucracies of the major combatants during World War II. Without a peacetime equivalent, the American system looked back to the processes that had been established during the Great War. Changes, however, quickly had to be made due to the number of casualties, as well as technological advances. Individual units alerted theatre headquarters of any dead, missing or wounded personnel. This information was then collated and sent by cablegram or radiogram to the War Department in Washington, DC, where individual forms for each service member would be manually recorded and a telegram prepared for the next of kin. To aid efficiency, the detail in the telegrams was very brief.

Japanese and Australian systems also relied on the postal telegraph system to inform next of kin.[16] In Australia, telegrams were sent by the government late in the afternoon. These were sent to the nearest post office of the next of kin. The message would then be delivered by the local post-man the following morning. At midday the following day, the postmaster would be contacted via a second telegram asking him to urgently respond and confirm the telegram had been delivered. Postal workers in Japan and the United States were also charged with this unpleasant duty.

In all three countries next-of-kin would often write back to the government seeking more information on the circumstances of their loved one's death. Such details were often not available – even if the government had had the ability to respond to each request individually. Information often came through informal channels from letters written by friends of the deceased or their commanding officer. It was not until 1944 that new American regulations were introduced that compelled letters of condolence to be written by a deceased member's unit, hospital personnel or a chaplain. These letters were to provide more details for families regarding the circumstances of the death. Given the scale and nature of the Pacific War, it was perhaps not surprising that the system of reporting casualties was not infallible.

The early unreliability of the American casualty reporting system is exampled in the case of James T. Hamlin. Hamlin was a crewman on board the battleship *USS California* on the morning of 7 December 1941. Nine days later, his parents, Mr. and Mrs. Green Hamlin, of the small town of Harlan, Kentucky, received a telegram from the Navy Department:

Washington, D.C., December 16 [1941]
Mr. Green Hamlin.

The Navy Department deeply regrets to inform you that your son, James Thomas Hamlin, Fireman First Class, U.S. Navy, was lost in action in the

performance of his duty and in the service of his country. The Department extends to you its sincerest sympathy in your great loss. To prevent possible aid to our enemies please do not divulge the name of his ship or station. If remains are recovered they will be interred temporarily in the locality where death occurred and you will be notified accordingly,
    Rear Admiral C. W. Nimitz, Chief of the Bureau of Navigation

On New Year's Eve, the distraught family received a second telegram from the Navy:

Washington, D.C., December 31 [1941]
Mr. Green Hamlin.

The Navy Department is glad to inform you that your son James Thomas Hamlin Fireman First Class US Navy previously reported missing following action in the performance of his duty is now reported to be a survivor. He will doubtless communicate direct with you at an early date informing you as to his welfare and whereabouts.

Rebuilding after Pearl Harbor

Almost as soon as the Japanese attack had finished on 7 December, Americans began rebuilding what remained of their base at Pearl Harbor. Although the Japanese had inflicted a terrible blow to US' naval power, the damage was less grievous than many Americans initially feared: as noted, the American fleet of aircraft carriers had been away from port when the Japanese struck, and as events soon proved, those carriers played a pivotal role in first halting, then reversing the Japanese advances across the Pacific. The most severe damage inflicted on the US Navy at Pearl Harbor was to the fleet of battleships, five of which were sunk. In several cases, however, vessels were successfully salvaged, and this 1943 article from the *New York Times* details the efforts and sacrifices made to bring the *West Virginia* back to battle-ready condition. This effort was one aspect of the United States' successful endeavour to deploy its industrial might to best effect. Japan's inability to match the United States in this regard was an important factor behind its eventual defeat. Articles of this type were written and published partly to provide information, and partly to build American morale.

Nowhere in the world, according to Navy officers here, have Navy and civilian workers toiled together in such close coordination and harmony on a monumental task. Their joint achievement has never been equaled, either as a feat in mechanics or as an example of cooperation between military and nonmilitary men.
    When the subject of the *West Virginia* is mentioned to the men who worked on its salvage, they seldom say anything. They just whistle.

The Japanese left this $27 million beauty a model for destruction. It will be amazing and disheartening to them now to learn that it will return to the war a better ship than it was before.

The West Virginia's 32,600-ton mass lay deep in the water when the Japanese flew away. It listed far to port, its starboard bilge hooked into the adjacent battleship Tennessee.

Seven torpedoes had hit its port side, blowing out a series of gashes above and below the armor belt 120 feet long and so wide from lip to lip that two tall men could stand, one on the other's shoulders, in the vent.

The boat deck was a shattered mass. Bombs laid open four decks that way an earthquake might tear away the wall of a four-story building, leaving the rooms indecently exposed. Up on the bridge, Capt. Mervyn S. Bennion had lain grievously wounded, refusing to be moved, and there he died. Posthumously he was awarded his country's highest honor, the Congressional Medal....

As the pumps strained to suck out the fouled sea inside, the West Virginia rose, inch by inch. Each new day disclosed a new surface ring of oil and black muck from the harbor bottom marking on the cofferdam the laborious progress of the ship's flotation.

During this time, the workers lived close ashore in rude huts built for them so they could stay near the job. They came to work on foot, over a bridge laid on floats. These were sailors all. The "yard workmen," civilians, had their customary quarters elsewhere, and were taken to and from the ship by boat.

When the time came to nurse the West Virginia over the sill and into dry dock, the engineers held their breath, for the battleship now was in great danger of striking some small obstruction that would rupture it again....

[T]he job before Admiral Furlong's big and hard-bitten organization could be stated simply, but the implications were staggering. They just had to rebuild a large portion of the ship. ... Discoveries odd and gruesome were frequent as the men set about righting and cleansing the charnel. This work was arduous and discouraging, but the work crews, supervised by the West Virginia's own officers and men who treated the maimed battleship as a mother would tend a sick child, carried on.

There were instances of heroism in the salvage that deserve to go permanently into the annals of Dec. 7. One day an unexploded 1,750-pound bomb was discovered. ... An officer risked his life to unscrew the live fuses....

Workmen prowling the ruins below decks made several tragic discoveries of the type that can only be expected when a city of more than a thousand men is hurled to the bottom of the sea in a space of minutes....

The electrical equipment, with its hundreds of miles of wiring, was also brought on deck and cleaned preparatory to overhaul. Some 50 specialists from General Electric … were brought from the mainland for the complex rewiring. The taxpayer may rest assured that the Navy isn't throwing away anything that can be fixed.

Summing up the *West Virginia* job, Admiral Furlong said: "We built her new from the inside out. We went right to the bottom, like a dentist drilling out a rotten tooth."

CHAPTER THREE
THE JAPANESE ADVANCE, 1941–1942

SURRENDER, and from my narrow view of affairs, a shameful surrender. … Feeling of utter disgust and shame, never saw a Jap, never fired a shot and there are thousands like us.

Alec Hodgson, 16 February 1942, following the Allied surrender at Singapore

The Japanese strike at Pearl Harbor was only one of a number of attacks launched on 7 December 1941. As the bombs and torpedoes struck the American Pacific fleet, American and British possessions elsewhere in the Asia-Pacific were also attacked. These attacks were part of a broader strategy for securing Japan's primary objective: the oil fields of the Dutch East Indies.

The US Pacific Fleet, which had posed the major threat to a Japanese advance southwards, had been severely damaged, but the flanks of a Japanese advance on the Indies also had to be cleared. On the right flank sat the British in Hong Kong, Malaya and Singapore, and on the left the Americans in the Philippines. Prior to the Japanese attack, the British, American, Dutch and Australian militaries had established a joint command structure for the defence of the Asia-Pacific, known as ABDACOM (American-British-Dutch-Australian Command), and established its headquarters in Singapore under the command of British General Archibald Wavell. Wavell's orders were straightforward: stop the Japanese from advancing, and prevent them reaching the oil fields of the Indies.[1]

Wavell's forces outnumbered the Japanese, but he faced two major problems. First, because of American neutrality and suspicions about where Dutch loyalties actually lay, there had been very little planning or coordination of the forces available. ABDACOM was, to a large degree, a public relations exercise – an attempt to create a posture of deterrence.[2] Second, to protect the Philippines, Malaya and the Dutch East Indies, the Allied forces were dispersed thinly.

Shortly after the beginning of the Pacific War, Winston Churchill and Franklin Roosevelt met in Washington. The ARCADIA Conference – as these talks were known – established Allied 'Grand Strategy' for the conduct of the war. It set up the Supreme Allied Command and reinforced the principle of 'Europe first', whereby Allied resources would be prioritised to 'beat Hitler first'. The Allies employed a 'strategic defensive' plan for the Pacific, but there were doubts concerning their ability to hold Malaya and the Philippines.

Mark Peattie has suggested that for Japan, war offered 'glittering opportunity and appalling risks'.[3] The ongoing war with China was a drain on manpower and resources, and the new front opened against the United States and its Allies to reach the oil, tin and rubber of the Dutch East Indies was a gamble for opportunity and time. With most of its naval air power committed to the Pearl Harbor strike, and the attack forces heading for Malaya and the Philippines outnumbered by the defenders, the element of surprise and the ability to concentrate forces in specific locations, while the British and Americans had been forced to stretch their resources to cover various attack possibilities, were crucial to Japanese success.

Japan's gains of 1942 exceeded the wildest expectations of their strategists as promulgated in their original plans of November 1941.

Japanese success can be explained by the Allies' lack of preparedness as much as by superior Japanese strategic preparation. Four years of war with China had oiled Japan's military decision-making machinery, and turned many of its soldiers into experienced combat veterans. Allied resistance had been much less vigorous than anticipated. Japanese success can also be explained through an examination of the nation's military doctrine. The Japanese were creative and experienced proponents of the art of war. Despite the often heated exchanges between senior Army and Navy officers during the 1930s, their successful operations in Southeast Asia were characterised by the successful coordination of land, sea and air forces. War in the Pacific was highly mobile and relied on amphibious operations. At the beginning of World War II, Japan was the only nation in the Pacific which had the requisite doctrine, tactical concepts and forces to conduct such operations.[4] These factors, coupled with equipment that was technically superior to their Allied counterparts, meant that with targeted deployments, good leadership and shrewd management of resources, the Japanese could compensate for their inferior numbers.[5]

On the other side of the ledger, Allied failures also explain the reasons for defeat. As a multinational force, the Allies had enormous difficulty integrating their forces. At sea, for example, the Allied combined fleet could not communicate effectively, let alone act in a concerted and uniform way. These problems were also evident within the armed forces of individual nations. Inter-service rivalries, divided responsibilities and lack of unified command dogged the American military at the start of the war.[6]

Japanese success also highlighted the dated quality of Allied military doctrine. Allied conceptions of warfare had been shaped by the Great War and were 'completely unsuited' to the conditions of the Asia-Pacific.[7] Much of the equipment issued to Allied forces in the Pacific was unsuited for the tasks that lay ahead. Moreover, in comparison to the Japanese, Allied service personnel were often poorly trained and lacked combat experience.[8] The most experienced British and Australian forces were still fighting in the Middle East.

In early 1942 the Japanese juggernaut appeared unstoppable, and Roosevelt openly discussed the possibility of the invasion and loss of Australia. Convinced that such was inevitable, the New Zealand government suggested that it, and not Australia, should be the major staging base for the Allied defence of the southwest Pacific.[9] Whether the Japanese ever had any intention of actually invading Australia remains a major historical debating point of the Pacific War.[10] These debates are fuelled in part by the Japanese bombing of Darwin and other northwest Australian towns from February 1942 onwards, but the general agreement now is that these attacks were meant to disrupt possible Allied counter-offensives to the Japanese invasion of Timor.

THE SOURCES

The Personal Letters of Gordon Bennett

The Australian Government assisted the British in the defence of Singapore and Malaya by sending elements of the 8th Division of the Second Australian Imperial Force (8/2AIF) to garrison the British colony in early 1941. By this time the government of Prime Minister Robert Menzies had been alerted to the deficiencies of Singapore as a bastion of British power in the Pacific and the guarantor of Australian defence. The 8th Division was commanded by Great War veteran H. Gordon Bennett. As he prepared his troops for a conflict which looked increasingly inevitable, Bennett shared his thoughts with Melbourne stock broker and Menzies confidant Staniforth Ricketson.

For service personnel, letters home were a tangible means of maintaining a link with their loved ones and acquaintances. It has been suggested, moreover, that letter writing allowed those at war to maintain contact with their 'pre-war selves'.[11] For historians, letters provide opportunities to explore themes usually not covered in official documents and allow previously under-explored dimensions of war, such as the emotional and psychological state of service personnel, to be examined.

Bennett's writing reveals that even in times of impending crisis, military leaders are intimately influenced by political considerations, of both the nation and high command. In public, senior Australian officers rarely engaged in political debate and even more rarely allowed themselves to be associated with a political party. However, their private words in letters such as this one reveal that senior officers were politicians as well as soldiers.

11th August 1941
Stan,

Being in the middle of a big move, I am unable to have this letter typed. Please excuse.

Your letter of 31st ultimo reached me this morning – and was very interesting. This morning's paper quotes, in headlines, the PM's reference to dangerous developments in the Far East. I agree that the trend is towards a local conflict. At least Japan will hold important air bases over the border in Thailand very soon. I suppose the PM's tactics are to clear away the petty squabbles of self-seeking interests so that Australia can get on with its share of winning the war. In fact, it can't be won unless all small minded pettiness is eliminated.

I have a feeling that a move is now afoot to create a Corps here with two Divisions, each consisting of a stiffening of an Australian brigade and a filling of Indians. I like the idea. But the Corps and both Divisions must be led by Australians. The P.M. should demand it and refuse to allow the watering down otherwise. It is reasonable and right. You might think that my urge is personal in the hope that the Corps will come my way. No! I think the Corps must be led by an Australian regardless of personal interests. At the same time I admit that the Corps command should be mine by right, I was senior to Blamey, Lavarack and Sturdee and the rest when this war started and was penalized because I was foolish enough to draw attention to our unpreparedness, especially on the industrial side. Time has proved I was right. I am senior; I know local conditions; I have produced a good result here; I get on extremely well with the local people. As to my fitness to command, it is not for me to comment – except to say that I feel confident that I can produce results and I have the confidence of all under me.

If you can do anything to see that this matter is dealt with fairly and honestly, I would appreciate it.

I was very upset at losing the service of Norman Marshall and am more upset that his illness is so serious. He has been a tower of strength. I could safely leave his task of training his Brigade to him. I know he has produced good results. Lind too has been ill but is again back at work. I fear that the conditions under which he is living will be too much for him. Gastric conditions do not like tropical food and tropical conditions.

Alf Berham, for some time after his arrival, was affected by the climate. He is now well again. He also has some domestic worries. Alf is thoroughly honest and reliable and I feel privileged to have him on my staff. I do find that men over 50, even 40, are unable to stand the strain of campaigning. In the Middle East they have found the same. At present, I am struggling to bring down age levels. I won't make an officer over 27 years of age. I would like them younger still. An example of the power of youth is Norm Marshall's young B.M. Pond. Pond is the best B.M. we have – full of energy and enterprise and with an active brain.

Regarding the general situation, I feel that we will have to fight the winner of the Russo-German bout when it is over and that fight must come in the Middle East. Both of those nations will be attracted past the fields of Iran and Irak [sic] down to the Persian Gulf. Such a strategic move will hurt Great Britain. It would open the road to India and Egypt. Britain's long line of communications would make it difficult for her to provide and maintain a large enough army there to deal with either Russia or Germany. That demands that Australia must exert herself to her utmost to equip a large army to relieve Great Britain. Only one thing matters. The Empire must win this war. And the people of Australia should subordinate everything to that end – including party feeling and prejudice. What is the use of our great ideals if we are unable to develop them? And we can only develop them if we are on top of the world. Labor slogans – usually idle words – do not make a nation great.

I must close for now. I have plenty of work to do. Many thanks for your interesting letter. Your letters do keep me informed of the things I want to know.

Regards,
Yours very sincerely
H. Gordon Bennett

Canadian Newspapers Report on the Allied Garrison at Hong Kong

The personal reservations of senior officers such as Bennett never found their way into the mainstream media. Newspaper reports before Pearl Harbor exuded confidence. The public was reassured that all would be well and that every confidence could be placed in the ability of the Allied forces to quickly dispatch any Japanese invader.

Despite having a sizeable Pacific coastline, most of Canada's efforts in World War II were directed towards the European theatre. Nevertheless, like the Australians and New Zealanders, Canadians were called on to garrison British possessions in the Asia-Pacific. The Canadian newspaper *The Globe and Mail* reported on Canadian efforts to hold Hong Kong in the early days of the war. Notwithstanding the swiftness and success of the early days of the Japanese onslaught, the newspaper's confidence in an Allied victory remained undaunted. Using examples of other successful campaigns of resistance from earlier in the European War was a common technique aimed at showing the strength of Allied resolve. Personalising the chances of success in the qualities of the commanding officer was another important morale-building technique.

American newspaper publisher Phillip Graham, who himself served in the Pacific during World War II, has been attributed with the claim that journalism was the 'first rough draft of history'.[12] These early newspaper reports of the Pacific War revealed how wrong the citizens of the Allied nations were about the capacity of their forces to successfully repulse a Japanese advance.

The Globe and Mail, 10 December 1941

Britain puts confidence in Hong Kong Command
(by Douglas Amaron)
London, Dec 9 (CP)

Hong Kong, the rocky Far Eastern stronghold which Canadian troops are helping to defend, may develop into a Tobruk of the Pacific.

Announcement that a Japanese attempt to cross the colony's mainland frontier has been halted by artillery fire is viewed by authoritative sources here as possibly the beginning of a siege similar to that which Empire forces withstood so successfully at the Libyan outpost.

No word as to the part the Canadians are playing in defence of the vital base has been received in London.

The Canadians serving in the Far East are under the higher command of Major General Michael Maltby, general officer commanding at Hong Kong and a veteran of the first Great War, with all the necessary qualities of leadership for the type of campaign to develop.

'I am confident Maltby will give a good account of himself' said a senior officer under whom General Maltby once served as a subaltern.

'He is the ideal officer to command a garrison of this nature. He is always cool and completely unruffled, and has a quiet sense of humour and tremendous powers of endurance. He is extremely popular not only with his senior, and junior officers, but with the British, Indian and Dominion troops'.

In the case of Canadian troops in Hong Kong, such reports elevated the hopes of loved ones when no hope was warranted. The public were shocked when surrender came. Suddenly, the task had been transformed into a battle fought under 'adverse conditions' – conditions that had not previously been apparent. Seeking to place some positive spin on a disaster, the *Hamilton Spectator* became fixated with the relative merits of conditional and unconditional surrender.

Hamilton Spectator, 26 December 1941

Garrison of 6,000 Troops, including Canadians, Capitulates to Japanese.
Enemy Destroyed Water Supply — Governor and Military Commander
to Discuss Terms of Surrender To-day

Ottawa. Dec. 26

An anxious nation waited to-day for more detailed word from Hong Kong of the fate of Canadian soldiers who fought night and day for two weeks against overwhelming numbers of Japanese. Beyond the announcement the fighting had ceased there was little definite news, but a statement by Defence Minister Ralston last night suggested that there has been no unconditional surrender.

To Discuss Terms

'An outstanding fact in to-day's news' Col. Ralston said, 'is that the garrison under these adverse conditions has so convinced the enemy of their determination to fight it out to the last and has succeeded in inflicting such severe losses upon the attackers that, instead of unconditional surrender, the governor and the military commander are, according to a Japanese report, in a position to discuss terms under which fighting shall cease'.

It was known here that Canadian casualties in the battle of Hong Kong were heavy, but it appeared definite word of their identity and numbers might not be available for some time.

'Everything possible is being done to obtain particulars of our casualties as quickly as communication will permit', Defence Minister Ralston said last night.

He said Hong Kong would stand as 'a somber but glorious page in the record of the Canadian army'.

Over 1,900 Canadians were involved in the failed defence of Hong Kong. More than 200 were killed during the battle, and another 200 died as prisoners of war.

Alec Hodgson's Diary

As the Canadians were surrendering in Hong Kong, Bennett's Australians were fighting the invading Japanese on the Malayan peninsula. The Japanese surprise attack on British colonies in Malaya and Singapore quickly destroyed British air power in Southeast Asia before it could play any decisive role. Lacking air support, British naval forces were vulnerable to Japanese attack. A major failing of British strategy and tactics was the belief that the jungles of Malaya were an effective barrier to an advancing army. It had been assumed that an invasion force would be confined to the few arterial roads of the country and that their advance could be easily stopped. On the main north–south road through the Malayan peninsula, however, the British and their Australian allies had not anticipated the Japanese use of tanks to force through defences and harass Allied forces behind the front line while they waited for the infantry to catch up. The Japanese form of Blitzkrieg was just as efficient as its German equivalent. Furthermore, off the road and in the jungle, the British, Indian and Australian forces had neither the experience nor tactics to successfully halt the Japanese advance.[13]

Through January 1942, the British, Australian and Indian forces holding Malaya fought a series of rearguard actions until they were forced back over the causeway and onto the island of Singapore in early February. British strategy maintained that a garrison could hold the island city until it was relieved by a naval force. The reality was very different. With the Allied forces deprived of air cover, the Japanese bombed the island into submission.

One member of the Australian forces on Singapore Island was Sergeant Alec Hodgson, a member of the 2/6 Field Company of the Royal Australian Corps of Engineers (RAE). Hodgson kept a diary through this campaign and his subsequent captivity.

Poor environmental conditions, coupled with relatively strict censorship regulations, meant that only a small proportion of the letters from the Pacific War that described combat reached their final destination, or survived for historians. In particular, the censorship of mail helps to explain why so many Allied service personnel began keeping diaries during the Pacific campaign.[14] Although they might be writing for no one but themselves, diarists usually wrote with a 'sense of audience'.[15] Furthermore, Earl Miner has noted that diarists are impelled by two motives: 'a strong consciousness of time and a desire to memorialize'.[16] Such considerations were especially powerful for wartime diarists. For many of those forced to adopt this style of writing because of the strictures of censorship, the audience was always in mind (and often explicitly discussed), and with the ever-present danger of death, the need to memorialise surrounded each entry. Reflecting a fatalistic assumption that they would not survive to recount their experience in the first person, many diarists assumed their writings would only be read after their death.

Fearing that the enemy would exploit captured diaries as sources of military intelligence, many commanders, including Bennett, expressly banned soldiers from keeping diaries. The act of keeping a diary was thus an illicit activity that increased the authors' sense that they were engaged in a hidden and secretive act of writing. Whilst the regulations prohibiting diary keeping were relaxed during the war, diaries and notebooks could not be sent through the mail system.[17]

Although letters home were often an intimate discourse with loved ones, they were usually characterised by some pretence of self-censorship, or they were censored for political and military purposes. By contrast, whilst diaries are not infallible sources for historians – Aaron Moore has questioned whether the product of diary writing was any more truthful than letter writing, and suggested its 'reliability' was no greater than fiction – they nonetheless offer candid insights into the experience of war.[18]

As well as highlighting that the minor issues of daily existence continued to require attention in even the most horrendous of circumstances, Hodgson's diary betrayed the confusion and disappointment felt by many Australian soldiers who had done little fighting but found themselves members of a defeated army.

5th Feb, 1942
Dive bombers very busy. Surprised to find how jittery some of the fellows are. Have to keep driving them to get out of their slit trenches and holes. Watched about 40 shells explode all around house opposite us without a hit. Went to Naval Base for salvage again. Plenty of rum, result, half the company full, don't like the stuff myself. Joe Young and Jack Maskiell wounded.

6th Feb, 1942
Heard machine guns and heavy shelling all night, and not surprised at news that Japs had forced landing. Watched dive bombers score hit on oil tanks very cleverly. Dive bombers kept us low nearly all day, plus high bombers and

shelling. Artillery man hit and killed about 40 yards away. Direct hit at 2/12 [Field Company, RAE] killed 6.

8th Feb, 1942 (or 9th)
Stood to all night and cowered like rats in holes all day. Japs don't seem to have much artillery nor many aeroplanes for that matter but are making skilful use of both. Haven't seen one of our planes for a couple of days.

Moved at dusk with what we could load. Usual chaos, company in two halves and spent night on road as did not know where to go. Hear Japs are progressing everywhere.

Picked up some of the 2/10 [Field Company, RAE], who had been in on the job at the landing (Japs nearly surrounded them), they are scattered everywhere and lost fairly heavily. It seems to happen to every unit when they come into immediate contact with the Japs, this scattering haphazardly. 2/10 chaps say the infantry just left them 'in the air' particularly 2/18th [infantry battalion].

Saw strings of Indian troops without even a rifle among them. Can't understand it, morale seems to have gone, even among white troops. Am inclined to think baby officers have a lot to do with it.

9th Feb, 1942 (or 10th)
After much messing about, eventually found company headquarters at Stevens Road. Plenty of breeze, [fear] and dashing about. More b____ slit trenches to dig. Tojo has had several goes at this joint judging by the houses and smashed cars about. Are bivouacked on a hillside which will be a nasty spot if he lobs shells this way.

Left behind Kota Tinggi or lost on the road a tin of letters and the photo Mary sent me.

10th Feb, 1942
Pretty hectic day. Dashed back to pick up Bill Hooper and Seringeour, who had been left behind in charge of explosives. J.U.E turned up during day full of mud. Some of the lads found some gin and Halls wine and there was a certain amount of convivial feeling. Pretty continuous waves of bombers but none came our way.

11th Feb, 1942
What a day of panic!! 15th RAA [Royal Australian Artillery] moved in during night and posted guns in bottom of gully only 50 yards from us. The din when they opened up was deafening and it wasn't very long before the dive-bombers started smelling them out. Lewis and Marshall could not be seen for hours at a time and Mute was away on some scrounge of his own.

Moved sections over to reverse slope of hill. Must doff my hat to gunners. Stuck to their jobs all day, but did they draw the crabs on us!

Marshall spent whole day in dugout. Somebody or other lost last remnant of nerves during afternoon and ordered whole company to get packed up.

Went to officer in charge to find out definite orders and was told to go and find where a sniper – one solitary sniper – was firing from. Found he was at least half a mile away, came back and found whole section and practically whole company missing. Lewis running around like a sick hen.

A few of us who were left scrounged around and loaded what gear we could find on to the only remaining truck (a foul thing) and managed to find three other trucks after dodging two or three snipers who must have had their eyes shut, as none even heard a bullet passing. After a couple of hours aimless wandering about, we eventually hid (no other word describes it) in a Chinese cemetery towards Changi and a D.R. [Despatch Rider] went in to try and find the remainder.

Lofty and I went out on the road to guide any in should they happen along. They did, nearly the whole team, in about an hour and a half, majority pretty full as they had been waiting at the U.J.C. We turned them in and had just got on the narrow track when Yellow Ned turned up. Had decided couldn't stay there. Changi guns were firing and there was a little machine gun fire about 1½ miles away, so I suppose we ran away from the noise. After more fruitless and aimless wandering about we spent remainder of night on roadside.

An Australian Newspaper and the Fall of Singapore

Back in Australia, the general public relied on reports on the situation that had first been sent to London. In the hectic early months of the Pacific War, newspaper reports relied on a variety of information sources, including those provided by the enemy. It is striking that some media reports of this period, particularly in Britain and Australia, deemed it appropriate to recount enemy interpretations of events that contradicted the Allied governments' positions. This approach would not last long.

Sydney Morning Herald, 12 February 1942

DEFENDERS COUNTER-ATTACK AT SINGAPORE
JAPANESE CLAIM TO BE IN CITY
AUSTRALIANS FIGHTING HEROICALLY
From our correspondent and A.A.P.

The general situation at Singapore is still serious but it has not deteriorated since Tuesday, it was stated authoritatively in London yesterday.

'We are counter-attacking towards the line first held between the River Kranji and the River Jurong', the authoritative spokesmen said, 'we also are counter-attacking against the second Japanese landing between River Mandai and the River Kranji'.

'There are no indications that Japanese have succeeded in putting a large number of troops across the Johore Causeway' he added.

The announcer of the Malayan Broadcasting Corporation said last night, however, that ships were ready to take off many of the garrison and as much equipment as possible should the fall of the island become inevitable.

Japanese imperial headquarters stated last night: 'Japanese forces stormed into Singapore city proper this (Wednesday) morning and are now engaged in fierce hand-to-hand fighting with the British troops in the city'. Unofficial reports state that they penetrated the western suburbs at 2pm (local time) and that they also have occupied Seleiar Airfield, on the northern coast. Tokyo Radio says they have occupied Singapore Racecourse (four miles from Government House).

British, Australian, New Zealand, Indian and Chinese volunteers are valiantly resisting tremendous Japanese pressure. The Japanese are ceaselessly dive-bombing and machine-gunning the forces, and their bombers, thousands of feet over the battle-front also are at work.

The Australian Minister for the Army, Mr Forde, announced in Canberra last night that he had received a message from the Australian GOC Major General Gordon Bennett, stating that the AIF was fighting 'heroically and stubbornly'.

'The outcome of the Battle of Singapore is now a matter of hours. The British Imperial Forces are putting up a very fierce opposition' declared the correspondent of the British United Press at Singapore in a message received last night.

Shimada Hōsaku's Recollections

Although some early newspaper reports of the war in Southeast Asia were based in part on information gleaned from Japanese sources, Western readers had scant exposure to first-hand Japanese reports of those campaigns. Into the post-war period the absence of Japanese perspectives perpetuated a perception that so tremendous and rapid had been the Japanese victory, and so complete the Allied defeat, that the Allies were the only ones to experience hardship and trauma.[19] There were few attempts to appreciate that winners also suffer loss. Some of the 'tremendous Japanese pressure' on the British and Australian forces on Singapore came from Shimada Hōusaku's tank battalion. Shimada's memoir was written several years after the war, and we have to make allowances for how the eventual defeat and the passage of time shaped his recollections. Nonetheless, his recollections suggest that Shimada, a hardened veteran of the China campaign, was as traumatised in victory as Sergeant Hodgson had been in defeat.

Lance Corporal Miyabe came running through enemy fire. He was the gunner in Masuda's tank. I raised the cover and yelled out: 'Miyabe, what's happened?' I saw blood running down his face.

'We got done'

He looked like he was about to cry.

'Can't you move that tank?'

'Yes, all of us got done'

'What do you mean, all of you of got done.'

Surprised by this unexpected news, I jumped off the tank. Miyabe, who'd recovered slightly, led me to the back of the second tank.

'Over there. We were hit by machine guns. By the time I opened fire, we were already hit. The platoon leader, the gunner, the driver, they copped it', he said, pointing out the emplacement of the enemy machine gun, hidden under leaves about 30 meters ahead of the platoon commander's tank. Enemy soldiers were lying there too.

Suddenly I got sick of fighting. Previously this kind of scene would have spurred me on, but suddenly the will to fight left me. I forgot even that I was on a battlefield; I was just standing there, stunned, staring at Masuda's tank in a daze.

From the back, the tank hadn't changed. You might even see the happy, laughing faces of the crew. But it was horrible when you got close. I wanted to think that they'd survived. I wanted to just wait, wait for the cover to open, wait for Masuda's face to appear. Bullets were flying right past, and I didn't even move. I started shouting.

'Masuda! Lieutenant Masuda! Sergeant Ōe! Corporal Takeichi!'

Miyabe was weeping. As if it was replying the tank started shaking.

'Look, the tank, its alive!'

I was about to run up when – BANG – the whole thing burst into flames. With the explosion, bullets started spraying out of the window from which Miyabe had escaped. Now the tank was burning fiercely.

Suddenly, Miyabe's voice rang out.

'I stuffed up'.

'What are you saying? You fought really well'.

'I've got to die with them'. Miyabe started running towards the burning tank.

'You bloody idiot! Stop!'

I managed to catch him.

'You fool! You can't die now! You're coming in my tank. Get in there, quick. This is a battle of revenge, now'.

I forced him into my tank and closed the cover from the outside. My fighting spirit had come back: it was now burning as ferociously as Masuda's tank.

Alec Hodgson's Diary and Defeat

Back in Singapore Alec Hodgson was still finding time to keep his diary. His entries in the final days before surrender continued to reflect his confusion and disappointment at the situation. He also began apportioning blame. The Japanese remained virtually invisible in his entries: they were a threat to be reckoned with but always out of sight and never confronted. The entry regarding the first hours after surrender is also important. Besides suggesting that many Australian soldiers assumed Gordon Bennett's escape to Australia was to 'arrange' their release, they also offer a perspective unclouded by the later Japanese treatment of Allied prisoners of war. Hodgson became a prisoner of war and endured the privations and brutality of incarceration under the Japanese. Whilst the punishment for owning such a record was far more drastic than that imposed by Australian authorities, the soldier continued to maintain his diary. We can assume that Hodgson, like other diarists, enjoyed the catharsis of writing – this was a part of himself removed from the Japanese – and came to view the diary as an essential part of his being.[20]

12th Feb. 1942

Arrived Bishop's Court on Tanglin Road. Had much needed shower and shave. Billeted in unoccupied house. Boys soon found tucker and booze. Plenty of aircraft, all Jap of course.

Had half Company out looking for snipers, which I'm beginning to be convinced are not snipers at all. Periodically there is a small crack from a different point each time, which might be a .22 but I am sure it is some stunt of Tojo's. Nobody ever gets hit or sees a sniper.

A good bed and a good sleep (I don't think). The blinking artillery followed us again and the din all night was terrific as Tojo lost no time in replying.

Unloaded all trucks for the 'nth' time. Mute wanted a list of all tools and stores we have. Oh these dud officers. I suppose Mute is the best of 'em but he has more faults than merits. Lewis is just a swollen headed egotist with no ability or knowledge of how to handle men, and Marshall – God 'elp us. Sloan seems to be a man at any rate.

23 years today since I was demobbed [demobilised from World War I]. Wonder how many years to next and last.

13th Feb, 1942

Still at Bishop's Court all day. Pretty lively with dive bombing and shelling but none of ours hit. This place has been occupied by Air Force before us, and by the looks of things they had cleared out even quicker than some of our exits. Clothing, food, equipment, tobacco scattered everywhere. Was able to make up a bit of my kit which had been missing ever since the Tanglin Club panic. I haven't a thing now which I treasured. Even my pen and wallet are gone and every photo.

Believe the Air Force followed Navy and skipped. I think we have about shot our bolt here. Japs have firmly established landings at several points, and their planes are playing havoc with the fellows' spirits. Haven't seen one of ours for a week.

Had a very busy hour with dive bombers. Shelling was continuous all night, seemed to be after a battery in front of us.

Had to go over to take charge of Workshops Section as an infantry platoon. Marshall useless. Mossy hopeless.

Three at least of chaps were terrified at the idea of becoming front line troops. Had just split into sections and was going to start training them when wanted by officer in charge. He, Spurling, Charlie Graham, Sis Cupitt and I went around to Firestone Park, where he showed us positions we had to take up and after a lot of questioning, managed to discover we were forming a perimeter and were drawing away from coast, allowing Japs to work down along S.W. coast into city.

Looks to me as if the game is up. Cannot begin to understand our generalship. Seem to have been directed towards helping Jap all the while, and now the final suicidal policy of allowing him to encircle us with superior numbers? Artillery and all the aircraft seen. He can just pound the hell out of us now. Surely the game would have been to scatter into say companies and go looking for him, not here on the island but up in Johore. His planes would have been useless then. Instead we have put up miles and miles of wire which he had bombed us out of.

Hear a very persistent rumour that Yanks and British have landed at every port from Penang downwards. Don't believe that and don't believe the Jap has anywhere near the number of troops we have actually on the island. Reckon if we were all sent to it we could chase him off.

Am not at all impressed with what I have seen of A.I.F. [Second Australian Imperial Force].

Warned at 6 o'clock might have an attack on my sector, so made arrangements. Found an 18 gallon keg of rum and tapped enough to give the lads a tot each.

Lewis came round about 11 and moaned because some of the men were asleep so had it ding dong. Told him they were dead beat with digging in, and if he had them standing to all night they would be useless when wanted.

Met Huon Barton of 2/10 on patrol, who told me Bill Clasper had half his face taken off and McCullough badly hit in chest. Night passed quietly as regards SA [small arms] fire. 13th artillery alongside us again. Hoot Gibson and party went.

14th Feb, 1942

More trenches dug, and fields of fire improved, but an awful position to defend. Dead ground everywhere and tommy gun range masking fire.

High level bombers pasting wharves and shipping all day as well as shells. Battery by us soon spotted and five bombers and shrapnel very close. One bomb collected 9, 3 Poms, 4 Indians on road alongside us. Lewis told me to take no notice of Marshall but carry on on my own. Lewis slept in bomb proof shelter. Marshall as close to it as he dared.

Sloan has gone back to 2/10 and I believe he cheered to himself to get away from this mob. Shortage of water but plenty of tucker.

Nothing much to vary things. Went around to Bishop's Court with party of volunteers and brought back some tea, tucker, what personal gear we could find and a few bottles we found.

From reports, Japs are closing in all round. Don't know what is happening elsewhere on Island, but Singapore is getting a whale of a time from shelling and bombers. Had to stand to all night. Japs are pressing 25th back. S.A. fire and mortars very close. A miracle that none has been hit so far with the dive bombers and shrapnel. Marshall wanted me to charge Bull, but refused.

15th Feb, 1942
Tojo got onto us today with great gusto. Shrapnel in morning and H.E. [high explosive] in p.m. with bombs and Ha Ha's all day. None hit in morning but Steele, Jim Scott, Bardeley and Norm Allen hit. Steele and Allen dead.

2/10 have lost about 20 killed and 50 wounded. Their hill caught more than we did. Luckily, I had moved my chaps out of slit trenches and under bank, otherwise must have lost more, as several trenches received practically direct hits. One H.E. lobbed between Lynch's and mine and scattered our little bit of gear far and wide. We happened to be eating our tea together in another trench 20 yards off.

Went down to tell Mute I was pulling my reserve sub-section out from behind him and got blown off my feet by the back blast of one, and a dud landed about 5 yards off Bill Olwer and I when were lopping a shrub which masked some fire. Have been warned to move my chaps up tonight to link up with Mixed Brigade.

The chaps have rum and are game for anything, but too b____ rowdy for night work. Shelling seemed to come from all around us this afternoon; I'm afraid we have a forlorn hope now. Unbelievable to me that any general would have allowed himself to be forced into the position we are in so damned easily. There has been an extraordinary quiet here since about 5.30. Not a gun and hardly a rifle firing.

Have just had orders to be stood by to move up with magazines empty to go in with the bayonet. Apparently the idea is to let our chaps through then do a death or glory stunt. Marshall is a bundle of nerves but has pulled himself together well. The boys are ready for anything. Am writing this in old shed by torchlight. Might be the finish but can only hope. Has been very little Ack Ack fire today.

16th Feb, 1942
SURRENDER, and from my narrow view of affairs, a shameful surrender. Apparently, and this I feel intensely, even while I was trying to build the chaps up to tackling anything, the armistice began at 7.30 last night, and we didn't know till about 10.30, probably the last unit to learn, as always.

Feeling of utter disgust and shame, never saw a Jap, never fired a shot and there are thousands like us.

Whole damn campaign has appeared to be a dismal tragedy of non-cooperation and blundering.

Am writing this in luxurious surroundings, with a cigar, glass of beer, and wireless going in next room.

Grabbed a truck first thing this morning and went down to try and spy out chances of getaway, but pretty hopeless. Jap patrols, planes and motorboats everywhere, so dived into sheds and wharves and loaded up with tucker and Cascade [Tasmanian beer]. Should estimate 30 cases of Cascade went into company today.

Japs very friendly to us, no trouble at all with their pickets, in fact, some had a drink with us. Gave away about two cases and Biscuits to some Punjabis who were absolutely parched and starved.

Heard wireless saying Percival's last message before surrender was 'No Petrol, water, food, or shells'. Bunkum! Trouble was that organization had broken down. Surrender apparently unconditional. What a smack for the British Lion, and what a wonderful job the Jap has done.

Rumours that G. Bennet [sic] has flown home to try and arrange something.

Shimada Hōsaku's Memoir and Victory

The great Japanese victory in Singapore did not translate into exuberant celebrations for Shimada and his men. The relief of the end of battle was tainted with a combination of anger and sadness at the losses endured, losses that would have been avoided, in their minds, had the enemy surrendered even a few minutes sooner.

I was thinking: 'once we've taken them, the next step will be fighting in the city streets. The enemy is tenacious all right. Maybe they'll fight to the last.'

Somebody yelled: 'I can see a white flag. It's a white flag'

'Where?'

I surveyed the enemy trench, but I couldn't see anything. I was half in doubt.

'Higher up'

As I raised my eyes, I saw a white flag going smoothly up a long pole which had suddenly appeared.

'You goddam bastards!'

The gunner let off a volley of bullets at the white flag. I didn't try and stop him. After all that, to finish it like this. ... This was something that could make you incredibly angry. But now the enemy had suddenly stopped shooting back, and you looked like an idiot if you kept shooting, and so naturally we stopped.

If you were going to surrender, why not do it earlier? Why couldn't you give up even just one hour earlier? Tears welled up. The fight was over. We had won. Tears were rolling down my cheeks. Masuda, we won! I looked back from the white flag to where Masuda's tank was still burning and I started sobbing. I didn't care who saw me. All the men were crying. Soldiers came out of the trees screaming 'Banzai'. But amongst us, not a single one yelled 'Banzai'; we were just crying.

After the battle ended, I relaxed under a roof for the first time in 70 days since landing and ate some rice porridge. The image of Masuda's burning tank under the white flag was burned onto my eyelids. Every so often I'd get upset and my eyes would well up with tears. The night was falling on a now peaceful Singapore, but in the barracks I was still battling my emotions. What made me even sadder was knowing that in the very moments we were fighting that battle, General Yamashita was presenting General Percival with surrender documents, pressing him for an unequivocal 'yes' or 'no'. I felt that I could really understand why he was so harsh in his negotiations.

CHAPTER FOUR
THE WATER AT SEA: CORAL SEA, MIDWAY AND BEYOND

[W]e were ordered to abandon ship. . . . I didn't realise it at the time but it was the end of an era. No longer would battleships be considered the masters of the ocean. They had been conquered by machines a mere fraction of their size. Aircraft were now masters of both air and sea.

Ralph Robson, after the sinking of the *HMS Repulse*

In the aftermath of their attack on Pearl Harbor, the Japanese appeared to be an almost unstoppable force. Just six months later, however, the tide of battle had begun to turn, and by mid-1942, although the Allies had a long struggle ahead to defeat Japan, there was considerable reason to be optimistic about the war's eventual outcome. Before the Australians' victories against the Japanese in New Guinea, the first significant successes for the Allies were at sea. In May 1942, at the Battle of the Coral Sea, off the north-eastern coast of Australia, and then in June, at Midway, in the Central Pacific, the Allies first thwarted and then inflicted a decisive defeat upon Japanese naval power.

These victories were achieved against considerable odds. Still attempting to overcome the restraints placed upon naval development by the arms limitations treaties of the inter-war years, Allied strategists in the Pacific confronted a confident and powerful foe.[1] Having come to reject naval limitation, as first prescribed in Washington in 1921 and then confirmed in London in 1930, by 1941 the Imperial Japanese Navy was arguably the most powerful in the world. Japan's formidable fleet of eleven battleships (and the soon-to-be completed *Yamato*, the largest and most heavily armed battleship in the world) and ten aircraft carriers, was complemented by a well-trained force of 1,500 naval aviators, who played a key role in Japan's early successes.[2] American strategists were aware of Japan's powerful fleet; they were less-well-appraised as to how effectively it would be deployed, particularly during the early stages of the Pacific War.

The Pacific War posed particular challenges for naval strategists on both sides. One issue was the sheer size of the battlefield.[3] The Pacific Ocean is vast, and as large as the navies were, locating and tracking enemy ships was never straightforward. Further complicating those logistical issues was the fact that the naval war extended into the Indian Ocean, further straining naval resources. The American war effort, moreover, was characterised by an ongoing competition for human and material resources between the European and Pacific theatres: in theory, the European theatre was the highest priority; in practice, the desperate nature of the early stages of the Pacific War meant more resources were deployed there than planners in Washington initially envisaged.

In part, the role of navies during World War II had changed little from earlier conflicts. Yet the vital task of ensuring that lines of communication and transportation remained open was even more crucial in an age of industrialised warfare. And the role of protecting soldiers being transported across the sea – and to the Japanese-held islands for which the Marines in particular paid such a heavy price – was crucial, for unlike subsequent conflicts, most of the service personnel dispatched to the Pacific were transported by ship rather than by plane. In theory, naval strategists were well versed with these tasks. There was less certainty, however, regarding the role of air power at sea. During the inter-war years, there were sometimes bitter debates, particularly in the United States, about the shape of future naval battles, with the proponents of battleships quarrelling with advocates of aircraft carriers. In part, those debates reflected a rivalry for scarce resources. But they also reflected fundamental differences over the merits of aircraft carriers. By war's end – indeed, by mid-1942 – that debate had been resolved, and the dominance of aircraft carriers in the Pacific War marked a watershed in the history of naval warfare.[4]

Consequently, whilst both the Japanese and American navies continued to build and deploy battleships, and although American battleships played an important role as sea-borne artillery support for their infantry as they 'island-hopped' across the Pacific, when the two navies clashed, aircraft carriers were the decisive force. The Pacific War thus marked a new type of naval conflict, in which air power – particularly air power projected by aircraft carriers – became a decisive force both at sea and on land. The Battle of the Coral Sea was the first naval engagement in which the protagonists on both sides did not see their enemy's ships: they only saw the aircraft launched by those ships. That shift in naval power, of course, had been first signalled by the Japanese attack on Pearl Harbor, and by their subsequent success in using air power to sink the British battleship *Prince of Wales* and battle-cruiser *Repulse*. Paradoxically, even as Japanese and Allies alike contemplated the scale of the Japanese success at Pearl Harbor, Japan's triumph there was undermined by its failure to sink the American aircraft carriers.[5] Within six months, that Japanese failure had far-reaching consequences, first in the Coral Sea, and subsequently at Midway.

In May 1942, soon after Japanese forces landed at Tulagi, in the Solomon Islands, a second invasion force headed toward Port Moresby. On 7 May, Japanese and Allied forces clashed in the Coral Sea. On paper the Japanese losses at the Battle of the Coral Sea did not seem decisive. Indeed, the Japanese appeared to have won the duel, having sunk the American aircraft carrier *Lexington* for the loss of the much smaller light carrier *Shōhō*. But, as well as preventing the Japanese sea-borne invasion of Port Moresby, the Battle of the Coral Sea signified the end of the expansion of the Japanese Empire.

A month later, at the Battle of Midway, there could be no doubting the scale of the American victory. For the loss of one aircraft carrier and a destroyer, the Americans sank four Japanese carriers and a heavy cruiser. The Japanese plan to drive the Americans from the Central Pacific had been based around the planned capture of Midway Island, which would give the Japanese command of the surrounding skies – and the sea – and would prevent the US Navy from extending its power into the Western Pacific. Japanese forces would also be in a position to threaten Hawaii. Initially, Admiral Yamamoto Isoroku had not sought to fight a decisive naval engagement with the Americans at Midway. Instead, hoping to confuse American commanders, he dispersed his forces over a wide area. Part of his diversionary plan entailed an attack on the Aleutian Islands and a surprise attack by midget submarines on Allied ships in Sydney Harbour. But thanks to the efforts of Allied intelligence – which had broken the codes used by Japanese naval commanders and hence provided insights into Japanese intentions – the Allies were forewarned of Yamamoto's strategy. By concentrating their forces at the right place, American strategists were able to overcome some of the advantage enjoyed by the Japanese in terms of numbers of carriers and aircraft.

The major engagements of the Battle of Midway were fought on 4 June 1942, and the battle is worth recounting in detail as a crucial moment in the Pacific War. The battle began before first light, when American aircraft attacked Japanese transport ships; a few hours later Japanese aircraft attacked the American base on Midway Island. The Japanese destroyed a number of American aircraft based on Midway, but they inflicted little damage on the US forces there. Later that morning, when American aircraft attacked Japanese carriers, they suffered dreadful losses and caused negligible damage to the Japanese fleet. A subsequent attack by American carrier-based torpedo-bombers was similarly unsuccessful. That attack, however, drew Japanese fighter aircraft away from their carriers, which were fatally exposed when a further attack by American aircraft – this time dive-bombers – caused massive damage to the carriers *Kaga*, *Akagi* and *Sōryū*. Subsequent attacks by Japanese aircraft launched from the *Hiryū*, their only remaining operational carrier, did cause grievous damage to the carrier *Yorktown*. But the battle was not yet over, as American aircraft from the *Enterprise* then attacked and sank the *Hiryū*. With his carrier strike force destroyed, and after some tentative and unsuccessful efforts to use his surface ships to locate and attack the American fleet – which had steamed eastwards to protect Midway Island – Yamamoto was forced to retire westwards. On 5 and 6 June, American forces continued to harass the retreating Japanese, damaging and sinking several surface ships. On 7 June a Japanese submarine attacked and sank the *Yorktown*, which the Americans had been attempting to salvage.[6]

The Japanese defeats in the Coral Sea and – in particular – at Midway had a profound impact on the course of the Pacific War. Just seven months after Pearl Harbor, the Allies had not only inflicted a serious psychological blow on the Japanese, and destroyed a significant part of their naval and air capacity, but had also made further Japanese advances on land much less likely. The gamble for control of Southeast Asia had failed: Japanese forces were now on the defensive both in China and in the Pacific. The Japanese loss of strategic initiative was compounded by the knowledge that the United States – the 'sleeping giant' to which Yamamoto had purportedly referred in the wake of the attack on Pearl Harbor – enjoyed a major industrial and logistical advantage.[7] Put simply, the United States could replace ships and aircraft much more quickly than Japan, whose war on two fronts was leaching it rapidly of resources and manpower. Indeed, at Midway alone the Japanese lost 200 of their best-trained and most experienced pilots.

Along with a measure of good fortune, the Allied successes at sea during mid-1942 resulted in part from sound planning and tactical and strategic doctrine, as well as the valour and determination of the men at the front lines. In his study of the carrier war in the Pacific in 1942, Douglas Smith has observed that 'in the most critical stages of the war in 1942 the American carrier commanders were invariably outnumbered, deficient technologically, and saddled with unproven doctrine and tactics'. Yet the US Navy prevailed. Smith suggests it was the 'operational acumen' of the American commanders that allowed this to happen. In the Coral Sea the American commander Admiral Jack Fletcher 'had the moral courage to formulate doctrine when none was in place'.[8] On these foundations the American Navy developed a formula for success with sound planning, and tactical and strategic doctrine forged by battle experience.

The Allies also enjoyed a distinct advantage in military intelligence. Allied code-breakers, often far removed from the scene of battle, were able to assess their adversary's intentions, and the Allies could deploy their own forces accordingly. Japan's naval leadership, by contrast, could only divine American intentions, and whilst Japanese ships and planes – and their sailors and pilots – were a match for the Allies, the defeats at Coral Sea and Midway suggested that the Japanese faith in resolute bravery and patriotism could not subdue a resurgent United States.

The Imperial Japanese Navy had started the war with the most powerful strike force in the world, but much of this power was soon blunted. Despite spending a staggering 27 percent of its national budget on the Navy, Japan could not keep pace with American naval output.[9] Such was the size of the American economy that by 1944, the US government could afford to cancel orders on new battleships and aircraft carriers. Whether the Japanese had 'man for man and ship for ship, the best sea fighters in the world' became irrelevant under the weight of American industrial production.[10]

Following their successes in the Coral Sea and at Midway, the Allies enjoyed the strategic initiative in the war at sea. As the American industrial juggernaut delivered new warships, merchant vessels and aircraft, Japan was forced into an increasingly defensive posture. Whilst the Japanese Navy remained a potent force, and although numerous Allied vessels were attacked and sunk during 1943–1945, Japanese naval power did not seriously impede the Allied offensives. And late in the war, when Japan dared to expose its capital ships to battle, they suffered at the hands of an Allied fleet that by 1944 enjoyed a superiority of numbers, along with advantages in technology and personnel. During 1944–1945, in a desperate attempt to counter those Allied advantages, the Japanese Navy began using 'Special Attack' weapons. These suicide torpedoes, or manned submarines packed with explosives, were intended to be rammed into Allied ships, and were naval versions of the better-known *Kamikaze* planes. Like the *Kamikaze*, the Navy's Special Attack craft represented the juncture between the Japanese Imperial forces' ethos of self-sacrifice, self-consciously adapted from medieval warrior traditions, and modern technology. At the point of battle, although the means of killing had changed dramatically, and whilst the enemy was often unseen, the moments of terror and the sometimes savage determination to kill the enemy were no different from earlier conflicts. Indeed, as the brutal and racially charged nature of land warfare during the Pacific War was a 'war without mercy', the war at sea could be an equally fierce affair.[11]

Due to the nature of naval warfare, warships spent long periods away from their home port. Most of this time was spent at sea in varying states of isolation. This environment, and the nature of naval service, combined to produce fighting words that differed from those generated on land, and which provide unique challenges for naval historians.

The three major navies in the Pacific War were the Imperial Japanese Navy (IJN), the United States Navy (USN) and the Royal Australian Navy (RAN). To varying degrees, each had been shaped by their exposure to Britain's Royal Navy.[12] A lasting British influence on all three navies was the procedures by which the activities of the ship were recorded in 'logs'. For the RAN the writing tradition remained identical to the Royal Navy's. Each ship or shore establishment maintained 'Letters of Proceedings' (later known as 'Reports of Proceedings'). These records were submitted to Naval Headquarters on a regular basis. Access to a port permitting, ships supplied the records on a monthly basis. Shore establishments supplied them on a quarterly basis. For ships, reports of proceedings recorded information on the operation and condition of the vessel, port visits, exercises or engagements, encounters with other vessels, the morale and health of the crew, distances steamed and fuel consumption.

The USN equivalent to the Report of Proceedings was the 'Deck Log'. The Deck Log was compiled on a daily basis and chronicled similar information, including the logging of the ship's latitude and longitude three times a day. Naval writing was a role reserved largely for officers and formed an important part of a junior officer's training. Reports of Proceedings or Deck Logs were not narratives. Their aim was to *record* rather than *describe* or *provide explanation*. The writing style was usually passive and devoid of any emotion. Whilst they can be a less-than-lively source, these bulky logs, kept on oversized paper and often running more than four pages a day, are of enormous value to naval historians. An entry in the Deck Log of the American light cruiser *USS Denver* for 1 August 1943 is illustrative:

Anchored as before. 1648 U.S.S. VIREO underway and shifted berth. 1649 U.S.S. MONTPELIER underway from alongside tanker, proceeded to and anchored in berth No. 14. 1740 Hoisted plane No. 7 aboard, pilot Lt. (jg) A. B. Haseltine, A-V(N), USNR, passenger NEAL, J. E., CAMM, USN. [*signed*] J. G. Lightburn, Lt. D-V(G), U.S.N.R. [13]

As well as the Deck Log, American ships and many shore establishments were requested in World War II to complete 'war diaries'. The aim of the war diary was to record ship-board activities that could be used subsequently for a variety of purposes – including ensuring there was an accurate historical record. Writing in 1943, one commentator observed: 'Their quality and value naturally varies with the aptitude and attitude of the officers charged with such recording. Some are far too busy or disinclined to write more than a "Nothing to report" week after week; some, on the other hand, are full-dress critical analyses … On the whole they form a highly valuable supplement to the formal reports.'[14] Some ships also had their war diaries published as a memento for the crew.[15]

The isolation of naval service also influenced the nature of private writing. The relative comfort of a warship and the small but regular periods of free time generally provided extended opportunities for private writing. Such writing, however, was often frustrating due to the extended periods of isolation. Weeks or even months might pass before the members of a ship's company would have the opportunity to post a letter via another ship or the visit to a port. Incoming mail bags were 'sacks of morale'.[16] In some Japanese cases no opportunities for sending mail were provided until the vessel returned to home port. Diaries were a popular substitute and usually faced fewer prescriptions or prohibitions in comparison to those being generated in forward areas on land.

The value and permanence of official and private records was conditional. Many ships' logs or private diaries from the Pacific War were lost when ships were sunk. The at-sea records of the IJN, especially from the latter years of the War, are scarce because of the enormous loss of warships to enemy engagements. In such cases often all that endured were the memories of surviving crewmen.

The selections below offer insights into how the momentous naval battles of mid-1942 – along with some of the less well-known encounters of the period that followed – were experienced and fought by Allied and Japanese sailors and airmen, and their commanders.

THE SOURCES

Air Power Ascendant: The Sinking of the *Prince of Wales* and the *Repulse*

On 10 December 1941, Japanese aircraft attacked and sank HMS *Prince of Wales* and HMS *Repulse*. Sent to Singapore to deter Japanese aggression, these ships were symbols of British power in the Far East, and their sinking, off the Malayan coast, was a major loss to Allied naval power, and a body blow to British prestige. The sinking of these two ships highlighted the vulnerability of battleships, and other surface ships, to air power. Ralph Robson was a crewman aboard the *Repulse*. Later, recounting the sinking of the ship, he referred to the uneven contest between Japanese air power and British naval power. For historians, the recollections of men such as Robson are an invaluable resource, since the crew's diaries and letters, along with the ships' official records, all went down with the *Prince of Wales* and *Repulse*.

On Monday, 8th December, following the dawn raid on Singapore, the *Prince of Wales* and *Repulse* quietly left Singapore at sunset. They sailed north up the east coast of Malaya hoping to intercept enemy transport ships....

Next day we continued to head north. Since we had no fighter protection we were glad of the low cloud and mist which screened our progress. But at about five o'clock visibility improved and we were spotted by three enemy aircraft carrying out a reconnaissance. As soon as it was dark the battleships altered course and proceeded south to Kuantan where, it had been reported, Japanese troops were landing.

As a clear day dawned we stood off Kuantan only to find that the information was incorrect and all was quiet. Admiral Phillips set course for Singapore. At 11.08 a.m. on that sunny day, nine bombers in close formation attacked the *Repulse* scoring one direct hit which started a fire. By 12.27 p.m. the *Repulse* had been struck by five torpedoes and began to sink....

Japanese twin-engined bombers were swooping down low and machine-gunning the ship. ... Taking a quick peep at the upper deck I saw a dead gunner bisected by machine-gun fire, his lower torso on the deck below. Blood was spattered over a wide area. I dived into the Signal Office, too numb with shock to even mention it.

About twenty minutes later the first torpedo struck. Some twenty minutes after that we were ordered to abandon ship. The *Repulse* was listing badly to port (left). I stood with one foot on the rail and one on the deck. Men were scrambling down as best they could. Some slithered on their backs. I managed to walk and eventually reached the water and walked into the sea.

It was vital to swim as far away from the ship as possible in case we were sucked under when she sank. There was no panic.

After we had swum for about a hundred yards, I turned to watch *Repulse*, waiting for her to go down. It was an awesome sight. Nearly an hour later we watched the *Price of Wales* as she too foundered about three miles away.

The destroyers *H.M.S. Electra* and *H.M.A.S. Vampire* began their rescue work. ... I noticed a seaman thrashing about in the water and swam over to help him. Later I always thought of him as 'The Blackman', because the poor bloke was smothered all over with fuel oil. He must have jumped off the ship into the middle of a swelling pool of oil. He didn't hear me approach and gave a startled gasp as I touched him. I did my best to calm him and convey to him that we were heading towards rescue. Grabbing him under the armpits I started to swim towards the *Electra*.

I seemed to have been swimming for miles before I got alongside the destroyer which was crammed with survivors. Thankfully I grabbed hold of the rope netting above which sailors were helping people on board. One sailor told me to climb aboard too. "I can," I called, "but this bloke can't." Two sailors immediately climbed down the boarding netting and with some difficulty hauled 'The Blackman' aboard. Wearily I followed.

Once on the deck of the *Electra*, I realised how limited my vision had been while swimming below. I gazed at the surface of the sea which was covered with the detritus of the sunken vessels. There were dead men, carley floats, launches, pieces of wood and other debris. 'The Blackman' was lying near one of the deck houses and I slumped down beside him, totally exhausted. Presently the nets were pulled on board and we got underway. I didn't realise it at the time but it was the end of an era. No longer would battleships be considered the masters of the ocean. They had been conquered by machines a mere fraction of their size. Aircraft were now masters of both air and sea.

The crew of the *Electra* had been engaged all this time in rescuing the survivors. 'The Blackman' had been taken below by a Sick Berth Attendant. I went to the rail and saw the same Attendant coming back along the deck. I asked him how 'The Blackman' was and he said, "Sorry mate, but he was dead when he was pulled aboard."...

While the rescue was taking place, Japanese planes could be seen high overhead but they made no attempt to molest us. In view of their behaviour before the sinkings and subsequent behaviour as the war progressed, this inaction seemed inexplicable. They were reputed to have returned the next day and thrown a wreath where the two British ships had sunk....

Some of the helpers who welcomed us ashore were under the impression that we had been in action against a large Japanese battle fleet. They were stunned when we disillusioned them. Indeed it seemed incredible that such a disaster had been caused by a few aeroplanes.

Striking at the Japanese Homeland: The Doolittle Raid

The first months of the Pacific War witnessed a procession of Japanese victories. As Japan's forces dominated on land, at sea and in the air, Allied planners searched for a means of striking back at the Japanese. On 18 April 1942, a squadron of B-25 bombers, under the command of Lieutenant Colonel James Doolittle, was launched from the aircraft carrier *USS Hornet*, for an attack on Tokyo, and other Japanese cities. This was a major logistical accomplishment, since the B-25s were not designed as carrier-borne aircraft, and because of the long distance to the targets. After dropping their bombs, all sixteen aircraft involved in the attack were lost: most landed in China, where some crewmembers were captured and executed by the Japanese; one aircraft landed in Vladivostok, where its crew was interned by the Russians. Yet whilst the Doolittle Raid inflicted only scant damage, it demonstrated that the Japanese homeland was not immune from Allied attack, and boosted Allied morale. In public, the Japanese authorities dismissed Doolittle's raid as insignificant. As the following extracts reveal, however, the Americans' ability to strike directly at Japan was a shock to the Japanese populace, and a disappointment to senior military commanders. Significantly, too, in the wake of the Doolittle Raid, there were calls in Japan to drive the American Navy from the Central Pacific. Those calls were one imperative behind the Japanese determination to seize Midway Island from the Americans.

In 1942 Koiwa Kazuei was working at the Yokosuka arsenal when it was bombed:

I was conducting business by navy telephone … shortly after noon on 18 April 1942.

Suddenly, the air raid alarm sounded. Soon loud booms shock the entire building. This attack on Tokyo was the first time the Japanese mainland had been bombed. … In my surprise I looked out the window and saw a ferocious cloud of black smoke rising rapidly from the Number-1 dock directly in front of my building. I went out on the roof and peered down to see that the warship *Daiho*, then in dry dock, had been hit. Large numbers of wounded were being carried on stretchers to the infirmary next to the docks.

As I gazed stupefied at the scene I heard a voice behind me say, "The enemy is quite something." I turned around to see a short flag officer smiling ruefully. It was the arsenal chief Naval Vice Admiral Tsuzuki Ishichi....

The sky was full of the unfamiliar low-flying squat black American military aircraft. Antiaircraft fire exploded in the sky high above them. Japanese fighter planes were flying up to meet the attack. For me as a nineteen year old it was the occurrence of a moment. But when I recall it now, I realize that I had happened upon an important historical event.

Ugaki Matome, an Admiral in the Japanese Navy, recorded the Doolittle Raid in his diary:

Saturday, 18 April 1942. An enemy task force attacked our homeland!...

At 13.00 we received news of an enemy air raid on Tokyo. ... They bombed nine spots in Tokyo with incendiary and other bombs. Twelve were killed, over one hundred wounded, fifty houses burned, and fifty more completely or partly destroyed....

[T]he enemy force seemingly withdrew to the east after launching the planes. We have missed him again and again. This is more than regrettable, because this shattered my firm determination never to let the enemy attack Tokyo or the mainland.

[W]e shall have to revise our countermeasures fundamentally, studying their type planes. In any case, this is one up to the enemy today.

The Battle of the Coral Sea: A Crewman Aboard the *Lexington* Describes a Japanese Attack

During the Second World War, as the Japanese successes at Pearl Harbor, and against the *Prince of Wales* and *Repulse* demonstrated, engagements between aircraft and ships were often uneven contests, particularly for ships lacking the protection of fighter aircraft. For the sailors aboard ships under attack from the air, battle was both terrifying and chaotic. Yet, whilst the contest between slow-moving and cumbersome ships, and nimble and speedy aircraft, was often an uneven one, the pilots of attacking torpedo-bombers – which flew relatively slowly, and at a predictable altitude above the waterline – had to steer a very precise and constant course toward their target. This made them vulnerable to anti-aircraft fire. As the war progressed, too, naval vessels deployed increasingly sophisticated anti-aircraft gunnery systems.

Recalling an attack on the *Lexington*, Stanley Johnson described the close-fought nature of the battle between aircraft and ships.

The forward 1.1 battery has the range on that first Jap. I see their shells, bright crimson tracers, tearing through the wings and fuselage. This plane wavers, begins a slow roll to its left and veers off just enough to pass in an inverted position just under our bow. As it glides by I see flames coming from the tail, and the machine smashes itself into the water 50 feet off our starboard bow.

The port forward 5-inch battery, manned by Marines, concentrates its fire on the second Jap. As this plane zooms to cross almost directly over these guns, they hit it squarely with a shell. The explosion blows it to bits, its engine plunging into the water almost at the foot of the battery. Shreds of its wings and tail surfaces slither along the carrier's deck like sheets of paper swept in front of a gale.

The Battle of the Coral Sea: A Japanese Pilot Describes the Perils of an Attack

The chaos aboard the *Lexington* was paralleled by the anxieties of Japanese pilots attacking American ships. In this extract, a Japanese pilot reveals that whilst they were often regarded by Allied servicemen as a fearless enemy, who had little regard for their own well-being, Japanese servicemen experienced the same stresses and anxieties as their Allied counterparts. Recalling the close proximity at which aircraft and ships engaged in battle, one Japanese pilot described the volume of anti-aircraft fire that his American adversaries were able to bring to bear during the Battle of the Coral Sea:

When we attacked the enemy carriers we ran into a virtual wall of anti-aircraft fire; the carriers and their supporting ships blackened the sky with their exploding shells and tracers. It seemed impossible that we could survive our bombing and torpedo runs through such incredible defences. ... I had to fly directly above the waves to escape the enemy shells and tracers. In fact, when I turned away from the carrier, I was so low that I almost struck the bow of the ship, for I was flying below the level of the flight deck. I could see the crewmen on the ship staring at the plane as it rushed by.

Australian Prime Minister John Curtin Describes the Significance of the Battle of the Coral Sea

In Australian popular memory the Battle of the Coral Sea has been constructed as the battle that both saved Australia from invasion and cemented the Australian–American alliance.[17] With the battle still raging, Australian Prime Minister John Curtin addressed the Australian Parliament on 8 May 1942. Curtin's task was a difficult one. He wished to alert the nation to the significance of the naval engagement, but could not risk revealing information that might be of strategic value to the Japanese. Consequently, he could refer neither to the location of the battle nor its nature. His carefully selected words, however, conveyed the significance of the battle and reminded Australians of their patriotic obligations. Ironically, what would be 'widely regarded' as Curtin's 'finest speech of the war' was delivered to a virtually empty House of Representatives. It was the journalists who had scrambled into the press gallery, and who were moved to tears by Curtin's words, who conveyed them to the Australian people.[18] It was only in the following weeks and months that Australians were made aware of the significance of the Battle of the Coral Sea for the course of the war in the Pacific. Curtin's speech was both a statement of the significance of the battle that was unfolding off the Australian coast, and a reminder to Australian civilians that they too had patriotic responsibilities.

[The] events that are taking place to-day are of crucial importance to the whole conduct of the war in this theater. I have no information as to how the engagement is developing, but I should like the nation to be assured that there will be, on the part of our forces and the American forces, that devotion to duty which is characteristic of the naval and air forces of the United States of America, Great Britain and the Commonwealth. I should add that at this moment nobody can tell what the result of the engagement may be. If it should go advantageously, we shall have cause for great gratitude and our position will then be somewhat clearer. But if we should not have the advantages from this battle for which we hope, all that confronts us is a sterner ordeal and a greater and graver responsibility. This battle will not decide the war; it will determine the immediate tactics which will be pursued by the Allied forces and by the common enemy. ... I ask the people of Australia, having regard to the grave consequences implicit in this engagement, to make a sober and realistic estimate of their duty to their nation. ... [I]t is not asking too much of every citizen who to-day is being defended by these gallant men in that engagement, to regard himself as engaged in the second line of service to Australia. The front line needs the support of every man and woman in the Commonwealth. ... Men are fighting for Australia to-day; those who are not fighting have no excuse for not working.

A Japanese Pilot Describes an American Attack During the Battle of Midway

On 4 June 1942, as the Battle of Midway raged, Fuchida Mitsuo experienced an American attack on the aircraft carrier *Akagi*. This was a reversal of roles for Fuchida, whom we have encountered earlier as the leader of the first wave of the Japanese attack at Pearl Harbor. The attack described by Fuchida was a key moment in the Midway encounter: following soon after an attack by American torpedo-bombers, which had been decisively thwarted by agile and speedy Japanese Zero fighter aircraft, the Americans attacked again, this time using their dive-bombers. As Fuchida describes, the timing of the second American attack was crucial, both in terms of the targets that were presented to them on the decks of the Japanese carriers, as well as the deployment of the Japanese fighter aircraft. Fuchida's description leaves no doubt about the chaos and carnage aboard the *Akagi*, but does not reveal that he broke his leg as he helped fight the fires raging aboard the ship, and that for the rest of the war he served as a staff officer:

Preparations for counterstrike against the enemy had continued on board our four carriers throughout the enemy torpedo attacks. One after another, planes were hoisted from the hangar and quickly arranged on the flight deck. At 10:24 the first Zero fighter gathered speed and whizzed off the deck.

At that instant a lookout screamed: "Hell-divers!" I looked up to see three black enemy planes plummeting toward our ship. Some of our machine guns managed to fire a few frantic bursts at them, but it was too late. The plump silhouettes of the American Dauntless dive-bombers quickly grew larger, and then a number of black objects suddenly floated eerily from their wings. Bombs! Down they came straight toward me! I fell instinctively to the deck and crawled behind a command post mantelet.

The terrifying scream of the dive-bombers reached me first, followed by the crashing explosion of a direct hit. There was a blinding flash and then a second explosion, much louder than the first. I was shaken by a weird blast of warm air. There was still another shock, but less severe, apparently a near miss. Then followed a startling quiet as the barking of guns suddenly ceased. I got up and looked at the sky. The enemy planes were already out of sight.

The attackers had gotten in unimpeded because our fighters, which had engaged the preceding wave of torpedo planes only a few moments earlier, had not yet had time to regain altitude. Consequently, it may be said that the American dive-bombers' success was made possible by the earlier martyrdom of their torpedo planes. We had been caught flatfooted in the most vulnerable condition possible – decks loaded with planes armed and fueled.

Looking about, I was horrified at the destruction that had been wrought in a matter of seconds. Planes stood tail up, belching livid flame and jet-black smoke. Reluctant tears streamed down my cheeks as I watched the fires spread. Explosions of fuel and munitions devastated whole sections of the ship. As the fire spread among planes lined up wing to wing on the after flight deck, their torpedoes began to explode, making it impossible to bring the fires under control. The entire hangar area was a blazing inferno, and the flames moved swiftly toward the bridge.

On the Wires: The Associated Press and the Battle of Midway

By the 1940s many people learned of distant events from the radio. But newspapers remained important sources of news and information, and provided detail that was often absent from radio broadcasts. The Associated Press (AP) was a cooperative of newspaper interests formed in New York City in the mid-nineteenth century with the aim of speeding up the flow of news from the Mexican–American War. Over time AP became a 'wire service' taking advantage of new technology to aid the flow of news. It was the Associated Press which introduced the news 'Flash'. By 1941 AP had expanded its reach around the world, having moved from the Morse code telegraph, then to the teletype, and then into radio. The first media outlet to learn about the attack on Pearl Harbor was the AP's San Francisco bureau which received a phone call from its Honolulu reporter Eugene Burns as the attack was beginning.[19]

For small town papers in isolated communities, the Associated Press
provided a level of coverage unavailable from any other source. One such
affiliate of the AP was the *Winona Republican-Herald* in Minnesota. As
well as news flashes, and other reports, AP supplied the paper with
analyses from leading journalists such as DeWitt Mackenzie. Mackenzie's
analysis of the battle highlighted the ways in which journalists sought to
understand events without having the full picture. Unaware that much
of the American success at Midway was due to their communications
intelligence (Comint) – including the breaking of Japanese naval codes,
which enabled American commanders to position their fleet where
it could best engage the Japanese at Midway – observers could only
explain the American victory as a consequence of good fortune and
an understanding of the Japanese psyche.[20] Such reporting was the
starting point for many popular myths of the Pacific War:

Midway Victory May Turn Tide in Battle of Pacific

Jap Attacks Seen As Answer to Raids on Tokyo
By DeWitt Mackenzie, Wide World War Analyst

The smashing American victory over the Japs off our base at Midway –
an atoll that is minute in size but vast in defensive importance – must have
far-reaching and perhaps decisive effects on the battle of the Pacific, which
the men of Nippon started six months ago.

On the face of returns thus far, so heavy is the punishment administered
to the enemy off Midway that one has the rather justifiable urge to wave
the flag a bit. However, naval operations also are proceeding off Dutch
Harbor, and we shall do well to restrain our enthusiasm until we have the
whole story.

While some points are still obscure, we get a fairly comprehensive picture
of the general situation to date by combining statements from Admiral King,
commander-in-chief of the United States fleet, Admiral Nimitz, commander-
in-chief of the Pacific fleet, and news dispatches from informed American
headquarters. If you will please refer to your maps we shall try to reconstruct
the position.

Planned Double Attack

The Japanese, combining necessity with strategic speculation, plotted to
restore their prestige, shattered by their defeat in the Coral Sea and our
unprecedented bombing raid over Tokyo and other cities of Nippon. They
picked Midway and Dutch Harbor as the objects of their attention.

In making this selection, the Japs figured they could at least repair their
damaged reputation by hit-and-run bombing of these two bases, and if things
went well they might develop the attacks into major operations. The point is
that both islands are of vast strategic value.

The midget Midway is the outpost of Hawaii and Pearl Harbor, and since the latter is the key to the Pacific, the little atoll becomes a mighty important part of the defenses of North America. If the Japs could capture it they would have secured a base from which they could launch a major offensive, with our West Coast and the Panama Canal as ultimate objectives.

Midway Guards Lifeline

But that isn't all. Midway is a sentinel over our lifeline to Australia, and possession of the island would facilitate Nipponese efforts to cut out shipping routes and thus cripple this continental base which is a rapidly-growing menace to consolidation of the Mikado's conquest

Thus in attacking Midway and Dutch Harbor the Nipponese were aiming blows at vital spots. The enemy naively hoped that he could spring a surprise and not only carry out the face-saving raids but capture at least Midway. The great strength massed for the operation against the atoll is clear indication of the Japanese ambitions.

But fate played a trick of its own. The American high command, being blessed with acumen and knowledge of Jap psychology, knew for a certainty that a face-saving operation would be undertaken. Thus we are ready for the attack, and the descendants of the Shoguns walked into a trap at Midway.

It's quite likely that other operations, perhaps even an assault on Russia, were dependant on the success of the Midway attack. Thus the beating which our forces have administered may well have spiked an ambitious program.

On the basis of present information it seems possible that the losses inflicted on the Japanese at Midway, coupled with their heavy setback in the Coral Sea, may severely limit their ability to stage further offensives, and it is important to note that they are dependant on their navy for operations. Certainly we can agree with observers at general MacArthur's headquarters in Australia that the Midway defeat has hastened the day when the United Nations can stage a major offensive in the southwestern Pacific'.

An American Ensign Uses V-Mail to Tell His Family of the Victory at the Battle of Midway

Despite the insights they provide, letters are not an unproblematic resource for the historian of the Pacific War. Writers tailored their narrative to suit the recipient of the letter. A soldier's letter to his mother might be very different from a letter to a best friend who was also in uniform. A sailor might betray emotions in a letter to his father that fitted a familiar masculine stereotype but which had been far removed from his real emotions at the time. Such self-censorship and manipulation means that letters cannot be explored uncritically.

As well as self-censorship, service personnel were subjected to official military censorship. This censorship usually operated at the unit level and was conducted by junior officers. A second screening process – outside the unit but still within the theatre of operations – also ensured unit censors did their job. The unit censors' main task was to ensure that service personnel were not providing their correspondents with information that if captured by the enemy would provide a military advantage. Furthermore, comments that might impact negatively on home-front morale were excised. If a letter passed the censor, it was stamped as such and sent on its way. Offending passages were either cut out with a razor or blacked out. If a letter revealed too much restricted material or was of intelligence value to the military itself, it could be detained. Detained letters could be used to provide qualitative data in morale and intelligence reports.

Because service personnel knew their letters would be read by another person before reaching their destination, a degree of self-censorship was often evident. As one soldier noted, the fact that one's superior was reading one's mail meant critical comments were often removed: 'it is seldom the smartest thing in the world to write ... "It's been months since I did an honest day's work" '.[21] Many soldiers avoided mailing letters in the field and only did so when they returned to base. On a base the base censor was not in the soldier's unit, affording a degree of anonymity.[22]

Many service personnel found ways to circumvent the military censors, and provide friends and family with more information than the military desired.[23] They might establish elaborate code systems. One of the censor's responsibilities was to break such codes if they could. An important consequence of the censorship system for all combatant nations in the Pacific was that it dramatically slowed the delivery of mail back to home countries. This might add days to the weeks and months mail would take to be delivered due to the sheer volume of letters being produced.

To help expedite the mail service and reduce the anxieties of separation, the US military adopted a British postal scheme which the Americans called 'V-Mail'.[24] The sender wrote a one-page letter that was then photographed by the military mail service, using a 16-mm camera. The roll of film was then air-mailed to a processing Post Office in the United States, where the film was enlarged and sent onto its final addressee. One ton of letters could be condensed into 11 kilograms of microfilm. One roll of film could include 1,500 letters. Each letter was limited to one page, but there was no limit to the number of letters a serviceman or servicewoman could send.

As the rush of battle subsided after the clash at Midway, Ensign Arthur Thomas Burke wrote from the USS Enterprise to his family, reassuring them of his safety and describing the extent of the American triumph. Several passages of his letter had been censored, in an effort to protect details that might jeopardise future operations. Note, too, that the censors also sought to deny that luck had played any role in the battle.

June 8, 1942 Dearest Mom & Dan,

How's everything by you all? I am still all right. (Just to let you know). Well, the Navy gave the Japs quite a licking, eh? It sure sounds like propaganda and exaggeration for (CENSORED - "Admiral Spruance"?) to say that all those Jap carriers, battleships, cruisers, and transports were sunk and damaged with US losses only a damaged (CENSORED - "carrier"?), doesn't it? But it is a very conservative communiqué. The Navy is making no false or colored statements and is being very careful not to have to take any statements back, so, incredible as it may seem, it's all true and as he says himself, all the returns aren't in yet. But I still (CENSORED - "shudder"?) to think of what might very well have been had (CENSORED - "our bombers been a few"?) minutes later in their (CENSORED - "dives. How many of our carriers"?) would have been (CENSORED - "sunk"?). Oh, well! Say hi to everyone for me, please. How are you making out, Dan? In the army yet? Honest folks, I am <u>tired</u> so I'll end this letter right here and write more when there is a chance of getting it off again.

Love,
Art
Arthur T. Burke

Submarine Warfare in the Pacific

Submarines played an important, if not decisive, role in the Pacific War. Whilst Japan had a substantial submarine fleet, it was frequently ineffectual, in large measure because it was often deployed in a scouting or reconnaissance role, rather than in a concerted attempt to disrupt Allied supply lines.[25] In addition, Japan used submarines as de facto cargo vessels, and also used midget submarines to attack Allied forces. Conversely, although many attacks from US submarines during the early part of the war were ineffective due to faulty torpedoes, Japan's heavy dependence on imported oil and other raw materials meant it was particularly vulnerable to submarine warfare. In the long run, the American Navy's decision to wage what amounted to unrestricted submarine warfare against Japanese targets – particularly its merchant marine – had a significant impact on Japan's war effort.[26] Submarines were often regarded as hunters, striking enemy vessels without warning. But those roles were sometimes reversed, and particularly as Allied radar and sonar technology improved during the war, the Japanese submarine fleet became vulnerable to attack from Allied ships and aircraft. To an even greater extent than was the case for sailors aboard surface vessels, submariners often went for long periods with no communications to, or from, home. To recreate the day-to-day experiences of the men who served aboard submarines, we rely heavily on veterans' recollections, often composed long after the battles and missions they described. Corin

('Mendy') Mendenhall served on two American submarines during the Pacific War, the *Sculpin* and the *Pintado*. This extract, taken from a diary of his wartime experiences, but not published until 1990, describes an engagement off the coast of New Britain. The submarine's effectiveness, as well as its vulnerability, is evident in Mendenhall's account.

28 September [1942]
[M]asts were sighted to the west, and *Sculpin* commenced closing. The possibility of an attack was evident after twenty minutes of tracking, so we went to battle stations. The target was a large tanker ... with only one small escort visible. They were zig-zagging wildly ... at a speed to eleven knots. After an hour of maneuvering to gain firing position, we fired a spread of four fish [torpedoes] at the tanker ... at a range of 1,860 yards.

The captain saw two hits, and three explosions were heard throughout the boat. After watching for only a few seconds longer, the captain took *Sculpin* to deep submergence as the escort headed for us with a bone in his teeth. Sonar reported hearing the screws of two escorts.

Long before reaching *Sculpin* he commenced dropping depth charges. We knew that he was way off target. All was quiet for about twenty minutes. The crew was released from battle stations, and I went to my bunk for some rest.

No sooner had I gotten in the bunk than I was almost knocked out of it by a string of four very close depth charges, seemingly right over me. I could hear water spewing into the compartment. I ran to the control room to report that water was coming into officers' country in the vicinity of the head (toilet), and then went back to find the leak.

A gauge line to sea ... was broken. Water was building up on the splash-tight deck, over the forward battery. We dared not let the saltwater get into the battery below, because deadly chlorine gas would be formed when the saltwater reacted with the hydrochloric acid in the battery....

It was incredible how much water could come in through a quarter-inch tube at a depth of 275 feet.

Baldwin arrived with plugs, turnbuckles, and other equipment to plug the leak....

I took on the job of dipping up buckets of water, handing them through the compartment door for the bucket brigade to pass aft and dump. ... The [bucket] brigade was dumping the water into a bilge and into the canned goods storeroom just aft of the control room.

We were able to keep the water level below twelve inches at our bailing location for the half hour that it took Baldwin to stop the leak. Then we bailed out the residual water and dried the deck. Fortunately, no water got into the battery.

Others throughout the boat were also making repairs, stopping leaks, and getting back to normal, while the captain directed evasive action over a period of two hours....

Torpedoed: The Sinking of the *USS Indianapolis*, July 1945

Although the US Navy made more extensive and effective use of submarines during the Pacific War, Japan's submarine fleet did achieve some successes – albeit too late to affect the war's outcome. In late July 1945, after stopping at the American base in Tinian Island to deliver vital parts of the atomic bomb that would subsequently be used against Hiroshima, the heavy cruiser *Indianapolis* was sailing to Leyte Gulf in the Philippines, in preparation for the planned invasion of Japan. In the early hours of 30 July 1945, the *Indianapolis* was hit by two torpedoes launched by the Japanese submarine I-58, commanded by Hashimoto Mochitsura. The *Indianapolis* sank just twelve minutes after being torpedoed, and although an estimated 900 members of the nearly 1,200-man crew were able to abandon ship, no rescue mission was launched until 2nd August when survivors were spotted by the pilot of an American aircraft on a routine anti-submarine patrol. Only 317 men survived their ordeal in the water; the rest had died of wounds, dehydration, drowning or from shark attacks. A subsequent investigation by the US Navy led to the court martial of the *Indianapolis's* commander, Charles Butler McVay III. McVay was found guilty of 'hazarding his ship by failing to zigzag'.

All the combatant nations engaged in the Pacific War relied on elaborate disciplinary codes to govern the actions and behaviour of their service personnel. Individuals who broke disciplinary codes, or military or civil law, were liable to prosecution and, perhaps, punishment. Minor offences were normally dealt with by administrative procedures within units. More serious offences were dealt with by a military 'court martial' – the military equivalent of an *ad hoc* magistrate's court. As with naval writing the Australian and American codes of military justice had been influenced by British traditions.[27] Indeed, the 1941 Australian Manual of Military Law was a derivative of British military justice. Japanese military codes reflected older Prussian as well as traditional Japanese approaches to discipline and the law. In the most serious case the punishment imposed by a court martial could be death. Within the American armed forces in the Pacific theatre, twenty-one service personnel were executed between 1942 and 1945. The crimes were either murder or rape, and eighteen of the executed were African-Americans.

The prosecution, defence and judge in courts martial were military or naval officers, who often had no legal background and only the briefest of introductions to military law. In the case of McVay's court martial, however, the prominence of the case and the rank of the defendant ensured full legal representation. Like their civilian counterparts, court documents in military or naval trials were written by lawyers and

reflected their binding legal status. McVay's indictment provides a clear
example of World War II military 'legalese':

In that Charles B. McVay, 3rd, captain, U.S. Navy, while so serving in command
of U.S.S. INDIANAPOLIS, making passage singly, without escort, from Guam,
Marianas Islands, to Leyte, Philippine Islands, through an area in which enemy
submarines might be encountered, did, during good visibility after moonrise
on 29 July 1945, at or about 10:30 p.m., minus nine and one-half zone time,
neglect and fail to exercise proper care and attention to the safety of said
vessel in that he neglected and failed, then and thereafter, to cause a zigzag
course to be steered, and he, the said McVay, through said negligence, did
suffer the said U.S.S. INDIANAPOLIS to be hazarded; the United States then
being in a state of war.

Having initially been made a scapegoat for the loss of the *Indianapolis*,
McVay's sentence was remitted in 1949. But the controversy surrounding
the sinking of the ship continued, and in 1968 McVay committed suicide.
In 2000 the US Congress resolved that McVay's record should state that
he was exonerated for the loss of the *Indianapolis*.[28]

The bitter arguments over the responsibility for the sinking of the
Indianapolis were fuelled by the Navy's delay in launching a mission
to rescue the survivors – and by those survivors' descriptions of their
harrowing ordeal. Woody Eugene James was one of the survivors:

Sunday, the 29th of July was a quiet day. The sea was runnin five or six feet …
waves, just a beautiful day out. Didn't do too much, read a book, did a little
tinkerin as usual. … Just got laid down good … and the first torpedo hit. …
I wondered, "what in the hell is goin on?"

I got out of my blanket and started to roll out from underneath the turret
and the other torpedo hit. … Within a minute and a half, maybe two minutes
at the most the bow is startin to do down. It filled up with water that fast. …
Complete chaos, total and complete chaos all over the whole ship. Screams
like you couldn't believe and nobody knew what was goin on. The word got
passed down, "ABANDON SHIP"!

Jim Newhall and I went over the side holding hands. I got tangled up in the
life line long side the ship. I got untangled and surfaced. I'm all alone so I swam
out away from the ship, probably fifty yards, maybe one hundred yards, I don't
know. I flipped over on my back and looked back and about two thirds of the
ship was in the water, bow first and leanin to the right, the propellers were
still turning. In the silhouette of the sinking ship I could see guys jumpin off
the fantail like crazy. I went over the side with a life jacket. I pulled it off and
gave it to one of the younger officers that was screamin his head off that
he didn't have one.

Anyway, there I am layin on my back lookin at that and no life jacket. I don't
hear anybody around me any place so I'm just kind of floatin and relaxin when

low and behold, a potato crate floats by. Potatoes were packaged in wooded crates then. It was just an empty potato crate, made a good buoyancy to hold on to. Works as good as a life jacket I guess. Then pretty soon I heard some voices. I yelled and who answers me, my buddy Jim Newhall. So I swam over to where he was and there was quite a group of them. It's chaos and everybody talkin and a lot of the guys were wounded, burned and we were trying to do the best we could.

Day 1
The next morning we kind of counted heads the best we could. There was about 150 people in the group. We were scattered around quite a bit. Well this isn't too bad, we thought, we'll be picked up today. They knew we were out here after all we were due in the Philippines this morning at 11:00 so when we don't show they'll know. If they didn't get a message off, but we're sure they got a message off, they'll still know where we are so no sweat, we'll be picked up before the days over.

So the day passed, night came and it was cold. IT WAS COLD. The next mornin the sun come up and warmed things up and then it got unbearably hot so you start praying for the sun to go down so you can cool off again.

Day 2
When the sharks showed up, in fact they showed up the afternoon before but I don't know of anybody being bit. Maybe one on the second day but we just know we'll be picked up today. They've got it all organized by now, they'll be out here pretty soon and get us, we all thought. The day wore on and the sharks were around. Come night time and nobody showed up. We had another night of cold, prayin for the sun to come up. What a long night.

Day 3
The sun finally did rise and it got warmed up again. Some of the guys been drinkin salt water by now, and they were goin berserk. They'd tell you big stories about the *Indianapolis* is not sunk, it's just right there under the surface. I was just down there and had a drink of water out of the drinkin fountain and the Geedunk is still open. The Geedunk bein the commissary where you buy ice cream, cigarettes, candy, what have you, "it's still open" they'd tell ya. "Come on we'll go get a drink of water," and then 3 or 4 guys would believe this story and go with them.

The day wore on and the sharks were around, hundreds of them. You'd hear guys scream, especially late in the afternoon. Seemed like the sharks were the worst late in the afternoon than they were during the day. Then they fed at night too. Everything would be quiet and then you'd hear somebody scream and you knew a shark had got him.

We were hungry, thirsty, no water, no food, no sleep, getting dehydrated, water logged and more of the guys were goin bezerk. There was fights goin on so Jim and I decided to heck with this, we'll get away from this bunch before we get hurt. So he and I kind of drifted off by ourselves. We tied our life jackets together so we'd stay together. Jim was in pretty good shape to begin with, but he was burned like crazy. His hand was burned, he couldn't hold on to anything, couldn't touch anything.

Day 4
Then the next day arrived. By this time I would have give my front seat in heaven and walked the rotten log all the way through hell for just one cool drink of water. My mouth was so dry it was like cotton. How I got up enough nerve to take a mouth full of salt water and rinse my mouth out and spit it out I don't know but I did. Did it a couple of times before the mornin was over. That's probably why I ended up with salt-water ulcers in my throat. When we got picked up my throat was bigger than my head.

Anyway, we're out there in the sun prayin for it to go down again, then low and behold there's a plane. Course there had been planes everyday since day one. They were real high and some of the floaters had mirrors that tried to attract them, but nothing. Anyway, this one showed up and flew by and we thought, "Oh hell, he didn't see us either. He's gone." Then we seen him turn and come back and we knew we had been spotted. What a relief that was.

About midnight, a little bit before there was a light shining off of the bottom of the cloud and we knew then we were saved. That was the spotlight of the *Cecil Doyle*. The Navy is on the scene. There's a ship comin. You can't believe how happy we were, guys screamin and yellin', "We're saved, We're saved."

Morning of the 5th Day
The *Doyle* arrived on the scene and started pickin survivors out of the water a little after midnight. It was daylight the next morning that he came along side us in our little raft. Boy, what a happy day that was to get my feet on the deck again.

Japan's 'Special Attack' Weapons

By 1944, the tide of war had turned against Japan. With much of their fleet sunk, and with thousands of their sailors and pilots dead, Japanese naval strategists sought a weapon that would offset the increasingly obvious Allied advantages. One such weapon was the kaiten, an improvised vessel constructed from two torpedoes, and launched from the decks of submarines. The idea was that a trained sailor would guide the torpedo – laden with explosives – toward an Allied ship. The sailor was expected to stay with their torpedo until impact: the kaiten was thus a suicide weapon, a naval equivalent of the better-known *kamikaze* aircraft. Convinced that his 'Motherland' faced 'imminent peril', and learning of the development of 'a weapon that will destroy the enemy', Yokota Yutaka volunteered for service, knowing – and accepting – that he should not expect to return alive from his mission. But Yokota did survive the war, and subsequently described his experiences and recollections. Although Allied propaganda depicted men such as Yokota as victims of indoctrination, with no regard for human life, the reality was more complex.

At the time of Pearl Harbor I had been a sixteen-year old, finishing middle school, really impressed by the nine war gods of the midget submarines who were credited by the papers with much of the success at Hawaii. They weren't, of course, actual human torpedoes, but even then, I'd thought to myself, I wouldn't mind dying like that. I was a militaristic youth. I'd been purely cultivated to serve....

When selected I felt a slight sense of sadness. My life had now no more than a year to go. ... I wasn't thinking of surviving the war. Rather than getting shot down by some plane, better to die grandly. Go out in glory....

We trained desperately ... It was agony. For everybody. Once you became a member of an attack force, you became deadly serious. Your eyes became set. Focused. If you had two lives, it wouldn't have mattered, but you were giving up your only life. Life is so precious. Your life was dedicated to self-sacrifice, committed to smashing into the enemy. That's why we trained like that. We practiced that hard because we valued our lives so highly....

The morning of our departure from Hikari we said farewell to life. We wore our dress uniforms. They gave us each a short sword, a *tantō*, just as if we'd graduated from Etajima, and a headband marked with the words, "Given Seven Lives, I'll Serve the Nation with Each of Them."...

When the motor launch first took us to our mother ship, we jumped onto our own torpedoes and, standing with our legs apart, waved our Japanese swords in circles in answer to the cheers. Before that ... I actually kissed the bow of the Kaiten that carried the explosive: "Do it for me. Get an enemy carrier for me."...

There's an old expression, "Bushidō is the search for a place to die." Well, that was our fervent desire, our long-cherished dream. A place to die for my country. I was happy to have been born a man. A man of Japan. I don't care if that makes me sound egotistical, but that's how I felt. The country was in my hands....

Our submarine, I-47, with its six Kaitens on deck, was part of a four-sub attack plan. ... But we never made it to Okinawa. We were discovered only two days out, bombed, and depth-charged. Afterwards our Kaitens looked like they'd been made of celluloid, all bent and twisted out of shape. We had to return to Hikari empty-handed.

I sailed for the second time on April 20 for the American supply lines between Ulithi and Okinawa....

We were young. We often talked about women. Dirty jokes were our stock in trade. We never talked about "loyalty," or "bravery," or "the nobility of the soul." We were just like brothers. Kakizaki never mentioned it, but he had a girl friend. He had a picture of a woman in his gear. After he'd carried out his mission, a letter from her arrived for him. He never got to read it. I always had a picture of my mother in my pocket. She's died when I was just four. Whenever I boarded my Kaiten the words, "Ma, I'll soon be there with you," escaped my lips.

"Kaiten pilots! Board! Prepare for Kaiten battle!" The sub's speakers blared. Our time had come. ... Because we were young men we were vain. It would have been a disgrace to lose composure ... You clambered up the ladder to the hatch leading to your Kaiten. You didn't have much time, but you still looked back down and forced yourself to smile. "I'm going now," was all you said. You wanted to be praised after you died, as much as you wanted it during your life. You wanted them to say, "Yokota was young, but he went with incredible bravery. He was dignified to the end." It would be terrible if they said, "He went shaking. So unlike a Kaiten pilot." There was only one like that in our whole group. He was a disgrace to the Kaiten Corps. I cut him out of the pictures I have of us preparing to depart....

On my third mission, all members of my attack group had been members of previous groups but had been unable to launch for various reasons. Before we departed, we swore to each other that we would not return. No matter what. But I returned because three of the Kaitens failed. There was a crack in my main fuel-gauge pipe. The other three launched. Kuge left a letter asking that nobody think of those of us who couldn't go as cowards....

It didn't help. I was really beaten up this time, called a disgrace to the Kaiten Corps for coming back alive! Because of that beating I still have difficulty hearing with my left ear, and I bear scars on my left hand, too....

One day, a maintenance mechanic told me that Japan had lost. "What are you saying, you filthy bastard?" I couldn't believe it. That night we were all assembled. The senior commander of the Special Attack Forces told us the news. He was in tears. I left the gathering ... tears sprang to my eyes. I cried bitterly. "I'll never launch! The war is over. Furukawa, Yamaguchi, Yanagiya, come back. Please return!" I cried and cried. Not because Japan had lost the war. "Why did you die, leaving me behind? Please come back!" I shouted toward the sea. My tears were not tears of resentment or indignation, nor were they in fear of Japan's future. They were shed for the loss of my fellow pilots.

CHAPTER FIVE
TURNING THE TIDE ON LAND, 1942–1943

There are only two definite things on earth. LIFE and DEATH. The difference between LIFE and DEATH is absolute. One cannot rely upon the dead; no one can make friends with the dead; the dead can neither speak nor mingle with the living.

Japanese Propaganda Leaflet, 1944

In the wake of the Battle of the Coral Sea, Japanese military commanders were forced to reconsider their plans for the Southwest Pacific. Port Moresby remained the primary target, but the direct invasion was now replaced by an audacious plan to seize the strategic Allied positions by land assault. This strategy called for a two-pronged approach. One invasion force would land at Milne Bay on the south-eastern tip of Papua, 370 kilometres from Port Moresby. After securing a beachhead at Milne Bay and destroying the Allied base under construction there, this force would move overland and advance along the coast to Port Moresby. A second invasion force would land on the northern coast of Papua, cross the treacherous Owen Stanley Range, and then attack Port Moresby from the rear.

The Allies sought to blunt the Japanese advance and establish bases from which sustained air attacks on Rabaul could be mounted as a precursor to an Allied counter-attack. The Allied base being constructed at Milne Bay was part of this plan. As well as this base, the Allied commander Douglas MacArthur wanted to build a second base on the north coast of Papua. With no understanding of the geography of Papua, MacArthur ordered that a force be sent from Port Moresby overland to the north coast village of Buna to begin preparations for the second air base. Like the Japanese plan, MacArthur's plan entailed crossing the Owen Stanley Range.

MacArthur's planned base was in roughly the same location as the landing point for the Japanese invasion of northern Papua. Australian and Japanese forces encountered each other near the administrative village of Kokoda. With superior numbers the Japanese pushed their enemy back towards Port Moresby.[1]

As the battle for the Owen Stanley Range raged, in late August 1942 the second Japanese force landed at Milne Bay. For five days the Japanese invaders threw everything they had (including light tanks) at the Australians. But by the beginning of September it was clear that a victory would not be secured and Japanese forces began to withdraw on 3 September 1942.

The Battle of Milne Bay was important for the Allies' cause because it marked the first defeat of Japanese land forces in the war.[2] Recalling his own experience of the Burma campaign, Field Marshall Sir William Slim noted: 'Some of us may forget that of all the Allies it was Australian soldiers who first broke the spell of the invincibility of the Japanese Army.'[3] Such a result is hardly surprising given that until early 1943 there were more Australians than Americans fighting the Japanese on land in Pacific.

On the Owen Stanley Range, the growing Australian defence, as well as the logistical problems of waging war across one of the most difficult terrains in the world, compelled Japanese forces to retreat. By November 1942 the battle for Port Moresby was over, and the Japanese were left clinging to the northern Papua coastline. Between November and

January 1943 a series of engagements known as the 'Battle for the Beachheads' took place between Gona and the nearby village of Buna. These battles culminated in further Allied victories.

Japanese reverses in Papua were concurrent with their efforts to secure the 'Solomons Chain' and isolate Australia from the United States. Prior to their defeats at Milne Bay and Kokoda the Japanese had enjoyed some success in their advance through these islands, the most strategically important of which was Guadalcanal. From Guadalcanal the Japanese could project their power as far south as New Caledonia and disrupt the lines of communication between its two main enemies in the Pacific. The American and Japanese struggle in Guadalcanal continued into 1943. After a bloody and hard-fought campaign the Americans prevailed.[4]

Guadalcanal was important for the course of the Pacific War for two principal reasons. First, as Milne Bay had proved to the Australians, Guadalcanal showed the Americans the advantages of joint service operations: the campaign included the first amphibious operation by the United States since the 1898 invasion of Cuba during the Spanish American War.[5] Second, with Guadalcanal secure, the Allies were ready to mount their counter-offensive. While the Coral Sea and Midway naval battles are often cited as the 'turning point' battles of the Pacific War, Charles W. Koburger has contended that the Solomons Campaign was 'the key to victory'.[6] Having resisted the Japanese advance in Papua and in the Solomons, the Australians and Americans were in a position to attack Rabaul and push Japan out of the south-western Pacific.

THE SOURCES

War Diary, 39th Battalion, Australian Military Forces

Japanese and Allied military units kept 'war diaries' or 'field diaries' during the course of the War. War diaries were official administrative records of the daily activities of the unit (usually of a battalion size or larger). These diaries were kept by a junior officer in the unit headquarters and were usually only maintained when the unit was deployed in a battle zone. The diary was a British tradition that had been adopted by the American and Japanese militaries. 'Field diaries' had emerged in the Japanese military during the late nineteenth century as a means of enforcing accountability amongst officers. The reportage protocols associated with diaries soon made them public documents, providing 'a new language for narrating the battlefield'.[7]

Each Australian unit fighting in Papua kept its 'war diary'. Whilst guidelines stipulated how entries were to be made, individual officers interpreted these guidelines in different ways and expended more or less effort in their completion. Consequently, the overall quality of these records differs markedly. Although these records were not personal diaries, they provide insights into the travails of the men of individual units. One of their purposes was to assist historians and others to piece together the experiences of individual units. Capitalisation was used for personal names, place names and for emphasis.

The first Australian unit to encounter the invading Japanese force near the village of Kokoda was an Australian militia battalion from Victoria. Poorly trained and equipped, they were led by Lieutenant Colonel W. T. Owen, who had managed to escape the massacre of the Australian garrison when the Japanese had seized Rabaul in January 1942. The Battalion's war diary documents the first encounters between the Australians and Japanese in Papua:

25 Jul. '42
Lt. Col. OWEN and Capt. TEMPLETON proceeded to AWALA and arrived at 0130 hours. It was then decided to make a stand at dawn and posns [positions] were occupied accordingly, - 800 yards EAST of GORARI. 11 and 12 Pls [platoons] on main track with P.I.B. [Papuan Infantry Battalion] details on flanks in the bush. LEWIS guns were sited to fire along track while TSMG's [Thompson Sub-machine Guns] were for the most part to be used in jungle.

Lt. Col. OWEN left for KOKODA at 1000 hrs to contact further troops due to arrive by air.

ENEMY patrol advanced along track at 1145 hrs. Fire was held until they had passed our flanking posns, and when fire was opened, fifteen ENEMY were killed....

Tps [troops] by this time were very tired, and approx six men were missing. Capt. STEVENSON was sent to KOKODA to report situation to Lt.Col. OWEN. ... Supplies were sent forward by forty native carriers, who returned to KOKODA with packs which were not required. Lt. Col. OWEN ordered OVI to be held at all costs — unless the Force was surrounded....

26 Jul. '42

Enemy approached along track at 1445 hours. ... Our L.M.G's [Light Machine Guns] opened fire at 1500 hrs. Fire was immediately returned from ENEMY M.M.G [Medium Machine Gun] on the flanks. ... After approximately five minutes, fire was coming from all around our position. Fire died down at 1730 hrs. ... Capt. TEMPLETON walked around a corner of the track towards the rear with a view to warning the remainder of 16 Pl which was expected, to keep a sharp lookout. A burst of fire was heard in the direction he had taken and he was NOT seen again. ... Heavy firing was continued throughout early part of the night, and at 2000 hrs it was decided to break out of the encirclement.

With a native Police Boy as guide, the Force moved out under mortar fire — for DENEKI ... They arrived in DENEKI the next afternoon....

27 Jul. '42

Lt. Col OWEN, after the destruction of all possible stores, material and buildings at KOKODA, withdrew with all tps then in that area – to DENIKI. As it was impossible to get all packs etc, out of KOKODA, the entire force was without blankets or groundsheets....

28 Jul. '42

Some tps, previously thought to be missing, arrived at DENEKI. They had slept in KOKODA on the previous night, as the ENEMY had NOT occupied KOKODA. Lt. Col. OWEN decided to do so. This occupation was completed by 1330 hrs. ... At 1330 hrs ENEMY trps were seen running across the track and moving on to our flanks....

29 Jul. '42

At 0230 ENEMY were reported to be advancing on our posns from the NORTH. Lt Col OWEN personally took command of this section – and it was while standing firing a rifle down the escarpment that he was hit just above the right eye by an ENEMY Sniper. He was dragged from his posn and carried to a nearby building – where he was attended by the M.O. [Medical Officer] attached to the P.I.B. [Capt. VERNON]. By this time the enemy was firing from our rear and closing in on the flanks. Our Tps then commenced to withdraw in fairly good order despite the difficulty of distinguishing friend from foe in the darkness. ... Lt. Col. OWEN was still alive, but unconscious at this time, and had to be left at the R.A.P. [Regimental Aid Post] from which our force was cut off. It was obvious, moreover, that he would only remain alive for a few more minutes....

Doc Vernon's War Diary

One of the Australian officers at the fall of Kokoda was Captain Geoffrey 'Doc' Vernon. The 60-year-old Australian was the medical officer in charge of native carriers on the trail. Vernon kept his own war diary. By mid-September the Australians had been pushed over the Owen Stanley Range and were within sight of Port Moresby. Vernon was still on the Trail.

Ioribaiwa was rapidly evacuated by all but combatants. Between the 11th and 16th Sept a determined stand was made. We were heartened by accounts of the entire destruction of small Japanese assault parties, but these successes were not lasting. It was from here that the fine work of our native stretcher bearers gained general recognition, and the Angels of the Owen Stanley track sprang into being....

AIF units were coming out of the combat area and I spoke to one officer. He told me our men were not really fighting, not to the degree he had known in the Middle East, and too many were picked off from long range by lack of skill in concealing themselves. This was just the opinion of one man. I asked [a medical corps] officer why we were evacuating Ioribaiwa, and he said it was because we were losing too many men....

There followed the worst walk I have ever taken. The heavens opened and, amid lightning and thunder, sheets of water wet us through in minutes. The big hill was so steep and slippery you often slid back for yards. The most curious feature of the trek was the hordes of men all pressing on in the same direction, and soon we had to fall into a queue that extended for miles....

Progress was by a slow crawl. When night fell it was so dark I could only keep on the track by putting my hands on the shoulders of the medical orderly in front of me. Most of the line was linked in this way to prevent a fall into a precipice of unknown depth. Next morning I returned along the same track. ... The whole length of it from Ioribaiwa had been seriously fouled. During the retreat in darkness, men were compelled to relieve themselves anywhere, and the whole route literally stank....

Watanabe Toshio's Diary

Like the Allies, the Japanese demonstrated a pitiful ignorance of the Papuan terrain and assumed that once they arrived on the north coast they could easily build a road over the Owen Stanley Range. Unlike the Australians, however, most of the Japanese were combat veterans from the China or Malaya campaigns and had been well trained in jungle warfare.

Few intimate written records of the Japanese experience in the Southwest Pacific survived the war. Those that have survived were for the most part captured documents, removed from prisoners or, more often, dead bodies. If a Japanese soldier (dead or alive) held a document, it was usually of a private nature – typically a letter from home or a diary.

As it was in the West, diary keeping was a long-established and popular pastime in Japan. Its popularity grew in the 1920s as a consequence of developments that gave self-narratives such as travelogues, confessionals and shishosetsu (I-novel) a prominent place in Japanese literary culture. Furthermore, the Japanese military saw some advantage in encouraging soldiers to keep diaries. The modern Japanese soldier needed to be self-disciplined and their commanders hoped 'guided diary writing' would inculcate a range of political and military ideas that would empower the soldier.[8]

Japanese diary practice, however, tended to differ from Western approaches. In his discussion of this subject, Lee Miner has noted: 'We may say roughly that Japanese diary literature emphasizes love rather than marriage, death rather than mortal battles, the family rather than public life.'[9] Such an emphasis is evident in Japanese wartime diaries of the Pacific Theatre, but such themes often compete for space with the more immediate concerns driven by the privations endured as a consequence of Allied interdiction in the waters around Rabaul and the ensuing restriction of Japanese resupply of forces in Papua, New Guinea and the Solomons. Accordingly, these wartime diaries served two functions: as a log of record; and as a site for philosophical and spiritual meanderings. As living conditions deteriorated to the point of starvation, these two streams often merged. The reported lack of food, for example, fuelled thoughts on the meaning of life and death.

Along with the educational background of the diarist, the contents of a diary could be influenced by its physicality. Many Japanese soldiers used small pocket diaries rather than the larger writing pads used for formal field diaries which would have allowed more expansive recording. A small diary was also more easily concealed. Despite the earlier urge to encourage diary keeping, the Japanese military imposed restrictions on diary keeping during the Pacific War. While some Japanese soldiers later wrote of their considerable efforts in hiding their diaries during inspections, the policing of Japanese regulations prohibiting service personnel keeping diaries was often even more lax than was the case amongst the Allies. This laxity may be explained by the general view amongst Japanese leaders to 'dismiss intelligence as having negligible importance'.[10] The reality, however, was very different. Japanese diary entries from these early campaigns of the Pacific War were of significant intelligence value. They highlighted the degree to which the tide of war was turning against the Japanese well before the Allied counter-offensives of 1943. Another reason for the prevalence of diaries amongst Japanese soldiers was the collapse of the Japanese logistical system in the South Pacific. For soldiers who were rarely able to share letters with loved ones, diaries were one means of recording their experiences.

After the war many Japanese soldiers destroyed their diaries as a way of trying to forget the disaster that had befallen them and the nation. Wartime thoughts were of little help in rebuilding Japan. Those who did not destroy their diaries, however, maintained a connection with an earlier mindset: 'The subsequent stubbornness of many veterans to accept the orthodox postwar narrative, wielding their diaries as they once did their rifles, is a direct result of the power of the diary as a self-disciplinary tool.'[11]

One Japanese diary keeper was Watanabe Toshio. He fought along the Kokoda Trail until his death near Templeton's Crossing (named after the Captain mentioned in the 39th Battalion's war diary) in October 1942. His diary, documenting his recent experiences, was removed from his body and translated by Allied intelligence. The intelligence value of Watanabe's words is clear. Allied authorities were given strong indications that Japanese logistics on the Trail were breaking down and that a lack of food was reducing the combat efficiency of the enemy.

May 4th, On the way to Port Moresby attacked and returned [The Battle of the Coral Sea]

July 21st, landed BUNA, advanced to Port Moresby, the first battalion alone

July 31st, arrived Kokoda aerodrome

August 10th, recaptured the aerodrome

August 16th, 2nd and 3rd battalions landed BUNA

August 23rd, for a month since the landing we have only had miso flour and soy with rice. Everybody feels run down. 2ND AND 3RD Battalions arrived at KOKODA,

Sept. 21st, we had to cross the OWEN STANLEY RANGE many times to get supplies. We are very much distressed by shortage of food. In the fighting between KOKODA and ISURAVA, our company was reduced from 180 to 80 men. Amongst 144 Rgt. [regiment] our company commander OGAWA was killed at Kokoda, the next commander HATANAKA was killed at ISURAVA and the 3rd commander is HIRANO. Every company reduced to half strength.

October 7th, On the 26th last month near BUTAI, the 2nd Bn. and no 2 company were left behind as 'STANLEY DETACHMENT' and the rest withdrew from the first line. 41st Regt. left one Bn. [battalion] in KOKODA and the other withdrew to BUNA. At present Detachment Headquarters, Regt. HQ, the 1st and 3rd Bns and independent engineering unit are all assembled in KOKODA and bivouacking in jungles. I believe PORT MORESBY operations have been discontinued and they have withdrawn.

10-10-42, Papaki Bridge fell. Our rice supply is gone and yesterday and the day before yesterday we had no rice at all. Lately we have been eating nothing but potatoes and we have never experienced so much shortage of food.

General Horii's Message to the Troops

In his study of war and leadership Owen Connelly has suggested that reading the words of military commanders is an excellent means of appreciating a nation's 'way of war',[12] Whilst censorship may have denied readers at home a true appreciation of some aspects of the Pacific campaign, military communications, by necessity, dealt with realities as they unfolded. At the same time, inter-unit communication still had the important task of maintaining morale while offering an accurate assessment of the situation. Maintaining this fine line, especially for an army enduring defeat, became a literary art form in itself. Major General Horii Tomitarō led Japanese troops on the ground during the Kokoda campaign. In September 1942, when it was clear the fortunes of the battle had turned against the Japanese, Horii sent a message to all his troops.

Whilst messages from Japanese commanders alluded to servicemen's responsibilities to overcome the hardships of war, they rarely acknowledged that the Japanese leadership had exacerbated these problems. This approach tapped into a wider Japanese national outlook that had insisted that the nation's 'spiritual strength' would be the decisive factor in securing victory. For soldiers, connecting the physical with the mental was the key to this personal and collective fortitude. Spiritual strength was not measured on performance of physical power or cleverness. Rather, it was based on meeting the 'difficulties that test a person's will'.[13] The key attribute was an ability to carry on when enduring fear, disillusionment, depression, boredom and loneliness. When an individual demonstrated spiritual strength, the fortunes of the whole unit would be improved.

A few weeks after writing the message, Horii died, not at the hands of the enemy, nor through disease, but as a result of drowning when he fell from a tree that had been hastily felled to cross a river.

Message to Troops by Horii Tomitarō, Officer Commanding the Detachment 20/9/42

1. After the departure of our detachment from RABAUL, it is now over one month since we took over from the Yokoyama unit which, sent here ahead of us, had put up a brave fight....

2. For more than 20 days of that period, every unit forced its way through deep forests and ravines, and climbed over scores of high peaks in pursuit of the enemy. Traversing mud more than knee-deep, clambering up steep precipices, bearing uncomplainingly the heavy weight of artillery ammunition, our men overcame the shortage of our supplies and succeeded in surmounting the STANLEY RANGE. No pen or word can depict adequately the magnitude of the hardships suffered. From the bottom of our hearts we appreciate these many hardships and deeply sympathise with the great numbers killed and wounded.

3. We realise the enemy in Tulagi and Guadalcanal Island have not yet been annihilated. ... Therefore we are staying here firmly maintaining our situation so that during this period we can perfect our organization and replenish our fighting strength, and then strike a hammer blow at the enemy stronghold of MORESBY. However, in the front of us, the enemy still crawls about. It is difficult to judge the direction of his movement, and many of you have not yet fully recovered your bodily strength. I feel keenly that it is increasingly important during the present period while we are waiting for an opportunity to strike, to strengthen our positions, re-organise our forces, replenish our stores, and recover our physical fitness.

4. You will all bear in mind how vital are the situation and character of the Detachment in the South Pacific, and how increasingly heavy are your responsibilities. You shall strengthen your morale, replenish your vigour, and having perfected all your preparations for battle, you shall, when next we go into action, ungrudgingly draw on the whole fighting power of the unit.

Ralph Honner's Speech at Menari

On the other side of the Owen Stanley Range another leader was speaking to his men. Lieutenant Colonel Ralph Honner had earlier seen war service in the Middle East. Appointed to command the 39th militia battalion on the death of Bill Owen, Honner arrived on the Kokoda Trail to find his new command hopelessly outnumbered and demoralised. Through inspired leadership he engineered a number of fighting withdrawals. The men of the 39th did not win a battlefield victory, but they bought time for the Allies. Their resistance allowed Australian commanders to send more men and supplies up the Trail and, eventually, reverse the course of the campaign. Exhausted after weeks of fighting, the 39th Battalion was finally removed from the front line. At the mountain village of Menari, Honner praised his men. Connelly has proposed that the words of leaders reveal their 'ontological, epistemological and teleological views'.[14] A teacher before becoming a lawyer, Honner was a man of letters and a lover of Shakespeare. One military historian has suggested that Honner's knowledge of the bard played a role in his battlefield leadership during the campaign.[15] The Menari speech was clearly inspired by *Henry V*. Here was a 'band of brothers'.

Men, the first thing I want to say is congratulations. Over the last two months you have performed magnificently under very difficult circumstances and have every right to be very proud of what you have achieved. You have done Australians proud, and you have done yourselves proud. Brigadier Potts [the Officer in command of Australian forces on the Trail] has specifically asked me to commend you on your performance, and to tell you that news of your magnificent deeds have travelled far. All of the Australian Army is proud of you.

For the rest of your days you will be able to look on these days with the warmth of knowledge that when the heat was on you did not buckle, did not take a backward step. None of us will ever forget our fallen comrades, but your own efforts have ensured that they will not have died in vain.

Some things it may be better to forget. I have heard some talk among you that some of you might feel you have been let down by other battalions and companies. While I understand that kind of talk under these difficult circumstances, I ask that you let it go. I remind you that those men are no better or worse than you, but their circumstances were different. Had they been side by side with you they may have performed magnificently. Had you been side by side with them you might have performed less well. I repeat; the fact that their leaders may have failed them, and yours didn't, doesn't mean they were any better or worse than you are'.

Japanese Diary from Milne Bay

At Milne Bay in September 1942 Australian soldiers found a diary belonging to a Company Commander of the Kure No 3 Special Landing Party. The diary highlighted the way Japanese soldiers often constructed warfare around the spiritual themes of life and death. Often there is the implicit – and sometimes explicit – suggestion that personal resolve will be recognised and rewarded by a higher power. Nonetheless, the confessional nature of the diary saw this Japanese officer ponder his own weaknesses, often in the face of Allied technological superiority.

August 23 Sunday
When we were about to make the first landing on GUADALCANAL Island, we heard the appearance of enemy attacking units and, in compliance with the orders of the commander of the 8th fleet, were forced to change our prearranged plan. It was decided that we were to return to TRUK, our South Sea Island Mandate Island. There was actually no opposition to the landing operation, but since our landing party has no attacking power at sea, regrettable as it was, we had to wait for further orders and opportunities. Our special landing unit has experienced disappointment three times in spite of our attentive and gallant determination and I can well understand the feelings of the officers and men. It is a gigantic battle of annihilation. A gamble of life and death. It is a battle with a powerful enemy which will cause the fear of death. It is an unspeakable experience in the mind of men and will no doubt contribute towards creating views of life in the future.

August 25 Tuesday
6 enemy planes attacked our convoy at 6.05 am while officers and men were smoking and resting on the top deck after a hasty breakfast. The first bomb scored a direct hit on the flagship JINTSU. Her bridge was in flames. We were ordered to the upper crew's quarters, but our ship also suffered a direct hit

to the bridge. I escaped to a corner of the crew's mess hall. Though I lost control of myself because of the fire caused by the explosion, I only sought for a safe spot ... the fire bombing has caused great confusion amongst the officers and men. After seeing that confusion I still fear an aerial attack....

Although our men and officers were rescued by patrol boats from the convoy and felt relieved for a while, the enemy attacked us again. They bombed our convoy but we escaped. We who have been through these attacks can scarcely believe that we have survived such fearful and difficult experiences.

Our casualties were great. ... For the landing Party, August 25 was one of the most dangerous days and must be remembered as our resurrection day.

'My Guadalcanal': Inui Genjuru's Diary

One Japanese soldier who did reach Guadalcanal was Inui Genjuru. As the Guadalcanal campaign continued, the Americans maintained their very effective interdiction of the Japanese supply line down the chain. Food and ammunition were soon in short supply for the Japanese making survival difficult and virtually ruling out the possibility of defeating the enemy. Inui's testimony challenges a number of enduring Western perceptions. First, that rigid discipline permitted little challenge to regulations and, second, that Japanese soldiers were little concerned about casualties. In the case of breaking the rules, Inui did not share this breach until after the war when he added a parenthetical comment. Despite his diary's intimate purpose, Inui had feared it might be read by officials:

Oct. 10, 1942
Dreamed of my parents, little sister Utako, Kikuko, brother Seizaburō and Shigeo. Shigeo was carried on Utako's back and got her sick. An odd dream. A peaceful day.

Oct. 11
The name of Ichiki-Shitai was changed to Kitao unit. I dug potatoes, did the washing and bathed for the first time in 25 days. I feel better lately.

1st Lt. Sakakibara brought us packs of cigarettes from Rabaul. 5 pieces to each, I took 7 'Hikari' cigarettes for myself. Takeda was on sentry duty, I and Oki had delicious rice and sweet potato porridge, and potato leaves boiled in soy sauce for lunch. Sick of the long nights.

Oct. 12
Made a report of the battle about the death of Kondo, Kihira, Kato and Yoshimura, changing their cause of death from illness into glorious death in the Battle of Tenaru R. on Sept. 13. I feel I've done my duty as an officer. ... (Of course, it was a fabrication of an official document that I had altered the cause of their death. But there were many differences between the payment from the social security systems according to the causes of death. Such

a fabrication was not a rare thing then, but I couldn't alter reports any more in the latter days of the battle when soldiers started dying from disease and or starvation one after another).

Oct. 13

Our planes were up in superior numbers to the enemy lately. Unloaded on a large scale, 4000 soldiers by 5 cruisers last night. Our army is steadily getting ready for a new battle. Somebody suggests that we should dig out our guns and join the battle, and another says that we can order the rest of our guns (3 guns) from Rabaul. A good idea.

But after I had suffered hardships beyond description, I wished that I could stay there for 10 or 20 days more having gourmet food, moderate exercise and peaceful rest without guarding against enemy.

To tell the truth, the gourmet dish is 15 cm pickled yellow Japanese radish or 10 days ration for 3 men. But I don't feel any discontentment with this furnishing of food when I think of the days of retreat in the mountain.

Counting the number of arms and clothing began. Capt. says he doesn't approve the loss of gas masks. He himself made soldiers carry his binoculars, katana-sword and gas mask with no consideration of their pains. Perhaps he thinks his soldiers' lives are lighter than his equipment.

Oct. 14

15:30, Departed Cape Esperance where we had lived so long and peacefully. We return to the 28 km front, Tasivarongo Point. The duty is the same.

Enemy planes don't attack this morning because our planes are making a violent attack. Takeda, Oki and I stayed behind in the jungle of Sekiro to assemble and organize the 3rd and 4th platoons. They carry a heavy load of kitchenware. I carry 11 lit. rice.

Oct. 15

Surprised to find 4 destroyers on the sea in the morning glow. Planes that flew over us seemed to be our force. At a rest point, a marine said that 6 transports were unloading at Tasivarongo under 10 destroyers' escort. The main force of Aoba regiment is unloading! Another large force is landing at Esperance.

Our battleships and convoy are anchoring in daylight. Only our planes are up and few enemy planes are flying! What a glorious and delightful day!

Because of the late arrival of the 3rd and the 4th platoon, the work was 10 hours behind schedule. They can't be reproached under their present condition....

Corp. Kawai brought us sweets (special nutritive of the Navy). He sometimes sends me kind present. I must get something for him in return for his kindness.

Oct. 16

A fierce attack on a landing spot in the morning. Supply bases in the jungle and near the Mbonehe R. were utterly destroyed. 3rd platoon was expected

to arrive at 7:30, and 4th platoon at 10:00, but the very end of the line had
not arrived till after 12:00. At the suggestion of the other platoon leaders,
I agreed that soldiers were not to start carrying provisions to the front until
tomorrow morning, because they were tired out. Every day they had conveyed
provisions on the extending supply route. 3rd platoon started one after
another. We started at dusk. No Japanese planes today, and enemy planes
destroyed as they liked.

Arrived at Tasivarongo on 21:40, and joined the main force....

At night, we marched along the beach near the unloading spot, and saw
3 Japanese transports burning, blazing red flames rising up into the sky. Bright
and greater flames rose from a ship and suddenly it listed with a terrific noise.
A Commander of the Independent Ship Engineering Regiment died in the battle.
A soldier of a Ship Engineering Company said "We unloaded all munitions and
provisions. But we were completely destroyed and only 8 survived. Please
avenge our buddy on them." 3 transports were stranded....

And on our way back after we parted from the main force, about 22:40,
we saw burning red sky and ships. When we approached the first ship, it
listed with a terrific noise, fierce flames bursting out and black smoke from
the forecastle deck. We could do nothing but look on the scene in utter
amazement, standing motionless on the path through coconut grove 30 meters
away from the ship. How miserable!

On our way back, Oki picked up some canned foods. Gathered copra
for fuel.

Oct. 17
Fierce air raid on Tasivarongo yesterday. It was funny that Oki was at a loss
what to do with the cans. Fierce bombardment by enemy warships. Our
planes didn't come. A fire at the ammunition dump spread to all the
ammunition and went up in a furious and miserable explosion, the desolate
scene of the night sky reflecting the red flame.

2nd Lt. Kinoshita went to the unloading point with 100 soldiers to order
the provisions. Furukawa 'detachment' got a lot of 'Pirate' cigarettes.

Oct. 18
17:40, led 259 soldiers of Kitao unit and carried 100 sacks of rice to
Kakambona. ... Arrived at 20:00, then let each unit go back to their camp.
An attack of fever of 40.00 degrees on 19:20. First I felt uneasy but some-
what better when I had arrived at Tanavasa. But after arrival at Kakambona,
I became worse and took a rest at Maj. Kajiki's tent. With 2nd Lt. Umeda.

Oct. 19
3:30, feeling good, left Kakambona. Luckily found a bicycle and got back
in an hour.

My fever went down and I have a big appetite. I had an excellent coffee
yesterday morning when I was hungry, for the first time since I had coffee

in Java. Had another this morning. All sorts of delicacies for a side dish and 'Chesterfield' cigarettes!

23:30, left our camp for Kakambona again.

Imamura's Recollections of Rabaul

With the situation deteriorating in the Solomons and Papua, General Imamura Hitoshi was sent to Rabaul. Having fought in China and the Dutch East Indies, it was hoped his wealth of experience could be the deciding factor. Arriving in the Southwest Pacific, however, Imamura found his men already contemplating defeat. Problems of communication and logistics that would subsequently plague the Japanese land campaigns in the Southwest Pacific had already taken their toll. Like Horii, Imamura had few resources at his disposal and had to rely on the well-worn Japanese argument that their superior spiritual strength would overcome the Allies' advantages in men and machines.

At 2pm I arrived in Rabaul and, received greetings of the remaining persons of the 17th Army. As personnel of my HQ were transported by ship, they could not be expected before two weeks later.

Having seen behaviours of the persons there for a few days, I recognised they were hopeless. They were dispirited like a dog in a house of death. Of course it was quite natural for them, who were worrying over a hard battle and hunger upon their CinC [commander in chief] HYAKUTAKE and other soldiers on Guadalcanal island. However, it was impossible to fight in such a condition. I gathered all officers in Rabaul and, gave instructions:

'From now on, turn all soldiers out of doors every evening and let them sing military songs, ballads OK? Put a big loud speaker of the propaganda section in the middle of town and send a cheerful melody. Don't make soldiers depressed'.

After that I sometimes heard soldiers singing.

Immediately after my arrival, I sent an instruction to Lt Gen HYAKUTAKE, the CinC of the 17th Army:

'Many thanks for your long and desperate efforts. Loading two crack divisions, which are expected here after one month, I will come with these and reconquer the island. Be courageous and patient. And keep the base for landing'.

From Lt Gen HYAKUTAKE I received a reply in cable:

'Recently, [the number of] starved amount to 100 per day, and expected to increase more. All coconuts on the beach have been completely finished. The island had changed to Gua – starving – island'....

The 6th and 51st Divisions, which should be shifted towards Guadalcanal Island for its reconquering, were coming from China, being expected at Rabaul before the end of December. I was intending to advance on the island, leading two divisions and, seek a decisive battle. However, if the 2nd Division and a part of the 38th Division, which were keeping the landing points in the island, were to die out from starvation or become immovable by emaciation, the landing of the 2 Divisions would be very difficult. The American forces on the island consisted of approximately three divisions and their equipped firepower was three times the estimation of the general staff officers....

I sent two staff officers of my HQ to the island by submarine to investigate the situation of friends and enemy, general land situation, landing points for the reinforcements, and enemy's positions which should be attacked. Ten days after, they returned by a submarine again, and reported to me as follows:

'Starving conditions of the CinC HYAKUTAKE and others far beyond the previous report from there. For instance; it is impossible to send soldiers on patrol without giving them 4 persons food stuffs to each one. In connection with food there are many immoral conducts increasing against military discipline and the number of the starved is coming up to 120 or 130 per day. However, true to their name as Japanese soldiers they brandish their bayonets when the American soldiers approach and, never surrender. The enemy keep out of serious fighting and, are watching for self-extermination, having cut off the supply.

Yoshida Kashichi's Poem

Japanese servicemen, like those of other nations, devised various ways to momentarily escape the horrors of battle and the boredom in between. It might be tempting to try and find a link between the poetry written by Japanese officers and the refined intellectual world of the much earlier samurai classes. And whilst Allied propaganda frequently depicted twentieth-century Japanese military men as fanatical heirs to the warrior values of the samurai class, the wartime propaganda of the Allies, as well that of the Japanese, was based on fundamentally racist understandings that essentialised both the enemy and the 'self'.[16] Even in writing on the Pacific War that is distant from the conflict, it is not unusual to encounter descriptions of the Japanese as fundamentally different and unrecognisable, highlighting the persistence of Orientalist notions beyond the end of the war. As Beatrice Trefalt has demonstrated, however, an insistence on Japanese difference – particularly by the commonly used trope of the medieval samurai as a specific and historically recognisable martial legacy – serves to perpetuate the language of wartime propaganda, by suggesting a form of fanaticism which obscures rather than enlightens us through other, more valid, ways of understanding Japanese militarism.[17]

Many Japanese officers were highly educated, and some found the composition of poetry an apt form of expressing their fears and anxieties about life and death, as well as a means of removing oneself mentally from the battleground. As the Japanese position in Guadalcanal deteriorated, Yoshida Kashichi shared his thoughts in a poem. The desperation of a now pointless mission provided a moment of poignant reflection:

When Will This March End?

No matter how far we walk
We don't know where we're going
Trudging along under dark jungle growth
When will this march end?
Hide during the day
Move at night
Deep in the lush Guadalcanal jungle
Our rice is gone
Eating roots and grass
Along the ridges and cliffs
Leaves hide the trail, we lose our way
Stumble and get up, fall and get up
Covered with mud from our falls
Blood oozes from our wounds
No cloth to bind our cuts
Flies swarm to the scabs
No strength to brush them away
Fall down and cannot move
How many times I've thought of suicide.

American Poets and Guadalcanal

Whilst a poem might be intended for public consumption, it often betrayed an honesty more closely associated with the more private forms such as diary writing. Jay Winter has contended that the poetry of 'soldier-poets' during World War I created a new language of 'truth telling' that challenged the 'lies' or 'Big Words' of the 'older generation that sent them'.[18] The desire to accurately and honestly relate the harsh reality of war helped produce a 'poetry of witness'.[19] Medic Jim Eppieson's poem, and the anonymous poem that follows, convey the commonality of the American experience in the Solomons. Often these poems were penned in response to the frustration of the censor's cut or the propaganda campaigns at home that papered over the privations of life on what the Marines quickly dubbed the 'Hell Hole of the Pacific'. Concomitant

with the notion that war was hell, Australian and American soldiers'
writing referred frequently to the idea that the soldiers were fighting
in Hades itself. The notion is clearly indicated in the title of both poems:
Guadalcanal is not an island one fights *on*, it is a place *into* which one
is drawn:

Life in Guadalcanal

Down in those muddy valleys,
We sure are in a spot,
Battling in the terrific heat,
In the land that God forgot.

Just laying hear and thinking
Of what we left behind,
We'd hate to put on paper
What's running through our minds.

Many miles we have marched,
And stood guard on many a post,
Hours and hours we've thought of
The things we want the most.

Down with the mosquitoes,
Down where a soldier gets blue,
Down at the very bottom
Six thousand miles from you.

Out in the jungle with a rifle,
Down in the ditch with a pick
And doing the work of a Medic
And too hungry and tired to kick.

Every night the bombing raids are coming,
It seems more than a man can stand,
Some times we think we are convicted,
But we are defenders of our land.

We are soldiers in the Army,
Earning our meagre pay
Fighting for people with millions,
For a lousy two bucks a day.

Living only for tomorrow,
And hungry for our gals,
Hoping when we return home,
They aren't married to our pals.

No, she at home knows we are living,
And some don't give a damn
Back home its soon forgotten
We've loaned our lives to UNCLE SAM

The obstacles that we have confronted,
Our censor won't let us tell,
Let's hope it's nice in heaven
We've served our time in hell.

Somewhere in Guadalcanal Island

Somewhere in Guadalcanal, where rain is a like a curse,
And each day is followed by another slightly worse,
Where your tent is always mouldy, and your clothing damp,
Where shaving is a torture, and a man feels like a tramp.

Somewhere in Guadalcanal, where a white man is never seen
Where the sky is always cloudy, and grass is wet and green
Where something besides a mosquito robs a man of sleep,
Where there isn't any whiskey, and the quinine is cheap.

Somewhere in Guadalcanal, where the moon's not made for love
And the sky is filled with searchlights, spotting TOJO's planes above,
Where the flashes like a comet show the ack ack is right,
And the Zero whining downward, one less for tomorrow night.

Somewhere in Guadalcanal, where the mail is always late,
And a Xmas card in April is considered up to date,
Where we never have a payday, and we never have a cent,
But we never miss the money, because we never get it spent.

Somewhere in Guadalcanal, where the ant, and goons play,
And a hundred fresh mosquitoes replace the ones you slay,
So take me back to good old Virginia, where I can hear the Cathedral bells.
For this God forsaken outpost is a substitute for hell.

The Pacific War as a Race War

The Pacific War was constructed as a race war. Japanese propaganda often depicted Japan's mission in terms of the need to rid Asia of the white races. Americans and Australians tapped into a wellspring of racial animosities which had been constructed around the notion of the 'Yellow Peril'. Racial animosities influenced not only propaganda but the conduct of war in the Pacific.[20] In 1943, while stationed on Guadalcanal, Lieutenant

Colonel W. D. Long wrote an Intelligence memo referring to the Pacific War as Race War:

Intelligence Memo Number 9
Americal Division APO 716
Headquarters, 17 May 1943

'Race War'

Regardless of our own individual attitude on this subject, our Japanese opponents regard the war in which we are now engaged as a 'Race War'. Through all the ages of history this type of war had always been most bitterly fought and the experience of our troops to date shows that the present war is no exception. It is indeed war in its simplest form in which it is either kill or be killed.

The Japanese hate us with a burning hatred. We must recognise this fact and conduct ourselves in battle accordingly. Not only this, we must, by thinking things over before hand, consider our own attitude towards the Japanese. If it is not a sensible and practical attitude then we must develop one that is, even though this temporarily compels us to depart for the duration from our usual standards and ideas. The Japanese … considers that anything is fair in war … Americans are prisoners of fair play. … This mental attitude of ours is so understandable but must be recognised as a menace to us in battle, and all officers and men must alter their mental attitude for the duration of the war.

Lt. Col. W. D. Long

Private Descriptions of the Brutalities of War

Major Ralph Noonan, a former school teacher from Massachusetts, served in the Quartermasters Corps of the Americal Division on Guadalcanal in early 1943. The privacy of his diary records an aspect of the Pacific War which the Allied militaries and governments sought to prevent from entering the public domain. A visit from an American Marine to Noonan's office suggests Long's missive was superfluous:

24 Jan. [1943]
Young Marine in the office today trying to sell some souvenirs. Had a Jap rifle and helmet, all kinds of Jap money and six gold teeth. [He] had captured … Japs during the night, slaughtered them for souvenirs, choked an officer so he wouldn't swallow his teeth when the Marines knocked them out. These kids are positively bloodthirsty. Two causes. First, they have found on dead Japs items that the Japs evidently took of Americans in Wake Island and the Philippines. Story that one Marine found his brother's pocket book and diary on a Jap. The Army fellows are just as bitter as the Marines. … Have reason to believe that the Japs are going cannibalistic. One definite case of an American

body being found with flesh on the thigh cut away. Second case where the Japs were driven out of an area, a patrol found a stew … and the meat was definitely human flesh.

'Fuzzy Wuzzy Angels'

Throughout the campaigns in the Southwest and Central Pacific the Allies and the Japanese made use of indigenous peoples to aid their war effort. Both sides were often compelled to use coercive measures when the requisite number of volunteers did not come forward. On the Allied side tasks for this labour ranged from stretcher bearing to ammunition carrying to active military service in organised units. During the Kokoda Campaign Australian soldiers dubbed the Papuans 'Fuzzy Wuzzy Angels', for their work as stretcher bearers. The phrase was immortalised in a poem by Bert Beros, an Australian 'sapper' (combat engineer):

Many a mother in Australia,
When the busy day is done,
Sends a prayer to the Almighty
For the keeping of her son,
Asking that an Angel guide him
And bring him safely back
Now we see those prayers are answered
On the Owen Stanley track,
For they haven't any halos,
Only holes slashed in the ears,
And with faces worked by tattoos,
With scratch pins in their hair,
Bringing back the wounded,
Just as steady as a hearse,
Using leaves to keep the rain off
And as gentle as a nurse.

Slow and careful in bad places,
On the awful mountain track,
And the look upon their faces,
Makes us think that Christ was black.
Not a move to hurt the carried,
As they treat him like a Saint,
It's a picture worth recording,
That an Artist's yet to paint.
Many a lad will see his Mother,
And the Husbands, Weans and Wives,
Just because the Fuzzy Wuzzy
Carried them to save their lives.

From mortar or machine gun fire,
Or a chance surprise attack,
To safety and the care of Doctors,
At the bottom of the track.
May the Mothers in Australia,
When they offer up a prayer,
Mention those impromptu Angels,
With the Fuzzy Wuzzy hair.

A Feature Writer's Perspective of the War on Land

As well as journalists filing stories for news agencies or for sub-editors at home to edit for news reports, a number of American and Australian war correspondents in the Pacific were feature writers for major magazines. Thanks in part to the extra words at their disposal, feature writers could look past the day to day activity of war reporting and convey a sense of the personal to their audiences. Many of these essays allowed readers at home to gain some appreciation of and empathy for those doing the fighting.

The Battle of 'Bloody Buna' saw American infantry committed to the ground war in MacArthur's Southwest Pacific Theatre for the first time. This baptism of fire for what was essentially a poorly trained former National Guard unit was a startling introduction to war. Seasoned Australian war journalist George Johnston reported on these battles for *Time* Magazine. As well as describing differences between the Allied and Japanese tactics, Johnston reflected on the differences between the American and Australian armies. In the brief extract below, he captured the physical and mental torment of those who had been wounded in one of the most remote battlefields of the war, as well as the contribution of the natives, who played an important role in the war in Papua-New Guinea. Note, too, his description of natives' and soldiers' attitude toward captured Japanese:

War in the Papuan Jungles
Time
Dec. 14, 1942

Down muddy, green-walled tracks stagger wounded men, the blood still running from beneath grimy bandages, their green uniforms stained grey with mud, their faces lined, insect-bitten, haggard, sometimes fever-yellowed. Men with torn limbs lie, eyes closed, on crude log stretchers, borne on the muscled shoulders of kindly, perpetually plodding, splayfooted natives....

Down the tracks occasionally come a few Jap prisoners. ... Americans and Australians look curiously, the natives with hatred, at the captured. Japs....

A Feature Writer's Perspective on the War at Sea

Crucial to the land campaigns in the Pacific were the naval engagements at sea which sought to secure lines of communication and supply. While the American and Australian navies won this struggle, victory came at a cost. One of the losses was the American aircraft carrier *USS Wasp*, torpedoed by a Japanese submarine off Guadalcanal in September 1942. A November 1942 article in *Time* magazine described the horror and chaos that followed the torpedoing of the *Wasp*. The extract below, beginning with the reflections of an officer, a pilot and a petty officer, all of whom watched from another ship as the *Wasp* sank, emphasises the discrepancy between the war as it was experienced by American naval personnel and the ways in which the conflict was sometimes described by military leaders often far-removed from the battlefield:

Time
2 November 1942

The Sinking of the *Wasp*

A wiry little officer said grimly: 'Some one's going to get relieved over this'. A flyer, an old hand with greying hair and a cynical look, said: 'Well, that's three I've seen go—the *Lex*, the *Yorktown* and now this baby'. [A] chief petty officer said: 'I'm thinking of those boys on Guadal'.

[Later] they read ... that a certain Admiral in Washington had told newspapers: 'The U.S. now has the balance of military and naval striking power in the Pacific'.

CHAPTER SIX
THE ALLIED COUNTER-OFFENSIVE, 1943–1945

Please congratulate me. I have been given a splendid opportunity to die. This is my last day. The destiny of our homeland hinges on the decisive battle in the seas to the south where I shall fall like a blossom from a radiant cherry tree. ... How I appreciate this chance to die like a man!

Matsuo Isao, 28 October 1944

With their successes on land and sea in 1942, the Allies were poised to commence a general counter-offensive against Japan. Whilst the Casablanca Conference of January 1943 reinforced the policy of 'Beat Hitler First' and promulgated a 30/70 resource split between the Pacific and European theatres, the United States secured agreement that 'constant pressure' could be applied to Japan.

After retaking Rabaul and some strategic islands in the Aleutians, the Allies would advance into Micronesia, removing the Japanese from the Gilbert, Marshall and Caroline groups as they headed for the next main target, the Japanese naval base at Truk. Having lost the initiative in the Southwest Pacific, the Japanese were now forced to defend Rabaul, rather than use it as a launching pad for offensive operations. The need to protect Rabaul's flank saw the Japanese attempt to commit troops to the nearby New Guinea coast. These troops, however, were quickly isolated and pushed along the northern New Guinea coast. Meanwhile, the Allies advanced up the Solomons Chain.[1]

As the fighting in New Guinea and the Solomons continued through late 1943, the Allies met again, this time in Cairo. The plans for Japanese defeat were now well advanced. Rabaul was no longer the primary target. Instead, it would be isolated as MacArthur and Nimitz headed for the Philippines via New Guinea and the Central Pacific, respectively. In Tokyo a review of Japan's position in Southeast Asia and the Pacific led to a 'New Operational Policy', which identified the loss of ships and aircraft, rather than territory, as the most serious setback unfortunate aspect of the Pacific campaigns. With lines of communication broken, the extremities of the Japanese advance could not be held. Time had to be bought through dogged defence to allow Japan to build a 'National Defence Zone'.[2]

During 1943 MacArthur and Nimitz adopted a tactic that became known as 'island hopping'.[3] Isolated and with no chance of escape, certain concentrations of the Japanese, either on the north coast of New Guinea or in the islands of Micronesia, were bypassed. The Allied selection of which bases to skip and which to attack was greatly assisted by the Allied cracking of Japanese military codes.[4]

By mid-1944, with the loss of the Marianas Island group in the Central Pacific, the Japanese 'National Defence Zone' had been penetrated. Consequently, a new operational plan known as SHO-GO (Victory) was issued. The Philippines was identified as the key to Southeast Asia, and plans continued for homeland defence. Along with a new strategy, the Japanese employed new tactics, the most important of which was to avoid engaging the invading Americans at the beach-heads but to wait inland, beyond the reach of the Allies' naval guns. The new tactic was employed during the battle for the island of Peleliu. While the result was never in question, the American Marines suffered heavy casualties.[5]

With the looming Allied invasion of the Philippines, the Imperial Japanese Navy made plans for a final, decisive battle against the Allies. Whilst the Battle of the Leyte Gulf (October 1944) culminated with the Allied invasion of the Philippines, and destroyed much of what remained of the Japanese Navy, it also witnessed the launch of another Japanese tactic – a new variant on 'Special Attack forces' that became known as Kamikaze.[6]

By the beginning of 1945 the Allies (by now almost exclusively American apart from some Australian and British ships) had secured much of the Philippines and the Central Pacific.[7] In Japan a new 'Defence of the Homeland' doctrine was implemented. Air defences, fortification and the return of combat troops from the Asian mainland were the main priorities. Furthermore, the 'outer perimeter' of Japanese islands would be sacrificed to protect the four principal 'home' islands.

As the Allies inched towards Japan, another meeting between Roosevelt and Churchill in Quebec endorsed a general strategy known as 'strangulation'. Admiral King and General H. H. 'Hap' Arnold, who devised the plan, hoped a combination of sea blockade and aerial bombardment might force a Japanese surrender without a costly invasion.

Except for the Doolittle Raid of early 1942, Japan had remained outside the operational range of Allied aircraft. This only changed in mid-1944 with the delivery of the Boeing B-29 'Superfortress'. In June 1944 from bases in India and China, and then in November from bases in the Marianas, B-29s commenced a concerted air war against Japan. Due to the distances involved, climactic conditions and improving Japanese air defences, this campaign was not particularly successful until the Americans shifted from precision, low-altitude daylight bombing to carpet, high-altitude night-time attacks using incendiary bombs. From February 1945 these 'firebomb' raids devastated Japanese cities and killed over 600,000 civilians.[8]

Lack of fighter support for the B-29s over Japan compelled the Americans to seek a base closer to Japan. Iwo Jima, a small island between the Marianas and Japan, was chosen. The American Marines who invaded the island on 19 February 1945 were unprepared for the level of Japanese resistance. Situated only 1,050 kilometres from Tokyo, Iwo Jima was considered Japanese soil and therefore its symbolic significance rivalled its strategic importance. The small island witnessed some of the fiercest fighting of the war. By the battle's end several weeks later, only 1,000 of the island's 22,000 defenders had survived. American causalities exceeded 27,000.[9]

As the Battle for Iwo Jima raged, the US Joint Chiefs of Staff shelved plans to invade Formosa, deciding instead that the Philippines would be used as the staging base for a strike north towards Japan. The first target and the last stepping stones for an invasion of Japan were the Ryuku Islands, the most important of which was Okinawa.

The invasion of Okinawa on 1 April 1945 was the largest amphibious assault of the Pacific War. Like Iwo Jima, Okinawa was considered part of Japan proper and therefore part of the 'Absolute National Defence Zone'. Japanese resistance paralleled that experienced on Iwo Jima. When the campaign ended on 2 July, another 12,520 Americans were dead or missing, with tens of thousands more wounded. Despite their horrendous casualties, the Americans had now secured a staging base for an attack on the Japanese home islands.[10] Even while the fighting on Okinawa was raging, MacArthur and Nimitz were planning for a full-scale invasion of Japan in late 1945. The 'Golden Gate by '48' was a popular catch-cry amongst American Marines and soldiers.

By early 1945 the Allied counter-offensive had largely destroyed Japanese military capacity in the Pacific. As well as the vast area lost and the obliteration of the Imperial Japanese Navy, more than 550,000 Japanese service personnel and civilians had been killed in the Southwest and Central Pacific. Battle deaths for the Allies in these two theatres were fewer than 50,000. Allied success reflected a number of factors. The Americans and Australians learned from their early mistakes and made significant changes to doctrine and tactics.[11] Logistics – the ability to move, and resupply forces – was a crucial struggle that the Allies won, thanks in part to their air and sea superiority.[12] The success of Allied submarine warfare, coupled with poor Japanese logistical doctrine, meant tens of thousands of Japanese soldiers were left isolated and weakened by lack of food and ammunition.

These problems with logistics reflected broader failings in Japanese military doctrine. The rigidity of many Japanese approaches to the art of war left their military unable to meet the new challenges that emerged when they shifted from offensive to defensive operations.[13] The Japanese, especially the Navy, also suffered from 'victory disease' – an inability to plan for failure or conserve resources.[14] Many Japanese strengths in 1942 were weaknesses by 1945.

Compounding these problems were the growing industrial and technology gaps between the Allies and the Japanese. At the beginning of the war, Japan's military technology – underpinned by a phenomenon described as 'technonationalism' – was more advanced than that of other countries.[15] Yet the limitations of the nation's industrial capacity meant military doctrine focused on the infantry unit as the core of operations. By 1945 the United States had decisively overcome any pre-war advantage that Japan might have had, and America's industrial capacity allowed it to develop a new military doctrine that looked to technological instead of tactical solutions.[16] Japanese propaganda had suggested that in 'some nations, proud of their technological progress, the machines have outstripped the men'. But in the end 'spiritual strength' – informed by popular myths regarding Japan's divine origins, its warrior codes, and its unfailing victories – was insufficient.[17] A new 'technological fanaticism' had developed in the United States, which used the Pacific War as a 'laboratory test site'.[18] Physicists, not generals, shaped the final months of the Pacific War, as the destruction of Hiroshima heralded the arrival of the 'Atomic Age'.

THE SOURCES

Fighting Words in the Sky: 22 SQN RAAF's Operations Record Book

Japanese and American air forces during the Pacific War were subsections of the Army or Navy. Consequently, their unit record keeping followed the policies of the parent service. By contrast, the Royal Australian Air Force (RAAF) was a separate branch of the armed forces. Established in 1921, the RAAF is the second oldest dedicated and permanent air force in the world after the Royal Air Force (RAF).

The Australians followed British practice for meeting the requirements of recording the events experienced by an air force. An RAAF squadron or unit maintained an Operations Record Book. These books included records from the time of the establishment of the squadron or unit and were the primary source for information on all operations. A principal aim of the book was to provide a repository for information that would later be of historical value. As with all such documents, the value of an Operations Record Book was dependent on the care and skill employed by its compiler. Instructions stated that the document was to be written from 'the historian's point of view', with *explanation*, as well as *description* of events. Each day's entry was completed on a form known as Form A50. Entries would be made under the headings Place, Date, Summary of Events and References to Appendices. A second form – the A51 Unit History Sheet – was also introduced. This form dealt specifically with operations and was also placed in the Record Book. At the end of each month a copy of the entries in the Record Book was sent to Headquarters.

The Unit History Sheet for 22 Squadron RAAF, dated 18 March 1943, chronicles the operation in which Flight Lieutenant W. E. ('Bill') Newton's aircraft was shot down during an attack on the Japanese garrison at Salamaua, New Guinea:

Descriptions of Operations

Bombed stores and buildings on foreshore at SALAMAUA. Bombed anti-aircraft positions at McDonald's Junction, results unobserved save timber and debris seen in air after the bursts. Remaining bombs in target area along foreshore starting two fires one small near west end of area and the other just west of the picture theatre. A large explosion after start of second fire which burnt very brightly with much flame and smoke but was only of short duration. Aircraft A28-3 seen smoking after leaving target area, later caught on fire and landed in water approximately one and a half miles south of LAPUI POINT and one mile out to sea and sunk in a few seconds. The crew of A28-3, F/L W.E. Newton (Pilot), Sgt. J Lyon and Sgt. B.G. Eastwood. Two unidentified members of the crew were seen in the water swimming towards the shore and when aircraft left the area were about six or seven hundred yards from shore....

Words of Commendation: Bravery Award Citations

Each of the major combatants had bravery awards systems. For the Japanese it was the grades of the Order of the Golden Kite. For the Americans it was the 'pyramid' of gallantry awards culminating in the Medal of Honor. For the Australians, the British bravery system, with the Victoria Cross as its pinnacle, prevailed.

The original Victoria Cross had been created during the Crimean War as both a means to recognise outstanding examples of valour, and to silence media critics.[19] The public relations exercise surrounding the award, therefore, was always of importance, as a tool for maintaining morale both within the services and at home. It is surprising, therefore, that many Victoria Cross citations were relatively bland documents that often failed to capture the essence of the bravery or situation they described. This might be explained by the fact that into World War II, there was little effort to massage the citation for greater public impact; usually, the words of the original nominating officer informed the citation.

The third Australian Victoria Cross of the Pacific War was awarded posthumously to Bill Newton, whom we encountered in the previous document. His citation read:

Flight Lieutenant Newton served with No 22 Squadron RAAF in New Guinea from May 1942 to March 1943 and completed 52 operational sorties. Throughout, he displayed great courage and determination to inflict the utmost damage on the enemy.

His splendid offensive flying and fighting were attended with brilliant success. Disdaining evasive tactics when under the heaviest of fire, he always went straight to his objective. He carried out many daring machine gun attacks on enemy positions involving low flying over long distances in the face of continuous fire at point blank range. On three occasions, he dived through intense anti-aircraft fire to release his bombs on important targets on the Salamaua Isthmus. On one of these occasions, his starboard engine failed over the target, but he succeeded in flying back to an airfield 160 miles [260 klms] away. When leading attack on an objective on March 16, 1943, he dived through intense and accurate shell fire and his aircraft was hit repeatedly. Never the less he held to his course and bombed his target from low level. The attack resulted in destruction of many buildings and dumps, including two 40,000 gallon fuel installations. Although his aircraft was crippled, with fuselage and wing sections torn, petrol tanks pierced, main planes and engines seriously damaged, and one of the tyres flat, Flight Lieutenant Newton managed to fly back to base and make a successful landing. Despite this harassing experience, he returned to the same location the next day, his target this time was a single building even more difficult, but he came in and attacked with his usual courage and resolution, flying a steady course through a barrage of fire. He scored a hit on the building, but at the same time his aircraft burst into flames. Flight Lieutenant Newton maintained control and calmly turned his aircraft away and flew along the shore. He saw it as his duty to keep the aircraft in the air as long as he could so as to take his crew as far away from the enemy as he possibly could. With great skill, he brought his blazing aircraft down in the water. Two members of the crew were able to extract themselves and were seen swimming to the shore, but the gallant pilot is missing. According to other aircrews who witnessed the occurrence, his escape hatch was not opened and his dinghy was not inflated. Without regard to his own safety, he had done all that a man could do to prevent his crew from falling into enemy hands. Flight Lieutenant Newton's many examples of conspicuous bravery have rarely been equalled and will serve as a shining inspiration to all who follow him.

The *New York Times* Reports on the Battle of Saipan

One of the most important battles in Chester Nimitz's island-hopping campaign through the Central Pacific was the Battle of Saipan, which demonstrated the hopelessness of the Japanese defensive situation, as well as their determination to resist the Allied advance. Once secured, Saipan allowed the Americans to project their power towards both the Philippines and Japan. Contemporary media reports noted the importance of the battle for the course of the war. The following report from the *New York Times* highlights the state of journalism pertaining to the Pacific War by 1944. As the number of war correspondents killed in the Pacific continued to grow, Honolulu was a much safer option for many journalists. With Nimitz's headquarters situated in Hawaii, journalists had ready access to the military's expansive public relations machine. Many media outlets, even with correspondents in the Pacific, relied on official communiqués as their major source of information. Moreover, thanks to the telephone line between Hawaii and the west coast of the United States, a news item could reach a sub-editor's desk in minutes. While the date of information released by the military was often days or, sometimes, weeks old, once released it could be printed in an American newspaper within hours.

The New York Times, Tuesday, June 20, 1944

JAPANESE LOSE 300 PLANES IN SAIPAN BATTLE, By GEORGE F. HORNE. By Telephone to THE NEW YORK TIMES.
PACIFIC FLEET HEADQUARTERS, Pearl Harbor, June 19—

The greatest air-sea battle since Midway was fought off the Marianas yesterday, when the American carrier task force supporting the ground attack on Saipan shot down more than 300. ... Japanese planes. ... American fliers and ship gunners so successfully fought off the severe attack. ... that. ... only one of our ships was damaged....

Kawaguchi Tarō's Diary from Saipan

As the American advance into the Central Pacific gained momentum and the destruction of the Imperial Japanese Navy rendered evacuation or resupply impossible, isolated Japanese soldiers fought more than just their American adversaries. Despite such conditions, the Japanese units on Saipan held out for weeks against the invading Americans. Kawaguchi Tarō was a member of the 43rd Division Hospital Unit stationed on Saipan during 1944. Kawaguchi died during the battle and his diary was found on 19 July 1944 by American Sergeant J. William Winter. The diary, translated by a Japanese-American in Winter's unit, highlights the degree to which many Japanese soldiers justified their ordeal and sacrifice around the higher ideal of protecting the Emperor and the nation.

June 25, 1944: Because of unfavorable situation near the vicinity, the unit received orders to move near the vicinity of Tara-Hoko. During the night moved the patients to Tara Hoko. It is regrettable but we had to abandon some supplies.

June 26, 1944: Spent the night below the cliffs with the patients. Conditions are getting ever increasingly unfavorable and because of concentration of artillery, took cover among the trees. No casualties. During the evening the unit received orders to move to Donnay. Some of the patients were committing suicide with hand grenades.

June 27, 1944: I slept good because of the Saki we took last night. Upon being awakened by Capt. Watanabe, immediately departed for Donnay. Proceeded to Donnay under terrific artillery file. We received heavy casualties ... Was ordered by hospital commander to be prepared to attack the enemy with rifles, hand grenades or bayonets attached to sticks....

June 28, 1944: ... Quenched our thirst with rain water.

June 29, 1944: Dug foxholes due to scare of previous night. Stayed in area until the afternoon and again received a terrific bombardment. When the firing was over everything was desolated. Took upon duty of treating the patients again. During the night orders were received to proceed to Taro-Hoko. ... When we reached the "Y" junction again, there was a feeling of sadness, pity and anger and we resolved to gain revenge for the dead.

June 30, 1944: Towards the morning we reached the Taro-Hako area. Immediately started on construction of air-raid shelter and received a rain of enemy bombs while constructing. ... Ate rice for the first time since the 25th and regained strength. Felt like stamping the ground and tears came to my eyes. On this day the hospital received concentrated fire and numerous casualties occurred. I received a slight wound on my left thigh.

July 1, 1944: While working everyone seemed to regain their strength and upon seeing this I became greatly relieved. Stayed in air-raid shelter all morning due to concentrated fire....

July 2, 1944: At dawn visited the place where my friend lay dead with a bayonet wound in his head. Covered him with grass and leaves....

July 3, 1944: At daybreak the sound of enemy artillery and rifle fire echoed throughout the valley. Immediately took up battle security disposition. The rifle reports seemed nearer and more terrific than yesterday, however the situation cannot be comprehended. If the enemy approaches the whole unit will repulse them with every weapon at hand....

July 4, 1944: Different from yesterday. Today was extremely quiet. ... I was bothered by the wounded leg. Orders were given by the unit commander to fight to the last in the bivouac area. "My foxhole is my grave."...

July 5, 1944: 1st Lt. Matsumai came to our dugout and saying "As long as I'm going to die, I want to die with the pharmacist's section," he joined us ... While waiting in the hole after breakfast the furious assault of the enemy commenced ... Seeing that we were surrounded in the front and rear, we approached the enemy with the determination of annihilating them. We fired at the enemy in the rear but there was no effect. ... Two men committed pathetic suicide due to severe wounds. The Lt. and the pharmacist's section bid farewell and promised to meet at the Yasukuni Shrine after death....

July 6, 1944: Received artillery barrage during the morning and took cover among the rocks. As each round approached nearer and nearer, I closed my eyes and awaited it. Rifle reports and tanks seemed nearer and everyone took cover within the forest and waited for the enemy to approach. Soon the voice of the enemy could be heard and machine gun fire could be heard over our heads. I thought this was the end and was ready to charge out with a hand grenade when ordered to take cover by the Capt. When I looked from the side of the rock I could see the hateful bearded face of the enemy shining in the sunlight. With a terrific report the rock in front of my eyes exploded, and the Sgt. that joined us last night was killed. Also the Cpl received severe wounds in his left thigh. However, I could not treat the wounds even if I wanted to. Everyone hugged the ground and kept quiet, waiting for an opening in the enemy. As I stood up to get the rifle from one of the dead a bullet hit between my legs and I thought sure I was hit, but after glancing down, to my happiness, nothing was wrong. A report was heard and as I looked back I saw my friend Cpl Ito lying on his back with a rifle in his hand. Oh! Cpl. Ito who has been in my section ever since Nagoya had died. After fierce counterfire, the enemy was repulsed so I approached the body of Ito who had a bullet hole through his left temple, with his eyes half open and lips tightly clenched. "I'll take Ito's revenge." Taking Ito's rifle which was clenched in his hands even after death, I waited for the enemy to attack. Cpl Yasukiro also had wounds in both legs. Pathetically he was saying, "Please kill me," so 1st Lt. Matsumai beautifully cut his head off. The Cpl pleaded before being cut to the Lt. "Please cut skillfully." The Lt. with sweat pouring down his hand, took one stroke, two strokes, and on the third stroke he cut his head off....

July 7, 1944: While shivering from wetness, orders to move were issued. Facing the dawn, the north, bowing reverently to the Imperial Palace and bidding farewell to the parents, aunt and wife I solemnly pledged to do my utmost. ... The enemy is surrounding us in all directions. Helplessly we took cover in the jungle. At the crack of dawn, enemy activity commenced below on the road with vehicles, tanks and walking soldiers. At last the end has come. ... Even though we wanted to attack we have no weapons, so with the determination of dying for the Emperor we spent our time by preparing for our remembrance. Looking back through the years. I am only 26 years old. Thanks to the Emperor, both my parents, and my aunt I have lived to this day and I am deeply gratified. At the same time it is deeply regrettable that I have nothing to report at this time when my life is fluttering away like a flower petal to become a part of the soil. Since the enemy landing, to have fought against the enemy endeavouring my utmost power in carrying out my duty and thus becoming a war lord, I am very happy. It is only regrettable that we have not fought enough and that the American devil is stomping on the Imperial soil. I, with my sacrificed body will become the white caps of the Pacific and will stay on this island until the friendly forces come to reclaim the soil of the Emperor.

A Pilot's Fighting Words: Marshall Chester's Diary

With Saipan and other islands of the Marianas secured by August 1944, plans were made to relocate B-29s to these islands for the assault on Japan. Marshall Chester was a young B-29 pilot who was part of the first Marianas-based B-29 attack on Japan in November 1944. He recorded his experiences in a diary. Once again the style of the diary resembles a letter:

After spending two nights in Hawaii, two nights at Kwajalein and losing one calendar day on crossing the International Date Line, we landed at 4:10 p.m. on November 16 on Saipan. The next day, we attended a briefing for the mission that would take place on November 18; it included an early morning takeoff. This mission was delayed for six days because of bad weather over the target area in Tokyo. Talk about tension builders! At last, the big day came, and we climbed aboard our planes. Were we excited? Yes! Afraid? You can put this down; whoever said he wasn't afraid, wasn't exactly telling it like it was!

Tokyo, here we come.

November 24, 1944. After last night's briefing update, some of the doubting Thomases placed wagers on another postponement. Some even offered odds that there would be another stand-down.

My old buddy, Lt. Herbert Kelly from Madison, Wisconsin, pilot on Leibman's crew, asked whether I thought we would go.

"Yep, we'll go," I said. "And my sure-fire reasoning is this: today is Thanksgiving back in the States. Crew 25 always reserves holidays for momentous flights. We left the States on a holiday [Armistice Day] and now, because this is Thanksgiving, we will bomb Tokyo today."

"Don't hand me that crap," Kelly said. "But anyway, Lightnin'" (my nickname), "I hope you're right; this wait is killing me."

5:45 a.m. As the morning begins to dawn, all activity is at a peak. ... As we look out across Magicienne Bay past Kagman Point, we can see the sun's first rays against spotted cirrus clouds that resemble a herd of sheep dancing across the sky.

It's now 15 minutes before we go, and soon, across the way, Gen. Emmet "Rosie" O'Donnell and Maj. Robert Morgan will start up *Dauntless Dotty* and get the mission to Tokyo-code name San Antonio I-under way.

Standing by their B-29s ready to board are 111 crews representing a strike force of 1,221 men. ... And they are about to write a new chapter in the history books by blazing a trail in the sky over Tokyo.

We have double- and triple-checked everything and had the crew inspection, and bombardier Herb Feldman has scribbled in large letters, "One for Rosie" on one of the 10, 500-pound bombs hanging snugly to the rear of the bomb-bay racks. The bombs are unarmed and will remain so until Herb later crawls into the bomb bays to pull out the arming pins before we start our climb to altitude.

Our gross weight is 137,000 pounds. That is almost maximum for the plane, and since we have never before taken off with a load that heavy, we anticipate having to use the entire length of the runway to gain as much speed as possible before liftoff....

6 a.m. The word is go. No postponement today! It is time to get this show on the road.

Japanese Combat Propaganda

For the combatants of the Pacific War propaganda was an important dimension of psychological warfare.[20] Hoping to weaken the enemy's resolve, both the Japanese and Allies sought to disseminate words that would influence their foe's opinions, attitudes and emotions. On both sides so-called 'combat propaganda' was mostly improvised and 'conducted according to hit-or-miss methods'.[21] Central agencies in both military and government were tasked with this role, but within theatres of operations such work was often carried out by intelligence officers.

The following Japanese-produced leaflet was found in the Central Pacific in 1944 as Nimitz and MacArthur's forces were preparing for the Leyte Gulf. Japanese propaganda generally, and combat propaganda in particular, was largely ineffective because of the reality of the Japanese position, language barriers and a failure to appreciate the motivations of Allied soldiers.[22] Yet Japanese propaganda continued to insist that the Allied advance was sheer folly and that the death of American and Australian soldiers was assured. This example of combat propaganda perpetuates the notion of an Asia now united to resist a return of the colonial powers.

Farewell, American Soldiers

You are still alive! What a miracle! And marching, too. But WHERE? To the Philippines? To Tokyo? But do you know what awaits you in the Philippines? Let me tell you. It is the Japanese forces with the combined support, both moral and material, of all the awakened Asiatics – the Manchukuoans, Chinese, Filipinos, Annamese, Thailanders, Burmese, Indians, Malayans and Indochinese. And the Japanese are there to pound you incessantly and relentlessly as you should have known. Perhaps they may retreat temporarily, but only to attack you again with double fierceness after your reinforcements have arrived. Day in and day out the Japanese troops are also pushing to the front in ever-increasing numbers. And remember, entire Asia is behind them! As long as you persist in marching west, the attacks will continue. Innumerable strongholds are all set to give you hearty welcome from the land, air and sea....

But this is not all. There is still another thing in store for you along the Philippines front. What is this thing? I will answer you. It is a grave. YOUR GRAVE! Nobody can say where it exactly is, but it is certain that it does exist somewhere in the Philippines, and you are bound to find it sooner or later, far or near. Today? Tomorrow? Who knows? But one thing is positive, you are heading west for your grave – as positive as the sun sets in the west. Officers and men, you still insist on marching west? If so, I shall have to carve an epitaph for you.

There are only two definite things on earth. LIFE and DEATH. The difference between LIFE and DEATH is absolute. One cannot rely upon the dead; no one can make friends with the dead; the dead can neither speak nor mingle with the living. If you insist on marching west, we (by we I mean all living things) must bid you goodbye and stop bothering with you, because we, the living, are too busy to have anything to do with the dead.

Your politicians are among those who survive and are enjoying life comfortably at home. General Marshall and General MacArthur can enjoy their reputation as heroes only because they are alive. But you ... You continue to march westwards to sure death, to keep your rendezvous with the grave. The same holds true for your comrades-in-arms who are pathetically struggling to escape their ultimate fate. The graves awaits you and you and

ALL OF YOU! So, officers and men, I bid you a pitiful goodbye. Today, you are with the living, tomorrow, with the dead. So again goodbye, American soldiers! … Farewell! … Farewell!…

Allied Combat Propaganda

Allied forces also used combat propaganda. In her study of Allied psychological warfare during the Pacific War, Allison B. Gilmore has concluded that despite language difficulties and the poor regard in which it was held by military leaders, this area of Allied operations experienced some success, because it did not succumb to racial demonisation of the enemy, and rejected the popular belief that words could not overcome Japanese fanaticism.[23] These campaigns took a variety of forms but were often based on quoting senior Japanese officials and then showing how they had lied or broken their promises. Often a Japanese figure from history might be cited to suggest a correct path of action in comparison to that taken by a current Japanese leader. Cherry blossoms and Mount Fuji were constant motifs in Allied propaganda as means of making an emotional connection with home. Unlike much Japanese propaganda, which questioned the wisdom of an Allied advance, Allied propaganda encouraged the surrender of Japanese soldiers – this was a clear reflection of Allied success contrasted to Japanese failure. American Office of War Information Leaflet 101 is one example:

Now is the season of beauty in your homeland and the glorious snow-capped peak of Mount Fuji beckons to the traveler and the visitor. Your parents and wives await you and your dear children wonder whether they will ever see you again.

But you are here on a miserable island, awaiting our overwhelming force of men and machines. Your military leaders grow fat at home as they continue to mislead your people. They enjoy the beauties of the season and the thrilling sight of Mount Fuji. Their children eat with them and bask in their love.

The Allies also used the popular Japanese technique of using the words of POWs to attempt to influence enemy soldiers. OWI leaflet 1049 was dropped on Wake Island in an effort to secure a surrender of the Japanese garrison:

A Comrade's Cry

Like you, I have eaten seaweed. I know how weeds taste. I have been exposed to bombing and shelling. I escaped from an isolated island in the MARSHALLS where I suffered the worst tortures of starvation and despair. As a result of the kindness of the Americans, which was greater than you can imagine, I made a complete recovery although I had been just a step this side of death.

Now, even though I am a prisoner of war, I spend the nights and days without feeling any discomfort. However, even now, while I am receiving this fine treatment, I cannot help feeling uneasy when I picture to myself the sight of you recklessly throwing away your precious lives by starvation on an isolated island.

Radio Propaganda

Radio propaganda was another important part of the Pacific War. Using captured American and Australian service personnel with broadcasting experience, the Japanese military established a shortwave propaganda service. In an attempt to damage Allied morale, Japanese authorities made use of English-speaking Japanese women. These women became collectively known as 'Tokyo Rose' or 'Orphan Ann'. The most famous of these women was the Japanese-American Iva Toguri. The American-born Toguri had been trapped in Japan at the start of the war and was the announcer on a programme known as the 'Zero Hour'. After the war Toguri was persecuted and charged with treason.[24]

Tokyo Rose: Hello you fighting orphans in the Pacific. How's tricks? This is "After her weekend, and oooh, back on the air, strictly under union hours." Reception okay? Why, it better be, because this is All-Requests night. And I've got a pretty nice program for my favorite little family, the wandering boneheads of the Pacific Islands. The first request is made by none other than the boss. And guess what? He wants Bonnie Baker in "My Resistance is Low." My, what taste you have, sir, she says.

The men of the First Marine Division responded to Rosie through their own radio programme.

Dear Tokyo Rose,
    Because for so many many months now you have entertained the Marine Corps in general and the First Division in particular, we feel that the only gentlemanly thing to do is return the compliment. So we have a little number we are going to play tonight dedicated just to you. But first, Rosie, in regard to those cracks you been making that the folks back home will forget us out her in the Pacific when Germany surrendered. Rose I'm surprised at you. Ordinarily you are a pretty smart propagandist but this time you've missed the boat. Why? Well it's this way. You Japs with your bowing and scraping to the man of the house have about as much family life as the jeeps parked out here in our motor pool. On the other hand, we and our mothers, and sisters, dads and brothers have not only a devotion and a love but we also have a mutual respect and that's something you Japs could not possibly understand. No Rosie they haven't forgotten us out here, nor will they, and we haven't forgotten them. And now as I say, just for you we play Rimsky-Korsakov's Flight of the Bumble B-29!

Kamikaze Writings

The Battle for the Leyte Gulf, which opened the American campaign to retake the Philippines, also marked the first use of 'Special Attack' aircraft, whose pilots became known as *Kamikaze*. Because of the secretive nature of their operations those members of special attack units were subjected to strict censorship. Such censorship was extended to the last letters these young men would write before setting out on their final fateful missions. The degree to which these pilots wrote what they hoped would pass unit censors raises issues about a possible disjuncture between what these men felt and what they actually wrote. That many of these men resorted to having their letters smuggled out of their camps to avoid censorship suggests they hoped to convey to their loved ones emotions and ideas deemed unacceptable by the Japanese military.[25] Moreover, it has been argued that the backgrounds of the men produced different results. Pilots from military colleges were more deeply inculcated in Japanese military culture than university students who had been conscripted.[26]

Notwithstanding whether they were writing a letter for the censor, or having a letter smuggled to a loved one, *Kamikaze* pilots still felt a need to rationalise their actions. These private letters, and other intimate writings such as diaries, provide clues to the mindset of these young men as they contemplated almost certain death. These primary sources also offer clear insights into the degree to which Japanese military doctrine influenced individual servicemen's attitudes towards death against a broader Japanese cultural perspective.

One of the first *Kamikaze*, Flying Petty Officer First Class Matsuo Isao of the 701st Air Group, wrote home to his parents in Nagasaki in October 1944.

28 October 1944
Dear Parents:
   Please congratulate me. I have been given a splendid opportunity to die. This is my last day. The destiny of our homeland hinges on the decisive battle in the seas to the south where I shall fall like a blossom from a radiant cherry tree. I shall be a shield for His Majesty and die cleanly along with my squadron leader and other friends. I wish that I could be born seven times, each time to smite the enemy. How I appreciate this chance to die like a man! I am grateful from the depths of my heart to the parents who have reared me with their constant prayers and tender love. And I am grateful as well to my squadron leader and superior officers who have looked after me as if I were their own son and given me such careful training. Thank you, my parents, for the 23 years during which you have cared for me and inspired me. I hope that my present deed will in some small way repay what you have done for me. Think well of me and know that your Isao died for our country. This is my last wish, and

there is nothing else that I desire. I shall return in spirit and look forward to your visit at the Yasukuni Shrine. Please take good care of yourselves. ... Movie cameramen have been here to take our pictures. It is possible that you may see us in newsreels at the theater. We are 16 warriors manning the bombers. May our death be as sudden and clean as the shattering of crystal.

Written at Manila on the eve of our sortie.

Isao

Soaring into the sky of the southern seas, it is our glorious mission to die as the shields of His Majesty. Cherry blossoms glisten as they open and fall.

Army Captain Uehara Ryōji, formerly an economics student at university, contemplated life and politics as he prepared for his last mission:

My Thoughts

I am keenly aware of the tremendous personal honor involved in my having been chosen to be a member of the Army Special Attack Corps, which is considered to be the most elite attack force in the service of our glorious fatherland. My thoughts about all these things derive from a logical standpoint which is more or less the fruit of my long career as a student and, perhaps, what some others might call a liberal. But I believe that the ultimate triumph of liberty is altogether obvious. As the Italian philosopher Benedetto Croce has proclaimed, 'liberty is so quintessential to human nature that it is absolutely impossible to destroy it.' I believe along with him that this is a simple fact, a fact so certain that liberty must of necessity continue its underground life even when it appears, on the surface, to be suppressed ... it will always win through in the end.

It is equally inevitable that an authoritarian and totalitarian nation, however much it may flourish temporarily, will eventually be defeated. In the present war we can see how this latter truth is borne out in the Axis Powers [the alliance of Japan, Germany and Italy] themselves. What more needs to be said about Fascist Italy? Nazi Germany too has already been defeated, and we see that all the authoritarian nations are now falling down one by one, exactly like buildings with faulty foundations. All these developments only serve to reveal all over again the universality of the truth that history has so often proven in the past: men's great love of liberty will live on into the future and into eternity itself.

Although there are aspects to all this which constitute something the fatherland has reason to feel apprehensive about, it is still a truly wonderful thing to feel that one's own personal beliefs have been validated. On every front, I believe that ideologies are at the bottom of all the fighting that is going on nowadays. Still further, I am firmly convinced that the outcome of each and every conflict is predictable on the basis of the ideologies held by the opposing sides.

My ambitious hope was to have lived to see my beloved fatherland – Japan – develop into a great empire like Great Britain in the past, but that hope has already been dashed. If those people who truly loved their country had been given a fair hearing, I do not believe that Japan would be in its present perilous position. This was my ideal and what I dreamt about: that the people of Japan might walk proudly anywhere in the world.

In a real sense it is certainly true that a pilot in our special aerial attack force is, as a friend of mine has said, nothing more than a piece of the machine. He is nothing more than that part of the machine which holds the plane's controls – endowed with no personal qualities, no emotions, certainly with no rationality – simply just an iron filament tucked inside a magnet itself designed to be sucked into an enemy air-craft carrier. The whole business would, within any context of rational behavior, appear to be unthinkable, and would seem to have no appeal whatsoever except to someone with a suicidal disposition. I suppose this entire range of phenomena is best seen as something peculiar to Japan, a nation of spirituality. So then we who are nothing more than pieces of machinery may have no right to say anything, but we only wish, ask, and hope for one thing: that all the Japanese people might combine to make our beloved country the greatest nation possible.

Were I to face the battles that lie ahead in this sort of emotional state, my death would be rendered meaningless. This is the reason then, as I have already stated, that I intend to concentrate on the honor involved in being designated a member of the Special Attack Corps.

When I am in a plane perhaps I am nothing more than just a piece of the machine, but as soon as I am on the ground again I find that I am a complete human being after all, complete with human emotions – and passions too. When the sweetheart whom I loved so much passed away, I experienced a kind of spiritual death myself. Death in itself is nothing when you look upon it, as I do, as merely a pass to the heaven where I will see her once again, the one who is waiting there for me.

Tomorrow we attack. It may be that my genuine feelings are extreme – and extremely private! But I have put them down as honestly as I can. Please forgive me for writing so loosely and without much logical order. Tomorrow one believer in liberty and liberalism will leave this world behind. His withdrawing figure may have a lonely look about it, but I assure you that his heart is filled with contentment.

An Allied Perspective on the *Kamikaze*

The Japanese public was informed of the activities of the Special Attack units, whose members were lionised as national heroes. Because Japanese radio broadcasts to Australia and the United States were usually jammed, and with stiff penalties for anyone caught listening to enemy radio broadcasts, the Australian and American public knew nothing of the *Kamikazes'* exploits until 5 May 1945. On that date, many months after the first *Kamikaze* attack, the American people read of this new style of warfare in the pages of *Liberty* magazine. The article was written by Irving Wallace, a member of the Army Air Force serving with Hollywood director Frank Capra's First Motion Picture Unit. With Japanese radio broadcasts monitored and translated for intelligence purposes, their contents were now considered classified. Having seen these classified translations, Wallace, who like many service personnel wrote articles in his spare time for major American magazines, was given permission to write a story based on their contents. Thus a somewhat unusual story resulted: an article written by an American serviceman based exclusively on Japanese radio broadcasts. Wallace's account perpetuates a number of Western perceptions of the Japanese – most notably that they valued life less than the Allies, and were easily compelled to undertake such acts.

Casting about for a last desperate weapon to stem the tide of defeat, Tokyo's war lords have come up with something that goes Hitler one better – human robot bombs.

Radio Tokyo is on the air.

"News flash! News flash from Tokyo! The Imperial Headquarters announced at two thirty o'clock this afternoon that the Kamikaze Special Attack Corps has sunk one American battleship, three large transports, and damaged one battleship or cruiser in Leyte Gulf.

"Our six fliers successfully penetrated enemy fighter-plane defenses and headed for enemy transports, which were escorted by battleships and cruisers.

"One of our planes plunged into an American battleship, and just as the big ship shook from the impact, a second plane crashed into it. A huge fire soon enveloped the vessel. The four other planes raced toward the enemy transports. In swift succession they plunged into them, sinking three and setting ablaze another large ship, which last was seen emitting a pillar of black smoke.

"Among the six Kamikaze fliers who died in this attack, three men – Matsui, Terashima, and Kawashima – are not yet twenty years old. The spirit of these young fliers crash-diving on their objectives is admirable."

This news report – typical of recent daily reports – discloses Japan's last hope.

With Allied sea and air power slowly strangling Japan, the Tokyo war lords cast about for some last-resort weapon....

Determined to capitalize on the willingness of their young men to die, the Japanese leaders organized the Navy's Kamikaze Special Attack Corps. Suicide assaults by Japanese infantrymen and fliers were already familiar occurrences. But with the Kamikaze, Japan made the first modern effort by any army or navy to send vast numbers of trained men to premeditated suicide.

Kamikaze is Japan's god of the wind. The word itself means "Divine Wind" and it stands for much in Japan. Six and a half centuries before Nimitz, the mighty Mongol, Kublai Khan, threatened Japan with 300 warships and 200,000 men. At the eleventh hour it happened that a real wind, a typhoon, bore down on his armada, smashing and sinking it. Ever since, the Japanese have been taught that when in danger a Divine Wind would save them.

But this time the Japanese leaders knew they could not depend on a typhoon. They knew they must create their Divine Wind. And so they created the Kamikaze Special Attack Corps, dedicated to death – for itself and Americans....

The Kamikaze Special Attack Corps was first thrown into action two weeks after General MacArthur waded onto Philippine soil with his infantry veterans.

General Tomoyuki Yamashita, German-educated conqueror of Singapore and Bataan, opposed MacArthur, proclaiming that the Kamikaze would turn the trick. Even as Leyte fell, he reassured the folks back home in Tokyo. "That our forces," he said, "with (comparatively) small strength and small amount of material supplies, were able to achieve such brilliant war results is all due to the traditional spirit of offering one's life and carrying out deliberate crash-dive attacks on the enemy. ... If one of our fighter planes should bring down one enemy B-29 by a deliberate crash-dive attack, it would be proportionately one to ten. Then again, if one plane should sink or damage one enemy aircraft carrier or one battleship, it would be one to 100, 1,000, or 10,000. No matter how the enemy would come against us with his superiority in materials, if the enemy is met with this deliberate crash-dive spirit, then it could be concluded that the enemy could be completely defeated."

Desperately the Kamikaze pilots catapulted their bomb-laden planes into our warships and supply ships off Leyte, Mindanao, and Luzon. The American Navy soberly admitted to some losses. The Japanese ecstatically claimed half of all our shipping. The truth? There is only one truth. Today, again, we dominate the Philippines. Today we stand astride the Pacific. Quite obviously Japan's Divine Wind has not been enough.

Yet there is every indication that Japan will, in the near future, throw her organized Kamikaze suicide fliers against us in greater numbers. Admitting shortages in everything else, she finds men ready to die in her cheapest effective weapon....

[T]he basis for the Kamikaze is Japanese fanaticism. There are many explanations for that. The most satisfactory is state Shinto, the so-called religion of Japan, the "way of the gods." Shinto is thoroughly politics, the spearhead of Japanese Fascism. It preaches a perverse morality that condones rape, murder, the stab in the back. It tells the Japanese they are the holy people, superior to all others on earth, and that one day they and their emperor must rule the rest of the civilized world. Above all, Shinto makes human life cheap, cheering its young men with the promise, "To die for the emperor is to live forever."

For almost a century the young men of Japan were prepared for this task of sacrificing their lives to the divine mission of the state. On the ground, the Japanese soldier dared not retreat. ... In action, the Japanese soldier had to live the legend of the three human bombs of Chapei, soldiers who carried dynamite into Chinese barbed-wire entanglements and blew themselves up with it.

It was not until ten years ago that this suicidal indoctrination was first channeled into flying. At that time Japanese militarists toyed with the idea of developing special aviators to plunge dynamite-packed planes into enemy warships. The plan was shelved, and suicide crash-dives occurred only when Japanese pilots found their planes shot out of control. Instead of dumping their bomb loads, they often dived into the nearest available military objective. Reports on these irregular desperation dives began to filter back to Tokyo. Japanese leaders learned that often they were successful. This revived again the old idea of an organized and trained suicide corps....

The average Kamikaze volunteer, a graduate of the Air Military Academy, is five feet three inches tall and weighs 118 pounds. He is between nineteen and twenty-five years of age. Before seeing action, he is put through a short preparatory course. On the first day of it a movie shows him how other Japanese heroes have sacrificed themselves for the emperor. He is persistently lectured on the three qualities each Kamikaze flier must possess: First, absolute obedience. Second, complete devotion to duty. "This means intellectual conclusions must not be made." Third, thorough knowledge that any given assignment must be carried out successfully. "Death counts as nothing before the importance of the completion of one's duty."

There is an unwritten law that Kamikaze trainees must not discuss or philosophize on the subject of life and death. They are kept busy: classes, flying, sports. The favorite sport is kendo, a Japanese pastime involving two men attired like baseball catchers who belabor each other with bats....

Recently a Tokyo newspaper, the *Yomiuri Hochi*, interviewed Colonel K. Tomomori just after he'd learned that most of his students had plunged to their death. Said the account:

"Colonel Tomomori's emotion was deep. 'I am overcome by tears of joy,' he related, as teardrops welled in his eyes."...

When the claims of the Kamikaze are tabulated, it will be found they claim to have destroyed every ship in the U.S. Navy and merchant marine – plus those scheduled to be launched up until 1955!...

The Kamikaze won't save Japan any more than it saved the Philippines. It may cause some damage, some loss of life, but our planes and carriers and battleships will continue to knock most of these suicide raiders out of the sky before they complete their missions.

A Japanese Account from Iwo Jima

First Lieutenant Sugihara Kinru was an officer in the 11th Antitank Battalion stationed on Iwo Jima. His diary covers the weeks before the American invasion and includes the battle until his presumed death sometime in late February 1945. The excerpt included here details the period until the American landing, when life for the Japanese was mostly confined to caves and air raid shelters as a result of sustained aerial and later naval bombardment.

24 January 1945 – Wednesday. Clear. Cloudy, and rain in the afternoon....

10.20 – Air raid. Later on it was reported that an enemy Task Force consisting of one battleship, five cruisers, and seven destroyers was observed 317 kilometres away. Prepared for bomb shelter life again. Took afternoon nap.

13.45 – Naval bombardment commenced. Two landing barge, one transport, and two coastal ships were anchored, and unloading cargo since this morning. My thoughts immediately turned towards our ships.

'This would have to happen now that the long-awaited transport has finally arrived, and cannot escape being sunk. We always have this hard luck', is what all the soldiers say, feeling a keen personal disappointment. At 15.00 the naval gunfire ceased.

15.07 – All clear sounded. Presently the ships' unloading crew returned and told me that all the ships were ablaze, and that the only materiel landed was cement and steel reinforcements. Although it is heartbreaking we cannot do anything about it....

Ate dinner at 16.00. Air raid alarm given twice in succession. Planes came over only on reconnaissance. Had several raids until 3 o'clock in the morning.

Today's casualties were seven killed and 11 wounded ...

26 January 1945 – Friday. Clear. Warm....

Forty of the 60 B-29s that bombed NAGOYA on the 14th passed over Kit peninsula and the SHIKOKU area on the way. It is too awful to relate that at this time they revealed their true beast-like nature and had the audacity to drop a few bombs on the TOYOUKE Shrine.

Defilement of the Gods is a complete renunciation of the sublime rights of mankind. In other words, the plan of the enemy is to undermine the solid foundation of the state (human morality) and to insidiously weaken the principles of solidarity of our people!...

29 January 1945 – Monday. Clear. Windy and slightly cold.

Wrote a letter home....

The situation in the PHILIPPINES is anything but favourable. It is reported that a part of the enemy force has fought its way in MANILLA. I wonder if we are forced to resort to the use of a delaying action, deceptions and "Bleeding'" tactics. The situation is gradually getting more and more critical ...

31 January 1945 – Wednesday. Clear. Southerly Winds....

Received a January 16th letter from my daughter, CHIYIKO. The letter stated as follows:

'Dear father, I am obeying mother and am studying hard to become a great lady. So please hurry and do away with Americans and return home to us'....

17 February 1945 – Saturday. Clear. Later cloudy

This dawn we were on alert and expected the enemy to land any minute. Nothing happened, however. The dawn broke gloriously. 06.00...

Intelligence Report: – Approximately 80 landing craft are heading this way ... Opportunity is at hand, but we have no planes.

09.00 – 1st Lt. HAYASHIHARA came over. A conference was held with regard to close combat (suicide patrol).

Conferred with battalion CO MUSASHINO and an agreement was made as to the disposition of suicide patrols....

The bombardment of SOUTH beach and MOTOYAMA is really frightful. I wonder if the enemy is actually going to attempt a real landing this time. The long-awaited hour is here. The opportunity to show our fighting ability is actually at hand....

18.60 – Went outside to get a breath of fresh air. In the air raid shelter it is just like staying in the hold of a ship. It is so stuffy from cooking etc and the temperature rises so, one cannot remain inside for a long period of time without getting a headache.

One must live in the nude while listening to the bombardment. When I went out to feel the cool evening air, I felt as though I had been reborn ...

19 February 1945 – Monday. Clear ...

Report: 0630 — 200 enemy LCs [Landing Craft] 2000 metres away, and advancing to make a landing. So the real landing has come at last!

An American Account from Iwo Jima

One US Marine who invaded Iwo Jima was 25-year-old Tom Kennedy from New Jersey. In a hastily scribbled letter to his wife, Milly, he offered insights into the fighting.

Some Japs crawled up out of their holes in the early hours of the morning and charged our foxholes. They crawled to within 10 feet of one fellow and started yelling, "Hey, Corpsman." Our fellow asked him for the password, but he still yelled, "Hey, Corpsman." All he wanted was for some fellow to show himself so the Jap could throw a hand grenade in his hole. The kid saw him and killed him. When they pull one of their banzai charges, they gather together in a big group and start yelling. Then some of their officers start waving swords above their heads and shout, "Banzai, banzai!" While they scream, they charge. Of course our guns cut them down like flies, Milly, but it is scary listening to them scream like that.

Photo as Text

Caroline Brothers has contended that in the twentieth century war became inextricably linked with photography.[27] As a type of 'enduring war relic', photographs can be read as text, thereby creating another

Iconic image as text: the Iwo Jima photograph. AP Photo/Joe Rosenthal.

narrative form providing insights sometimes impossible to convey by word alone.[28] Like words, however, photographs can mislead.[29] Arguably the most famous photograph of the Pacific War was taken on Iwo Jima.[30] It depicted an American sailor and five Marines raising the American flag on Mount Surabachi. That image became one of the most profound images of the war. At a time when many Americans feared the war would last well beyond 1945, the importance of the Iwo Jima photograph as a means of sustaining morale, including morale on the home front, was evident to military and civic leaders. Similarly, Joe Rosenthal, who took the picture even as shots continued to be fired, was praised for his gallantry and devotion to duty.

But although the photograph's iconic status was affirmed from the moment it appeared in the American media, questions were raised about its authenticity, and the image that was popularised was not of the first raising of the flag on Mount Suribachi.[31] Instead, as was pointed out in a March 1945 report in *Time* magazine, Rosenthal's famous photograph was of a second raising of the flag. *Time* noted: 'For all his pains', Rosenthal's 'shot of Iwo's first flag raising was far from dramatic. A few hours later. . . a second band of marines ... planted a larger flag in the same spot. This time Rosenthal ... got his great picture.'[32]

The story of 'The Photograph' of the flag being raised on Mount Suribachi raises important questions concerning the relationship between visual images, patriotism and the role of the media during wartime. Media has taken new forms since the end of the Pacific War, but the issues arising from the raising of the American flag on Iwo Jima in 1945 continue to resonate during the twenty-first century. And as the success of James Bradley's 2000 book *Flags of our Fathers*, along with the 2006 movie of the same name, revealed, the story of the creation and manipulation of the images of the raising of the flags on Iwo Jima has extended well beyond academic circles.

Bradley's father, John Bradley, was one of the men seen raising the American flag in Rosenthal's photograph. James Bradley thus had a very direct and personal interest in the events on Mount Suribachi. Early in his book he points out that of the six Americans pictured in Rosenthal's photograph, three were killed in action as the battle for Iwo Jima continued and another two were 'overtaken and eventually destroyed – dead of drink and heartbreak'.[33] John Bradley was thus the only 'survivor' amongst the flag-raisers. Much of *Flags of our Fathers* is devoted to telling the story of the men in 'The Photograph', and the ways in which the photograph drew political and national attention. But James Bradley also reflects on the ways in which his father eschewed the limelight, and played down his own role on Iwo Jima.

The fate of the late-twentieth and twenty-first centuries was being forged in blood on that island and others like it. The combatants, on either side, were kids... My young father and his five comrades were typical of these kids. Tired, scared, thirsty, brave; tiny integers in the vast confusion of war-making, trying to do their duty, trying to survive.

But something unusual happened to these six. History turned all of its focus, for 1/400th of a second, on them. It froze them in an elegant instant of battles: froze them in a camera lens as they hoisted an American flag on a makeshift pole. Their collective image, blurred and indistinct, yet unforgettable, became the most recognized, the most reproduced, in the history of photography. It gave them a kind of immortality – a faceless immortality. The flagraising on Iwo Jima became a symbol of the island, the mountain, the battle; of World War II; of the highest ideals of the nation, of valor incarnate. It became everything except the salvation of the boys who formed it. [...]

When he [John Bradley] died in January 1994 ... he might have believed he was taking the unwanted story of his part in the flagraising with him to the grave, where he apparently felt he belonged. He had trained us, as children, to deflect the phone-call requests for media interviews that never diminished over the years. We were to tell the caller that our father was on a fishing trip. But John Bradley never fished. No copy of the famous photograph hung in our house. When we did manage to extract from him a remark about the incident, his responses were short and simple and he quickly changed the subject. [...]

"The real heroes of Iwo Jima," he once said ... "are the guys who didn't come back."

Subsequently, in an Afterword to the 2006 edition of *Flags of Our Fathers*, James Bradley published 'A Letter' to his late father, wherein he reflected both on his father's legacies and the continuing power of 'The Photograph':

Dear Dad,

You witnessed the six-decade-long power of The Photograph, a power constantly rejuvenated by the deepest thoughts and feelings of millions.

And its luminous power shone even before you were aware of what Joe Rosenthal had captured in that 1/400th of a second. [...]

When Americans celebrate the Fourth of July with an Iwo Jima Flagraising float, they perceive it's their inspiration. They don't realize that they are among the millions who have been caught up in the power of that 1/400th of a second.

A few years ago I wrote a book. Now I understand that I served The Photograph.

John Wayne also served The Photograph in *Sands of Iwo Jima* [...]. The concrete fragments of Wayne's fist and shoes are in the famous forecourt of Hollywood's Grauman's Chinese Theater. The two million people who visit Grauman's annually notice that John Wayne's plaque is different from those of other movie stars. His plaque is black. America's number one movie star asked for black concrete, made from black sand. From the black sands of Iwo Jima.

The power of The Photograph flows through past, present, and future.

Women's War: Nursing the Wounded

Early in the Pacific War Allied service women were confined to bases no closer to the front lines than Australia and Hawaii. From late 1943, however, plans were made to allow some female service personnel, notably nursing staff, to be stationed in 'forward areas'. Two such nurses were Lieutenants Olivione B. St. Peter and Alice Aurora Goudreau, of the US Navy. Both had joined the Naval Nursing Corps in 1942. In 1945 they shared their experiences in a Navy hospital on Guam with readers of the *American Journal of Nursing*. Professional journals published during this period often provided in-depth specialist insights into various aspects of war and were usually written by specialists for specialists. Consequently, the need to discuss an issue for the benefit of a profession overcame any broader concerns about the content. St. Peter and Goudreau's articles offer insights into rarely reported and often forgotten aspects of war during some of the worst fighting of the conflict.

St. Peter

After thirty days at sea, we reached Guam. We found the hospital partly built and partially occupied with medical cases and a few surgical patients.

Goudreau

The day after their arrival on the island, the nurses were on duty. Some were still suffering from the remnants of seasickness, heat exhaustion, and a generally wobbly feeling acquired during many weary weeks at sea. Added to this was that acute form of homesickness that strikes suddenly when you first realise you are thousands of miles from home, in a new and alien land.

St. Peter

The hospital was nearly empty, other wards and the surgery were being completed and prepared for occupancy, the surgery personnel worked in shifts to make up the linen for the anticipated need, and supplies were being stored up, for there was a rumor of a battle on Iwo Jima. Then one evening the casualties began to come in by ship. Doctors, nurses, and corpsmen admitted patients until the early hours of the morning. Baths were given, wounds expected, and some amputations and other emergency surgery done. Penicillin was continued as previously administered on ship and in medical field units, narcotics and hypnotics administered as necessary, and Phenobarbital given to a few patients to assist them in calming down after the excitement of battle.

Goudreau

As all the world knows, no one was prepared for the horror of IWO JIMA. Base 18 was not expecting such overwhelming numbers of casualties, but each and every man admitted received the finest medical and nursing care. Because of the high standards set by the Navy doctors and nurses, everyone worked long, weary hours to give the wounded almost personal attention....

A hospital ship entering the harbor was the signal for every member of the staff to report for duty. On such occasions during the Iwo campaign these were daily routine; the nurses remained on duty fourteen to sixteen hours a day....

St. Peter

Many cases needed amputations, but in many others refrigeration could be used. Some limbs were completely saved, in other cases several inches of limb were saved. ... Refrigeration was used because the patient was in too much shock to survive operation; or had other injuries that needed care first; or needed to be built up physically by the use of blood plasma, whole blood, and fluids....

After the airplanes could land fairly safely on Iwo Jima, patients were admitted to the hospital approximately four to six hours after injury. The greatest problem we had was that patients were brought in after nine o'clock. Lights had to be out so that other patients could sleep. The patients in the ward were anxious about the progress of the war and there were discussions over and over again. Just as these were settled, more would come in. As they were taken off stretchers, the boys in bed would say: 'Mate, are you Army or Marine? I got mine on Bonzai ridge, where did you get yours?' Et cetera, et cetera, on and on, fighting and refighting the war step by step because they were not in there still doing their part....

Goudreau

Our brain surgery ward was filled to capacity during the entire campaign. Most of these patients were on the "critical" list. All professionally trained nurses realise the constant care such patients demand. Our patients were evacuated as soon as possible, but even the "convalescents" were an ever-present source of worry. A young marine with a healing head would, carrying a sliver of shrapnel deep in the brain, might be a gay, happy youngster in the morning and become violent, irrational, or go into a series of convulsions before the day was over.

The terrific strain of nursing patients with gunshot and shell wounds of the head is beyond description. For this duty, our nurses were carefully selected. All were experienced in surgical nursing and several had been especially trained in neurosurgery....

The majority of our ambulatory admissions were classified as neuropsy-chiatric patients. ... These were the traditionally tough marines, experienced campaigners, who with outstanding gallantry had established beach head after beach head in the islands of the Pacific. Most of them, some little more than boys, were in such a severe state of shock that they had to be led by the hand from the planes and ambulances.

Although our resources in an advanced base hospital were of necessity limited, the care of war neuroses patients was modern and adequate.[34] The typical "shell chock" victim presents uniform symptoms; loss of appetite with associated loss of weight, insomnia, headache, and "startle" reactions to the slightest noise. The sharp slam of a screen door produced uncontrollable quivers in every muscle....

The cause of war neuroses varied with the experiences of the patients. "Fear of the shells" was the most frequent. The constant, hellish din of bursting shells during the early days of the campaign was described by many observers as almost beyond human endurance. Some were victims of bomb blasts. Others had lost control with a close shell burst blasted their "buddies" to bits before their eyes. One Marine's vivid impression of the beach on D-Day-plus-two was: 'it was as if a giant meat grinder had passed through our lines and left thousands of chopped bodies in its wake'. It is any wonder that we admitted so many patients with a diagnosis of psychoneurosis?

Gordeau

In addition to her nursing duties, the Navy nurse listened to many a heartsick, lonely boy's story. Even the toughest marine, when wounded, was just another homesick American boy yearning for home and his loved ones

The Air War: Over Tokyo

As the Marines wrested control of Iwo Jima and Okinawa, the B-29s continued their devastating attacks upon Japanese cities. In an April 1945 letter to his parents Lieutenant F. H. 'Pete' Reed shared his experiences of his fourteenth raid over Japan. By April the securing of Iwo Jima meant that the B-29s had fighter escorts in the form of the Lockheed P-51 Mustangs.

10 April 1945

Dearest Mom and Dad:

Wonderful letters from you all yesterday. I am quite surprised that you enjoyed the tale of Osaka that much....

The biggest thrill in the daytime was on the Big T raid the other day with P-51 protection for the first time.

On the way up, we ran through some foul weather, and couldn't even see beyond our wing tips for a long time. Naturally we were apprehensive about the fighters getting through it, as well as our own formations, intact. ... When we finally broke out of the "stuff," we were able to get together, and climbed on to our bombing altitude – which for daytime bombing would make your hair stand on end – it was anything but high altitude! By this time the weather had dissipated, and 'neath a bright sun (what a rarity!) Mt. Fuji could be seen clearly, as well as the saw-toothed mountain ridges running up Honshu's back....

After one or two circles, the time for the fighters to appear was only moments away. We knew it would be well-nigh suicide to go in at our altitude without them. And no kidding, for wonder of wonders, (just like in the movies), a group of small specks appeared high on the horizon – and then more and more. After a heart-stopping thought that they might be Jap fighters, we just knew they were ours....

As I looked ahead towards the object of our trip, I suddenly saw a flash of flame at about our altitude – then a billow of white and looking again after rubbing my eyes, I saw a Jap fighter spinning in flames, the pilot way off to one side swinging from his chute, and 4 P-51s circling back up. First kill! And off the coast too!! And a few moments later some "eager" lad in a 'Tony' came steaming in for the last ship in our formation, and 4 P-51s piled all over him so fast he undoubtedly never knew what happened. Down he went in pieces. I couldn't get over the kick it gave me to try to visualize the surprise it must have been to those Japs to get hopped by our fighters when they probably didn't dream of anything like that happening – ever!

By now we were about ready to turn on the bomb run and the other groups were already on it. From a clear sky, the picture suddenly became flecked with ugly black spots – in fact, it seemed to have become filled with them! It was hard to realize that those big black puffs were ugly pieces of jagged, razor-sharp steel shrapnel. And it was equally hard to realize that the pretty puffs of milky-white stuff were in reality the bursts of a phosphorous shell, that would burn any part of a plane that went through it. And all the time, the wonderful P-51s were scooting all over the sky, pouring it to the Japs.

Now we were on the bomb run, and here I found that plenty of Jap fighters were still "feeling fine" and very active. A twin-engine Nick came hurtling through the formation from 2 o'clock high – a beautiful silver job. His guns were blazing, and tracers were flying by us. He swished immediately underneath our ship, and out of sight. ... From here on the guns were going all the time – and the flak was bursting all the time. Way up in front, a 29 fell below his formation, and 4 P-51's went hurtling down to him – he blew up into three flaming sections. After what seemed like years, our bomb doors were opened and finally bombs were away.

As we turned from the target, I looked out on my right ... believe me I was scared stiff ever since we started the bomb run ... And saw a ship of our formation with my best buddies in it streaming flames from the section of wing behind #2 engine. (I found out later they were hit there at the beginning of the bomb run but had gone on in anyway, thinking that it might go out- but instead it kept burning more fiercely.) He feathered the prop, but it still burned on – and big chunks began breaking off from the affected spot. By now the ship had fallen back and to the side of the formation – and fighters were jumping on him in spite of the 51's nearby. We all turned to his side – and it was obvious that they should jump – but Big T was underneath, and I guess the hope that they might make their way out to sea and ditch and somehow get picked up was over-shadowing common sense. For just a minute or two later the wing came off, and the plane blew and spun down in pieces. Some chutes opened – but not as many as were in the plane – and no one knows who got out and who stayed.

I was pretty sick – and fighters were still jumping us as we passed over the coast....

A few hours later the 14th mission was over. Whew!! Fifteen solid hours – it took me about 24 hours to want to go back again.

Love,
Pete

P. S. Anyone flying a P-51 should be President.

CHAPTER SEVEN
OCCUPATION EXPERIENCES

For all their talk of 'co-prosperity' and freedom for the peoples of Asia, the Japanese made little serious effort to win the support of the Malayan people. Their rule was based on terror.

Sybil Kathigasu

The Pacific War is often told as simply the story of a struggle between Japanese and Americans. However, millions of other people were also caught up in the events that dominated the region. The Pacific War delivered Japan – albeit temporarily – an enormous empire in the Asia-Pacific. Millions of Asians found themselves 'liberated' from European colonial regimes and new members of the 'Greater East Asia Co-Prosperity Sphere'.[1]

Prior to the Great War, 'pan-Asianism' was 'little more than an unorganised tendency' with a vague political agenda.[2] By the 1930s, however, the Japanese government had done much to posit 'regional cooperation in opposition to European imperialism'.[3] Encouraging nationalist movements in Asia was an expression of this sentiment. Such encouragement included offering political exile, bringing potential nationalist leaders to Japan for further education and providing financial and moral support to specific nationalist groups.

By encouraging local nationalists to overthrow their European masters, Japanese leaders envisaged that such developments in Asia would extend their nation's influence. Using jingoistic discourses of national superiority based on racial purity and divine origins, or arguments based on the rapidity and success of Japan's modernisation and industrialisation, and its military might, many Japanese intellectuals contended their nation was the obvious choice to head a new, liberated Asia.[4] After Japan left the European-dominated League of Nations in 1933, critics suggested Japan was planning to create an Asian equivalent to the increasingly hapless League. Japanese propagandists claimed the destruction of European colonialism was a central plank of Japan's 'New Order' in Asia, and testament to their nation's role as the 'the protector of Asia, the leader of Asia, and the light of Asia'.[5] However, it was not until after the war with China had started that the discourse shifted from the intellectual to the political sphere.

Despite the continuing use of the phrase 'Pan-Asianism' after the Pacific War, historians have often regarded the term as a rhetorical tool by which Japan sought to serve its own interests, and 'a cover for Japanese imperial ambitions in east Asia'.[6] This argument suggests that the advance into Southeast Asia was motivated primarily by the imperative of securing the region's raw materials for war. Writing in the 1930s, left-wing Chinese writer Du Zhongyuan insisted that 'Pan-Asianism is Japanese imperialism, nothing more, and nothing less'. Particularly in Southeast Asia, however, the idea 'expanded the welcome the Japanese initially received'.[7] In the Dutch East Indies, for example, the majority of Indonesians welcomed the Japanese as liberators.[8] But Japanese support of local nationalist movements was conditional upon whether they helped the war effort. For instance, in places such as Malaya and Sumatra, where there were crucial raw materials to be exploited or denied to the enemy, tight political control was exercised and less autonomy given to nationalist groups. By contrast, in Java, where the island's human resources were considered crucial to the war effort, nationalist leaders and their organisations were given a greater degree of support.

Even if the desire of many Japanese to liberate Asia for the benefit of the colonised was a genuine ambition, such ideology never translated into practice.[9] Japanese occupation policy was largely influenced by the form of administration adopted by the military in Manchuria, rather than by the nation's long-term colonial experience in Korea or Taiwan. Although a Ministry for Great East Asia and a Department of Military Administration were created in Tokyo, and whilst officers of these bureaucracies were sent to occupied areas, there was little integrated planning. Enormous discretionary power was left in the hands of local military commanders. When placed beside practical wartime considerations and a number of variables including geography, class, ethnicity, religion, gender and age, Japanese occupation had wide and varied impacts on the peoples of Southeast Asia.

One experience shared by most peoples of the Greater East Asia Co-Prosperity Sphere during the war years was hunger. The Allies' 'scorched earth' policies, the Japanese military practice of foraging to sustain a unit in the field and orders for areas to be self-sufficient or assist Japanese agricultural shortfalls, along with the disruption of local economies and regional trade through the dislocation of war, brought great hardship. Lack of food led to rationing. In Singapore the rice allowance per person was progressively reduced as the war progressed so that by 1944, the ration amount for one month barely met the pre–war-recommended consumption figure for one day.[10]

To inculcate local populations to embrace the Co-Prosperity Sphere, the Japanese oversaw massive changes to local education systems. Many pre-war school systems, especially those whose instruction had been in a European language, were closed. Some local and religious vernacular schools were permitted to remain open, although their syllabus now focused on areas such as 'industrial technological instruction', which would aid Japan's war effort. All school teachers were expected to learn Japanese, and Japanese became an important new subject in schools. Adult classes in Japanese were also established.

Like the European colonials before them, the Japanese created schemes to take advantage of local labour. These programmes were often assisted by local nationalist leaders. The largest of these schemes operated in the Dutch East Indies, where it is estimated that between four and ten million Javanese and other Indonesians served in a labour corps known as the *rōmusha* (labourers). Over 270,000 of these *rōmusha* were sent abroad to assist the Japanese war effort. Like Allied POWs, these labourers were brutalised and mistreated, but their mortality rates were much higher than those suffered by POWs.

Despite some of the pronouncements of American president Franklin D. Roosevelt, and notwithstanding the 1941 Atlantic Charter, which suggested that a new independent future for Asia would come with peace, the colonial powers assumed they would reclaim their former colonial empires. Indeed, even before the tide of war had turned in favour of the Allies, the colonial powers were making plans for their return. As Japan's hopes were stymied, the Japanese made greater concessions to nationalists in the hope that independence might slow down the Allied advance.

The development and detonation of the atomic bomb, and the quick end to the war, left most of Southeast Asia still under Japanese control, with Allied units unable to assert immediate control. In Indonesia the result was a declaration of independence by the nationalists who had been complicit in the occupation. In Vietnam those nationalists who had opposed the Japanese secured control. These declarations of independence, however, did not deter the returning colonial powers.

Using force of arms where necessary to ensure their return, the former colonials promptly set about re-establishing their dominance. Colonial peoples were quickly divided between resisters and collaborators. Such distinctions, however, reflected the motivations and actions of only a very small percentage of the population.[11] For the overwhelming majority of Asians who found themselves under Japanese control, passivity rather than active resistance or collaboration reflected their approach.[12] Paul Kratoska has suggested with regard to Malaysia that 'nearly everyone collaborated, but few did so because of a commitment to Japanese objectives as presented by the Japanese'.[13]

Most of the armed resistance to the Japanese was led by communists. Aided by Allied intelligence, groups such as Viet Minh in Indochina, the Hukbalahaps in the Philippines and the Chinese communist guerrillas in Malaya fought against the Japanese to free their countries, rather than return them to colonial power.[14] One Japanese historian, examining anti-Japanese resistance in the Malay state of Perak – where opposition was strongest – has concluded that such efforts were little more than an 'irritating nuisance' and that the principal purpose was to prepare for resistance to the return of the British.[15]

Historians have disagreed on whether the Pacific War constituted a turning point in the history of the region. The so-called 'transformation school' and the 'continuity school' have argued over the extent to which the war brought significant change to the region.[16] It is undeniable, however, that the war changed Southeast Asia forever and encouraged decolonisation. Nicholas Tarling has noted that the 'Japanese invasions of Southeast Asia overthrew the colonial system. That in itself had more impact, no doubt, than the residual pan-Asianism it carried with it'.[17]

In some places, including Indonesia and Vietnam, the failure of the returning colonials to accept the changed reality of their circumstances precipitated revolutionary struggle. Moreover, Japan's Greater East Asia Co-Prosperity Sphere had been Asia's first attempt at regional integration. Ironically, however, Japan's efforts in building such regional identity produced its own alienation as it played the role of 'the last imperialists in Asia'.[18]

THE SOURCES

H. J. Heijnen's Account of the Last Days of Dutch Colonial Rule in 1942

The Japanese conquest of Southeast Asia rocked the former colonial societies to their core. This impact was particularly evident in the Dutch East Indies. Upon their arrival in the archipelago, the Japanese first secured important strategic centres. Smaller island groups were left undisturbed for weeks, sometimes months; in some cases islands were considered of such strategic insignificance that their inhabitants never saw a Japanese soldier. On the small island of Geser, on the eastern tip of Ceram in the eastern archipelago, a Dutch administrator waited for an uncertain future as his control and authority was progressively undermined. A few weeks after his escape to Australia, H. J. Heijnen recounted the last days of Dutch control on Geser. He committed his recent experiences to paper as evidence for an inquiry examining his decision to leave his post in the face of the Japanese advance. These sources must be examined carefully, given that their objective was to defend the author's actions. Nonetheless, the testimonies given in written or oral form to commissions of inquiry, or to military courts martial, comprise an often-underutilised source for examining the personal experiences of war.[19]

Written by a bureaucrat well versed in imperial administration, the text provides insights into the prevailing colonial discourse. As he makes clear, confronting the Japanese was not straightforward, given the imbalance of forces and underlying uncertainties about colonial authority and power. In the end it was not the physical arrival of the Japanese, but their words – and the ideas they encapsulated and encouraged – that compelled Heijnen to escape.

Survey of events in the period from 8 Dec 1941 to 3 April 1942

After the outbreak of war I took over the military camp from the acting detachment commander, European Sgt W. Zijlstra on 9 December. … That day the soldiers left for Boeal on a prauw and the drilling site of the BPM [a Dutch oil company]. The only means of power which I still had at Boeal was a military police detective and three admin police officers armed with klewangs [swords]. All the police officers were used for control jobs and tax collection in my territory so that most of the time they were not at Geser.

The population was still at that time loyal. The enemy was far away and one did not need to fear any violent act. I never noticed any Japanese political activity. It is true that the regent of Dobo was charged in an anonymous letter of having pro-Japanese feelings but in my investigations nothing of that appeared....

On 9 December I confiscated all important provisions namely rice, flour, sugar milk, petrol and cigarettes, which after an inventory were stocked centrally in the customs building located on the landing at Geser. We immediately introduced a distribution system with coupons, the preparations of which was already partially in place. For all population groups equal quantities were sold depending on the number of family members. ... The arrangement worked to everyone's satisfaction....

Around 12 December a Council was introduced which advised me on all local matters. The following people were members: the local supervisor of natives, the supervisor of the Chinese and a local Arab, plus the Regent of Keloe and about five of the most respected and trusted civilians of all population groups. This Council did a good job....

All needed measures were introduced without too much panic. After bombings on Tarempa we began digging trenches. This news brought the first elements that inspired fear of the Japanese among the population. After the order to dig trenches was announced many women and children left for other islands or went to Ceram. They were driven by fear. As it might have caused panic to keep them from going I just introduced the condition that the evacuated persons had to be registered....

On first February 1942 the attack on Ambon became public knowledge. On my own initiative I proceeded with distribution to the regional leaders a document regarding the attitude to be adopted upon the occupation of their district. This document was titled 'Penoedoek Indonesia'. The fear of a coming occupation of Geser was noticed immediately in a new evacuation of women and children. All men of military age were prohibited to leave the island without permission as they were needed to double the guards. I had already installed lookouts on 8 Dec.

A lot of doubt was expressed about the power of NEI [Netherlands East Indies] Army and this defeatism started to grow. It is true that it was not expressed very clearly because of the risk of criminal charges but a few reliable persons who were respected by the population and always well oriented about what went on in the population informed me. ... I believe that this opinion did reflect the feelings of many native peoples. ... The fact that the Japanese were capable of bringing a huge amount of naval, air and infantry forces to Ambon drew more and more attention. Also ... the surrender of the Dutch army had taken place after one day and the Australian surrender after four days. Power is always attractive, especially for primitive people who are not in the least aware of the use of modern weapons and the modern conduct of war.

These fears and doubts led to a new evacuation on a larger scale during the first three weeks of Feb. Women were no longer present at Geser. The public and secondary school were closed because of a lack of students.

Between 11 to 17 Feb about 25 men from the Geser detachment returned from Ambon. They had run away during the surrender. Some had escaped from captivity. ... I gave all of them advances so that they could buy clothes

and I planned to send all of them to Toeal or Timor-Kopeang as this was
the only open way to join their army again. I informed them of my plan on
16 February after consulting Zijstra [a European sergeant who has escaped
Ambon]. There was a lot of unwillingness to follow this order. I explained the
consequences of refusal; court martial, loss of rank, pension etc and gave them
time till next morning to think. Early the following morning First Lieutenant
Hieronymus [a Dutch officer] returned to Geser. After explaining the
situation he ordered that all soldiers would gather in the camp at 11am. Only
three men gathered. ... They were given till 12 to change their mind. They
declared a reluctance to join the Lieutenant and Ziljstra. Assistant police
rounded them up and told them to go with the Lieutenant. All refused even
after the Lieutenant pointed out the consequences. The three men who had
been prepared to go now changed their mind.

The reasons for refusal were as follows
1. We have done our duty
2. We have fought and lost and this is the end of the war for us. We will stay
with our family
3. When we had weapons and could fight the commander at Ambon had
already surrendered. Now we do not have weapons so will not fight any
more....

The Lieutenant, I and Zijlstra thought about what to do. We discussed at
length whether it would be possible to force the unwilling to go taking into
account the available arms. We had one rifle and my revolver. Finally we
decided not to force them to go because even if we succeeded in arresting
them they could not be locked up or guarded by reliable guards. ... So they
could only be released and I tried to spread them along the shore of Ceram
so they could not organise themselves for rebellion....

On 18 Feb the Hieronymous and Zijlstra left for Toeal....

Into March the Japanese had still not sent forces from Ambon to Geser.

The tax clerk Abdullah Wairooy returned by the end of March from a tax
trip along the coast of Ceram and stated that not a single regent had paid
taxes and that all pretended that the population did not want to pay anymore
after the Japanese had come to power. The regent of Atiiahoe had tried to
collect the taxes but had been prevented from doing so by village heads under
threat that charges would be pressed against him with Japanese authorities in
Ambon. Some regents headed off for Ambon to offer their subjection to
Japanese authority and obedience.

These were the first signs that respect for Dutch authority was
disappearing. I did have the power to bring back this respect but not the fast
transportation to go to these places to try and stop this and provoke loyalty
by my presence. ... The spirit of disobedience was spreading fast.

By end of March no one greeted me. They just passed me by with grumpy
faces. ... It was clear that the stream of disloyalty and fear born at Ambon and

transferred by those who fled Ambon was expanding further to the east and we could expect serious difficulties in Geser....

On 7 April at 7.15am the district master of the native population at Geser, Mohamad Kelian, came to my house and showed me a letter he had received on second of April from Daeng Bula who arrived back from Boela. The letter was in Malay:

Announcement

The Japanese administration in Amboina temporarily confirms the appointment of Mr Mohamad Kelian as the kampong head of the city of Geser (Ceram). It is his duty to execute the orders of the Japanese at Ambon. He does not have to follow the orders of the Controller at Geser. It is strictly forbidden by the native residents of Geser to give assistance to the Dutch, Australian or other Europeans or to go to another place by prauw.

Ambon 20 March 1942
The Japanese administrator in Ambon
Signed Ida

I went to the office and arranged a few things. Picked up some personal records and some secret letters which I would bring away or destroy....

This declaration was made public with Malay translations:

'The undersigned HJ Heijnen, Commander of East Ceram, declares his resignation from his position on the grounds that in the Japanese letter from Ambon dated 20 March 1942 instructions were given to the people of Geser not to follow his orders any more, a fact which means that Dutch sovereignty is not recognised by the occupiers any more'

Lieutenant Nievera's Open Letter

Like Indonesian soldiers, Filipino soldiers serving with the Americans contemplated their continued support for their colonial masters. Japanese propaganda sought to drive a wedge between Filipino soldiers and the American military, often by printing open letters written by recently captured Filipinos. One such letter was allegedly written by Lieutenant José Nievera, who was captured in late January 1942.

I am addressing myself to my comrades in Bataan. I cannot stop myself from talking from the bottom of my heart. Your day has come. I have returned to Manila under the whole hearted protection of the Japanese soldiers. And what joy met me when I found myself in the midst of my family. I saw my beloved wife and children of whom I was thinking constantly and who even appeared in my dreams. I also met my old friends who are now constantly talking to me in the midst of our happiness.

Now I am eating the best of foods such as adobo, michado, sinigang etc. ... which I have been longing for in the foxholes. I am smoking the best cigarettes. I walk the streets unhampered by anybody and my heart is leaping with joy. It seems to me that I have just awakened from a bad nightmare.

The Japanese Army is not our enemy; our real enemy is the American Army that is always behind us in the battlefield; that is fooling us, and scaring us and wrestling away from us our happiness.

Watanabe Wataru's Directives for the Occupation of Southeast Asia

At the same time as orders for Japanese soldiers in Southeast Asia perpetuated notions of pan-Asianism, they also maintained social relations and racial hierarchies that had been used by European colonists. General Watanabe Wataru drafted many of the policies that informed the administration of Malaya and Singapore, some of which are included below.

1. Where the local people's religious and cultural habits/traditions are concerned, do not interfere directly. Any changes necessary should be discussed by the people themselves. Even if something has to be changed, take it step by step

2. Do not maintain anything that was established by force by the British and the Dutch, so as to effect a change in attitudes towards the Japanese, such as policies on language, or the system of inherited bureaucratic positions. ... Never put yourself in an equal position to the native. Control natives with your mind and your beliefs, but be neither contemptuous nor overly friendly, because you won't be able to control them that way. In other words, do not put yourself in an equal position....

3. Basic policies for interaction with Sumatra natives.
   a) The principles of the Great East Asia War. There have to be improvements to their sense of mission that Asians will lead Asians.
   b) Adapt your attitudes to each particular ethnic group. Some ethnic groups could be encouraged, others need to be controlled more strictly.
   c) Quickly capture and use the feeling of liberation amongst the population, which has been encouraged by the current war. [In] addition: if necessary establish people's liberation halls in the big cities, which can be used as General HQ for guidance, policy making and implementation, and the collection of information about the native population. (But exclude Chinese and Indian ethnic groups from this movement, or you'll provide a facility for conspiracy against Japanese).

Japanese Propaganda and Filipino Civilians

Japanese propaganda towards the civilian populations in Southeast
Asia utilised radio, newspapers and magazines as popular forms of
dissemination. In Manila, Filipinos were enjoined to reject their
Americanisation and embrace their 'Oriental' traditions – an outlook
and way of living shared by the Japanese.

The Filipinos ... should return to the original features of an oriental people ...
and their dependent mentality ... [and] return native life to one of simplicity
and reorganise industries which make possible the cooperation of this country
with its neighbours. ... A nation which indulges in pretty dresses, nice foods,
physical enjoyment and expensive fashion can never succeed in establishing
a strong nation.

Such re-evaluations of Filipino life were even extended to civic pride.

Manila wipes its nose

Manila has been known to be one of the most beautiful cities in the Orient –
also one of the least clean. This ugly blot on the reputation of Manila was
mainly due to the failure of the past regime to inculcate in the masses the
proper community spirit necessary to enlist their cooperation in matters
affecting the common welfare....

The new order of things, however, has changed the whole picture. For
instance, cocheros are now required to carry with them refuse receptacles
and scoop up their own horse's manure from the streets....

Private individuals also actively cooperate in making the city clean by
sweeping the streets in front of their houses and by either burning or burying
their garbage instead of waiting for the garbage collectors to come around.

Through catchy posters, the public is enjoined to keep public places, public
conveyances, and private domiciles clean and sanitary. Prizes are offered to the
cleanest districts'.

The Singing Imamura Hitoshi

In Batavia, Japanese officer Imamura Hitoshi attempted to find ways
to unite the Indonesian and Japanese peoples.

Civilisation of the Indonesian people was far higher than that of the British
Indians, which I had witnessed before, and near to Formosans. Their nature
was moderate and peaceful. If the Japanese lost their hearts, the Military
Administration must be wrong. And whether we would get their hearts or
not, it depended upon soldiers' behaviour. For the purpose of spreading my
ideas upon the natives, especially upon the Japanese soldiers, I requested
the propaganda section to collect 'songs of racial melting' from both sides.
Mr OKI Atsuo acted in this work chiefly. Considerable amount of prizes

were offered and many poems were collected. No 1 on both sides were published and musical settings for these poems were offered with prizes again. The No.1 on the Japanese side was a song with words by a certain superior private and with music by a military band. ... The word 'Yaeshio' – vast ocean – in the poem name was taken to be the theme.

Yaeshio – the vast ocean

1. Calling out for the Japanese:
    'From afar beyond the divine land in the vast ocean, we have marched our troops on this island with our compatriots, in obedience to the Imperial rescript'.

2. Answer of the Indonesians:
    'The Japanese empire is the light of Asia. We being honoured with the Majesty's favour, will swear fealty to him from an island in the south, where coconut trees grow.'

3. Chorus of the both
    'The vast ocean is the highway of every luck. We are strengthened by the surf. Let us, awakened nations, rouse ourselves to establish the Great Asia Co-Prosperity Sphere'

Southeast Asian Memories

Examining public commemorations and memorialisations helps historians understand wars and their impacts.[20] The way a war is remembered in a monument provides telling insights into how individuals – and a culture – recall and understand war. Southeast Asia, however, is remarkable because of its distinct absence of public commemoration of World War II.[21] This is perhaps understandable, given that the traditional justification for the construction of such sites of memory is to remember those who fell in battle. (That perspective, of course, places to one side the thousands of Asians who served in Dutch, British and American colonial armies.) More generally, the Japanese occupation of Southeast Asia has been more difficult to document than many other aspects of the Pacific War. Because traditional documentary sources dealing with the Japanese occupation are scarce, historians have been compelled to rely upon individuals' memories of the period to describe and analyse the experiences of those whose nations were occupied. There are parallels here with the prisoner-of-war experience, where historians have also relied heavily on the memories and memoirs of those who were captured by the Japanese.[22] Unlike that field of inquiry, however, there has been relatively little interest in the experiences of those nations occupied by the Japanese.

Paul Kratoska has noted that in 'Malaysia and Singapore those who experienced occupation have kept its memory alive, but each succeeding generation find their war stories less compelling and young people know little about the events of the war years'.[23]

Memories as expressed through memoirs therefore play an important role in documenting the lived experience of the Pacific War. Whilst 'the history of the colonised' in Southeast Asia has 'rarely appeared in documents', the region is 'alive in oral sources'.[24] Nonetheless, while the surviving and scattered documents of Japanese and local origin are often 'extremely sketchy', they provide helpful insights for historians.[25]

The fact that many Japanese soldiers' behaviour antagonised local populations reflected Japanese notions of their racial superiority, along with the chauvinism of the military victor. In Malaya, one Japanese officer believed victory gave him extraordinary rights. Lim Kwee Phaik recalls her family's encounter with one Japanese officer in Penang. Contrary to Kratoska's assertions, the Japanese occupation was an important chapter in this family's history, and remained an oral tradition until it was converted to paper in a memoir.

During the Japanese occupation of Malaya, my grandfather had to vacate his house. It was requisitioned and taken over by the Japanese to make part of its headquarters and command post. ... My grandfather moved his whole household to live on one of his estates much further inland where it was considered safe as it was surrounded by the jungle....

One day, my grandfather's employee came to the house in haste. Ashen-faced, he informed my grandfather that his former Japanese employee who had worked as a clerk at one of my grandfather's warehouses had been made a captain of the Japanese imperial order. He had been making inquiries about my mother. According to informed sources he had fallen in love with my mother when working as a clerk. Now he wanted her as his woman.

Panic rippled through the house. My grandfather sprang into action and made arrangements for my mother, together with my brother and me, to be taken to hide in his house in Penang Hill. The house was situated quite a distance from the Moniot Road station. ... From the station it would take about an hour to walk to the house along a jungle path. However, we could not travel by train as the Japanese already occupied the train station. The other route was to hike up the hill from the foothills at Ayer Itam or from the Botanical Gardens. ... Grandfather was determined to make sure of the safety of my mother so he called upon his most loyal workers and arranged for several strong bodied men to carry her, my brother and me up the hill in a sedan chair. ... My father could not join us in case he was followed, so he returned to stay in his mother's house.

A few days after we had left, the Japanese Captain came to my grandfather's house looking for my mother. Grandfather told him that my mother had been killed when the bombs fell. With disbelief in his eyes, the Captain ordered a search of the premises and the interrogation of the household staff. Of course the workers, having been instructed by my grandmother to say my mother was dead repeated this.

Since my mother could not be found, the Captain vowed to keep looking for her. He told my grandfather that he had information that my mother was seen alive after the bombing raids. My father was anxious to rejoin us up on the hills but knew his movements were being watched. He waited for some time to pass; meanwhile he continued working at the clinic. When he found that he was no longer under twenty-four hour surveillance, he hatched a scheme to rejoin us. He disguised himself as a coolie and carried bags of rice to the foothills. Under the cover of night he hiked from Ayer Itam up the hill to the house. From this point it was dense jungle and no Japanese troops were patrolling this area....

One day a group of Japanese soldiers was seen assembling at the foothills train station. ... Through a relay of workers stationed at various points, the news of the Captain's arrival was sent to my mother at the house up the hill. A contingency plan had earlier been put in place in case this happened. A clearing in the jungle had been made some distance from the house. ... The entrance to the hut was concealed by the thick growth and foliage of the jungle....

The moment my mother received the message she quickly bundled us and with our nanny and minimum rations we went to hide in this hut. We waited in fear for the arrival of the Japanese soldiers. Not knowing they had arrived we stayed there for several days. During this crisis my mother ran out of milk. I was fed with boiled rice porridge water, but the water was reddish since it came from the earth pond. ... I could not tolerate this and became very sick and kept on crying and whimpering. ... When my crying became too loud, my mouth had to be covered and I was nearly smothered to death.

After a few days, the caretaker came and told us the Japanese Captain had left so we came out of hiding and returned to the house. He told my mother what had happened. The soldiers searched everywhere. Leaving no stone unturned [they] could not find any evidence of my mother's presence. Baby things were found but the caretaker told them they belonged to his wife who had just given birth. The superstitious Japanese did not want to go near any women who had given birth as they considered them to be 'dirty' since they would be still bleeding. So they left quickly after their thorough search. Everyone was so relieved. News reached my grandfather that the Japanese Captain had stopped searching for my mother. He was finally convinced that she had been killed. Shortly after that the Japanese captain was transferred to another posting in another part of Malaya and was not heard of or seen again. When my grandfather was absolutely sure that he had gone he sent for my mother to return home.

Speaking Allegiance

In many Asian societies where the colonial system had only permitted rudimentary education systems, the spoken word remained significant as a force for change. Perhaps the most pragmatic and charismatic of word plays, public speaking had a pedagogical power that had largely waned in Europe during the nineteenth century (although orators such as Churchill and Hitler went some way toward reviving the art during the 1930s and 1940s).[26]

War and occupation compelled local nationalist leaders to pledge their allegiance to one side or the other. Their decisions, and their justifications, typically rested upon assertions that they were motivated by the best interests of their peoples. In the Philippines, limited independence had been granted, and a timetable set for full independence. Prior to the Japanese invasion, Filipino president Manuel L. Quezon affirmed his support for the United States.

I am not worried that the Filipinos will take with Japan. The Japanese can never offer us anything like the Americans have offered us, and no amount of mistrust on the part of the High Commissioner or double crossing on the part of a few congressmen will make me lose faith in fundamental Americanism. I think that its code is the code which holds out the most hope for us and I choose it deliberately. I think that it can be said that there is more merit in my loyalty than there is in that of Americans who are born to their creed.

Speaking in Central Luzon in early 1943, fellow Filipino Benigno S. Aquino expressed a different point of view.

I would not hesitate to say that I do not care if I were called a traitor to America, first because I am not an American, and second, because, if by treachery to America I could serve my country and my people, if by treachery to America, peace and tranquillity could be restored to the Philippines so that the people might live again their normal lives; if by treachery to America all our institutions might return to their state of normality and thus restore to the hearts of the people the aspirations for a happy future, then I would say once again that I would rather be one thousand times a traitor to America if by being so I show complete loyalty to my country.

As the Japanese position in the Pacific deteriorated, increasing pressure was placed on local populations to support the Japanese cause. In the Philippines in late 1944, the 'Fence Sitters' were called to their 'Hour of Decision'. Such calls reflected the unrealistic Japanese evaluations of the strategic situation, which were quickly undermined when proven false.

This is written during a lull after three of the most exciting weeks we have experienced in our neighbourhood since the outbreak of the present war. The excitement in question is none other than the brilliant victory achieved by the

Imperial Japanese Forces over the American marauders who attacked Japan's inner defences on the pretext of liberating the Philippines.

But we are not allowing recent victories to turn our heads. We are in no holiday mood. On the contrary we are in a bellicose frame of mind. We are apt to be rough with some people. Even if we step on their toes, we will not be stopping to apologise.

We are far from believing that the recent military engagement of Taiwan and the Philippines were an indication that the end of the war is in sight. We think they were by preludes suggestive of the magnitude of the battles yet to come....

Nevertheless we do think that, for many Filipinos, the great victory won by the Imperial Japanese Forces in the last few weeks should bear a special significance. It gives many of us a good opportunity in which to take stock ourselves and to make up our minds once and for all, as to exactly where we stand as individuals, and as Filipinos, and as Asians....

We would like to speak plainly to that recalcitrant group still sitting on the fence and we speak in behalf of those comprising the opposite group who have shown themselves as true friends and endeavoured to maintain a steadfast belief in our cause and have really contributed their time in one way or another. We feel that we can no longer tolerate the continued vacillating attitude of the pseudo-Filipinos who have done nothing but contribute eloquent lip service and cleverly pretend to go through the motions. We feel that we should waste no more of our time or sympathy. They have been coddled long enough. We feel that it would be better for all concerned if they were bundled up and tagged and shipped to Leyte now to share the same destiny that is awaiting the Americans who have landed there. That would be disposing of the proverbial two birds with one stone.

Some of those who experienced the Japanese occupation wrote of their experiences in fictionalised forms. Indonesian nationalist Pramoedya Ananta Toer offered insights into Indonesian thinking on the Japanese occupation in his 1950 novel *Perburuan*. He conveyed a popular wartime collaborationist view that accommodation of the Japanese was a means to an end. This justification became popular after the Japanese defeat.

The former District Officer grumbled slowly: 'It's all the fault of the Japanese. They are proud of themselves and insist on us treating them with respect, but they treat their enemies like animals. They are digging their own grave. They think that Indonesians can't see how foul and corrupt they really are. Indonesians know how cruel their teacher is'.

Remembering the Black Market

Singapore was hit particularly hard by food shortages during the Japanese occupation. One Japanese witness who had pre-war experience of the island was the consular official Shinozaki Mamoru. During the occupation he remained as a special adviser to the military government. After the war he wrote of his experiences and the important role the 'black market' played in the life of the former British colony.

As the months passed, life in Syonan became more difficult. For many it became a struggle for survival. Probably the man with the most difficult job was the Controller of Food.

Most of the food came from Thailand in lorries, in trains and in ships. But there was never enough to fill the bellies of a million hungry people.

Food shortage changed the appearance of the city as much as that of the people. Tapioca and sweet potato plants replaced flowering plants in practically every garden, every patch of available land. The city authorities closed their eyes to the black market – At least some food was available for those who could afford it.

The black market is a curious phenomenon; in times of stress it operates everywhere. … The Japanese military administration in Syonan could not stamp out the black market, and so they too went to the black market to buy what they needed.

Of course the city administration tried to control the situation: they made changes in the trade laws; there were taxes on luxuries, there was a law prohibiting the removal of important machinery, boats and cars, there were regulations on savings, the promotion of self-sufficiency state lotteries, taxation, price control, licence fees, gambling farms – but all to no avail. The black market thrived, as it did elsewhere in the world.

A short supply of commodities encouraged invention and there were many Japanese technicians, engineers and chemists in Singapore. They invented many things, using Singapore products and materials, and some new industries were thus created. I believe that this experience partly helped to develop industrial Japan after the war.

Did the people of Singapore benefit from their terrible experiences during Japanese occupation? I believe they did in some ways. The people of Singapore proved they could look after themselves in adversity. They produced shark-liver oil, they ran a taxi service with taxies operating on charcoal. Singapore paper and Chinese sauces were made.

I think the Japanese occupation was probably a historical necessity in Singapore's political and subsequent economic development.

Words of Resistance

Among those people of Southeast Asia who resisted the Japanese occupation was Sybil Kathigasu. With her Ceylonese doctor husband, the 'Eurasian' Kathigasu provided medical aid for the anti-Japanese guerrilla forces operating in Malaya. Several times she was arrested and interrogated by Japanese authorities. Her memoirs of these years were left unfinished when she died in the early post-war era as a result of wounds sustained at the hands of her captors. In depicting the environment in which people lived their lives, Kathigasu emphasised the difficulties experienced by ethnic Chinese.

Under the Japanese, the informer was everywhere, and everywhere was hatred and fear. For all their talk of 'co-prosperity' and freedom for the peoples of Asia, the Japanese made little serious effort to win the support of the Malayan people. Their rule was based on terror, and this was particularly so in respect of the Chinese. It was as if they expected hostility rather than loyal support – as well they might, considering their naked aggression in China. Nearly all the guerrillas in the hills were Chinese, and though the Chinese community subscribed heavily to Japanese war funds, feted and feasted their conquerors and appeared willing to do anything that was required of them, the Japs were not taken in. In truth, they feared the Chinese, and gave expression to their fear in savage persecution and constant spying. They were determined that the Chinese should fear them and be kept docile by fear. Hence the public executions which were a barbarous feature of the Japanese rule.

Islander Oral History

An under-examined aspect of the war in the Pacific remains its impact on the Islander peoples of the Pacific. Lin Poyer has contended that part of the reason for this absence is that the 'local view' is confined to primary sources that are 'primarily oral and performative'.[27] Within these Islander communities the Pacific War has enjoyed an enduring legacy. Lamont Lindstrom and Geoffrey White have noted that memories of the war have 'frozen into narrative accounts' and 'these war stories compose a historical archive'.[28] It is impossible to generalise the experience of Pacific Islanders in any coherent form. From Polynesia to Melanesia to Micronesia, and from island to island within these regions, the war was experienced in a variety of ways.[29] To better understand Islanders' experiences of war, western scholars have tapped into the 'rich oral tradition of war history'.[30]

Mary Hane Jemes experienced the Pacific War as a young woman on the Carolines Island of Ponape. The former German territory had been acquired by the Japanese during World War I. In an oral history interview Jemes recalled working for the Japanese.

I was beaten up by the police master because my daughter was sick and I told the police master that I would take off that day, but he said no, then I said 'pakero' to him. He came and beat me up. The word pakero means stupid. The police master didn't hear the word I said, but a man from Madolenihmw told him. Two days after that, my husband went to Madolenihmw and told my boss that the word I said was not meant for him but for the Pohnpeian. Working for the Japanese was the worst.

On Mili Atoll one of the few revolts against the Japanese took place when a group of Marshallese and Korean labourers rebelled. Elson Ebel recalls:

Now it was the Marshallese and the Koreans together, because their low social level was not the equal of the Japanese. After those fellows were shot and died, the Marshallese and Koreans met together and said 'Good'. ... Next they said 'Well next week we will begin the battle'. A week in advance they talked it over. Next all of the men prepared red pieces of cloth for the night they were going to fight. And then afterward precisely that night at one and two o'clock in the middle of the night, they began to move. There were 101 Japanese on the islet, but 59 Marshallese and Koreans, 400-some, I do not know precisely how many. The Japanese were asleep and they went and entered their house and they began fighting. They shot many of them. Some few of them were manning the cannon, there were seven men and they called to them and got them drunk on coconut toddy. Well then, this was fine with those fellows and so they went ahead and drank and became inebriated, and when they were drunk they killed them. They went into the houses of the Japanese and killed them. The Japanese Tailo, they killed, but you see his cook escaped. They shot him and he was injured but he ran off and dove into the water and swam to Lukonwor, and there he reported, "There are no Japanese. All the soldiers have died, all the Japanese are dead."

Declaring Independence

When the new republics of Indonesia and Vietnam declared their independence in the days and weeks after Japanese defeat, they looked to American rather than Japanese precedents.

Ho Chi Minh's declaration of independence

"All men are created equal. They are endowed by their Creator with certain inalienable rights, among these are Life, Liberty, and the pursuit of Happiness."

This immortal statement was made in the Declaration of Independence of the United States of America in 1776. In a broader sense, this means: All the peoples on the earth are equal from birth, all the peoples have a right to live, to be happy and free.

The Declaration of the French Revolution made in 1791 on the Rights of Man and the Citizen also states: "All men are born free and with equal rights, and must always remain free and have equal rights." Those are undeniable truths.

Nevertheless, for more than eighty years, the French imperialists, abusing the standard of Liberty, Equality, and Fraternity, have violated our Fatherland

and oppressed our fellow-citizens. They have acted contrary to the ideals
of humanity and justice. In the field of politics, they have deprived our people
of every democratic liberty.

They have enforced inhuman laws; they have set up three distinct political
regimes in the North, the Center and the South of Vietnam in order to wreck
our national unity and prevent our people from being united.

They have built more prisons than schools. They have mercilessly slain
our patriots - they have drowned our uprisings in rivers of blood. They have
fettered public opinion; they have practised obscurantism against our people.
To weaken our race they have forced us to use opium and alcohol.

In the fields of economics, they have fleeced us to the backbone, impoverished
our people, and devastated our land.

They have robbed us of our rice fields, our mines, our forests, and our raw
materials. They have monopolised the issuing of bank-notes and the export
trade.

They have invented numerous unjustifiable taxes and reduced our people,
especially our peasantry, to a state of extreme poverty.

They have hampered the prospering of our national bourgeoisie; they have
mercilessly exploited our workers.

In the autumn of 1940, when the Japanese Fascists violated Indochina's
territory to establish new bases in their fight against the Allies, the French
imperialists went down on their bended knees and handed over our country
to them.

Thus, from that date, our people were subjected to the double yoke
of the French and the Japanese. Their sufferings and miseries increased.
The result was that from the end of last year to the beginning of this year,
from Quang Tri province to the North of Vietnam, more than two million
of our fellow-citizens died from starvation. On March 9, the French troops
were disarmed by the Japanese. The French colonialists either fled or surrendered, showing that not only were they incapable of "protecting" us,
but that, in the span of five years, they had twice sold our country to the
Japanese.

On several occasions before March 9, the Vietminh League urged the
French to ally themselves with it against the Japanese. Instead of agreeing to
this proposal, the French colonialists so intensified their terrorist activities
against the Vietminh members that before fleeing they massacred a great
number of our political prisoners detained at Yen Bay and Cao Bang.

Not withstanding all this, our fellow-citizens have always manifested
toward the French a tolerant and humane attitude. Even after the Japanese
putsch of March 1945, the Vietminh League helped many Frenchmen to cross
the frontier, rescued some of them from Japanese jails, and protected French
lives and property.

From the autumn of 1940, our country had in fact ceased to be a French
colony and had become a Japanese possession.

After the Japanese had surrendered to the Allies, our whole people rose to regain our national sovereignty and to found the Democratic Republic of Vietnam.

The truth is that we have wrested our independence from the Japanese and not from the French

The French have fled, the Japanese have capitulated, [and] Emperor Bao Dai has abdicated. Our people have broken the chains which for nearly a century have fettered them and have won independence for the Fatherland. Our people at the same time have overthrown the monarchic regime that has reigned supreme for dozens of centuries. In its place has been established the present Democratic Republic.

For these reasons, we, members of the Provisional Government, representing the whole Vietnamese people, declare that from now on we break off all relations of a colonial character with France; we repeal all the international obligation that France has so far subscribed to on behalf of Vietnam and we abolish all the special rights the French have unlawfully acquired in our Fatherland.

The whole Vietnamese people, animated by a common purpose, are determined to fight to the bitter end against any attempt by the French colonialists to re-conquer their country.

We are convinced that the Allied nations which at Tehran and San Francisco have acknowledged the principles of self-determination and equality of nations, will not refuse to acknowledge the independence of Vietnam.

A people who have courageously opposed French domination for more than eighty years, a people who have fought side by side with the Allies against the Fascists during these last years, such a people must be free and independent.

For these reasons, we, members of the Provisional Government of the Democratic Republic of Vietnam, solemnly declare to the world that Vietnam has the right to be a free and independent country and in fact it is so already. The entire Vietnamese people are determined to mobilise all their physical and mental strength, to sacrifice their lives and property in order to safeguard their independence and liberty.

CHAPTER EIGHT
HOME-FRONT EXPERIENCES

There's a girl behind the man behind the gun. All over this nation, in war plants great and small, in vast factories and modest shops, American girls are meeting the challenges of war by working in war industries.

Katherine Donovan

Throughout the Allied nations, and in Japan, the Pacific War precipitated dramatic social, cultural and economic change. Through a variety of means, ranging from encouragement to coercion, civilians contributed to their nation's war efforts.[1] In the United States, in particular, the resurgent industrial economy provided much of the materiel that enabled Allied forces to overwhelm Japanese forces on the battlefield. But civilians in Australia, New Zealand and other Allied nations which had been at war since September 1939 also made important contributions. With millions of men serving in the military, new sources of labour were required, and although the prevailing culture still suggested women's appropriate place was in the domestic sphere, the exigencies of the war meant that millions of Allied women joined the paid workforce for the first time.

The war also challenged prevailing cultural and social norms in Japan. During the 1930s and 1940s Japanese society presented a sometimes contradictory mixture of traditional and modern values. Since the 1860s Japan had embarked on a successful quest to modernise, and by World War II, had developed a bustling industrial economy, and a military system to match. In other respects, however, Japan remained a deeply traditional society, with a fragile democratic culture that was unable to withstand challenges from the military, which by the 1940s had gained control of the political system. In the wake of the 1937 invasion of China, Japan began to organise its economy on a war footing. The growing demand for labour was met from a variety of sources, including Korea, which had become a formal Japanese colony in 1910: by 1945 about 1.5 million Koreans were working – often in appalling conditions – in Japan. Women were another source of labour, but there was considerable resistance in Japan – far more than in the Allied nations – to the employment of women outside the home. As the tide of war turned against Japan, however, women, and children as young as ten, were employed in ever-greater numbers in factories and in agriculture.

The Japanese economy did not match the prodigious outputs achieved in the United States. With few natural resources, and with the Allied submarine campaign reducing the supply of raw materials, Japan was unable to replace weapons and equipment as quickly as the Allies. In 1943, for example, when Japan lost seven aircraft carriers in battle, only three new carriers were launched. That year the United States had twenty-two carriers under construction. To overcome their economic shortcomings, the Japanese government encouraged *seishin sōdōin* ('spiritual mobilisation').[2] It was hoped that the efforts of the Japanese people would make up for the more practical shortfalls. Japanese citizens worked longer hours, and were increasingly regimented, with more sections of the community mobilised for labour. But in the end, spirit was not enough.

Wartime governments sought to ensure stability and unity at home. Their efforts took a variety of forms, from public appeals designed to maintain morale, and attempts to control the press, to extra-legal efforts to quell dissent, both real and imagined. In Japan, an active network of secret and military police moved quickly, and sometimes brutally, to suppress dissenters. But the Allies, too, compromised civil liberties during the war, and the internment of Japanese-Americans, along with the continuing denial of equality to African-Americans, suggested that wars on behalf of democracy can diminish, rather than extend, civil rights. Significantly, however, as these documents attest, African-Americans and Japanese-Americans continued to believe in the ideal of American democracy.

The war brought hardship to all the nations fighting the Pacific War. However, hardship was not uniform, and whilst there were shortages in the United States, Americans' wartime experiences were very different from those of their Japanese adversaries, or even those of civilians in countries such as Australia and New Zealand, where rationing was more stringent, and lasted longer, than in the United States. Despite legal and social discouragement, black markets existed in all nations. Shortage of goods and services were in many cases merely an inconvenience – and for government propagandists, sometimes even a means of encouraging mass participation in the war effort.

In Japan, the privations of rationing were not the only difficulties. From late 1944 the Japanese home islands became part of the front line. For questionable military gains, the American bombing campaign rained death and destruction on Japan's cities. But even as the bombs fell, and as hundreds of thousands of civilians lost their families and their homes, Japanese civilians – including children – found ways to cope. The United States and Australia were spared most of the horrors that were inflicted on Japan, but when Japanese forces were able to attack the Allied nations directly – such as in May 1942, when Japanese forces launched an attack in Sydney Harbour – the public reacted with predictable fear.

The Pacific War brought serious and lasting consequences for the economies of the major combatants. The expansion in wartime Australia fuelled the establishment of new sectors of the economy that continued to grow in the post-war period. In the United States, the war left a lasting imprint on the American economy and produced what Dwight Eisenhower later labelled the military–industrial complex – a force for good and ill in post-war America. For both countries the war disconnected the economy from the Great Depression and helped produce post-war economic prosperity on a hitherto unseen scale. Not everyone, however, shared this prosperity, producing growing inequality. Ironically, post-war Japan experienced its own 'economic miracle', achieving through the market an international status and influence it had been unable to secure through territorial aggrandisement and war.[3]

THE SOURCES

Civil Liberties in Wartime: Interning Japanese-Americans

In the aftermath of Pearl Harbor, many Americans' suspicions regarding the loyalty of Japanese-Americans coalesced with a deeply entrenched anti-Asian racism, and envy towards Japanese-Americans' economic successes. Particularly on the West Coast, there were popular calls to remove foreign-born Japanese-Americans (*issei* or 'first-generation' Japanese-Americans) as well as the naturalised or native-born citizens of the United States (*nisei*). On 19 February 1942 President Roosevelt issued Executive Order 9066, authorising the removal and internment of Japanese-Americans. Within six months, 112,000 men, women and children were first moved to assembly areas, and then on to remote relocation centres.[4] The treatment of Japanese-Americans in these 'internment camps' contrasted to the generally benign treatment of German-Americans and Italian-Americans.

Japanese internees faced strict censorship regulations. Some internees were arrested after their mail had been read.[5] Moreover, there was pressure to ensure all written communication in the camps – from letters to small newspapers – were written in English.[6] Charles Kikuchi, an American-born internee, kept a diary detailing his experiences at Tanforan, a temporary internment camp in southern California. In the privacy of his diary – no newspaper would publish such an account during the war – Kikuchi described his experiences in the camp, and contemplated the meaning of Japanese-American identity.

April 30, 1942, Berkeley:
Today is the day we are going to get kicked out of Berkeley. It certainly is degrading. I am down in the control station, and there is nothing to do. The Army Lieutenant over there doesn't want any of the photographers to take pictures of these miserable people waiting for the Greyhound bus because he thinks that the American people might get a sympathetic attitude towards them....

I understand we are going to live in horse stalls. I hope that the army has the courtesy to remove the manure first.

This morning I went over to the bank to close my account and the bank teller whom I have never seen before solemnly shook my hand and said, "goodbye, have a nice time." I wonder if that isn't the attitude of the American people? They didn't seem to be bitter against us, and I certainly don't think I am different from them....

May 3, 1942, Sunday:
A lot of Nisei kids come in and mix their Japanese in with their English. Now that we are cut off from the Caucasian contacts, there will be a tendency to

speak more and more Japanese unless we carefully guard against it. Someday these Nisei will once again go out into the greater American society and it is so important that they be able to speak English well – that's why education is so important. I still think it is a mistake to evacuate *all* the Japanese. Segregation is the least desirable thing that could happen and it certainly is going to increase the problems of future social adjustments. How can we expect to develop Americanization when they are all put together with the stigma of disloyalty pointed at them? I am convinced that the Nisei could become good Americans, and will be, if they are not treated with much suspicion. The presence here of all those pro-Japan Issei certainly will not help things out any....

There was a terrific rainstorm last night and we have had to wade through the "slush alleys" again. Everyone sinks up to their ankles in mud. Some trucks came in today with lumber to build new barracks, but the earth was so soft that the trucks sank over the hubs and they had a hell of a time getting it out. The Army certainly is rushing things. ... Now that S.F. [San Francisco] has been almost cleared, the American Legion, the Native Sons of the Golden West, and the California Joint Immigration Committee are filing charges that the Nisei should be disfranchised because we obtained citizenship under false pretenses and that "we are loyal subjects of Japan" and therefore should never have been allowed to obtain citizenship. That sort of thing will gain momentum and we are not in a very advantageous position to combat it. ... I think that they are stabbing us in the back and that there should be a separate concentration camp for these so-called Americans. They are a lot more dangerous than the Japanese in the U.S. ever will or have been....

July 8, 1942:
I keep saying to myself that I must view everything intellectually and rationally, but sometimes I feel sentiments compounded of blind feelings and irra-tionality. Here all of my life I have identified my every act with America but when the war broke out I suddenly find that I won't be allowed to become an integral part of the whole in these times of national danger. I find I am put aside and viewed suspiciously. My set of values gets twisted; I don't know what to think. Yes, an American certainly is a queer thing. I know what I want, I think, yet it looks beyond my reach at times, but I won't accept defeat. Americanism is my only solution and I may even get frantic about it if thwarted....

There are so many interesting people in the camp. They are Americans! Sometimes they may say things that arise out of their bewildered feelings, but they can't throw off the environmental effects of the American way of life which is ingrained in them. The injustices of evacuation will some day come to light. It is a blot upon our national life – like the Negro problem, the way labor gets kicked around, the unequal distribution of wealth, the sad plight of the farmers, the slums of our large cities, and a multitude of things.

Civil Liberties in Wartime: The Japanese Home Front

During the war, a combination of government coercion and persuasion meant few Japanese were prepared to risk open criticism of their government. Those who dared speak out against the government, or who expressed doubt about Japanese victory, risked detainment, imprisonment, torture or even death. It is not surprising, therefore, that relatively few wartime expressions of dissent have survived for historians. After 1945, however, many Japanese citizens recalled the wartime mistreatment they had suffered at the hands of the authorities. Besides their attempts to control political and cultural currents, the authorities also sought to manage economic life. Prior to his death in 1984, Ariyama Sachi described an incident that occurred shortly before the war's end.

A military policeman suddenly came to our house. At that time, under the National General Mobilization Law promulgated during the War, my family had been forced to discontinue our hereditary textile-weaving business and convert to a machine parts factory. We were in the midst of hard times doing unaccustomed work.

After looking over our factory and finding fault with such things as the number of buckets for firefighting purposes and the lack of sandbags, the soldier said he had something to ask my father. He told him to present himself at ten o'clock the following morning at the military police substation....

I ran after him to ask what the summons was for, but he only said we would find out when my father got there. Apparently, on the way back he stopped by a store near our house and asked about our family's reputation.

Father went off the next day to the military police substation. He didn't return even after nightfall. I had a sinister premonition. At about 9P.M., I went alone to the substation. When I gave my reason for being there, the man who had come to the entranceway suddenly yelled at me, "We won't kill him! Go on home!" There was nowhere I could turn.

Father was finally released around midnight. According to him, someone in our neighborhood had informed on him. Father had said that Saipan had fallen to the American forces, so things were serious. He had mentioned this in conversation at a farewell party for a soldier being sent to the front. Someone in the neighborhood had reported this to the military police.

Father was questioned persistently about the source of his information about Saipan. Only after he was forced to give a written explanation was he released. After that our family was constantly under military police observation. These unpleasant days continued until the War's end. I learned from this experience that war tears apart people's hearts and leaves deep scars.

Race Relations in Wartime: African-Americans at War

One of the contradictions of World War II was that whilst the Allies were fighting for democracy, they did not always live up to their lofty rhetoric. In the United States, that contradiction was most starkly shown in the treatment of African-Americans. As they had in America's previous wars, African-Americans volunteered their services to fight for their nation. But they were not welcomed as equals into the armed forces. The individual and institutional racism they encountered in the armed forces reflected a broader pattern of racism within American society. Rapid economic expansion and the relocation of many rural African-Americans to war jobs in predominantly white urban centres, coupled with old prejudices, fueled race riots. There were numerous cases of violence directed against black service personnel stationed in the South, and in the North, a 1943 race riot in Detroit left twenty-five African-Americans and nine whites dead.[7] There were also serious outbreaks of violence in Harlem (New York City) and Columbia, Tennessee, in 1943.[8] One collective black response to such racism and violence was African-Americans' 'Double-V' campaign, designed to highlight the need to fight for freedom at home as well as abroad.

As the following letter suggests, individual African-Americans also fought for their rights. In May 1944, Private Charles F. Wilson wrote directly to President Roosevelt, outlining the injustices experienced by African-American service personnel, and highlighting the contradiction between America's stated war aims and its treatment of its black citizens. Although Roosevelt was a far more 'accessible' president than his predecessors, the fact that individual African-Americans believed that a direct approach to their president was not only possible but might also bring results suggests something about Roosevelt's presidency, as well as the American democratic culture. Individual Japanese soldiers would never have written to their prime minister, or the emperor.

9 May 1944

To: President Franklin D. Roosevelt
White House
Washington, D.C.

[T]he picture in our country is marred by one of the strangest paradoxes in our whole fight against world Fascism. The United States Armed Forces, to fight for World Democracy, is itself undemocratic. The undemocratic policy of Jim Crow and segregation is practiced by our Armed Forces against its Negro members. Totally inadequate opportunities are given to the Negro members of the our Armed Forces, nearly one-tenth of the whole, to participate with "equality" … "regardless of race and color" in the fight of our war aims. In fact it appears that the army intends to follow the very policy the

FEPC [Fair Employment Practices Commission] is battling against in civilian life, the pattern of assigning Negroes to the lowest types of work.

Let me give you an example of the lack of democracy in our Field, where I am now stationed. Negro soldiers are completely segregated from the white soldiers on the base. And to make double sure that no mistakes are made about this, the barracks and other housing facilities (supply room mess hall, etc) of the Negro Section C are covered with black tar paper, while all other barracks and housing facilities on the base are painted white.

It is the stated policy of the Second Air Force that "every potential fighting man must be used as a fighting man. If you have such a man in a base job, you have no choice. His job must be eliminated or filled with a limited service man, WAC, or civilian." And yet, leaving out the Negro soldiers working with the Medical Section, fully 50% of the Negro soldiers are working in base jobs, such as, for example, at the Resident Officers' Mess, Bachelor Officers' Quarters, and Officers' Club, as mess personnel, BOQ orderlies, and bar tenders....

Let us assume as a basis for discussion that there are no civilian or limited service men to do the menial work on the base. The democratic way, based upon "equality and justice" would be to assign work to both Negro and white. Instead, the discriminatory and undemocratic method is used whereby all of this work is assigned to the Negro soldiers....

How can we convince nearly one-tenth of the Armed Forces, the Negro members, that your pronouncement of the war aims of the United Nations means what it says, when their experiences with one of the United Nations, the United States, is just the opposite?...

With your issuance of Executive Order 8802, and the setting up of the Fair Employment Practices Committee, you established the foundation for fighting for democracy in the industrial forces of our country, in the interest of victory for the United Nations. In the interest of victory for the United Nations, another Executive Order is now needed. An Executive Order which will lay the base for fighting for democracy in the Armed Forces of our country. An Executive Order which would bring about the result here at David-Monthan Field whereby the Negro soldiers would be integrated into all of the Sections on the base, as fighting men, instead of in the segregated Section C as housekeepers.

Private Charles F. Wilson, Air Corps

Women's Domestic Labours Assist the War Effort

The realities of 'total war' meant civilians were called upon to work on behalf of the nation's war effort.[9] Women, as well as men, were expected to contribute to victory: significant numbers joined the armed forces, but many more remained 'at home', where their domestic labours were presented as crucial to the war effort. In the following extract, Elsie Curtin – wife of Prime Minister John Curtin of Australia – enjoined women to be frugal. By depicting female labour in the private sphere as analogous to the efforts of men at the front lines, she linked women's domestic responsibilities to notions of patriotism and civic responsibility. These connections, especially common in the Allied nations, challenged traditional assumptions concerning the relationship between masculinity and citizenship.

Prime Minister's Wife Gives Lead to Nation
By Mrs. John Curtin

The Australian housewife would find it hard to imagine herself as a shock trooper, but that is the role she can play in the new army which the government is recruiting.

That new army is the Austerity Army and its job is to wage war on wastage, one of the worst enemies of any nation at war.

How can the housewife practice austerity in the home? In countless ways, and here are some of them:

She can use cheaper cuts of meat and dress them up skilfully so that they taste as well as the more expensive cuts.

She can use mutton and lamb, of which we have plenty, instead of beef and pork which we need for canning for our own and American forces in Australia and for export to our Allies.

She can use fresh fruits, green vegetables and honey, which are plentiful, instead of foods in short supply such as potatoes and rice.

By rigid economy she can make the weekly allowance of butter and sugar go further, thus releasing more butter and sugar to help meet Britain's urgent needs.

She can release labor for war work by refraining from buying processed food....

Above all she can follow the golden rule for austerity shopping – buy only the things you really need and at the time you really need them....

Women at Work in American Industry

Alongside their efforts within the domestic sphere, millions of women in the Allied nations entered the paid workforce for the first time. The following articles, published in Boston newspapers in 1942 and 1943, describe the ways in which women were performing tasks previously regarded as being beyond women's capacities, and link women's physical labours to their patriotic obligations.[10] As well as encouraging patriotism, such articles encouraged more women to participate in the public economy and contribute to the industrial effort to defeat Japan. Many women workers assumed their participation in the public sphere was only temporary, and that when the war ended they would resume the domestic existence that had long been celebrated in western culture. But in moving beyond the domestic sphere, if only temporarily, these women challenged prevailing codes of gender relations. Indeed, for many women, even as their domestic labours were lauded as essential to the nation's war effort, their forays into the public sphere proved to be transformative experiences, as their patriotic obligations alerted them to their own, and other women's, abilities. Only a tiny handful of women workers were self-conscious 'feminists', yet women's entrance into the public sphere empowered them, and was an important precedent for the post-war women's movement.

Bay State Victory Girls Meet the Challenge of War
By Katherine Donovan

There's a girl behind the man behind the gun. All over this nation, in war plants great and small, in vast factories and modest shops, American girls are meeting the challenges of war by working in war industries. There are scores of thousands of these girls in Massachusetts alone, and soon there will be more.

Long hours, intricate precision-demanding labor, arduous jobs requiring physical stamina and mental alertness – to this critical challenge America's girl war workers have responded with heart-warming patriotism.

They're an inspiring group – a smiling, workmanlike, competent, responsible group of young women, keenly aware of the value of their contribution to victory and freedom, rightly proud of their status as the "home fronters," replacing and releasing men for the fighting services.

It was the poet Virgil who sang of "arms and the man." Today it is equally "arms and the woman." For the making and manufacture of armaments, as never before in our history, is today a woman's job.

They are of all ages, of all classes, of all degrees of training and education. They are the wives and sweethearts and sisters, the mothers and even the grandmothers of men in the armed forces.

These women are pledged to the vital task of seeing to it that those they love get what they need for victory – the guns and the tanks, the planes and the ships, the shells and the bullets.

As President Roosevelt has pointed out, there isn't a single article of war going to American servicemen and their Allies in the production of which women have not had a share.

For it is the women – young and old, wealthy and poor – who make all the difference between success and failure in meeting the supply needs of America's fighting men and those of the United Nations.

These women have a name for themselves. They're the WOWS – the Women Ordnance Workers' Service. And they're all out to "wow" the Axis.

They are working side by side in a stimulating freemasonry of those pledged to a common cause – girls with college degrees, youngsters fresh out of high school, trained technicians, debutantes and girls from humble homes, professional women and unskilled but earnest recruits....

Only a year ago, when it was first suggested that women be used on men's jobs, many an employer viewed with alarm, or laughed heartily and ignored the suggestion....

But with the expansion of industry and the increasing shortage in manpower, employers had no alternative but to call upon women. Skeptical at first, their attitude rapidly developed into one of amazed admiration....

Girls Man Huge Cranes
30 per cent of Arsenal Workers are Women
By Carl De Leuw

The answer to the current problem of women replacing men in essential war plants has definitely been given at the Watertown arsenal, where girls now comprise 30 per cent. of the workers.

Not only are women replacing men by the hundreds at this plant, but officials have found they are capable of doing the job as well as, if not better than, the men they are replacing.

On a specially conducted all-day tour of the arsenal, under the direction of army ordnance officers, New England newspapermen saw for themselves that women are capable of operating the intricate and precision machinery of an up-to-date war plant.

More than 1200 men have been released for active military service, and several hundred more will be released and replaced by women during the next year, due to an extensive training program started at the arsenal more than 18 months ago.

Mere wisps of girls are operating huge 10-ton hoisting cranes, and using all types of machinery and tools. They are even working on the melting platforms in the foundry, helping to cast 5000-pound gun tubes....

Encountering the Home Front: Americans in Australia and New Zealand

During the Pacific War, millions of service personnel found themselves stationed in, or visiting, foreign nations.[11] For many of these men and women, who had barely travelled from their home towns and cities, the war provided them with opportunities to experience other peoples and other cultures first-hand. To assist with this process the American government produced a number of 'pocket guides' – in effect, tourist guides – for their service personnel. Scores of these booklets were published by the Special Service Division of the US Army. One such guide, prepared for servicemen and women dispatched to Australia, included advice on negotiating the Australian accent and idiom.

It's the Same Language Too.

We all speak the language – the British, the Australians, and us – our versions of it. Probably the only difficulty you'll run into here is the habit Australians have of pronouncing "a" as "i" – for instance, "the trine is lite todi". Some people say it sounds like the way London cockneys talk, but good Australians resent that – and it isn't true anyway.

Thanks to our movies, the average Australian has some working knowledge of our slang, but it'll take you a while to get on to theirs. To them a "right guy" is a "fair dinkum"; a hard worker is a "grafter" and "to feel crook" means to feel lousy; while "beaut" means swell. Australian slang is so colorful, and confusing, that a whole chapter is devoted to it at the end of this book.

Also, the Australian has few equals in the world at swearing except maybe the famous American mule skinner in World War I. The commonest swear words are bastard (pronounced "Barstud"), "bugger," and "bloody," and the Australians have a genius for using the latter....

Australian Songs and Singing.

Australians, like Russians, are natural group singers. It's one of the great differences you'll notice between American camps and Australian – the singing.

Aussie soldiers and girls know every American popular song from Stephen Foster's My Old Kentucky Home to the latest tune of a year or so ago. The very latest jive may confuse them a bit, but they're catching on after listening to American regimental swing bands. The hit song in Australia today is Bless Them All, which has become almost a national epidemic – the Aussies sing it with curious variations from the original lyrics....

A standard favorite all over the country is Australia's own folk song, Waltzing Matilda. In fact the Aussies have made it a classic all over the world. When the Anzac troops made their first assault on Bardia, they did it to the tune of Waltzing Matilda [actually the tune was the Wizard of Oz]. ... The swagman (hobo) of the song represents the common man struggling against the oppressive exploiter. He prefers death to slavery and it is this defiant attitude which the Aussies hold dear....

"Cobbers"

There isn't any need for a lot of do's and don'ts for Americans in Australia. Common sense and good will go a long way there as they do everywhere else. As a matter of fact, the Australians, especially the girls, are a bit amazed at the politeness of American soldiers. And they say that when an American gets on a friendly footing with an Australian family he's usually found in the kitchen, teaching the Mrs. how to make coffee, or washing the dishes.

American troops have been welcomed in Australia with a good deal of warmth and a feeling of close kinship. The feeling that we and the Australians are "cobbers" means a fast finish for Mr. Jap.

Official guidebooks presented foreign cultures and peoples as fascinating subjects to be encountered. But many servicemen's encounters with other peoples reflected less anthropological priorities, with the result that fraternal feelings were sometimes frayed. It was suggested there were only three problems with Americans in Australia: they were 'over-sexed, over-paid and over-here'. Similar sentiments were evident in New Zealand, which also became an important base for American forces.[12]

Partly to avoid such misunderstandings, and partly to entertain and inform their service personnel, US military authorities published papers such as *Stars and Stripes* and *Yank: The Army Weekly*. Pitched as the 'authentic voice' of the GI, *Yank* became the world's first 'global periodical'.[13] To cater to specific theatres, specialised editions were published. In the Pacific a dedicated edition titled *Yank Downunder* was published.[14] While the paper's byline was 'By the men for the men in the service', *Yank* actually had a large staff of dedicated journalists. One such reporter in uniform was Mack Morriss. Having covered the war in Guadalcanal, in February 1943 Morriss secured leave in New Zealand. Whilst *Yank* would become famous for the 'glamour girl pin-ups' contained in its issues, Morriss' diary entries demonstrate that a photograph of Betty Grable or some other Hollywood starlet only went so far. The cities of the Antipodes offered romantic or carnal distractions from the horrors of war.[15] As his diary records, Morriss and his friend 'Brodie' sampled some of what wartime Auckland had to offer; he did not share these encounters with the readers of *Yank*.

20 February
This is the Army's liberty town and nobody bothers to make anything else out of it. When we came in yesterday we were given a long official song and dance on what we could and couldn't do, but it didn't mean a thing. We reported in at Victoria Park and were told that we could stay at a hotel if we liked. ... So we registered at the Royal – all we have to do is report to the top sergeant at Victoria every morning before 11:00. Our first night passed with only a mild drunk – very mild. Ran into Dowling – he gave us gin and scotch. We couldn't seem to really get started, even with gin and beer by the gallon. It was wonderful to sit down to a meal – a real honest meal – with chinaware and silver. Oh boy!

21 February
I am writing on my bed – clean white sheets – at 12:15 a.m. This has been the damnedest day I have spent in months. I am so full of solid food I'm almost popping – what a place this joint is....
Brodie and I were in the lounge when we spotted two wenches giving us the eye. We invited them to lunch. After eating they took us to their apartment. We had already drunk until our teeth floated, altho' we never did

get drunk, but we drank more and pawed around awhile. The babe I had was married and she expected her husband, so Brodie made a date with her friend for 8:00 and I was to come back this morning. So we came back to the hotel, Brodie and I ate, and lay down. Naturally, we slept through Brodie's date – oh boy, was he burned up. I was supposed to wake him – ha. Anyway this morning we went around. To make a bad story short, we got it. I have never seen anything like these women – my God, what animals. I'll believe anything. Not to go into the gory details – I probably established a world record for fast work … me and the rabbits. Four months layoff does things. I was not, shall we say, exactly pleased with mine – she was as evil minded a bitch as I ever saw – both of them – they had sex books of the dime variety all over the house. For pure carnal knowledge, which was all we had in mind, they were all right, but I couldn't stand a steady diet of that stuff. Phew!

This day has been one of meals – we eat like kings. New Zealanders are meat lovers and that's down my alley – steak and eggs, fillet, pork – anything. I'm stuffed – and on top of that there's the beer.…

The War Comes Home: Sydney Under Attack

The speed of the Japanese advance through Southeast Asia and the Pacific caused widespread alarm in Australia. With some of the nation's best troops far away in the Middle East, and with the arrival of significant American forces still some months away, the early months of 1942 were anxious ones for Australians. In February 1942, Japanese aircraft bombed Darwin, and over succeeding months, Japanese naval and air forces launched a number of attacks on Australia. Despite government censorship of many of the details of these raids, Australians believed their nation was vulnerable to Japanese forces. Those fears were exacerbated when three Japanese midget submarines attacked Allied ships inside Sydney Harbour on the evening of 31 May 1942. Whilst the raid was not a prelude to a Japanese invasion, as many people feared (rather, it was part of Admiral Yamamoto's strategy to divert Allied attention from the looming clash at Midway), it did cause near panic up and down the east coast. The Japanese submarines did not sink their main target, the American heavy cruiser *Chicago*, but they did sink the *Kuttabul*, a ferry being used as a dormitory ship by the Australian Navy. Twenty-one sailors died.[16] Two of the Japanese submarines were sunk in Sydney Harbour, and wreckage of the third was found off Sydney's northern beaches in 2006. The account reprinted below, published in the Melbourne *Age* in the aftermath of the attack, captured the drama and apprehension associated with the attack.

GUNFIRE SHAKES SYDNEY: GRAPHIC STORIES OF THE RAID

SYDNEY, Monday: For the first time in its history, Sydney actually had war on its front door step last night. The harbour and city were shaken time and again by the explosions of depth charges and gunfire from light calibre units ashore and afloat. Searchlights swept the harbour, and then there was another burst of gunfire from the heavier guns. The thunder of guns rolled over the harbour, across the city, and out into the suburbs. Graphic stories were told by eye-witnesses who were out on the harbour at the time.

One passenger who was on a ferry vessel crossing the harbour about 11 p.m. said: "We were making our way across the harbour, when all of a sudden we heard two shots from a nearby gun. The sound was deafening, but we have heard so much practice gun firing around Sydney of late that most of us did not take any notice of it. Almost immediately afterwards the harbour was lit up by the sudden sweep of innumerable searchlights. They seemed to be everywhere, turning the darkness of the harbour into bright light. We knew then that something was doing.

"A little while later we heard the sharp crackle of pom-pom guns, and then a terrific explosion, as shells were fired from heavier guns. Tracer bullets flew across the water. We saw in the distance the periscope and upper portion of the conning tower of a submarine. It was sticking out of the water in front of us and right in the glare of the concentrated searchlight rays. They followed it as it moved along, and the tracer bullets kept flying in its direction.

"Our ferry slackened speed, and we swung away with the current, so as to keep out of the way of gunfire. The guns kept on blazing, but we did not actually see the submarine hit. The mere sight of it gliding through the water in the night gave us a nasty turn. It seemed incredible that it was actually a Japanese submarine right here in our own home waters in Sydney. But the way those guns kept roaring and the play of the searchlights across the water left no doubt in our minds that this was the real thing. It was very ugly while it lasted."

Obviously, they [the submariners] hoped to move into the harbour under cover of darkness, as at Pearl Harbour, to do as much damage as possible in a quick, daring raid, and relying upon the element of surprise and the darkness to assist them to make a getaway.

Children's War

Children have always been affected by war. But the 'total' nature of the Pacific War meant that to a greater extent than ever before, children were exposed to the suffering associated with war. Notwithstanding the terror and misery of the war, however, Japanese children – who suffered far greater deprivation and trauma than their Allied counterparts – found ways of coping with, and sometimes even enjoying, their wartime experiences. As the Allies advanced towards the Japanese homeland, Satō Hideo was one of the several hundred thousand children evacuated from the cities to the relative safety of the countryside. Although Satō's memories of the war were recorded long after the conflict, they reveal much about the impact of the war on Japanese children.

A Japanese Evacuee's Wartime Experiences

From the end of my fourth grade, from 1943, I began to hear the word "evacuation." My whole home was going to move, and even to my child's mind, this gave rise to uneasy feelings. One day three or four large trucks came and began loading up our household belongings. Mother was told she must arrange all our things into boxes they gave her, and just like that, acting in great haste, we left Tokyo for Shinozuma in Ibaraki prefecture. The last day of our school classes in March, I was forced to bid farewell. Everyone said, "Satō will be evacuating." Only three out of fifty of us left at that time, so I felt exceptionally lonely. All my other classmates were evacuated later to Nagano.

The thing that struck me most about my time at Ibaraki was the bullying we evacuated children faced. I was persecuted thoroughly. My whole fifth year at elementary school was spent that way. We didn't have any relatives there. We were total strangers with no connections to use to get extra food. My lunch was full of barely and other rice substitutes. The kids sitting next to me brought "silver rice" – pure white, shining rice. They were from farming families....

Month by month, the number of evacuees from Tokyo increased. ... The year of the defeat, 1945, I was a sixth-grader. We no longer had many classes at school. The main thing we did was dig an antitank ditch in the corner of the schoolyard. "Dig a hole," they told us sixth-graders. The older children were no longer around. From April 1945 on, everyone above us was mobilized daily for work in war plants, while we spent days building "octopus holes." That was terrible work for an elementary-school lad. It took three days to hollow out a single foxhole deep enough so that when the teacher jumped in, it would be over his head....

Children can easily adjust to war. It almost becomes a sport. It's just an extension of naughty games they all play anyway. You would put your courage to the test. On hearing the planes banking, you'd see how long you could go without flinching. How brave could you be?

The army built an airfield near our school in the fall of 1944. Even my mother went there for volunteer mobilization work and dug bunkers to conceal military planes. We, too, were called in to carry the soil used to cover them over....

From March 1945 on, we experienced air-raid warnings and actual raids every day. ... They came about an hour after sunrise. ... We came to feel strongly that the Japanese military was not protecting us, that they thought only about themselves....

Throughout the war years ... the Emperor remained special. Our image of the Emperor never flickered. ... Whenever I saw a picture of the Emperor riding his white horse, I gushed, "How wonderful!"...

The defeat wasn't such a grave thing to us sixth-graders. The idea that I wouldn't be strafed any more was a relief. Until then, the Americans had been a nation of demons. I really mean that. I liked drawing, so I often drew caricatures of Churchill, Roosevelt, and others, copying them from newspapers. Our teachers told us that Americans were monsters and lowly creatures....

I was born in war. It was always around. But war is fun. Boys like war. War can become the material for play. ... I loved playing war.

When the war ended, we just turned around, almost without noticing it. Overnight. I experienced no real inner conflict. ... I never felt any humiliation, as some said they did....

Life Under the Bombs: Japanese Experiences

Appropriately, historians have emphasised the impact of the atomic weapons used against Hiroshima and Nagasaki in August 1945. Such an emphasis, however, can obscure the fact that from mid-1944, the United States waged a relentless bombing campaign against Japanese cities. Japanese propaganda had claimed the nation's air-defence system would prevent large-scale American bombing, and there had been some relocation of civilians and industries to rural and remote areas. But Japan's cities, with their wooden houses and poor civil defence, were vulnerable to incendiary bombs, and the American bombing campaign devastated dozens of cities and towns and killed hundreds of thousands of civilians. Partly because the Japanese had launched the war with their surprise attack at Pearl Harbor, partly because Allied propaganda had dehumanised and demonised the Japanese, and partly because information was emerging about the brutal way in which the Japanese were prosecuting the war, there was little concern amongst the Allies for the suffering endured by Japanese victims of Allied bombing.

The words that follow were written to accompany the drawings and paintings collected by the Sumida Ward Museum in central Tokyo for the sixtieth anniversary of the firebombing of Tokyo (10 March 1945). The authors of these lines and of these paintings are the now-ageing survivors of the bombings. For many, the drawing of an image – particularly the awful images so vividly etched in their minds sixty years ago – was a necessary prelude to describing the memory in words. Even in their brevity, these words paint vivid pictures of the horrors and the suffering endured by Japanese victims of the American bombing campaign. Memory can be an unreliable source for historians, but these extracts make it unambiguously clear that the Japanese, too, experienced 'total war'.

A picture by Itō Mitsuo (11 years old at the time) titled: *Orphan siblings, running away across the mountains from their evacuation house.*

During the war, we lived in Kikukawa in Honjō ward (previously Sumida Ward).[17] In 1944, I was evacuated to Chiba prefecture, together with younger sister and brother. My father, mother, my older brother and my littlest baby sister died – in order words, the entire family that had remained in Tokyo – died in the bombing of 10 March. We never found their bodies, so they have been "missing" since that time.

In May that year, we were moved from my mother's ancestral home to my father's ancestral home in the mountain village of Nagaoka in Niigata Prefecture. However, life was hard there too, and we were moved once more to a relative's place in the next village. I was really worried that we were going to be moved once more, so after thinking about it overnight I decided to run away with my brother and sister. The pictures (painted for the exhibition) show us running away to the mountains. Underneath, is a picture of us crying thinking about our parents when we stopped to drink water from a spring near the mountain top. In the 70 years of my life, this was the hardest experience. After the war, we were separated and sent to live with different relatives.

A picture by Kobayashi Hiroshi (16 years old at the time) titled: *a man, fallen, hit by an incendiary.*

At the time of the bombing, I lived with my family – dad, mum and my older brother, in Kotobukicho, Sumida Ward. On the dawn of the 10th, incendiary bombs fell two houses away from ours. Dad put a wet towel in my hands, saying 'you run away first', so I escaped by myself. My painting represents a scene I witnessed in front of the gate of the Kaya temple, in Kuramae 3 district, Asakusa ward, near Umaya bridge. I've painted the gate on the top left of the picture. In front of the gate there was a man bleeding from the side, he'd been hit directly by an incendiary. Next to him was a woman who was staring at the fallen man. However, the people who were walking past didn't even look at these people, they were thinking only of escape. Nearby there were some futons that someone had left while running away. An incendiary had fallen on them and they were burning.

A picture by Miyahara Tachirō (18 years old at the time) titled: *the town I saw from the air after the great firebombing*

In the last week of March 1945, I was given orders to transfer from the second training battalion of the Army Flying corps in Korea to the 18th Battalion at Kashiwa city in Chiba, and arrived for air defence duties in the Kantō (eastern Japan) area. Before and after our transfer, there had been no let-up in the American bombardments, and with many planes destroyed in sorties and no production of new planes, there were fewer operational machines. At that point, even if we sent twenty planes up, they'd face several hundred American large bombers and accompanying fighters, so it could hardly be called 'combat' as such.

Around that time, I was flying over the area around downtown Tokyo (today Sumida and Kōtō) everyday. It was a completely flattened surface, light brown with bits of white, exactly like the ashes of a fire, a plain with just a few burnt-out shells of concrete buildings. It was the same story for the other cities hit by the bombing, Chiba, Kōfu....

At that time, as a young soldier, I didn't think much about the fact that throughout Japan untold thousands had been burnt to death in these bombings. But I can still even now recall with absolute clarity those burnt-out plains.

Sustaining Love: Advice on How to Write to Servicemen

Margaretta Jolly has suggested that in the history of literacy, World War II 'must count as an ironically progressive moment'.[18] Millions of people were forced to sustain their relationships with nothing more than pen, paper and the written word. Consequently, letter writing was popularised across all social classes. As noted, letters are of enormous value for historians of the Pacific War. But beside the aforementioned historiographical issues, there is another significant practical issue for historians utilising wartime letters: the vast majority that survive were written *by* service personnel and not by their family and friends at home. Service personnel had few opportunities to keep their letters for sustained periods and so very few collections document both sides of a correspondence.

Military and government authorities knew that letters to service personnel were vital to the maintenance of morale. Campaigns encouraged civilians to write to service personnel. In some cases programmes were established whereby individuals were encouraged to write a letter that would be randomly sent to a soldier, sailor or airman serving overseas. In Japan this correspondence became known as 'comfort letters' and were usually written by young women. Women, especially, were advised what they should include in their letters. This had less to do with military censorship than with maintaining morale. Soldiers' morale, for instance, would be damaged after receiving a 'Dear John' letter where a sweetheart informed the servicemen that she was ending the relationship.

In 1942 Ethel Gorham wrote *So Your Husband's Gone to War!*, an advice manual for the wives of American service personnel. Along with information on a myriad of subjects, letter writing was covered in some detail. Gorham described how the *process* of writing as the only form of communication between a couple changed both the relationship and the individual.

How long since you have written a real letter, a letter that told what you were doing, what you were thinking, what the world around you was like?

[N]ow it is one more thing you must learn to do. It is one more thing you want to do. For it is the only way you can keep in touch with your husband and let him know what you are doing and thinking. It is for most of you your only constant means of communications these days, and it has to be cherished and nourished like another sense that needs developing when the senses of sight and smell have gone.

The fuller and stronger you make this new written bond between you, the closer your relationship will grow. So ripe and healthy can this become that soon you begin to think of your husband in terms of it. It was the most curious sensation after three weeks of steady letter writing to have my husband suddenly telephone one afternoon. I had been thinking of him in terms of letters. I knew his mood on this page and his humor on that page and the manoeuvres they were going through in the letter [of the] day before yesterday. His written word had become as familiar as the touch of his hand in other days....

Other senses get jarred as this new written sense develops. For instance, the whole feeling for time differs. You are answering today a letter written perhaps one day or one week or one month before, and what you say about yourself and your child and the people around you won't reach your husband for that length of time again.

So accustomed as you are to the immediacy of reaction over a telephone or across telegraph wires that it takes adjustment to get used to the delayed reaction time of letter writing....

One of the best rules to remember, if you want to spare yourself the unhappiness of wishing you hadn't sent yesterday's letter is to leave out all personal upheavals. ... Why mention it? Are you feeling lonely and upset and vaguely suicidal? Don't put it into written words unless you're prepared to jump out the window and this is your last message on it all....

Letters should be as warm and intimate as you yourself have been with the man to whom you are writing.

Incidentally, if he is not your husband, you know what he is. Friend, companion, the boy next door. Treat him as such in your letters, and don't be afraid of the effect. This is no time for coy girlish reticence. If everybody misses him, say so. If you miss him, say so, too. You may never have another chance.

After a while, as you concentrate on this business of letter writing, you will find yourself developing a personality that is completely dependent on the written word.

CHAPTER NINE
PRISONER-OF-WAR EXPERIENCES

All of this was like an unreal horrible nightmare.
Sergeant Gene S. Jacobsen recalls the Bataan Death March

For the Allies, one of the most horrific aspects of the Pacific War was the Japanese treatment of prisoners of war (POWs). Forced labour, starvation, untreated disease and unjustifiable brutality and torture resulted in unimaginably high death rates. The rights of POWs and the rules governing their treatment had been codified in the 1929 Geneva Convention; the Allies generally abided by these rules and expected the opposing side to reciprocate. The Japanese failure to treat prisoners humanely was seen, then and now, as an unjust and unforgivable aspect of the war.

For both former Allied and Japanese POWs, the experience of imprisonment has remained a vexed question, albeit for vastly different reasons. The Allied survivors of Japan's prison camps have had to deal with long-term mental and physical ailments that were long unrecognised by their own governments and societies, and by the Japanese government, which has refused to consider compensation for the forced labour and the hardships suffered by Allied POWs. Furthermore, while some POWs have found it difficult to recount what were immensely traumatic experiences, others feel that, despite their attempts to share their experiences at home, there was for many years little interest in their stories. Being a POW was, after all, hardly the kind of glorious martial masculine experience of combat that was routinely associated with war.[1] For the lucky ones, POW life was full of boredom and petty routines; for the unlucky ones, it was a life of hard labour, illness, brutality, starvation and, for a great percentage of them, miserable death.

Many Allied POWs managed in retrospect to find positive aspects of their experience in the strong bonds they forged with comrades, in the daily acts of sabotage performed against Japan (even if such acts consisted only of collecting bedbugs and other insects and carefully releasing them in the huts of the prison guards) and in the humour and hope that helped them survive their incarceration.[2] Yet the unprecedented death rate of prisoners in Japanese hands, and the cruelty and mistreatment meted out by their Japanese captors, was one of the most repugnant experiences of the Pacific War. As these sources show, whether the POWs were on the Burma–Thailand Railway, in the Philippines, or in Borneo, in the 'hellships' that transported them to Japan or indeed in Japan itself, the constants were exhaustion, violence and cruelty, starvation, disease and death.

The reported numbers of Allied POWs vary wildly, depending on whether colonial Allied soldiers (Indian, Indonesian, Filipino) and Allied Chinese Nationalist soldiers are included, and on whether a clear distinction can be made between military prisoners and civilian internees. Some of these questions are intensely political. (For example, Filipino soldiers of the American Army taken prisoner by the Japanese after Bataan have not been accorded the same recognition as American

soldiers captured at the same time.) Most authors agree on a figure
of 140,000 to 200,000 for Allied POWs, of whom at least 30,000 died
in captivity. The death rates in particular areas were much higher: on the
Burma–Thailand Railway, one in three prisoners did not survive.

The experiences of Japanese POWs were very different. Despite their
captors' often undisguised hatred of the enemy, Japanese prisoners were
well treated, well fed and generally free of forced labour duties. For them,
the problem was not the physical environment of the prison camp but
what had come before, and what they thought would come after. Unlike
the Allied armies, for whom surrendering was not, in theory at least,
a shameful act of cowardice, the Japanese armed forces explicitly forbade
surrender. Japanese soldiers were expected to fight to the death. Recruits
were told that this was a proud Japanese tradition, even though the links
with the *Bushidō*, the code of the former warrior caste, had clearly been
reinvented in the lead-up to the war. By 1941, the soldier's manual made
it explicit that becoming a POW was a source of great shame. Certainly,
only a tiny proportion of Japanese soldiers surrendered: the death-to-
captured ratio of the Japanese army could be as high as 175/1, compared
to Allied standards of 1/4, even taking into account that in the harshest
battlefields, neither side was taking prisoners.[3] But lofty ideals were not
always the sole reason for the small surrender rate of Japanese soldiers:
fear of being accused and executed as deserters by their own side, of
torture and slow death in enemy hands and of retribution in the long
term for them and their family, all conspired to make so-called 'Banzai
charges' or suicidal last-ditch stands more common than surrender
amongst Japanese soldiers. Those who did become prisoners were
sometimes plagued by feelings of shame and self-loathing, but more
frequently by the desperate thought that they would never see their
homeland and their families again. Even after Japan's unconditional
surrender and their repatriation, many ex-prisoners continued to feel the
stigma of their own untimely surrender, and sometimes hid even from
their closest friends the fact that they had survived the war as prisoners
of the Allies.

It is not surprising, therefore, that precise figures on the number
of Japanese POWs are elusive. This is partly because the Japanese
government routinely listed as dead – whether they were indeed dead
or had surrendered – those who were no longer part of their fighting unit.
It is also partly because so many Japanese prisoners gave false names
during their incarceration, or tried to 'pass' as a 'normal' demobilised
soldier (for example, one who had surrendered after 15 August 1945).
Ulrich Strauss has counted 38,666 Japanese POWs in American and
Commonwealth forces' hands at the end of the war; Yamamoto Taketoshi
has counted about 208,000, including the prisoners of Chinese Nationalist
or Communist Armies and the Soviet Union. Both researchers agree the

Japanese army had a tiny ratio of captured to dead compared to Allied armies (excluding the Soviet Union).[4] Prisoners in Allied hands were held at a number of locations in the United States, Australia, New Zealand and New Guinea. While Japanese prisoners were generally well behaved, there were a number of outbreaks of violence amongst Japanese POWs, the greatest and most famous of which was the so-called 'Cowra Breakout' in Australia. On 5 August 1944, 400 out of 2,233 inmates stormed the camp's perimeter outside the little town of Cowra, New South Wales: 234 prisoners and 4 Australian soldiers were killed. Most researchers agree that, rather than a serious attempt to escape, the breakout reflected a desire to die an honourable death.

The Japanese military notion that surrender was shameful helped explain – as distinct from justify – the abysmal treatment of Allied POWs. But there are other factors to consider, including a pervasive culture of violence in the lower ranks of the Japanese military. From the moment they entered the barracks recruits were routinely abused verbally and physically by their superiors. This violence extended down the hierarchical ladder to the Allied POWs. But the most important factor was undoubtedly the haphazard and improvised nature of the Japanese invasion and occupation of Southeast Asia and the Pacific. The administration of occupied territories (and of prison camps) was not centrally coordinated, and was often left to local military commanders whose principal concerns were the defence of the area and providing food for their troops amidst dwindling supplies from the homeland. Civilians in occupied areas found their own food and supplies indiscriminately and often violently requisitioned by Japanese troops for their own use; again, this left Allied POWs at the very bottom of the supply ladder. Allied POWs were thus victims of a poorly planned war as well as of the Japanese Army's own culture. This is also true for those POWs who survived transportation to Japan and worked on the mainland itself: the dwindling supply of food (expected even by the planners of the war) translated at the local level into exhortations to produce ever more with ever less. It led to malnutrition, illness, over-exertion and violence amongst the Allied POWs and the Chinese and Korean forced labourers with whom they worked.

The experiences of Allied and Japanese prisoners were thus very different. In the end, there is probably only one thing they had in common: the lack of communication with the outside world and their families. Told that their son, husband or brother was dead, families of thousands of Japanese POWs grieved their loss, only to experience shock and delight at their unexpected return after the war's end. For the families of Allied POWs, there were fewer certainties. In most camps there was no communication with the outside world, and Red Cross parcels rarely reached their intended recipients. Furthermore, it was only when camps were liberated towards the end of the war that their atrocious conditions became widely known. The hopeful thought that someone was safe because they were no longer at the front line was dramatically shattered once it became clear that no assurances could be made about the return of a loved one from a Japanese prison camp.

The excerpts below provide samples of the literature on the POW experience. These excerpts have been chosen for the way in which they portray different experiences of the POWs. The imbalance in the quantity of text on Allied and Japanese POWs reflects the imbalance in wartime numbers of respective POWs, as well as the greater diversity in Allied experiences.

THE SOURCES

An Allied Prisoner in Singapore

Hugh Clarke was captured in Singapore and survived incarceration in Thailand and transportation to Nagasaki. The introduction to his book contains a remarkably succinct explanation of the 'choices' available to Allied POWs.

Being a prisoner of war of the Japanese was to become an involuntary subscriber to an extraordinary lottery. You could remain hungry and bored in Changi, but relatively undisturbed by the Japanese captors; you could work on the wharves and food dumps and grow fat, if prepared to risk the inevitable bashings or worse if caught scrounging; you could journey to Japan in the early years of the war (Allied submarines permitting) and live in conditions not much worse than a Japanese miner or factory worker; or you could crack the bad-luck jackpot and end up on the railway. There were other prizes too, some better and others far worse – like Sandakan in Borneo were only six men out of 2500 survived a death march; or the sea voyages to Japan taken by survivors of the Burma-Thailand railway and others in 1944 when more ships were sunk by American submarines than arrived; or in the case of one group of prisoners which, after surviving a sinking, experienced first-hand the atomic bombing of Nagasaki.

The Ordeal of the Bataan Death March

One such 'bad-luck jackpot' befell those American and Filipino soldiers captured on Bataan in the Philippines and forcibly marched to prison camps and transport ships. Army Sergeant Gene S. Jacobsen was one of those.

During the entire march, the Japanese changed their guards at regular intervals, keeping fresh troops to watch us at all times. These well-fed men badgered us constantly insisting that we move along rapidly, yet constantly making it difficult for us to walk at all. Crowded together as we were and in our poor physical condition, it was almost humanly impossible to keep up the pace they demanded. The thing that kept most of us going then was our hatred for our captors and the feeling of assurance that the Yanks and tanks would arrive shortly and avenge this terrible wrong.

As we continued our march off Bataan, our numbers daily grew fewer as those too sick or weary could not go farther. Dysentery and malaria, not new diseases to us on Bataan, had been reasonably well controlled, but now they began to take their toll in large numbers. While we were on Bataan, the medics furnished quinine pills, but now on our own and without preventive medicine, the malaria-carrying mosquito was able to effectively take its toll.

At the time of surrender, one of the medics assigned to our squadron had given me a tiny aluminium can in which he had placed fifteen five-grain quinine pills.

"Don't let these get away from you," he warned strongly, "and don't use them until it is absolutely necessary for you to do so".

As the days passed, I saw many sick with malaria, but none of my close friends, so I continued to heed the counsel the medic had so forcefully given me. Each time we were searched by the Japanese, I placed the small can in the top of my shoe and removed it only when I was sure that it would be safe in the pocket of my sweat-caked overalls.

Water and sugarcane were two items over which there was a constant contest between us and the Japanese guards. The rules seemed to be that we could have both if we were willing to take the chance of being bayoneted or shot or severely beaten, if caught. However, if we could get water or cane and get back into ranks before a guard could get to us, we seemed to be safe for the moment. The guards were always on the alert and taunted us with fixed bayonets, daring us to make attempts for water or food.

In spite of the threat of death, or worse, some men gambled and won. Those who did get stalks of the cane found that while the juice did help to sustain them and give them energy, their mouths quickly became raw from chewing on the coarse cane fibers.

Because all of this was like an unreal horrible nightmare, it was difficult for us to keep track of the days. No one cared about the time of day. Our thoughts were constantly on food and water and hatred for the Japanese. There was little conversation among the men, each saving his strength to carry him through the ordeal. Adding to the depression was the gnawing fear that Japanese might execute all of us. We had ample evidence they were capable of doing just that.

Surviving the Horrors of Sandakan

Charlie Johnstone, an Australian serving in the British Royal Air Force, was incarcerated in Sandakan (Borneo), but removed to Kuching with other officers before the Sandakan death march. His diary depicts the ways in which those who forced to work as slave labourers tried to maintain their spirits despite their increasingly weakened physical state during 1944.

Ever since we had been in Kuching we had endeavoured to keep our minds active and be mentally alert. Being confined to the camp most of the time was monotonous and uninteresting. We had talks and lectures on all sorts of subjects, word-finding games, played cards and so on. If it was noticed anyone was becoming morbid or withdrawn some effort was made to get them out of their condition. These activities continued until we were released and I am sure helped us both physically and mentally. In most camps I was in, and where the officers were held with the men, efforts were made by the officers to sustain the morale of the men.

[Since I was an] Australian serving with the British forces some of my fellows showed interest in learning about Australia. I gave lectures on Australia and its people; sheep shearing and wool sorting at the sheds; the automobile business; and tractor and farm implements in Australia. Such talks sparked off debate, which lasted for some weeks keeping our minds active. It took our minds off our predicament. All servicemen leaving Australia were given a booklet full of information and statistics on our country. I had been out west with shearing teams for two years in my younger days. Most of my time was spend in the automobile and tractor business, so I knew what I was talking about.

Illness was with us all the time. The most prevalent were dysentery and beri-beri, followed by leg ulcers, skin complains, vitamin deficiency, malaria and undiagnosed complaints. Starvation and malnutrition was now just a common, ordinary condition. At this juncture we were having a very serious outbreak of dysentery in our camp. The only cure was to eat nothing for three days then take a good dose of Epsom salts, which was the only medicine we could acquire from the Japanese. It was a case of kill or cure. Most people in the camp suffered from the complaint. It overloaded our toilet facilities, which consisted of two wooden seats over removable buckets inside a small attap hut. We were compelled to use a sandy patch of ground about 70 yards from our hut along a path soon known as the 'speed track': and it was. We would dash from the hut to the sand patch grabbing tree leaves on the way, quickly scratch a hole and squat down. Afterwards we looked into the excrement to count the worms. Usually there were two or three about 8–10 inches long wriggling around. The hole was then covered in and a stick stuck up to indicate foul ground.

Transportation to Japan: One Prisoner's Experience

Even as Japanese shipping was becoming increasingly rare and vulnerable to Allied attack, prisoners of war continued to be loaded onto ships for transport to labour-short Japan. Countless POWs died of suffocation, hunger, illness and thirst in the overcrowded holds of the 'hell ships', and more died when these ships were torpedoed and bombed in Allied attacks. John M. Wright recounts the first few days on his third 'hell ship' after spending time ashore disposing of the bodies of comrades who had died in a previous attack.

When the work detail returned to the harbor, we found that the entire group aboard the *Enoura Maru* had been transferred to the *Brazil Maru*. ... We arrived in time to carry the last of the wounded from a barge onto the new ship. When we went aboard that third hell ship, there were already more than a dozen dead piled on the deck. They had been so seriously wounded that they were unable to survive the pain and shock incident to the move....

As usual, we were all crowded into one hold too small to properly accommodate the group. By that time, the original group of 1619 had been slashed to about nine hundred of whom at least two hundred were badly wounded. The twenty man work detail was the last of the group to board the ships, and since those men were among the strongest and healthiest, they were kept together and assigned to one bay in the hold.

The hold had been divided into about fifteen stalls, each stall having a shelf that divided it into upper and lower bays. The bays averaged in size about fifteen feet by ten feet. From twenty-two to twenty-five men were crowded into each bay. In the centre of the hold, directly below the hatch, was an open space about twenty feet square. In that open space were laid the men with broken arms and legs, and the men who were so far gone with dysentery and other diseases that they were not expected to live long. The hold was loaded so fast that there was no sufficient time to organize the group. By the time we were all aboard, the so-called hospital section in the centre was so crowded that it was impossible to walk among the patients without stepping on them. There were no electric lights in the hold, the only light being the daylight which came through an opening in the hatch about three feet by six feet, at the top of one ladder leading out of the hold. Thoroughly exhausted, we went to sleep that night in spite of constant screaming from the wounded as they were inadvertently stepped on in the blackness....

Through the day and night of January 14th, about thirty men died. Most of those who died were men who had been wounded and were finally overcome by shock and exposure. The weather was getting colder everyday as we sailed north toward Japan. Many men were still clothed only in the rags in which they had abandoned the *Oryoku Maru* [the first transport ship to be bombed on their trip], although all clothing was stripped from the dead and supposedly issued to men who needed it most. As men died during the night, their clothes were often stolen by the first person who discovered the corpse, and the clothing was not distributed to the most needy. There were a few rice sacks in the hold when we boarded: they were thrown over the wounded men in the hospital area.

Three days north of Takao, the death rate was about twenty a day. It was a pitiful experience to walk among the men in the centre of the hold, the men in the death section. They knew they were dying. They never whimpered. They knew how to die bravely. Lieutenant Hector J. Polla, West Point 41, lay on the hatch for several days, close enough to my bay that I could hear him saying over and over again, "Please, fellow, be careful. You're kicking my broken leg." Hector died as bravely as he had fought on Bataan....

For the first two days out of Takao, we went through another very critical period of thirst. No liquids of any kind were issued. From the 16th through the 29th, water was issued by the spoonful, usually twice a day. The water was black, salty and unpalatable. There was not a scarcity of water on the ship. In fact, there as so much fresh water that the guards bathed in a stream which gushed from a faucet. The water swirled across the deck and into the scuppers in front of the eyes of men who were going mad for lack of it.

The guards realised how thirsty we were and capitalized on the situation. Guards brought buckets of water into the hold to trade water for American jewellery. There was very little of value left, after we had abandoned two ships. But from somewhere appeared a few West Point rings, gold watches and previous jewels. Also, American shoes were valuable. A West Point ring bought one cup of drinking water. A pair of shoes bought a cup of water and a can of fish. Other deals were worked out for straw mats, cigarettes, rice, and soup from the Japanese galley.

On the *Brazil Maru*, we were somewhat better off as far as sanitation was concerned. There was an outside latrine. Three wood boxes with holes cut in the bottoms were tied to the rail and hung over the side of the ship. For men who were too weak to climb the dozen steps to get out of the hold, there were four or five wood tubs at the foot of the ladders. In spite of those facilities, men with dysentery frequently defecated in the bays or in the passageways, and quite often the tubs were tipped over during darkness. Invariably, the tubs were used until they overflowed before the guards allowed a detail to go on deck to empty them.

Indian Prisoners of War Recall Their Incarceration by the Japanese

Although thousands of Indian soldiers of the Commonwealth forces became POWs, little attention has been paid to their experiences, not least because their incarceration as British colonial subjects had political ramifications that lasted beyond Indian independence. Those who did not join the pro-Japanese Indian National Army were as badly mistreated as other Allies and suffered dreadful casualty rates during transport and in the camps. In his memoir John Baptist Crasta remembers the political divisions that emerged amongst Indian prisoners in the early days of incarceration.

The next day [17 February 1942], we marched to Ferrers Park, where over 60,000 prisoners had gathered for the surrender ceremony. Lt. Col. W.R. Hunt informed us that we were their prisoners and were being handed over to the Japanese, and were to be subject to their discipline. Then on behalf of the British General Staff, he handed us to Major Fujiwara, officer of the Japanese General Staff; and having signed the surrender papers, left. Major Fujiwara spoke to us in Japanese (his speech translated into English by Lt. Kunizuku) at length as to how the mighty British forces in Malaya and the invincible fortress of Singapore had been destroyed in such a short time. He added that they were fighting the common Anglo-Saxon enemy of the Asiatics, and theirs was a noble cause. The Whites, who mercilessly exploited the Asiatics, must be driven out of the entire continent. This sacred war championed by Nippon was not for selfish reasons, but for the sake of all Asians. The Emperor had commanded that all Indians be treated like their brothers, and he hoped that Indians would themselves try to throw off the yoke of slavery. He would now hand us over to the command of our officers, and had released Captain Mohan Singh for that purpose. We must carry out the latter's orders as if they came from the Japanese themselves.

Amidst thunderous applause "Captain" Mohan Singh mounted the rostrum and spoke for over two hours. He told us that British Imperialism had reduced India to a state of abject poverty, degradation and humiliation in the eyes of the world. Even a much smaller nation like Japan had taken up cudgels and was out to crush the Anglo-Saxon might. They were succeeding because the spirit of unity and self-sacrifice was imbibed by them. The Japanese soldier led a very simple life; his pay was only a meagre sum of four to seven rupees a month. His discipline and honesty were of the highest order. … He wanted Indian soldiers to emulate the Japanese. They were our Asiatic brothers, he said, and they had promised full support to drive out the British from India. Many Indians had helped the Japanese in the early stages of the war, but even without Indian help, the Japanese would have conquered Malaya, although their victory would have been delayed by a week. "We are going to start a national army which every Indian must join. And with the help of the Japanese we are going to drive out the British." Brotherly treatment would be meted out to those who joined. He would look after our comforts. This, however, did not mean complete exemption from manual labour!

Jemadar Chint Singh chose to remain loyal to the Commonwealth. He was one of the few survivors of the prison camp at Wewak. Ironically, whilst his letter was deemed to be of questionable historical interest by the Australian Army's Military History Section in 1946, it is one of the rare primary sources we have on this issue.

Letter from Jemadar Chint Singh: Farewell to the Aust. 6th Division.

Today the 13th of January 1946, I find myself the luckiest man in the world, who worked here for 2½ years as a P.O.W. and for 3 months as a free man in the free world – which was full of terror and darkness when my contact ceased with it.

To the best of my knowledge 201 Indian Ps.O.W were rescued from time to time in the New Guinea Campaign by the 6th Aust. Div., (later on 10 died in the plane crash, leaving only 191 the survivors out of 3000 who were brought by the Japanese at Wewak on 16th May 1943) are greatly indebted to the Australian Forces. We were suffering from terrible diseases and there was no hope of life – at this hour of our calamity, the Division worked as

Angels for us. We were fed, clothed and looked after in the hospitals and in camps by doctors, Nurses and the camp staff, to them owe our lives. Every member of the Div shared with our miseries and helped us, pleased us in this wilderness, where we have no hope to live.

Today I feel very happy that the Almighty Father has fulfilled my ambitions. (i) to take the right retribution with those who are responsible for the death of 2500 Indians. (ii) to tell the world about the fate of 3000 Indians who went under so many privations and lost their lives. (iii) to see Australia to where I am flying today. But I feel sorry at the recollection of my comrades who had the same ambitions and we together used to make schemes for the visit to Australia. The bad luck did not favour and only a few got this opportunity. The sympathy, love and affection shown by the every individual of the Div will always be with us and we and our countrymen will be very proud of it.

With all the best wishes for the many years to come and hoping that the friendship of your country and India will continue for all the time.

13/1/46   Jemadar Chint Singh

Life and Death on the Burma–Thailand Railway

The preceding document suggests that the death rate of Indian POWs in New Guinea was amongst the highest of all POW camps, although this is not well known. Indeed, until the horrors of Sandakan became known during the 1980s, the site most famous for high casualty rates was the Burma–Thailand Railway. Australian Tom Fagan's diary entry, dated 15 July 1943, provides a glimpse into the grim reality of daily life along the line.

The ulcer on my shinbone has worsened and I am officially hospitalised as it is a sheer impossibility for me to put my foot to the ground. The throbbing prevents me getting more than a couple of hours' sleep at night; the ache and red hot jabs of pain are there all the time. The hut, hospital to give it its title, is crammed to the bamboo rafters with ulcer and dysentery patients. One disease seems to go with the other. Life is hardly worth trying to hang onto. I must, though. I have my loved ones home and awaiting my return.

A very popular officer died last night, Captain Watts, of the Engineers; he was a highly regarded officer who always stood up for his men. His passing is a great loss. He was only 25 years of age.

Despite the daily pilgrimages by our medical officers to the Japanese Camp Commander, not one particle of medicine, nor a drug, has been made available, even though promised time and time again. You can't believe one word the Nips say. They are liars, torturers and completely unpredictable. Sadism seems to have been born into them. They thrive on it.

Don't know where it came from, certainly not from the hated Japs, but we have a small quantity of lime to which is added portions of charcoal, then applied to ulcered areas. Whether it will help or not remains to be seen.

When we arrived at this disease-infested blot (105 kilo) in the jungles of Burma, we had a strength of 800 men, in varying states of health. That number has now dwindled to 200. Deaths, and evacuations to the 55 kilo camp has been responsible.

Something serious has gone wrong as far as the Nips are concerned: they appear to be in a spate of madness. Almost daily they blitz the hut and literally pull very sick men off the bamboo-slatted bed platforms. Bashings are on all the time. Some poor devils, for no reason at all, are singled out, made to stand to attention and then cop an unmerciful belting.

Not a day passes without one, sometimes more, prisoners seen standing, quite often on a round stone and holding a heavy one above their head. At every hourly guard change we can hear screams of rage and the thud of some heavy waddy whacking skin and bone bodies.

My blood runs cold and the procedure goes on and on. Intervention by anybody is added satisfaction to the murderous and brutal guards. Another one to tear into, boots, rifle butts or anything that can be used to inflict hurt.

A Japanese Perspective

As the following excerpt makes clear, for the Japanese units building the Burma–Thailand Railway, the essential work of building the railway on time far outweighed any concern for the POWs. Second Lieutenant Tarumoto Jūji, the author, was later condemned to life imprisonment for his treatment of POWs in C-Level War Crimes Trials in Singapore.

In June new orders were issued by the high command to complete the railway by August. This must have been because an important military operation was planned in Burma, but I wondered whether it would be possible to shorten the time for completing the whole line by two months. We could hardly even complete the work by the initial date of October. Was there an ingenious secret plan? Some infantry battalions, engineers, house-building units and work units were added to the command of the 9th Railway Regiment, and the number of coolies was increased. This was all that could be done by the Japanese army at that time, and in fact it was only an increase of manpower. I did not think the shortening by two months could be achieved by this increase, but I determined to do all I could to comply with these orders. My platoon had to complete the given task at all costs. That was all I could do. But the consequences were to be expected. One by one our soldiers collapsed from sickness. At the most 35 men out of a total of 60 in the platoon were able to work. The number of men sent to hospital in the rear increased. And those who got sick never recovered their previous state of health. Except for a few, most of the men had to rest for several days after they had worked for a week or so. Every day I had to worry about how many men could come to work, and I got a shock whenever the doctor told me that a man had had to be sent behind the lines. Most of them suffered from malaria, and many were suffering also from abdominal pains or a sickness of indeterminate character. All the parts of every man's body became weak in the last extremity of fatigue. I had a fever once every ten days. One day when I was at a work site a private suddenly started to shiver violently so I sent him back to the barracks in the rain. Soon afterwards I myself started to shiver with cold.

It was the same for the PoWs. The ones who came to work were different every day: they could not work for three days in a row. The number of those who turned pale while working and had to rest increased. Some went back to the barracks supported by a comrade. Often a PoW was sent to the company command unit at Matoma from the barracks by the first bridge. When I met him on the way and looked into his face, he seemed to be almost dead with sunken goggling eyes. Some were very thin and seemed to have no hope of recovery. Was it my responsibility for keeping them working until that stage? I could dare deny it [sic].

Prisoners of War in Japan

While many of the prisoners in Japan were generally better fed, housed and cared for than their comrades overseas, towards the end of the war, the situation was made more dangerous by Allied bombing. During 1945 many prisoners died in the bombings, including the atomic bombings of Hiroshima and Nagasaki. Herbert Zincke, of the United States Army Air Corps, had been working in various factories since arriving in Japan in 1942, but in mid-1945, there was a definite shift in atmosphere.

After we stopped going to the factories we went in and out of the camp as we pleased without a guard, and nobody cared if we worked or not. Sgt. Mizuno didn't seem to care what we did, within reason. He, his young cousin (whom we called "Little Mizuno"), and the new quartermaster Hojami all spoke English as well, if not better, than the new interpreter, Yamazaki. The relationship between the Japanese staff and us warmed so much that I wondered if my more optimistic friends were right in thinking the war was over.

Each night for about two months I had had my Dutch knapsack packed and all my equipment handy to grab in case of a serious air raid. Every other night I put fresh water in my canteen. I was ready for a quick evacuation, as I had a hunch that our little vacation from air raids was about over, and that all hell would break loose very soon. What a spot to be in! So damn helpless, and sitting right in the centre of one of the most important industrial areas in Japan. We surely would have been a poor risk if we were trying to take out life insurance.

The Execution of Flight Lieutenant Bill Newton VC

The vast majority of surviving sources and historical interest in POWs has focused on the experiences of the tens of thousands of Allied service personnel captured with the fall of Singapore and the Philippines. The POW experience of Allied service personnel captured elsewhere has received much less attention. In New Guinea prisoners were rarely taken. Most of those who fell into Japanese hands were airmen. After interrogation, most were executed.

Contrary to the suggestions in his Victoria Cross citation, and its surrounding publicity, Flight Lieutenant Bill Newton did survive the crash of his aircraft. With Flight Sergeant John Lyon he was captured.[5] With no chance of sending the Australian airmen to Rabaul for imprisonment, it was decided to execute them. One unknown Japanese soldier recorded the execution of Newton in his diary.

All four of us – Kurokawa, Nishiguchi, Yawate and myself – assembled in front of Headquarters at 1500 hrs. ... The "Tai" commander Komai, who came to the observation post today, told us personally that in accordance with the compassionate sentiments of Japanese Bushido, he was going to kill the prisoner himself, with his favorite sword. So we gathered to observe this. After we had waited a little more than ten minutes, the truck came along.

The prisoner who is at the side of the guard house is given his last drink of water. The surgeon, Major Komai, and Headquarters Platoon Commander come out of the Officers' Mess, wearing their military swords. The time has come. The prisoner with his arms bound and his long hair now cropped short totters forward. He probably suspects what is afoot but he is more composed than I thought he would be. Without more ado, he is put on the truck and we set out for our destination.

I have a seat next to the surgeon. About ten guards ride with us. To the pleasant rumble of the engine, we run swiftly along the road in the growing twilight. The glowing sun has set behind the western hills. Gigantic clouds rise before us and dusk is falling all around. It will not last long. As I picture the scene we are about to witness, my heart beats faster.

I glance at the prisoner. He has probably resigned himself to his fate. As though saying farewell to the world, he looks about as he sits in the truck, at the hills the sea, and seems deep in thought. I feel a surge of pity and turn my eyes away. The truck runs along the seashore now. We have left the Navy guard behind us and now come into the Army sector. Here and there we see sentries in the grassy fields and I thank them in my heart for their toil, as we drive on; they must have 'got it' in the bombing the night before last; there were great gaping holes by the side of the road, full of water from the rain. In a little over twenty minutes, we arrive at our destination and all get off.

Major Komai stands up and says to the prisoner, "We are going to kill you." When he tells the prisoner that in accordance with Japanese Bushido he would be killed with a Japanese sword and that we would have two or three minutes' grace, he listens with bowed head. He says a few words in a low voice. He is an officer, probably a Flight Lieutenant. Apparently, he wants to be killed with one stroke of the sword. I hear him say the word "one"'; the Major's face becomes tense as he replies: "Yes."

Now the time has come and the prisoner is made to kneel on the bank of a bomb crater, filled with water. He is apparently resigned. The precaution is taken of surrounding him with guards with fixed bayonets, but he remains calm. He even stretches his neck out. He is a very brave man indeed. When I put myself in the prisoners' place and think that in one minute it will be good-bye to this world, although the daily bombings have filled me with hate, ordinary human feelings make me pity him.

The Major has drawn his favourite sword. It is the famous masamune sword which he has shown us at the observation stations. It glitters in the light and sends a cold shiver down my spine. He taps the prisoner's neck lightly with the back of the blade, then raises it above his head with both arms and brings it down with a powerful sweep. I had been standing with muscles tenses but in that moment I closed my eyes.

A hissing sound – it must be the sounds of spurting blood, spurting from the arteries: the body falls forward. It is amazing – he has killed him with one stroke.

The onlookers crowd forward. The head, detached from the trunk, rolls forward in front of it. The dark blood gushes out. It is all over. The head is dead white, like a doll. The savageness which I felt only a little while ago is gone, and now I feel nothing but the true compassion of Japanese Bushido.

A corporal laughs: "*Well, he will be entering Nirvana now.*" A seaman of the medical unit takes the surgeon's sword and, intent on paying off old scores, turns the headless body over on its back and cuts the abdomen open with one clean stroke. They are thick-skinned, these *keto* [hairy foreigner - term of opprobrium for a white man]; even the skin of their bellies is thick. Not a drop of blood comes out of the body. It is pushed into the crater at once and buried.

Now the wind blows mournfully and I see the scene again in my mind's eye. We get on the truck again and start back. It is dark now. We get off in front of Headquarters. I say good-bye to the Major and climb up the hill with Technician Kurokawa. This will be something to remember all my life. If I ever get back alive, it will make a good story to tell; so I have written it down.

Japanese Prisoners' Perspectives

As noted, Japanese POWs faced entirely different demons. This extract is from a secretly recorded conversation between two Japanese prisoners of war, Lieutenant Iizuka Yutaka and Aircraftsman Nagatomo (Sho) Katsuro, a year after their capture in 1942. It is kept in the records of the Allied Translator and Interpreter Service.

Sho: Where were you captured at?

Iizuka: At Guadalcanal. Where were you?

Sho: During the first attack on Port Moresby. Feb 28 of last year when we attacked Kavieng we bombed the place and on the second occasion, started a fire. Anyway, I was captured after being forced down during the first attack on Port Moresby. ... We could not see enemy fighters or bombes then. Later, we encountered them and I shot down the No. I plane, so I looked at my shotai cho [platoon leader] and he signalled me "O.K." I was going to fight until my fuel was exhausted but ... [Sho describes how his plane caught fire and he tried to extinguish them to no avail, then lost consciousness]. When I regained consciousness, it was 3 o'clock the following day and I enquired as to how I had been rescued. There were New Guinea natives and Australian soldiers near who said they had rescued me around 4 o'clock the previous day from the sea. I looked at my body, found I was burned and that my wounds were bleeding – yet they said I was fortunate to be alive. However I felt angry at that moment for being rescued....

Iizuka: I was thinking that if they'd let me return, I'd go back even though I know it is considered shameful to have been a p.w. Then, as the war will last for 5 to 10 years, I'd go to China or some place and teach flying for the duration. Aircraft will be scarce by the time the war is over. I hear that at Nomohan [sic] they are exchanging PsW now.

Sho: Even if we are still alive when the war ends, I don't think we can go home. Even if they tell us to come back, I'll have to commit suicide or something.

Iizuka: I don't think the war will end in less than 10 years.

Sho: I think 10 years is too long. Maybe in five years.

Iizuka: Why for another five years we can make opposed landings on enemy territories. That proves it must last another five years. Probably after five years we'll start exchanging PsW, even now at Nomohan they're doing it.

Japanese Prisoners Contemplate Defeat

Ōoka Shōhei, captured unconscious in the Philippines on 25 January 1945, became one of Japan's foremost storytellers on the war. In the book from which this extract is taken, he reflected at length on the fortuitous circumstances leading to his survival. Here, he paints a vivid picture of the tensions emerging in POW camps after the Japanese surrender, as those who laid down arms on the order of the Emperor after 15 August 1945 confronted those who had been captured earlier.

The friction that arose between the new prisoners and the old must be considered one of the more bizarre effects wrought upon Japanese citizens by the Pacific War. Inasmuch as new and old alike now lived in the custody of American forces and were sustained by American provisions, both groups should have been equal. The new prisoners had a great deal of difficulty accepting this circumstance straightforwardly, however. Still under the sway of the Army Combatants' Code that declared the shame of capture a fate worse than death, they lost no opportunity to show their contempt for the old prisoners.

One night a former second lieutenant who had been stationed on Negros barged into one of our platoon barracks in violation of the prohibition against officers mixing with the rank and file.

"Why haven't you disembowelled yourselves" he shouted. "How can you let yourselves be captured and then go on living? Cut open your bellies!"

The rowdy Odaka was always quick to speak up at times like this. "Oh yeah? You're a fine one to talk, when all you did was run around the mountains trying to keep out of harm's way. May I remind you that we're the ones who took the heat out front and got wounded and couldn't help getting captured? And incidentally, though they may choose to keep their mouths shut, we have some first lieutenants and captains in here, too, so a pipsqueak second lieutenant like you had better watch his tongue."

The claim that we had first lieutenants and captains among us was actually empty show. Some of the officers had claimed at first to be NCOs so as not to be held responsible, but in most cases they slipped up during the interrogations and got sent to the separate officers' sector of the camp. Nevertheless, the claim effectively parried the brunt of the lieutenant's attack. "Hrumph," he grunted and turned to leave, but Odaka was still steaming.

"Get outta here, you shithead!" he screamed after the lieutenant. "And don't come back, if you know what's good for you!"

The lieutenant spun on his heels. "What did you say?" he growled.

"Whatto issu whatto?" Odaka drawled in heavily accented English, and the onlookers burst out laughing. This was one of his favourite English phrases – a literal English translation of the standard Japanese fighting retort to "What did you say?" The lieutenant stood there fuming for several moments but then disappeared into the darkness outside without saying another word.

For good measure, Odaka sought the lieutenant out in the officers' sector the next day and yelled at him some more. On his return, he seemed quite pleased with himself, noting that there had been quite a few colonels and lieutenant colonels in the tent. One of the leading colonels had spoken sympathetically: "What you say is true," he said, "but now that we've given up like this, it's all the same. There were a lot of things wrong with our armed forces, and that was why we lost. From there on out, we need to look to the future with an open mind and work together to rebuild our country." He then gave Odaka a cigar, saying it had been a special gift from the commandant.

"I guess colonels have more common sense," Odaka remarked to me. "Upstart lieutenants don't know what they're talking about. The S.O.B. turned out to be the colonel's orderly, serving him meals and stuff like that".

CHAPTER TEN
HIROSHIMA AND THE DEFEAT OF JAPAN

A nation which sets the precedent of using these newly liberated forces of nature for purposes of destruction may have to bear the responsibility of opening the door to an era of devastation on an unimaginable scale.

Leo Szilard and 58 co-signers petition
President Truman, 3 July 1945

On 6 and 9 August 1945, respectively, the cities of Hiroshima and Nagasaki were literally flattened by two atomic bombs. The precise number of Japanese casualties is unclear, partly because of the fluidity of urban populations (particularly in military supply centres like Hiroshima), and partly because deaths due to the A-bombs ranged from, at one extreme, instant vaporisation at and around the epicentre of the explosions to, at the other, lingering deaths from the after-effects of radiation exposure years later. It is generally surmised that about 100,000 people died at Hiroshima either on 6 August or in the few days following, and slightly fewer in Nagasaki, with some 80,000 victims either on that day or in the following days.

Japan's vulnerability to Allied bombing was nothing new. Throughout the previous months, relentless Allied bombing had destroyed most of Japan's larger cities.[1] The firebombing of Tokyo on the night of 10 March 1945 had had a similarly devastating effect as the A-bomb insofar as some 100,000 people died and the city was reduced to rubble. However, on 6 August 1945 in Hiroshima, it was immediately clear that this was different. From the first flash of blinding light and deafening explosion through to the development of symptoms (including hair loss and bleeding gums) that signalled radiation poisoning, those who survived the nuclear attacks knew this was a new type of weapon, one of indescribable and unprecedented destructive strength. For those who witnessed the A-bombs, the attacks confirmed that Japan was shortly about to be defeated or completely annihilated.

US president Harry S Truman announced the use of A-bomb on Hiroshima a few hours after the attack. Reactions throughout the world were ambivalent: perhaps less important than the impact on Japan itself was the realisation that this had ushered in a new age where the annihilation of the whole human race had become a real possibility. The power of the bomb, in that sense, was twofold. It was the weapon that destroyed Hiroshima and Nagasaki and contributed to the Japanese surrender; but it was also the dark and unrelenting threat lurking behind international relations and creating visions of dystopia. In that regard, the A-bombs' power was also played out in the realm of culture, through new visions of the 'end of the world' (subsequently rehearsed in films such as the *Mad Max* series, for example), in anti-nuclear grass-roots politics and trans-national activist pacifism, and in ongoing academic debates about the actual intention of the use of the bombs (was the American intention to defeat Japan, or was it a pre-emptive diplomatic strike on the USSR?). As John Canaday has suggested, '[d]espite their physical substance, since World War II nuclear weapons have exercised their power in the purely literary form of their fictional use in the future'.[2]

As any glance through the mass of literature on the A-bombs reveals, there is an ongoing debate on whether the use of such a weapon was justified, on strategic, diplomatic or moral and ethical grounds. It is worth remembering that it was only in the wake of their use in Hiroshima and Nagasaki that the nature and extent of their destructive power on the ground was clearly and widely understood. The extent of destruction was nevertheless predictable enough that questions about the morality of the use of the bomb arose immediately. Michael Kort has provided a useful summary of the key questions and debates concerning the use of the bomb. These include the likelihood of a Japanese surrender in July–August 1945 if the bomb had not been used; American information about Japanese overtures for peace at the time the decision to drop the bomb was taken; American casualty estimates for an invasion of Japan (since the use of the bomb has come to equate lives saved both on the American and Japanese sides); the relative importance of the A-bombs and the Soviet entry into the war in Japan's decision to surrender; and the arguments on the use of the A-bomb as 'atomic diplomacy' – that is, as a show of force against the Soviet Union in the early days of the Cold War.[3]

In Japan, debates about the bomb have understandably had their own shape, dictated by fluid and competing narratives about the war. On one level, the experience of the A-bomb victims (*hibakusha* in Japanese) has spawned a mass of literature, poetry and other art forms that attempt to communicate the unprecedented suffering of those on the ground at Hiroshima and Nagasaki. As the victims of the world's first and only experiment with nuclear warfare, the *hibakusha* famously speak not on behalf of Hiroshima or on behalf of Japan, but on behalf of the human race as a whole, making 'Hiroshima' (as a shorthand for both cities) an international peace symbol. Japan's nascent pacifist and anti-nuclear movement grew in the wake of the Occupation and with the lifting of censorship on the bomb, and was further bolstered in 1954 when a Japanese fishing vessel was caught in the atomic fallout of a nuclear test in the Bikini Atoll. Hiroshima came to have particular power as a global symbol of the anti-nuclear movement, a process which also shaped the ways in which its history was understood.

Perceptions of the bombings of Hiroshima and Nagasaki are also inextricably tied to shifting debates about war guilt. For some, the focus on the horrors of the bomb and on the plight of the A-bomb victims undesirably diverts attention away from the fact that Japan had been at war with China at least for eight years and with the United States and its allies for more than three and a half years, and that it had failed to accept previous opportunities to surrender. According to some critics, a focus on Japanese victims of the war (symbolised by the A-bomb victims) has allowed Japan to ignore its own war crimes, along with its long-standing victimisation of its neighbours. The most potent symbols of this line of argument are the Korean victims of the A-bomb, whose presence in Hiroshima in August 1945 as forced labourers, often in work related to the military effort, not only contradicts the claims that Hiroshima was predominantly civilian and residential (like most Japanese cities then and today, there was limited separation between residential and industrial parts), but also serves as a reminder of Japan's brutal colonisation of Korea and the exploitation of the Korean population for Japanese ends. Furthermore, the failure to commemorate the Korean *hibakusha* within the actual boundaries of the post-war Hiroshima Peace Park symbolises an endemic post-war failure to engage with Japanese war crimes in any form. Hiroshima can thus come to represent, contradictorily, both the dreadful sacrifice of civilians in wartime at a universal level and, at a national level, the failure to understand and reflect on the wider ramifications of Japan's war guilt.

A further uncomfortable legacy of Hiroshima in Japan was the marginalisation of the *hibakusha* in the post-war period. Some of this was for the reasons spelled out above: John Whittier Treat, for example, has suggested that some non-*hibakusha* Japanese contrast their under-standing of the bomb with that of the *hibakusha* by stating that they, at least, were glad the war ended, suggesting that the suffering caused by the A-bomb was diminished by the fact that the war did end because of the bomb.[4] There is a clear resonance here with those arguments justifying the use of the bomb to save the American and Japanese lives that would have been lost in an invasion.

More pervasive and immediate, however, were widespread beliefs that those exposed to radiation had been 'poisoned', were thus impure, and even contagious. The situation was exacerbated by the failure of either Japanese or American doctors to significantly alleviate the plight of the victims. It took more than ten years for the Japanese government to acknowledge the particular nature of the *hibakusha*'s health problems: until then the victims could only avail themselves of the services of local doctors and hospitals whose knowledge of radiation sickness was limited. For the American side, intense interest in the long-term effects of the bomb was mitigated by reluctance to offer any form of alleviation of the symptoms, lest it be understood as an admission of guilt.

The atomic bombings of Hiroshima and Nagasaki have thus spawned countless multi-layered and complex narratives and debates, ranging from elaborate historical arguments on strategy, decision making and political will in the elite of the American government to highly emotive and disturbing accounts of the bombing at ground zero, to political and politicised debates about how best to remember the A-bombs and understand their significance and the plight of their victims. The most famous example of this issue is no doubt the Enola Gay controversy at the Smithsonian Institution in 1995, where curators, historians, politicians and veterans' groups debated whether the destruction at ground zero should be displayed with the fuselage of the airplane that dropped the Hiroshima bomb.[5] This selection of sources gives a sense of the breadth of these issues.

THE SOURCES

Scientists Protest the Use of Atomic Power

Some of the scientists involved in research in atomic power were
convinced that it was much too powerful to be used in the context of
the war against Japan, and that its use would be premature. Leo Szilard,
a physicist with the Manhattan Project, was particularly apprehensive
about the ramifications of the use of atomic weapons, and drafted a
petition to Truman advocating against its use against Japan. This was
signed by more than fifty other scientists.

A PETITION TO THE PRESIDENT OF THE UNITED STATES

Discoveries of which the people of the United States are not aware may
affect the welfare of this nation in the near future. The liberation of atomic
power which has been achieved places atomic bombs in the hands of the
Army. It places in your hands, as Commander-in-Chief, the fateful decision
whether or not to sanction the use of such bombs in the present phase
of the war against Japan.

We, the undersigned scientists, have been working in the field of atomic
power for a number of years. Until recently we have had to reckon with the
possibility that the United States might be attacked by atomic bombs during
this war and that her only defense might lie in a counterattack by the same
means. Today with this danger averted we feel impelled to say what follows:

The war has to be brought speedily to a successful conclusion and the
destruction of Japanese cities by means of atomic bombs may very well be
an effective method of warfare. We feel, however, that such an attack on Japan
could not be justified in the present circumstances. We believe that the
United States ought not to resort to the use of atomic bombs in the present
phase of the war, at least not unless the terms which will be imposed upon
Japan after the war are publicly announced and subsequently Japan is given
an opportunity to surrender.

If such public announcement gave assurance to the Japanese that they
could look forward to a life devoted to peaceful pursuits in their homeland
and if Japan still refused to surrender, our nation would then be faced with a
situation which might require a re-examination of her position with respect
to the use of atomic bombs in the war.

Atomic bombs are primarily a means for the ruthless annihilation of cities.
Once they were introduced as an instrument of war it would be difficult to
resist for long the temptation of putting them to such use.

The last few years show a marked tendency toward increasing ruthlessness.
At present our Air Forces, striking at the Japanese cities, are using the same
methods of warfare which were condemned by American public opinion only
a few years ago when applied by the Germans to the cities of England. Our

use of atomic bombs in this war would carry the world a long way further on this path of ruthlessness.

Atomic power will provide the nations with new means of destruction. The atomic bombs at our disposal represent only the first step in this direction and there is almost no limit to the destructive power which will become available in the course of this development. Thus a nation which sets the precedent of using these newly liberated forces of nature for purposes of destruction may have to bear the responsibility of opening the door to an era of devastation on an unimaginable scale.

In view of the foregoing, we, the undersigned, respectfully petition that you exercise your power as Commander-in-Chief to rule that the United States shall not, in the present phase of the war, resort to the use of atomic bombs.

Leo Szilard and 58 co-signers

Extract from Harry Truman's Diary (Potsdam, 25 July 1945)

In July 1945 the leaders of the major Allied powers convened at Potsdam, where they settled upon an agreed strategy to defeat Japan, and continued to debate the nature of international relations in the post-war period. Writing in the privacy of his diary, Truman summarised the potent power of the atomic bomb, and referred to the developing tensions with the Soviet Union. Truman's claims regarding suitable targets for the use of the bomb were not realised, however, and the 'warning' never appeared in a meaningful form for fear the Japanese might attempt to prevent the bomb's use. The diary remains an important piece of evidence in enduring debates about America's decision to use the bomb.[6] Truman was not a diligent diarist and often only made hasty notes, days or weeks after an event. As D. M. Giangreco has noted, Truman wrote about whatever was important to him at the time of the writing. This highly personal material was written for himself and his family, and he frequently used his diary as a vehicle to play with ideas for later use in speeches, or to simply get things off his chest. While such material provides valuable insights into Truman's views and makes fascinating reading, it also opens the door to misinterpretations, misunderstandings and misuse.[7]

We met at 11 A.M. today. That is Stalin, Churchill and the U.S. President. But I had a most important session with Lord Mountbatten & General Marshall before that. We have discovered the most terrible bomb in the history of the world. It may be the fire destruction prophesied in the Euphrates Valley Era, after Noah and his fabulous Ark.

Anyway we "think" we have found the way to cause a disintegration of the atom. An experiment in the New Mexican desert was startling – to put it mildly. Thirteen pounds of the explosive caused the complete disintegration of a steel tower 60 feet high, created a crater 6 feet deep and 1,200 feet in diameter, knocked over a steel tower ½ mile away, and knocked men down 10,000 yards away. The explosion was visible for more than 200 miles and audible for 40 miles and more.

This weapon is to be used against Japan between now and August 10th. I have told the Sec. of War, Mr. Stimson, to use it so that military objectives and soldiers and sailors are the target and not women and children. Even if the Japs are savages, ruthless, merciless and fanatic, we as the leader of the world for the common welfare cannot drop this terrible bomb on the old capital or the new.

He & I are in accord. The target will be a purely military one and we will issue a warning statement asking the Japs to surrender and save lives. I'm sure they will not do that, but we will have given them the chance. It is certainly a good thing for the world that Hitler's crowd or Stalin's did not discover this atomic bomb. It seems to be the most terrible thing ever discovered, but it can be made the most useful.

At 10:15 I had Gen. Marshall come in and discuss with me the tactical and political situation. He is a level headed man – so is Mountbatten.

At the Conference Poland and the Bolsheviki land grab came up. Russia helped herself to a slice of Poland and gave Poland a nice slice of Germany, taking also a good slice of East Prussia for herself. Poland has moved in up to the Oder and the west Neisse, taking Stettin and Silesia as a fact accomplished. My position is that, according to commitments made at Yalta by my predecessor, Germany was to be divided into four occupation zones, one each for Britain, Russia and France and the U.S. If Russia chooses to allow Poland to occupy a part o her zone I am agreeable but title to territory cannot and will not be settled here. For the fourth time I restated my position and explained that territorial cessions had to be made by treaty and ratified by the Senate.

We discussed reparations and movement of populations from East Germany, Czechoslovakia, Austria, Italy and elsewhere. Churchill said Maisky had so defined war booty as to include the German fleet and Merchant Marine. It was a bomb shell and sort of paralysed the Russkies, but it has a lot of merit.

Truman's Announcement of the Atomic Bombing of Hiroshima

The first public statement on the use of the Atomic bomb came from the White House several hours after the explosion over Hiroshima. Many newspapers, including the *New York Times*, carried the full text of President Truman's statement.

Washington, August 6 (U.P.) – following is the text of President Truman's statement announcing the first use of the atomic bomb:

Sixteen hours ago an American airplane dropped one bomb on Hiroshima, an important Japanese Army base. That bomb had more power than 20,000 tons of TNT. It had more than two thousand times the blast power of the British "Grand Slam" which is the largest bomb ever yet used in the history of warfare.

The Japanese began the war from the air at Pearl Harbor. They have been repaid manyfold. And the end is not yet. With this bomb we have now added a new and revolutionary increase in destruction, to supplement the growing power of our armed forces. In their present form these bombs are now in production and even more powerful forms are in development.

It is an atomic bomb. It is a harnessing of the basic power of the universe. The force from which the sun draws its powers has been loosed against those who brought war to the Far East.

Before 1939, it was the accepted belief of scientists that it was theoretically possible to release atomic energy. But no one knew any practical method of doing it. By 1942, however, we knew that the Germans were working feverishly to find a way to add atomic energy to the other engines of war with which they hoped to enslave the world. But they failed. We may be grateful to Providence that the Germans got the V-1's and V-2's late and in limited quantities and even more grateful that they did not get the atomic bomb at all.

Battle of Laboratories won:

The battle of the laboratories held fateful risks for us as well as the battles of the air, land and sea, and we have now won the battle of the laboratories as we have won the other battles.

Beginning in 1940, before Pearl Harbor, scientific knowledge useful in war was pooled between the United States and Great Britain, and many priceless helps to our victories have come from that arrangement. Under that general policy the research on the atomic bomb was begun. With American and British scientists working together, we entered the race of discovery against the Germans.

The United States had available a large number of scientists of distinction in the many needed areas of knowledge. It had the tremendous industrial and financial resources necessary for the project and they could be devoted to it without undue impairment of other vital war work. In the United States the laboratory work and the production plants, on which a substantial start had already been made, would be out of reach of enemy bombing, while at the time Britain was exposed to constant air attack and was still threatened with the possibility of invasion.

For these reasons Prime Minister Churchill and President Roosevelt agreed that it was wise to carry on the project here. We now have two great plants and many lesser works devoted to the production of atomic power. Employment during peak construction numbered 125,000, and over 65,000 individuals are even now engaged in operating the plants. Many have worked there for two and a half years. Few know what they have been producing. They see great quantities of material going in and they see nothing coming out of these plants, for the physical size of the explosive charge is exceedingly small. We have spent two billion dollars on the greatest scientific gamble in history – and won.

A Japanese Newspaper Describes the
Atomic Attack on Hiroshima

Unlike the American press that was wedded to cities or regional population centres, the Japanese press evolved as a national enterprise – a true 'mass media'.[8] The *Asahi Shinbun* remains one of Japan's main mass circulation national daily newspapers. This is the first report on the A-bomb that those Japanese outside the affected areas had on these bombs, in the midst of news coverage equally divided between the damage done to various areas with 'standard' bombing, the prospect of an American invasion and the courage and dedication of 'Special Attack pilots' (the so-called *kamikaze*). Unlike American press stories, which would lead from a headline, Japanese newspaper articles can be framed on several sides by extensive headlines relating to the story, thanks to a writing system that allows both vertical and horizontal lines.

NEW TYPE OF ENEMY BOMB ON HIROSHIMA

Attack with a small number of B-29; Extensive damage, details currently under investigation
(Imperial Headquarters announcement, 7 August 1945, 1530 hours)

1. massive damage in wake of air-raid on Hiroshima with a small number of B-29
2. details currently investigated regarding the possibility of the enemy using new type of bomb

PARACHUTE ATTACHED; EXPLOSION IN MID-AIR

Cruel new type of bomb; disregard for humanity

On 6 August, just after 8 am, a small number of enemy B-29 bombers attacked Hiroshima, and dropped a small amount of bombs. This resulted in extensive destruction of buildings, and also provoked many fires. It appears that the enemy used a new type of bomb in this attack, and that this bomb exploded in mid-air, having been dropped attached to a parachute. The extent of the damage is currently under investigation, but there are aspects that must be addressed.

The enemy has obviously made an atrocious plan to kill and injure the mass of innocent citizens with this new type of bomb. It is impossible to disregard, behind this inhuman act, the enemy's impatience towards the resolution of this war. The enemy, daring such an inhuman atrocity, will never again be able to speak of righteousness and humanity.

It is anticipated that the enemy will continue using such weapons, and Imperial Headquarters is expected to provide commands regarding strategic response at the earliest opportunity. Until then, the air raid protection strategies used until now will be continued, such as evacuation from urban areas, and continued construction of air-raid shelters. Be wary of the danger of underestimating the enemy from now on, even if an incoming air-raid is heralded by only a small number of planes.

The initial use of this new type of bomb has been accompanied by grandiose propaganda. Truman himself has made statements on this new type of weapon. It is important not to be befuddled by these things: each person, strengthening their resolve against the enemy, must fortify our air-raid defences.

An Australian Newspaper Reports the Attack on Hiroshima

In Australia, the editorial of one of the biggest dailies, the Melbourne-based *Age* newspaper, on 8 August 1945, reflected the ambivalence that permeated world opinion on the use of this type of bomb. It also foreshadowed how the bomb's character as a threat to humanity as a whole was to replace in importance its impact on Japan proper.

Triumph and Menace

Imagination is stirred by the achievements of American and British Scientists which have resulted in the use of atomic energy in the bombing of Japan. Because of its enormous potentialities for good or ill, the advance is epoch making, opening a new era in man's mastery over the 'secret forces of Nature'. Not only have war and the means of waging war been radically changed, but its essential madness as a form of racial destruction is thrown into starker relief. Since 1939, if not earlier, there has been a relentless battle not only by land, sea and air, but in the laboratories and workshops of scientists and technicians, to be first in the field with the colossal power accruing from the successful transformation of matter into energy.

'By God's mercy, British and American science outpaced all German efforts', declares Mr. Churchill. Some inkling of the prolonged and dangerous research work conducted in America to produce the atomic bomb was given by President Truman, who states that the 'greatest scientific gamble in history' involved an expenditure of 2000 million dollars, or over £600,000,0000 (Australian). The break-up of the atom and release of atomic energy have been quests of scientists for decades and the present achievement for purposes of war and destruction points either to further great progress in man's mastery over his surroundings, or annihilation by his fellows.

Detailed comparisons of the atomic bomb with others hitherto used conjure appalling pictures of destructive force, which makes light of even the "earthquake" bomb and the "blockbusters" that played havoc with the work of Todt construction experts and razed acres of German cities.

A revolutionary achievement such as this shows that war becomes more and more appalling. The allied landings in Western Europe were scarcely a day too soon in preventing cataracts of V-1 and V-2 bombs and high explosives being hurled against Britain and perhaps North America. Given another six months, it is reckoned that German scientists would have worked out the atomic bomb. Under the terrific urgencies and desperate impulses of self preservation in war, the pace of invention and scientific advance is accelerated. It is a cause of profound gratitude and thanksgiving that this race was won by Britain and American, and it would not be surprising if before long the use of the atomic bomb were to achieve in the war against Japan the major effect intended. Already the rulers of Japan have been given a time-limit within which to surrender, or witness catastrophic destruction on a scale never before seen either in war or in the cataclysms that have periodically rocked Japan by earthquakes or seared it with fires.

Lessons of tremendous import to the human race emerge. Human conflict ceases to be an affair of personal courage or physical prowess. It now assumes the guise of a terrific unleashing of impersonal forces capable of engulfing whole communities in general destruction. Doubtless what has been produced is but the forerunner of more destructive and powerful applications of atomic energy. If there were to be rivalry in developing such agencies, and risks of further wars, mankind would have created a Frankenstein monster for its own destruction. Such vast powers may be in the hands of moral and physical pygmies.

Unless man can control his own impulses and use the powers of science for beneficent purposes, his life becomes a brutish affair. So terrifying is the prospect of new wars that the only chance of maintaining decent existence anywhere on the planet is to apply effective deterrents to war. In bygone times, the fate of empires was decided in battles fought at a distance, while the home population went about its affairs with little disturbance. These immunities have irrevocably gone, and the ordinary citizen everywhere has a direct take in effectively ridding the world of the horrors implicit in a competitive use of the astounding products of invention. It is no longer a question of humanising war or of requiring belligerents to comport themselves with a decent regard to non-combatants. As the range of weapons and propellants increases, no part of the earth's surface would be exempt from sudden cataclysmic destruction.

Whether atomic energies can be harnessed to other ends than war and destruction remains to be seen. Probably, as Sir John Anderson says, much more research will be necessary before present sources of power in electric generating stations oil-burning engines or coal-fired boilers become obsolete. The control of this great energy to achieve a smooth, even release, instead of a terrific destructive effect, may take a long time. The holocaust of Hiroshima is a grim warning to Japan, and the threat of worse to come unless the Allies' demands be met must weigh heavily with the warlords responsible for continuing a lost cause.

A Survivor's Description of the Attack on Hiroshima

The extent of destruction and suffering on the ground in both Hiroshima and Nagasaki is difficult to express in words. Following the attacks, survivors sought to convey the horror of their experience through a variety of media, including oral and written narratives, poetry, drawings and paintings. The countless memoirs and artworks that paint the experiences of that day all emphasise, first, the blinding light and the earth-shattering sound of the explosion, then the eerie silence that followed before the survivors' pain erupted in screams and cries for help. The heat of the explosion seemed to be transferred right into the bodies of the survivors, so that the unquenchable thirst and the search for water becomes another leitmotiv of the survivors' accounts. Another point of commonality is the description of injuries peculiar to the A-bomb – the extensive burns, the skin peeling and hanging in strips, and later the haemorrhages, bleeding gums, and high fever symptomatic of radiation poisoning. The search for missing relatives, the daze induced by the extent of the destruction and the unexpected and unexplainable appearance of odd symptoms are all typical of the narrative of the A-bomb experience on the ground, as is the location of the experience in terms of relative distance from the epicentre.

Hiroshima was home to thousands of Koreans. Many of them had been born in Japan; others had been brought to Hiroshima from their home (a Japanese colony since 1910) during the war as forced labourers to work in war industries. Koreans occupied a lowly place in Japanese society as a whole before and during the war, and they continued to be discriminated against as an ethnic minority after the war. One area in which this discrimination is clearly visible is in the absence of the Korean *hibakusha* or 'A-bomb victim' both in early Japanese tallies of deaths in Hiroshima and often in subsequent memories and commemoration of the bomb. In this extract, a Korean labourer, Oh Bongsu, remembers that morning in Hiroshima.

On that particular day, I was going to Hiroshima, to Kamiyachō (1 km from the epicentre), wasn't I. Someone I knew had their house ripped down to make a firebreak, and was told to take the beams and the planks and whatever away, so I went to help take these, on my bicycle. It's quite a distance from here (in the outskirts of Hiroshima, about 5 km from the epicentre) to Kamiyachō. I got up at 4 am, brought water from the river to the fields, ate some breakfast and left the house. It was incredibly beautiful weather – it wasn't even 8 am yet and it was really bright. There were people everywhere on the roads. Everyone was off to work in Hiroshima: there were students, girl students, ooh, even those on labour service, though it was the suburbs, everyone was off to their factories or their work for the army or whatever.

Working in Kamiyachō, I was bent down, tying up sawn off planks, wasn't I. Then suddenly, AHHH there was this incredibly bright light and I was thrown two or three meters. I couldn't see anything – something was burning in my eyes. I couldn't hear a sound, as if I'd gone deaf. It was pitch black. I don't know how much time passed. It was incredibly smelly, a stink of sulphur. Then, gradually, I started hearing again and seeing again.

But then, what a sight, ooh, I couldn't believe it. Everything had collapsed. Everything was upside down. Everything was gone. Everything was flattened. There was nothing left. And then, from here and there, the cries, 'help me, help me', eyes blackened, noses gone, the skin gone from the flesh even, the skin hanging in strips from the limbs, screaming crying, well you couldn't look at it. I can't even describe it properly. Well, the things that happened then. ... Street cars were fallen over and burning. Horses burned to death, still standing. ... I ran away, didn't I, crazy, half-dead. ... I ran across the burning bridge at Yokokawa, and it was an iron bridge and that bomb, well, even the metal and the stones were burning ... I was so hot, it felt like I had a fire burning in me, like I was on fire ... sparks were falling on me, there was fire everywhere ... all the people running away, they were looking for water. ... Me too, it was incredible this fire burning inside me, my throat was burning and I thought if I drink water I will die.[9] ... and then my skin, ahh, my burnt skin, first I was picking it off, thought it was my clothes. ... I was dazed, thinking I must get home I can't die. I didn't even know I was barefoot my socks had come off.

I came as far as Koi, to a school where the army had a first aid station, it was full of people. There were lots of dead, too. A mountain of dead, fallen with blood flowing and crushed eyes. I was still alive ... When my turn came, there was this military doctor, and while he was dressing my wounds he asked 'Where were you?' This guy asked me this, and so I replied, didn't I, said 'I was in Kamiyachō'. So he says: 'you ... !!! You're a Korean!', and now he was looking at me like he wanted to kill me, he was glaring at me, wasn't he, hoooo!

I thought: 'Right! Like I need help from a bastard like you!' and I left, didn't I.

Japanese Memories of the Nuclear Attacks

As noted, the A-bomb experience has provoked countless artistic forms, including paintings, novels and films, but also including poetry. More than 50,000 A-bomb-related tanka (a traditional form of Japanese poetry) have been written.

Poem by Etsuchi Ayako
Like a demon or ghost
A man runs away –
Staggering-
With both hands
Hung loosely in front of him.

Poem by Ishii Sadako
One that lies down
Is not a corpse
He is still breathing,
Wriggling-
Here lies a living being.

Poem by Imai Tokuzaburō
The streets
Still smoldering
Are deserted
"let me hear a voice
Calling your father!"

Poem by Izumi Asao
On newspapers
Spread on depot platforms
We sleep
With those
Already dead.

Prisoners of War Under the Bomb

Another set of victims of the atomic bombs were Allied prisoners of war (POWs). Eric Hooper was an Australian POW in a camp in Nagasaki. He remembers the day the bomb fell. Hooper is laconic about his lucky escape, although his account reveals the death of many other Allied prisoners in the bomb. There are several striking aspects to his account, not least his description of a town empty of all living beings.

We heard the plane overhead that dropped the bomb on August 9th. The whole place came down on top of us, we were sheltered from the ray on account of being in the building. Of the 24 Aussies there, only one, Reg McConnell from Gosford, was the only one that had a slight ray burn....

Most buildings were blown down and the timber ones burnt. After the bomb fell we were free for sometime. I said to someone where was everyone and he said they had gone to the hills. I said, 'Well, we may as well go also'. I was stunned for a while. I found Peter Kerr in a room also stunned, but we both recovered after a while.

There was a horse and lorry standing in the camp as if nothing had happened. We knew there were Red Cross parcels in a room, so six or seven of us loaded as many parcels as possible on the lorry and set sail. We didn't know where to, but we just went. I, being a horseman, was in charge of the horse, the others were around the lorry holding the parcels on. There was debris everywhere, even electric light poles across the roads, but we and our faithful steed took everything in our stride....

We got clear of Nagasaki and we decided the horse and lorry were of no further use to us so we abandoned the transport and went across paddocks to the hills. I forget what we did with the old horse. Not one of our party had anything of the parcels to eat. We said we wouldn't touch them until we met up with the rest of the boys. We were eating raw vegetables from the paddocks. About mid-afternoon the guards picked us up and took us where they had the rest of the boys. The guards took possession of the parcels and throughout the night we could hear them opening cans etc. and eating the contents. We were very hostile that, at least, we didn't have a feed ourselves.

Next day we were taken to the square in the middle of Nagasaki where we stayed for about a week, cleaning up our factory site etc. There were twenty Englishmen in the camp. One got killed in the bomb and we cremated him on a heap of wood. We collected a few ashes, I suppose most would be wood ashes. After about a week, the Nips took us out about seven or eight miles to another camp. There were about 60 odd Dutch POWs. Eight died and many were burnt and injured. We had to make makeshift stretchers, and four of us to a stretcher had to carry the injured Dutch to the new camp. One day before we left Nagasaki we were cleaning up at the factory and a Yank plane dived at us. We thought we had had it, but they were only looking. There were big water tanks about three feet high for incendiaries and when the plane came over we all went for cover. One of the boys dived into the water. It was very comical afterwards. Back to the stretchers, how we did it beats me, because we weren't in good shape. I suppose the rifle the Nips had helped. Eventually we arrived at our new camp. On the 18th August 1945, the Nips told us of the capitulation. After that the guards were bowing to us instead of the way it was for about 3½ years. A complete turnabout face.

Living With the Scars

At the time the bombs were dropped there was little knowledge anywhere about the extent of its impact or the long-term effects of radiation on its victims. In Japan, concerns about long-term health issues as well as foetal deformations marginalised those affected by 'pikadon' ('flashbang', or the A-bomb) in post-war Japan. While there were a number of real health issues affecting bomb victims, there was also a great deal of misinformation, leading to discrimination. The girl whose story is recounted here, Konishi Yukiko, had been employed and schooled in the Hiroshima tram transport system and was working near the town centre at the time of the explosion. After the end of the war, the girls were squeezed out of the tram workforce by the return of soldiers, and Konishi found work in a more traditionally female job, in a textile factory, where she lodged in a company dormitory with about 1,000 other girls, and where her scarred body led to discrimination.

[Konishi Yukiko] went to the communal baths. There were lots of others there. Yukiko's body was covered in scars, and especially on her back the scaring was raw.

'What happened to her back?' 'oh yuck!'

Her friends speculated noisily about what might have happened. Then one girl asked her directly: 'What happened?'

'I was hurt by Pikadon', Konishi replied truthfully.

At once, everyone around her said 'Run away!' and scattered like birds. They mistakenly thought that Pikadon was poisonous, that it was contagious.

After that, whenever Konishi went to the baths, everyone looked at her strangely. No one came near her. Konishi washed herself apart from the others, and entered the bath apart from the others. For Yukiko, the communal baths became hell.

CHAPTER ELEVEN
SURRENDER

It will mean the end of these prolonged privations and pain.

President Harry Truman to the Japanese people,
8 May 1945

The Japanese government surrendered on 15 August 1945, ending an eight-year war against China and a three and a half-year war against the United States and its allies. The process of negotiating the surrender was a long one, which in retrospect is open to many interpretations. It had started with the Cairo Declaration of November 1943, in which the United States, Great Britain and China had announced that nothing but an unconditional surrender from Japan would end the war, and that the territory of Japan would be limited to the four home islands, with colonial possessions returned to China or granted independence. Eighteen months later, on 26 July 1945, the same governments, later joined by the Soviet Union, issued the Potsdam Declaration, which restated the aims set out at Cairo, and clarified the Allied plans for the post-surrender transformation of Japan. This included provisions for a military occupation of Japan, for the abolition of its military forces, and also for the political transformation of Japan into a democratic state.

The implied threat to the basic framework of the Japanese state and, by extension, to the Imperial institution (often described as the 'Japanese polity' or the 'national polity') was unacceptable to the Japanese government. It was only after the two atomic bombs fell on 6 and 9 August and the Soviet invasion of Manchuria from 8 August that Japan relented, having in the meantime clarified the terms of the Declaration in such a way that they could be understood to allow for the preservation of the Imperial house, without undermining the Allies' insistence that the surrender be unconditional. On 14 August 1945, at a fateful meeting of the Japanese leaders, evenly divided between those who wanted to accept the surrender and those who would keep fighting, Emperor Hirohito sided with peace. This finally brought the war to an end, while also beginning a protracted debate regarding the extent of the emperor's ability to influence the decisions of his government during the war and, by extension, the nature of his war guilt.

By August 1945, Japan had been within the range of American bombers for nearly a year. Its cities had been attacked relentlessly. The deadly bombing raid on Tokyo on 10 March 1945, which killed 100,000 people in one night, was only one amongst many deadly raids, destroying as much as half of all Japanese housing and industry. In April 1945, the Allies had landed in Okinawa, the southernmost part of the Japanese territory. The ensuing battles are famous for their bloodshed and loss of life.

For the Japanese people, the growing intensity of the bombing and the news of the invasion of Okinawa belied the optimistic twist that the newspapers were still attempting to give to predominantly bad news. Shortages of food, clothing and other goods were making life difficult. Soldiers were recruited amongst older men and university students: the latter often ended up training, and dying, as Special Attack pilots. Their planes were so inferior and fuel so scarce that the training was almost as deadly as the missions themselves. And yet, nobody talked publicly of surrender, although many did privately, notwithstanding Japanese and Allied propaganda to the contrary. Rather, the fiction was maintained that Japan would fight 'to the end'. Some neighbourhood associations even began training its members with bamboo spears in preparation for the invasion. For the Allies, the kind of resistance encountered first in Saipan and then in Okinawa suggested that an invasion of the Japanese mainland would be long, bloody and immensely destructive. This helped confirm the decision to use nuclear weapons on Japan.

One of the major debates about the Asia-Pacific war centres on what it was that pushed Japan to surrender, finally, on 15 August 1945. Most historians now agree that it was a combination of the devastating impact of the A-bombs, the Soviet invasion and the general exhaustion of Japan militarily, economically and psychologically. But there is an ongoing and lively debate concerning which of these factors was more compelling for the Japanese government. As Barton Bernstein has shown recently, although the debate about the A-bomb and the debates about the reasons for the surrender are clearly related, there are surprisingly few points of intersection between these debates, which are generally tackled separately. Bernstein's survey of the current state of debate on the Japanese decision to surrender provides a good understanding of how intricate the debate can become, how much of it is a matter of interpretation – in some cases leading two scholars reading the same document to arrive at completely different conclusions – and how much of it remains contingent on the discovery of new archives, especially in the former Soviet Union.[1]

Another aspect of the surrender receiving increasing historiographical attention is the notion that 15 August 1945 was only the official end of the war. This is partly the result of a turn towards social and cultural histories of the war rather than simply military ones. In these interpretations, there are continuities between the wartime and the post-war period that deserve attention, such as the impact of war injuries, the loss of family members, as well as other social transformations clearly linked to the war. In the case of Japan, 15 August 1945 marks a clear separation in both symbolic and practical ways between two distinct periods in twentieth-century history. Recently, however, many historians have challenged the absolute nature of that separation, and identified significant continuities between the wartime and post-war periods, including the organisation of local grass-roots welfare systems, or aspects of the central government.

However, these are issues that would have made little sense, and been of little interest, to those who witnessed the surrender. For ordinary people, whether they were living in Allied countries, in Japan or in areas occupied by Japan, the end of this long and devastating war was a momentous event. Although the defeat of Germany a few months before had presaged the inevitable defeat of Japan, amongst the Allies, the long-awaited VP (Victory in the Pacific) or VJ (Victory over Japan) day allowed for unbridled celebrations, though no doubt also tinged with sadness for the fallen, and also anger at an enemy who had not only fought viciously, but for much longer than necessary in the face of certain defeat.

The reactions in Japan were similarly complex, although it is difficult to measure adequately the sense of trauma that accompanied the news of the defeat. The shocking surrender was announced in the famous radio broadcast of an emperor whose distance from the people made him literally difficult to understand. Yet if the words delivered by the high-pitched voice belonged to the rarefied world of the Japanese elite, the meaning of the emperor's message was all too clear to those assembled around the available radio receivers. Most Japanese memoirs remember the stunned silence into which the emperor's words fell, broken by the sobs of adults and children alike. Even if there had been little hope for victory for many months, the announcement of the defeat was nevertheless deeply disturbing. But most memoirs also mention the glimmer of hope that accompanied the news of the surrender, the sense of relief that was mixed with uncertainty about the future. If nothing else, at least for now the bombing would stop, as would the relentless work in munitions factories and other war-related industries, perhaps even the hunger (although food shortages, as it turned out, would continue for the first two years of the Occupation). Despite the generally peaceful acceptance of the surrender by the population at large, there were also many members of the Japanese armed forces who resented the decision to surrender, including those who attempted a last-ditch *coup-d'état* and tried to storm the radio station from which the emperor's recording would be broadcast, and, as some documents in this chapters show, those who continued to hope for resistance even after the surrender.

Japanese people had come through years of exhortations towards victory, and had heard and perhaps contributed to propaganda claiming Japan could only win. Many had been preparing for last-ditch battles on the homeland: whether or not they really believed that the only alternative to victory was annihilation, it seems clear that very few thought their government would ever capitulate. For some, the loss of faith that this sudden turnaround prompted was too difficult to live with, leading to suicides, or murder-suicides. However, on the whole, the proportion of Japanese people who took their own lives on account of the surrender was minimal, even if amongst the Allies, there had been an expectation of mass suicides such as those that Allied forces had witnessed on Saipan or in Okinawa. Rather, it seems that in the first few months after the war, the exhaustion and the shock of the surrender translated into a patchy and on the whole short-lived, but at times intense, contempt for soldiers and what they represented. Some of this was due to the fact that some soldiers were helping themselves to stores of military goods when the civilian population had very little food or belongings left. To this was added the simple pressure that the return of three million soldiers from overseas put on the meagre resources of those at home. But some of the contempt was clearly also due to a sense that soldiers had been exacting the admiration and respect of the civilian population for all these years on false pretences. It was the military arm of the government – so the Japanese population was told in leaflets dropped by the Allies before the defeat – that had been responsible for dragging out the war, and in a sense demobilised soldiers were simply the most immediately available target of all the scorn, the resentment and the anger that many felt towards the military institution as a whole.

For soldiers in Allied armies, the surrender allowed for a less-complicated return home. If nothing else, membership of those forces on the victorious side allowed for a relatively uncomplicated celebration of the surrender. Whilst the celebrations were tainted with sadness at the death of comrades, there was at least the consolation that their death had been a sacrifice for a good and valuable cause. But even for victorious soldiers, reintegration into civilian life had its own problems: many felt alienated from their communities, partly because of long separations from family and friends and partly because of the gulf between the violence of the battlefield and the relatively 'normal' life of those at home. Many demobilised soldiers were unable to share their experiences with their families, or declined to do so because these were not topics to be brought up in polite conversation. The refuge provided by the presence of other demobilised soldiers at the local club or in various veterans' organisation thus acquired immense importance for some. Needless to say, all these reintegration problems also affected Japanese veterans, but for them, the situation was complicated by the fact that they had lost the war, and that their military institutions were being dismantled under the Occupation. The Army and Navy Ministries survived the end of the war by a few months as Demobilisation Ministries No. 1 and 2; after the bulk of demobilisation had been handled, the remaining soldiers overseas were processed on their return by civilian institutions.

In any case, the official date of the surrender was in many ways not the end of the war itself. In some areas, Allied attacks, coupled with the lack of reliable food supplies, forced Japanese soldiers to combine into small groups which hid from the Allies and foraged for food. Far from their own hierarchical structures, these groups had no reliable information about the progress of the war. Famously, some Japanese soldiers would not emerge from such hiding spots for many years, but more immediately, it meant that fighting continued well after 15 August 1945 until all Japanese soldiers had been rounded up and told about the surrender. In other areas, the need for peacekeeping forces overrode the importance of Japanese demobilisation, which meant that, in China at least, Japanese troops were not disarmed immediately but were used by the Nationalist armies to supplement their strength against resurgent communist armies. In Indonesia and Indochina, Japanese soldiers took part in the wars of independence that followed the end of the war itself, willingly or not. For Allied soldiers, too, a swift return home was hindered, sometimes for shipping reasons, sometimes because it was clear that soldiers would also be needed in the Occupation of Japan.

In that sense, then, the surrender of Japan does not mark a neat break in the history of the war – neither for the Allied soldiers nor for their Japanese counterparts. Needless to say, the break was perhaps even less defined in those countries that had been occupied by Japan. Although the news of the surrender there had been, for the most part, as joyfully received as in Allied countries, it was also greeted with new hopes for independence in a world with changed power balances. The Japanese surrender brought a short-lived and precarious peace in a world already divided by the rival domestic and international interests of the Cold War. The people of China and Korea barely experienced peace at all before their countries were once more torn apart by war. In other places, the disruption created by the Japanese invasion festered for many years before erupting into war again. And over all these new, smaller wars loomed the new threat of nuclear warfare.

THE SOURCES

President Truman Addresses the Japanese People

The Allies used not only bombing to destroy the Japanese fighting capability: psychological warfare was also an important means to persuade Japan to surrender. Leaflets such as the one below, which was widely dropped on Japan to announce the destruction of Nazi Germany, were designed to sow seeds of doubt about the certain victory that the Japanese government had promised its people. The personal greeting of President Truman was supplemented by a photo of Truman, on the phone, as a kindly 'man in a suit behind a desk'. The Japanese version used a writing style supplemented with syllabic characters, designed to make it readable to even the least educated Japanese. This one was dropped on 8 May 1945.

A message to the People of Japan from the President of the United States Harry S Truman.

Nazi Germany has been annihilated. The people of Japan must recognise the immensely destructive power of the American Army, Navy and Airforce. As long as the politicians and the military leaders of your precious country continue this war, we will massively intensify our attacks and their destructive power. There will be no relief until we have thoroughly destroyed the munitions factories, the transport system, even the human resources that support your war efforts. A war of attrition will only increase the misery and the pain of the Japanese people. Nothing can be gained by the Japanese people. Our attacks will not cease until the Japanese military has accepted uncon-ditional surrender and has laid down its arms. How will the military's unconditional surrender affect the population of Japan? In one word, it will mean the end of the war. It will mean the end of the authority of the military, which is responsible for the current destruction of Japan. It will mean the possibility that the soldiers of the Army and Navy, who are currently fighting in terrible conditions at the frontlines, will swiftly return to their loving families, their farms, their workplaces. Moreover, it will mean the end of these prolonged privations and pain, in which victory can only appear as a fleeting dream. Some will falsely claim that the unconditional surrender might mean the obliteration or the enslavement of the Japanese people: do not believe them.

The Allies Demand Unconditional Surrender from Japan

On 26 July 1945 at Potsdam, the Allies (initially minus the Soviet Union) declared the terms of the surrender for the Japanese government. The Potsdam Declaration contained the programme for post-war Occupation of Japan, and it was the Japanese government's understanding of a threat to the 'Japanese polity' – especially the Imperial House – that led it to hesitate and pursue earlier peace feelers. The hesitation carried through the bombing of Hiroshima, the news of the Russian attack on Japanese troops in Manchuria and the bombing of Nagasaki. Also note in the Declaration the apportioning of blame for the war.

The Potsdam Declaration

Proclamation Defining Terms for Japanese Surrender
Issued, at Potsdam, July 26, 1945

1. We-the President of the United States, the President of the National Government of the Republic of China, and the Prime Minister of Great Britain, representing the hundreds of millions of our countrymen, have conferred and agree that Japan shall be given an opportunity to end this war.

2. The prodigious land, sea and air forces of the United States, the British Empire and of China, many times reinforced by their armies and air fleets from the west, are poised to strike the final blows upon Japan. This military power is sustained and inspired by the determination of all the Allied Nations to prosecute the war against Japan until she ceases to resist.

3. The result of the futile and senseless German resistance to the might of the aroused free peoples of the world stands forth in awful clarity as an example to the people of Japan. The might that now converges on Japan is immeasurably greater than that which, when applied to the resisting Nazis, necessarily laid waste to the lands, the industry and the method of life of the whole German people. The full application of our military power, backed by our resolve, will mean the inevitable and complete destruction of the Japanese armed forces and just as inevitably the utter devastation of the Japanese homeland.

4. The time has come for Japan to decide whether she will continue to be controlled by those self-willed militaristic advisers whose unintelligent calculations have brought the Empire of Japan to the threshold of annihilation, or whether she will follow the path of reason.

5. Following are our terms. We will not deviate from them. There are no alternatives. We shall brook no delay.

6. There must be eliminated for all time the authority and influence of those who have deceived and misled the people of Japan into embarking on world conquest, for we insist that a new order of peace, security and justice will be impossible until irresponsible militarism is driven from the world.

7. Until such a new order is established and until there is convincing proof that Japan's war-making power is destroyed, points in Japanese territory to be designated by the Allies shall be occupied to secure the achievement of the basic objectives we are here setting forth.

8. The terms of the Cairo Declaration shall be carried out and Japanese sovereignty shall be limited to the islands of Honshu, Hokkaido, Kyushu, Shikoku and such minor islands as we determine.

9. The Japanese military forces, after being completely disarmed, shall be permitted to return to their homes with the opportunity to lead peaceful and productive lives.

10. We do not intend that the Japanese shall be enslaved as a race or destroyed as a nation, but stern justice shall be meted out to all war criminals, including those who have visited cruelties upon our prisoners. The Japanese Government shall remove all obstacles to the revival and strengthening of democratic tendencies among the Japanese people. Freedom of speech, of religion, and of thought, as well as respect for the fundamental human rights shall be established.

11. Japan shall be permitted to maintain such industries as will sustain her economy and permit the exaction of just reparations in kind, but not those which would enable her to re-arm for war. To this end, access to, as distinguished from control of, raw materials shall be permitted. Eventual Japanese participation in world trade relations shall be permitted.

12. The occupying forces of the Allies shall be withdrawn from Japan as soon as these objectives have been accomplished and there has been established in accordance with the freely expressed will of the Japanese people a peacefully inclined and responsible government.

13. We call upon the government of Japan to proclaim now the unconditional surrender of all Japanese armed forces, and to provide proper and adequate assurances of their good faith in such action. The alternative for Japan is prompt and utter destruction.

Emperor Hirohito Announces Japan's Surrender

The following is an extract of the message that the Japanese people heard on 15 August announcing the Japanese defeat. Hirohito's speech was not delivered live but had been made into a record for fear that military opponents of surrender might try to stop the broadcast. The emperor had not been heard on radio since the late 1920s, leaving most Japanese unable to recognise his voice. Moreover, he spoke in very formal Japanese. Many of the emperor's subjects had little idea what he was saying. His message was also not helped by an abundance of euphemisms intended to cushion the blow.

To our good and loyal subjects:

After pondering deeply the general trends of the world and the actual conditions obtaining in our Empire today, we have decided to effect a settlement of the present situation by resorting to an extraordinary measure.

We have ordered our Government to communicate to the Governments of the Untied States, Great Britain, China and the Soviet Union that our Empire accepts the provisions of their joint declaration.

To strive for the common prosperity and happiness of all nations as well as the security and well-being of our subjects is the solemn obligation which has been handed down by Our Imperial Ancestors and we lay it close to the heart.

Indeed, we declared war on America and Britain out of our sincere desire to ensure Japan's self-preservation and the stabilisation of East Asia, it being far from our thought either to infringe upon the upon the sovereignty of other nations or to embark upon territorial aggrandizement.

But now the war has lasted for nearly four years. Despite the best that has been done by everyone – the gallant fighting of the military and naval forces, the diligence and assiduity of our servants of the State and the devoted service of our one hundred million people – the war situation has developed not necessarily to Japan's advantage, while the general trends of the world have all turned against her interest.

Moreover, the enemy has begun to employ a new and most cruel bomb, the power of which to do damage is, indeed, incalculable, taking the toll of many innocent lives. Should we continue to fight, it would not only result in an ultimate collapse and obliteration of the Japanese nation, but also it would lead to the total extinction of the human race....

We are keenly aware of the inmost feelings of all you, our subjects. However it is according to the dictate of time and fate that we have resolved to pave the way for a grand peace for all the generations to come by enduring the unendurable and suffering what is unsufferable. Having been able to save and maintain the structure of the Imperial State, we are always with you, our good and loyal subjects, relying upon your sincerity and integrity.

Beware most strictly of any outbursts of emotion that may engender needless complications, and of any fraternal contention and strife that may create confusion, lead you astray and cause you to lose the confidence of the world.

Let the entire nation continue as one family from generation to generation, ever firm in its faith in the imperishableness of its divine land, and mindful of its heavy burden of responsibilities, and the long road before it. Unite your total strength to be devoted to the construction for the future. Cultivate the ways of rectitude, nobility of spirit, and work with resolution so that you may enhance the innate glory of the Imperial State and keep pace with the progress of the world.

All you, our subjects, we command you to act in accordance with our wishes.

Hirohito
(the Seal of the Emperor)
14 August 1945
(Countersignature of the Ministers of State)

The Experiences of a Japanese Factory Manager Based in China

The following is an extract from an unpublished manuscript by Kawazoe Sōichi, an American-trained Japanese engineer who had been managing a munitions factory near Mukden in Manchuria. After the Japanese surrender, Kawazoe and his family were prevented from returning to Japan because his technical skills were invaluable to the Chinese Communist Party. After several years in China, Kawazoe was eventually repatriated. Later he lived in the United States as a representative of a Japanese car manufacturing company.

On August 12, 1945, I left Mukden on a truck. I had already sent some 500 Chinese mechanics and 100 Japanese workers to Antung by freight train. I crated 500 machines and they were all on freight trains at the Mukden Station. All the passenger trains leaving Mukden southbound were occupied by families of Japanese Army personnel and V.I.P.'s in the government. None of us, civilian, could even get near the trains.

Later we realised that they already knew of the coming Japanese surrender and were trying desperately to reach Japan before the end. It was only we ignorant Chauvinists who blindly believed in the Japanese government and who, until the very last moment, were trying so hard to serve the country, who were left behind. Incidentally, the trains never made it to Japan. They were all caught in Korea when the war ended and the women and children fared lots worse than ours in Manchuria. Some of them escaped to come back to Manchuria and the stories were heard were simply unbelievable. They were all so dirty, skinny, sick and on the verge of starvation that we just did not have the heart to say that it served them right for abandoning us. We took them all into our families and gave them food, clothing and medication.

On August 12, 1945, as mentioned above, I left Mukden with my family and few other people including Mrs Komuta and her baby on a truck surrounded by our personal effects. It took us three days and we finally arrived in Sandorando on the morning of August 15th. At noon, as we were having lunch, we heard the voice of our Emperor announcing our surrender and the end of the war. There was a dead silence in the Dining Room; the only sound was the children eating noodles. We were shocked to hear the most unexpected.

When we recovered, I gathered all the workers together. I told the Chinese workers that they were free to go but to leave a representative with me as I wanted to discuss the matters of pay, rations and housing. I then held meetings with my Japanese engineers and mechanics. There was the Manager of Antung Plant of Manchurian Motor Company at Sandorando but the next day, as I tried to reach him, I found that he had run away the night before. He certainly did not waste much time as the Chinese workers started to hunt important Japanese of each company to avenge themselves for mistreatment. I was a plant manager too but a newcomer and besides, I never even imagined that my Chinese men would mistreat me so I tried to organize the chaos. I was being looked up to as the leader by both the Japanese and the Chinese workers who came with me from Mukden.

After the unconditional surrender of the Japanese Empire, we did not know how the Chinese people were going to treat us, but the men I sent to the city brought back bad news. Japanese women were being raped. All Japanese police chiefs, high government officials, presidents of companies either disappeared or were killed by Chinese mobs. Many Japanese farmers around Antung were robbed of all their belongings. Some resisted and were killed. Others took refuge in the Japanese community in the city. There were no police, no law. The Japanese families who had good Chinese friends fared best. Those hated were stripped of all belongings and thrown out of their homes.

Japanese Reactions to the Surrender

In the immediate aftermath of the surrender, the shock of capitulation revealed itself in a variety of behaviours and emotions. While most of the population accepted the defeat as inevitable and greeted it with a sense of relief, others had not understood the magnitude of the defeat. The following selections from regional military police reports, written a few days after the surrender, suggest both the confusion and variety of reactions occasioned by the end of the war, and the edginess of the military police in the face of apparently unpredictable reactions.

Military Police Headquarters, 20 August 1945,
Report on Law and Order
(Report from Tokai Squad HQ, 19 August 1945, 17:00)

1) re: military
   Some troops within the jurisdiction of the Tokai Military Police Headquarters are proclaiming that they will resist to the end. They are currently organising drills and crisis squadrons.
   a) In the air force squadron of the Navy at Suzuka, about 70 Special Attack Pilots have announced that at the time of the enemy's arrival they will barricade themselves into the mountains and continue to resist.
   b) At the Tokai battalion 94, after the unit commander announced on the 15th 'all troops must fight to the end', the unit members' spirits were uplifted and his subordinates organised crisis squadrons. In the same battalion, a section of soldiers born on the peninsula resented being excluded by the above mentioned soldiers, and are appealing for inclusion in these groups.
   c) Further:
      Re: Noda Sukemichi (29) Army Pharmacy Lieutenant attached to the technical sub-branch of the Seventh Army, Kanazawa office.
      In the early morning of 16 August at his home, the above-mentioned killed three members of his family (Grandmother, mother and younger sister) and himself with a sword, leaving a note that reads: 'I am unable to fulfil my duty of respectfully and reverentially accepting the Imperial Decision'

2) General conditions:

Although those who are patriots are hoping for the recovery of the army, there is a gradual change towards outspoken contempt for the army in general.

For example:

a) In the neighbourhood of Shinshiroshi in the district of Minami Shitara in Aichi prefecture, several members of the public attacked soldiers.

b) On a tram in the town of Kanazawa, there was an incident in which a uniformed warrant officer was contemptuously told: 'Soldier, get rid of your sword'.

c) Other events:

i. On the 17th, a rumour circulated that the chief of staff present at the meeting of the air force division 501 had said that 'when the enemy lands, they'll get their hands on young girls'. As a result, the mayor of Gifu ordered that all of girls in Gifu aged between 15 and 25 be evacuated to the nearby mountains, which temporarily caused extreme agitation. The prefectural police handled the matter carefully and by the 18th the city had returned to calm.

ii. In every region there appears to be an increase of people withdrawing their entire savings.

Demobilising the Japanese Military: Experiences and Tensions

Tensions between Japanese civilians and soldiers, which had been growing during the war as the home front came under fire, exploded into the public sphere after the surrender, provoking headaches for those responsible for public order. Here we discern the kind of comments by demobilised soldiers that were seen as disturbing the peace by the chief of police in a prefecture on the Japan Sea Coast, near one of Japan's major repatriation centres, into which now poured thousands of demobilised soldiers from nearby Korea and Manchuria.

20 September 1945. From Okura Masahiro, Chief of Police, Tottori Prefecture. To the director of security, Office of Police, Ministry of the Interior To the first division chief responsible for the region of central Japan.

Item relating to the reaction of a section of the population to returned demobilised soldiers.

The previous report suggested the attitudes of the general public and the behaviour of soldiers on the occasion of the homecoming and demobilisation of Army and Navy personnel, especially in regards to them carrying off clothes, food stuffs of course, but even cars and horses. As previously stated, the behaviour of returned soldiers is extremely irritating to the people around here, and tends to further inflame anti-military feelings. The more extreme of these behaviours have been referred to the responsible arm of the military police directly. Generally speaking, unfounded and exaggerated rumours unnecessarily inflame anti-military sentiment; and we clearly recognise that this also adversely influences sympathetic feelings towards war-bereaved families and war-wounded soldiers. It is important to provide leadership in this. The main issues that have arisen in the meantime are listed below.

Behaviour of returned soldiers:

1) At Dakyōji in Kurayoshi city,
A member of the Miho section of the engineer corps, Maizuru Naval Base, Yamane Nobuo, then 43.

Regarding the Japanese surrender, various rumours are circulated about the behaviour of the army, but at the Miho airbase we have certainly not disbanded. Of course on the surface we look like we are disbanded, but put us together with the Yonago railway management section and that can form an entire navy battalion. At Miho airfield, we heard in news from Manchuria and Korea that on the day of the Imperial Rescript, two officers of the Manchurian Army were dispatched as representatives to Tokyo to complain about the surrender. It looks like the complete disarmament of the Japanese Forces will be on 10 October, but around that last day, you bet there will be something happening.

2) At Tottori Squadron Liaison Headquarters,
Major Hirokichi

I myself came back from Manchuria, and my job is to guide demobilised soldiers into employment. I worry about the issue of food shortages and unemployment in Japan. Within the next three years, 10 million people will die of starvation. If we don't protect the employment of returned soldiers, there will no doubt be a crisis when they get balanced out by the return of [civilian] compatriots. If we don't collect rice from the farmers of the entire country, it will be the clodhoppers that will destroy Japan next. The farmers are saying it's the military that took the government and brought Japan to defeat, so they'd better see if they can take the government and save the people from starvation.

3) Tottori city, Yokkata town,
Lance Corporal Yamada Akiyoshi

I came back from Korea. The Soviet Army occupied Tientsin on 26 August, and I was really surprised that half of them weren't even armed. They were inferior quality soldiers: as soon as they occupied Tientsin they became violent and started plundering. We'd been disarmed and demobilised as per orders. They robbed us at gun-point, took our watches, clothing and shoes. I was so angry I could have shot them. It was a really terrible thing to see such miserable bastards in the middle of the Korean population.

I was drafted into the army in Korea, and was released in Korea and told to make my own way home. I'd only just been released when I was robbed by a Soviet soldier, and lost everything, then I paid through the nose for a ride in a fishing boat to Shimonoseki. There isn't one person who doesn't complain about the heartless treatment they've received. It's hardly a compassionate step to take to leave people to their own devices after demobilisation – just because you lost the war. When I got home, I saw that soldiers on the mainland were making money hand over fist taking clothing and food [from army stores]. I tell you, there will be a great deal of disturbances once another few million overseas soldiers come home.

An American Pilot's Exhilaration and Pride at the End of the War

The contrast between the disheartening post-surrender days of Japanese soldiers and the exhilaration of Allied soldiers is best illustrated by the juxtaposition of the above document and this letter, describing vividly the first post-war encounter with Japan of a B-29 bomber pilot.

THE THIRTIETH MISSION

The following letter reached its recipient in the Atlanta Office just before we went to press. The writer, Lt. F. H. Reed, a B-29 pilot who has been stationed on Saipan since last October, tells of his post-armistice flight over Tokyo August 28 to drop provisions in the P.W. camp at Kawasaki.

Dearest Mom & Dad:

I cannot possibly describe to you the adventure I had yesterday! I want to say so much, to describe so much, to let you know and realize so much – and I cannot do it! I cannot grasp all I saw myself! If I could only make you feel the way I felt – but you couldn't! It doesn't mean that much to you! You know the war is over – that Tokyo, Kawasaki, Yokohama, etc., have been terribly burned and bombed – but it doesn't go any farther – you know that we hit targets in the Tokyo area, and that Tokyo and the area around it symbolizes the toughest target area to B-29 crewmen of the "Fuji-44" class, but do you really comprehend? You know our prisoners of war (POWs) are there and that we dropped supplies to them – but can you appreciate the feeling we got and what we saw, when we found the camp and dropped the supplies?

So I'll just tell what I did, and for ever more realize how much it meant to me. We took off on Tuesday morning at 0900 to drop drums of supplies (attached to parachutes) to PWs. Our camp was known to be in Kawasaki, (a sort of southern suburb of Tokyo), separated by a river, though it had never been seen or photographed. It was supposed to be in an area that had been burned badly – and we were skeptical. We came into Tokyo Bay at about 5000 feet, at 1500 hours. The sun was beaming down, and we could see the fleet scattered all over Sagami Bay and some in Tokyo Bay already. F6Fs were flying around, and some F4As. We went up the Bay on the east side, drinking all the country-side in (indescribably beautiful), and noticing all the airfields, and planes sitting on them like a girl left waiting at the church. And finally came opposite Kawasaki, and the mouth of the big river that runs between it and Tokyo and empties into the Bay. We turned toward it, and began looking. What desolation! Acres and acres of nothing but a rusty looking soil and ashy rubbish, marked by the faint lines where walls had once stood. Now and then a few square blocks stood unscathed, but only serving to impress one with the total devastation. Some railways were in operation, as I saw an inter-urban train like the S.P. trains in California running through the ruins, and all heads were outside the windows and looking at us. The highways were OK; and looked beautiful, and quite a bit of auto traffic was apparent, considering the destruction. But then for the world's third largest city and its environs I guess it wasn't too much – even if they were in ruins. All of a sudden the bombardier picked out the PW camp. It was a two-story building with yellow pointed roofs, built in a square, with a large open compound or patio in the center. On one side was a large field bounded by a highway, and on the other side a jam-packed area of small houses that somehow had escaped the fire. There were the following signs on the roofs of the camp: PW. NEWS? NEWS? COME AND GET US, THANK YOU. The roof was crammed, the top windows jammed and the courtyard was full of prisoners all waving, gesticulating – delirious in their efforts to tell us how happy they were. We dropped the supplies in a field nearby; and the boys were evidently free to get outside of the compound, for they ran after them like mad. Some of the chutes failed to open, and it is a good thing we did drop them in the field, for the drums would have killed our own prisoners. Some did hit a Jap home on our second run, and plummeted right on through. We also noticed another building on the waterfront, a two- or three-story warehouse, that had the following writing or printing on the sides and top: AUSTRALIANS – TAKE US HOME, THREE CHEERS US NAVY. What a lump in my throat – as I say, I cannot describe my feelings. Then we went up and flew over the Emperor's Palace, and even out to our old Nemesis of a target – the one I have told you about so often – and we were flying at between 500 and 1000 feet! Tokyo is dead. Just acres of rusty looking ashes; and in the industrial areas, twisted, rusted gutted factories of all types. Now and then an untouched square of blocks, just to set off the contrast. Street-cars burned up, autos in parking lots burned, big government buildings like the Civic Center in San Francisco that looked unscathed, but with scorched markings, some worse than others. The down-town district of modern many-storied buildings reminded one of New York or San Francisco except not so tall. But to fly right over it! Everything flat as a pancake between the cement buildings, again that rusty, ashy looking dreariness, a close look showing that the big buildings still standing are gutted, burned out inside for the most part. Although there is little traffic, the city is literally dead. The Emperor's Palace grounds are in fair condition, though some buildings have been flattened, and others damaged. We flew on toward Fuji, indescribably beautiful in the distance, and found our aircraft plant beyond the outskirts of the city – demolished! Again the countryside so beautiful I cannot attempt to portray it. So neat. So compact. Such wonderful colors. Back to the Big City: people walking around in some districts look up at us; again some bicycles; some motor transportation; but mostly pedestrians, to whom the surrounding devastation gave an utterly dazed appearance. The sky was full of Navy fighters and B-29s (between 100 – 1000 feet) going every which way as they took their sightseeing, and gave themselves and the poor Japs a close-up of each other. Back to the PW camp for a final "buzz" job – then out over Tokyo Bay and down to the Yokosuka Naval Base, – destruction all along the waterfront; oil refineries demolished. I even saw hundreds of Japs out in the shallow water of the Bay, and it looked like they were planting rice! What could it have been? Many airfields, all resembling Hamilton Field, some with planes shot up, others untouched; hangars burned up, desolation supreme. Over the big Naval Base at the southern end of the Bay we saw a Jap battle wagon sitting useless, and a sub over-turned and rusting; destruction, utter and universal. The point towards Atsugi Airfield was our next heading. We flew nearly over it, and then turned left our over Sagami Bay, and buzzed the Fleet at 1000 feet, finally heading for Iwo, where we landed at about 2200. We had spent 1 hour and 45 minutes dropping our supplies and sightseeing – the biggest thrill of my life!

We spent the night at Iwo, and I flew back this morning. It may well be my last mission, though there is a possibility of a few more. (It made 30 for me. I'm pooped out – exhausted – thrilled beyond words!

Love,
Pete

P. S. No matter what they say, the biggest FACTOR in Japan's defeat is the B-29!

Return Anxiety: Welcoming Returned Servicemen Back to Their Pre-War Lives

With the end of war, many service personnel suffered what has been labelled 'return anxiety' as they considered their futures.[2] Loved ones and their communities shared such anxieties. In the minds of many were the troubles of reintegration and resettlement that had plagued the aftermath of the Great War. The victors had failed to deliver a 'Land fit for Heroes', and it appeared that the rise of Nazism and, by extension, World War II had much to do with disgruntled German veterans.[3] Even before victory was assured, the Australian and American governments focused on the job of post-war reconstruction.

Local community organisations sought to play their part in the post-war resettlement of their serving members. In Sydney, Australia, one such organisation was the Bondi Surf Bathers Life Saving Club, home of the iconic Bondi Lifesaver. With memories of its own reintegration difficulties in the wake of the Great War, the Club expended considerable resources to keep up the morale of its members in uniform and ensure they would return to the club on the war's conclusion.[4] One initiative was the production of a monthly newssheet called *The Doins*. Sent to each member in uniform, the newsletter kept members in touch with the club and their mates. Despite its conversational tone, the August 1945 edition shows the Club's concerns for its returning members.

Dear Mates,

Well, the job's done and despite their filthy, treacherous tactics the boastful Fascist bullies have tasted bitter defeat. It's now up to the Allied Statesmen to see that the lesson is a lasting one. Of course these Fascist fanatics with their twisted mentality could not realize that ordinary blokes who were quite content with simple leisure like a drowsy sunbake, an invigorating surf, a few schooners [glasses of beer] at the pub, and good companionship, could suddenly turn into deadly enemies when threatened with the loss of these things....

Well clubmates, that's all passed now and let's hope it won't be long before we are able to drift into the same old life we knew before the dreadful calamity of war blighted the world. Although the joy of victory is almost overwhelming and the desire to forget the horrors of war very great, we will always cherish the memory of our gallant mates who made the supreme sacrifice for the cause they believed to be just.

When they became members, each of these men was enjoined to do everything possible in conduct and competition to bring credit on the club. By their splendid war records they have brought not only credit but an undying glory to the club which was proud to have them....

Now comes the question of rehabilitation and in this regard your club is out to do everything humanly possible to help you. A strong committee has been elected to guide the club through the forthcoming big season, which might well be a record in the club's history. We want you to feel that you are coming back to a club which is proud of you and wants to show its appreciation in a tangible manner.

It was mentioned at the first Committee meeting that some of our clubmates coming back have felt a bit strange – almost a bit shy – when they saw so many new faces round the club. It was realised, with concern, that some of you might even feel inclined to drift away from the club. That's the last thing we want to happen, and in an effort to try and express just how welcome you are two men have been appointed more or less as official entertainers, receptionists, or liaison officers. Whatever you like to call them, their job is to try and show you just how happy we are to have you back. These men are Bill Jenkings and Frank Herron. We have selected the left hand corner of the public bar at the Astra (where Sylvia serves) as Bondi Surf Club corner and we'll always try to have someone there to meet you.

An Australian Reflects on His Wartime Experiences and Contemplates the Future

For some people, the war's end was also the beginning of a new life and of other new previously unimagined opportunities. Basil Archer spent the war years stationed in Western Australia, and remembers that it was by pure chance that he noticed a leaflet tacked on a fence post, advertising the need for soldiers in the Occupation of post-war Japan. After completing a crash course in Japanese, he was sent, via Morotai, to Japan as a member of the British Commonwealth Occupation Forces. Basil was a meticulous diarist, and his entry for the last day of the year the war ended is a vivid illustration of how much was only just starting.

31 DECEMBER MONDAY 1945

Tis the last day of 1945 today and as I write this in a semi closed in structure made of the island's timber and tent flies I can't help reflecting on what has been achieved during 1945. At the beginning of this year my career as an artilleryman ceased[5] and I was to become an infanteer. We were on the right side but I still ate the operation rations and took training stunts seriously. Perhaps I may be wrong and I may be right when I say fate decreed I should learn Japanese. Living in a hotel at one of Sydney's fashionable seaside resorts [the Coogee Bay Hotel] was an impossibility come true. V.E. day came and went and we all anxiously looked for V.P. day. Unexpectedly it came too and I too was one of the hilariously happy people who were pushed along Swanston St [Melbourne]. Work was still necessary but the pressure was off now and we eased down the rate a little and thought it would be only a matter of time before all were discharged. Came the unexpected decision that we would be necessary for a long [time] and [would need] to settle down to the prospect of yet another couple of years in khaki. Now as the year ends I find myself swatting various insects, mosquitoes etc. on Morotai. Vast distances have been covered this year and as I try to imagine the future I think next year's travel and experiences will dwarf those of this year. As tonight passes I have no regrets as to decisions made during the year and what is more I have experienced friendships that are not common to lots of people.

Loss, Grief and Mourning

The end of the war prompted a range of responses. For many Japanese families, defeat gave no closure, since their government could not provide information regarding the fate of their loved ones. There was no body and no grave. Some Japanese troops, refusing to believe the war had ended, or embarrassed about their survival when their compatriots had fought to the end, fled to the jungles of Asia or Pacific Islands. The most famous of those 'stragglers', Onoda Hirō, would not emerge from the jungle of Lubang in the Philippines until 1974, and the last, Nakamura Teruo, was found on Morotai a few months after Onoda.[6] But Onoda and other stragglers were atypical: most soldiers, including those Japanese troops still alive in August 1945, looked forward to returning home.

For hundreds of thousands of soldiers, Allied as well as Japanese, there would be no homecoming. In August 1942, Angeline Gallagher, whose other son had already been killed in a train accident, was at home in

Wyandotte, Michigan, when a car stopped outside her house. The driver delivered a telegram:

Deeply regret to inform you that your son Private First Class William Albert Gallagher US Marine Corps Reserve was killed in action. ... Present situation necessitates interment temporarily in the locality where death occurred and you will be notified accordingly.

The 'temporary internment' to which the telegram referred lasted until 1999, when Gallagher's remains were located on Makin Atoll, in the Gilbert Islands. Using DNA data, a still-identifiable gap between his front teeth and a slight indentation on his forehead that had occurred after another boy had thrown a stone at Gallagher during a childhood game, the Army's Central Identification Laboratory in Hawaii was able to confirm that the remains were in fact those of Private Gallagher. In August 2001, Bill Gallagher was buried with full military honours in Arlington National Cemetery, Washington, DC.

During the war tens of thousands of service personnel – along with significant numbers of civilians caught up in the fighting – were captured, or simply went missing amid wartime chaos and confusion. For their families, there was often no, or only scant, information about their loved ones. At war's end, many POWs and civilian internees returned home. In August 1945, shortly after the war ended, Australian Nellie Simpson wrote to her husband, Tom, from whom she had not heard since his capture by the Japanese over three years earlier. Despite the emerging stories of Japanese mistreatment of Allied POWs, like thousands of other women, Nellie hoped her husband had survived, and would soon return home.

At last peace, and how we are all anxiously awaiting news of our loved ones of whom no word during those dark terrible years. We have been told today we can write to you with some degree of certainty of our letters being delivered.... All those years we have talked, hoped, prayed and continuously thought about "our daddy".... Margaret is now 4¹/₂ years and such a grown-up little girlie. And your son Jon Nevison has just turned 3. You never knew you had a son, Tom. Such a bonny little chap. ... He is going to be like daddy. You will have such a welcome home.

Several weeks later, Nellie's letter was returned. But Tom did not.

A Wife Waits: Searching for the Unaccounted

In the United States and Australia, efforts continued in the post-war period to account for service personnel still classified as missing. Some of these investigative efforts became entwined with the efforts to punish individual Japanese through war crimes trials. In Australia, Mae Lyon was still waiting for any news on the whereabouts of her husband. John Lyon had been the RAAF Flight Sergeant who had been shot down with Flight Lieutenant Bill Newton over Salamaua, New Guinea, in March 1943. On 25 March, Mae Lyon received a telegram informing her that her husband was missing. In September she received another telegram offering some hope, after a 'confidential source' suggested her husband was a POW.

The Royal Australian Air Force maintained contact with the families of missing airmen through a unit known as the Casualty Section. Each missing airmen was the subject of a 'Casualty File' which contained any information attained about the missing member and all correspondence or interactions with their family. One RAAF officer recorded his visit to Mae Lyon in October 1943.

On instruction from O.i/c [Officer In Charge] Casualty Section, I called on Mrs. Lyon at 64 Bunbury Street, Footscray, were she is residing with her infant children at the home of her mother. I informed her that I had just called to inform Flight Lieutenant Newton's mother that this Department believed F/LT Newton was the victim of the enemy atrocity referred to in recent newspaper reports, but that we had been unable to secure any further information in respect of her husband....
12/10/43

Through 1944 there was periodic communication between the Casualty Section, and Mae Lyon and John Lyon's father. Then in February 1945 another Air Force officer visited the family. Mae Lyon, concerned that the International Committee of the Red Cross had no records of her husband's imprisonment, was contemplating writing a letter:

Interviewed Mrs Lyon in company with Mrs Newton (Mother of the late F/Lt W.E. Newton V.C. who arranged the appointment) and informed Mrs Lyon in regard to the circular received from the Red Cross, that, in my view, little good would come from the sending of the cablegram to her husband, but that, in my opinion, no harm would be done because two years had elapsed since her husband was first reported to be in the hands of the Japanese and that I did not think at this stage anything that she might do in regard to sending a message would prejudice his chances, and that the Department of Air would have no objection to her sending such a message. She considered, however, that she would prefer not to send such message.
In answer to Mrs. Lyon's inquiry as to whether her husband might be on Rabaul, I said this was a possibility, but we had nothing definite.

The end of the war saw no further resolution for Mae Lyon. Years passed with still no news. Then, in February 1948 she was given a copy of a clipping from a newspaper showing a photograph of a Japanese soldier executing what was believed to be an Australian airman. It was suggested the photograph dated from March 1943. Mrs. Lyon and members of her family saw a physical resemblance. She wrote to the Casualty Section:

Dear Sir,

I have had a Sydney Paper of last year sent to me by my brother in Sydney which has a photo of a Japanese execution of an Australian Airman.

In it it states that the Airman was one of two members of the crew of a plane which was shot down on the 18th of March 1943.

I have shown the newspaper cutting to several people including my husband's parents and relations also to a member of 22 Squadron who trained with my husband and they are all of the same opinion as myself that it is my husband. …

Trusting this will throw some light on the disappearance of my husband [about] whom it seems we cannot get any other definite information

I remain
Mrs. Mae Lyon

The photo was not of John Lyon. Nor was it Bill Newton (although a rumour that it was Newton lasted a number of years).

War Crime Investigators continued to examine the case of John Lyon's disappearance. In June 1948 a report suggested that not only could it confirm that Lyon had been executed, but that investigators had identified the executioner. Superior Petty Officer Kanda Kenichi provided testimony that he was responsible for Lyon's death.

'In May or Jun 43 I heard an Australian airmen Sgt had been captured at sea when his bomber crashed East of Lae. … I saw the airman the day he was captured. … When Lt Sato about four days later, told me the PW was to be executed I suggested beheading would be more merciful than bayoneting. … I beheaded the PW with one cut. I am an expert swordsman and am sure the PW died without pain. The spectators applauded my stroke. … Between February and May 1943. 2 American airmen Prisoners of War were brought from Salamaua to Lae. … I heard—

i. One prisoner of War was sent back to SALAMAUA and there, I heard later, was executed by Lieutenant Komai;

ii. The other Prisoner of War was kept for a while by No 2 Company and then executed.

Following the interview, the investigating officer reported: 'There seems little doubt that the airman was the late Flight Sergeant Lyon, J. despite the fact his photograph was not identified by Kanda.' There were, however, other doubts raised by Kanda's testimony. The chronology was wrong and his description of the fate of the two earlier 'American' airmen more closely resembled the fate of Lyon and Newton (who had been shot down over Salamua with Lyon, and was executed by Lt. Komai). Further evidence that Kanda was not Lyon's executioner emerged on 9 July 1948 when Lyon's remains were discovered in Lae.

Mae Lyon was visited by officials of the Department of Air on 20 July 1948. A follow-up letter was sent a few days later.

Dear Madam,

I desire to confirm the details conveyed to you and Mr. and Mrs. Lyon, Snr., verbally by officers of this Department on the 20th. July 1948, concerning the unfortunate death of your late husband, Flight Sergeant John Lyon.

As you are aware your husband's aircraft was shot down over Salamaua, after being hit by anti-aircraft fire on the 19th. March 1943. … The aircraft sank rapidly, and two of the crew were seen by members of the accompanying aircraft to be swimming strongly for the shore. I am attaching hereto an actual photograph taken of the two members by the accompanying aircraft. …

It was … suspected that your husband was taken to Lae, when captured, but his ultimate fate could not be determined despite widespread investigations. This assumption has now been confirmed by the recovery of his body at Lae, by natives on the 9th July 1948. I deeply regret to say that Medical examination of the body reveals death was caused instantly by bayoneting through the back. The body of your husband was located by natives. …

I desire to assure you that the report of the finding of your husband's body and the medical evidence concerning his fate, has been forwarded to Australian War Crimes, Tokio, requesting that further interrogation of the Japanese be carried out, in order to bring to trial the Japanese responsible for your husband's death. It is known that the chief responsibility for the killing of Australian personnel at Lae rested with Rear Admiral Fujita, who committed suicide after the termination of hostilities, to avoid arrest by Australian War Crimes Authorities. …

It is greatly regretted that it has been found necessary to convey such tragic news to you, and I desire to assure you of the continued sympathy of the Minister for Air and members of the Air Board in your sad bereavement.

Yours faithfully
Mr C. Langslow
SECRETARY

Without Mae Lyon's foreknowledge, John Lyon was afforded a military funeral at the Lae War Cemetery in 1948. In May 1950 the Ministry of Air sent Mae Lyon a photograph of her husband's grave.

CHAPTER TWELVE
LEGACIES

What's taking place is a tug of war for the perceptions of future generations.

The Washington Post, 26 September 1994, commenting on conflicting memories of the atomic attack on Hiroshima

The legacies of World War II in Asia and the Pacific continue to reverberate throughout and across local and national communities. Even as the people directly involved age and pass away, succeeding generations have taken up disputes about commemoration and amnesia, about appropriate acknowledgement and compensation, and about the need for or the quality of sincere apologies and true forgiveness. Although the fiftieth anniversary of the end of the war in 1995 proved an apogee of sorts for debates about war guilt and reparation, scars are still raw, or at least visible enough to be harnessed for a variety of political and cultural moments. Consider, for example, the anger and violence that erupts in China and Korea when the Japanese Ministry of Education endorses school history textbooks that gloss over Japanese wartime atrocities; the continued attempts by aging and gradually dwindling victims of the Japanese military brothel system to receive official recognition and compensation for their torture; the debates about commemoration that still simmer around the Nanjing massacre, the atomic bombs in the United States or the Yasukuni Shrine in Tokyo. But some of these battles are more personal: the now middle-aged children of the war dead still strive for answers about how and when their parents died. War graves commissions still search for those whose remains have lain hidden, and sometimes manage to bring long-awaited answers to family members about the circumstances of their loss. Despite the passage of time, the legacies of violence, loss, grief and dislocation are still clearly visible in all the nations that experienced World War II in the Asia-Pacific regions.

With its acceptance of unconditional surrender, Japan lost its overseas territories and submitted to occupation. Some of the external territories that Japan relinquished were occupied by Soviet forces, including the northern half of the Korean Peninsula, Sakhalin, the Kuriles and the former state of Manchukuo in northeast China. For many of those Japanese in territories under Soviet occupation, the next few years were spent trying to find a way to be repatriated to Japan across borders closed by the Cold War. The precise number of those who died in labour camps in Siberia and Central Asia is unknown, but runs into the tens of thousands.[1] The much-restricted Japanese territory (the four home islands) was occupied predominantly by American troops. A small contingent of Australian, British, Indian and New Zealand troops – organised as the British Commonwealth Occupation Forces (BCOF) – was stationed near Hiroshima. For those Occupation soldiers stationed around Hiroshima, the legacies of the war would turn up, much later, in the form of illness: the rate of early death from cancers and leukaemia remains suspiciously high amongst those exposed to remaining radiation in Hiroshima.

The reform and reconstruction of Japan was placed in the hands of the Supreme Commander of the Allied Powers (SCAP). The Japanese leadership hoped it had saved the 'national polity', but the Occupation brought a number of reforms under the headings of democratisation and demilitarisation. The most important were constitutional and legal reforms which vested sovereignty in the Japanese people (including women) rather than in the emperor, the abolition of the imperial military forces and the establishment of constitutionally decreed limits on a new national 'self-defence' force. Under Australian guidance, an extensive land reform programme was commenced, along with a wide-ranging – albeit short-lived – purge of those politicians and bureaucrats who had been associated with the war effort. In many ways, the Occupation also laid the basis for many new types of relationships between former enemies. Although the Occupation was marred by a variety of crimes (including murder, rape and robbery), and was characterised by lingering resentment on all sides, it was also the beginning of many important and life-long friendships between Japanese people and Allied soldiers, not least through the many marriages that brought Japanese women to live in Australia or the United States, challenging the pre-war migration exclusion policies of both nations. The need for Japanese literacy, both for the purpose of decoding during the war and for the broader requirements of communication during the Occupation, also created a new generation of scholars who transformed the field of Japanese studies in the West, particularly in the United States and Australia. These scholars fostered new knowledge about Japan, about its arts and literature, and about its politics and history, that challenged entrenched wartime stereotypes, and thus helped create a new basis for international communication – beyond fighting words. In a way, every scholar who continues to endeavour to broaden knowledge about Japan beyond its national borders, and every student who chooses to learn Japanese at school or at university today, is linked to that legacy.

It was also during the Occupation that war crimes were defined and criminals pursued. In Japan, the International Military Tribunal of the Far East convened between 1946 and 1948 to bring to justice twenty-five of Japan's wartime leaders who had recklessly engaged in crimes against peace and humanity. Seven were executed. Throughout Asia military courts convened to try individual officers and soldiers for all kinds of atrocities. These trials lasted into the early 1950s and resulted in several hundred executions as well as prison terms of varying lengths. However, despite the best intentions of those involved, the trials failed to convey a sense of impartial justice for many reasons. For example, the Japanese Emperor Hirohito was not indicted as a war criminal, for political expediency as much as because the extent of his wartime political power was – and is – unclear. The definition of crimes against peace and humanity was questioned at the time and has been put to the test since. The composition of the bench, the definition of war crimes (excluding, for example, a number of crimes such as the sexual slavery of Asian women in Japanese military brothels) and the ability of many officers to evade indictment by letting the blame fall on lesser-ranked individuals are all aspects of the war crimes trials that contributed to widespread cynicism about them. Despite their obvious failures, however, the Tokyo War Crimes Trials (like the Nuremberg Trials before them) were crucial in providing the basis for the continuing development of international courts for war crimes.

Similar cynicism taints assessments of Japanese reparations to the countries that were victims of its aggression and occupation. Negotiated at around the same time as the Peace Treaty, reparation policies were fundamentally shaped by the need of the 'Free World' to have in Japan an economically strong and politically conservative ally against its communist neighbours. Predominantly shaped as investment and technological transfer, these reparations have been seen as inadequate at best and, at worst, as an insidious post-war basis for the Japanese economic domination of the region. Japan's resurgent power in the early post-war period, due to rehabilitation policies influenced by the fears of the Cold War, thus meant that reparations for war damages and atrocities could not be exacted easily. This is vividly illustrated in the Korean case, where the 1965 Treaty of Basic Relations ratified the end of all reparation obligations on Japan's part, thus making it impossible for Korean citizens to use their government to seek compensation for Japanese war crimes. For the Korean women who survived being enslaved in Japanese military brothels during the war (so-called 'comfort women'), this has been one of many serious hurdles to gain recognition, apology and compensation.

The concerns of changing regional and global tensions affected the Occupation and its end with the San Francisco Peace Treaty (which took effect in April 1952) as a whole, not just in reparation policies. The Cold War, particularly the Communist victory in China in 1949 and the beginning of the Korean War in June 1950, gave international affairs an urgency and intensity that made Japan a crucial partner in the fight against communism. The ongoing process of decolonisation in Southeast Asia reinforced the need for a strategically aligned Japan.

The San Francisco Peace Treaty returned Japanese sovereignty, but with the accompanying United States–Japan Security Treaty, it also tied Japan inextricably to the United States and its foreign policy. Moreover, it created repercussions concerning the ways in which legacies and memories of the war were negotiated. For example, the 1952 diplomatic recognition of Nationalist China in Taiwan over the People's Republic of China meant that Japanese atrocities in Nanjing became well known and publicised in Japan during the early 1970s, when recognition of the People's Republic of China was being negotiated. The formal end of the war with the San Francisco Peace Treaty, seven years after the Japanese surrender (or later in the case of those countries not signatories to the

San Francisco Peace Treaty), was thus the product of a new set of international tensions.

This fact did not relieve the bitterness and cynicism with which many saw Japan's apparently lightning-quick post-war rehabilitation. The significant point, however, was that despite the widespread destruction of Japan, it had been one of the world's great powers before the war. It had a solid industrial basis and a literate and available labour force, which enabled it to take advantage of the opportunities presented by the Occupation, the Korean War and the global post-war economic boom to become the famous economic superpower that it remains today. Needless to say, nations emerging from colonialism or semi-colonialism (whether it be European or Japanese) did not enjoy the same advantages, and were for many reasons more vulnerable to the tensions brought on by the Cold War. During the post-war period, both Korea and China split into two rival nations; in other places independence was achieved gradually or violently, but never without reference to the impact of the Japanese invasion. This is not to say that Japan 'liberated' Southeast Asia – an untenable argument for obvious reasons – but that the impact and experience of World War II as a whole encouraged the conditions for decolonisation. And while the soldiers of the major combatant nations received veterans' pensions for their service to the state, former colonial soldiers, now citizens of a new country, became ineligible for the same pensions.

The rebuilding of nations and of personal lives were therefore intricately linked. Employment was needed for the thousands of demobilised soldiers. Welfare funds were needed for war widows and orphans, for disabled soldiers and for veterans' pensions in general. Japan also had to absorb some three million civilians returning from its previous overseas colonies. The post-war economic boom that so profited industrialised nations allowed for those still young enough – unless too physically or mentally damaged by the war – to enter the workforce and make a life for themselves and their families. But the bright and happy optimism of the post-war period often covered only superficially the ongoing ills, grief and dislocation caused by the war. Indeed, these continued for decades after the war, and resurfaced particularly strongly when the wartime generation reached retirement age and had the time finally to devote to making sense, from a distance, of their wartime experiences. At the same time, many of the children and grandchildren of the now fading wartime generation still seek clues to the circumstances of their parents' or grandparents' deaths, whether in prison camps, at sea, during bombings, or wherever else thousands of deaths went unrecorded. The boom in war stories and memoirs in all the former combatant countries from the 1980s onwards is a testament to this process.

But memory is not just an individual endeavour. Many of us who were not born during the war have an emotional and intellectual investment in that past and 'remember' it as a community. Such popular memories, and the way in which they help define nations and communities in the present, are the subject of growing interest on the part of historians, who can no longer take for granted their own 'ownership' of the 'truth' about the past. Knowing the past is not only about gathering known facts, but also about interpreting them, understanding them and making meaning out of them.

When these meanings validate the identity of a group, politicians, rather than historians, become the arbiters of the past's interpretation. Knowing the past 'properly' becomes a matter of political legitimisation and power. Consequently, if a defined moment in the past is understood to be especially formative to group identity, its proper interpretation, and its proper place in public life – perhaps even its resurrection from amnesia – becomes crucially important. A number of ongoing debates in Japan, in the United States, in Australia, and elsewhere, attest to this process. A famous example of this in Japan is the status of the Yasukuni Shrine (which enshrines all war dead, including some war criminals). Since the 1947 constitution separated church and state, it became a private shrine, although one which had been the central commemorative space for fallen soldiers for its entire existence until that point. Visits by politicians and public servants are thus illegal, a point that many of the families of fallen soldiers believe demeans the sacrifice they made for the nation, and which they have subsequently disputed.

In the United States, a famous 1995 debate centred on whether the exhibition of the bomber 'Enola Gay' at the Smithsonian Museum should include information about the damage wrought by the atomic bomb it dropped on Hiroshima on 6 August 1945. In Australia, there are regular debates about whether Britain 'abandoned' Australia at the fall of Singapore and whether the Japanese actually intended to invade.

How such debates might evolve as the wartime generation passes away is difficult to predict. The search for explanations for Japanese atrocities against prisoners of war (POWs), forced labourers and civilians in occupied areas will continue to occupy scholars of conflict and violence. Yet historians are also increasingly interested in the immediate aftermath of the war as part of a growing appreciation of the social and cultural legacies of the conflict. It took years and often decades to overcome individual or communal grief, to recover from war-related physical and mental disability ('post-traumatic stress disorder' was a term coined later) or to come to terms with loss and dislocation. In that regard, aspects of the experiences of the wartime generation were inherited by the generations that followed, and the process of commemoration became an increasingly important way in which the past was negotiated into daily life.

In the most immediate sense, however, the end of the war brought with it the Occupation of Japan, and this is where the last selection of our primary sources begins.

THE SOURCES

An American Journalist's Diary of the Occupation Period

The Occupation clearly illustrates how the end of a war is not the end of the propaganda. Both through censorship and through public education programmes, the Occupation Forces ensured that everyone in Japan knew what to think, or at least what they should be thinking. But when it came to actual policy making, lofty ideals rubbed against more realistic and grubby realities in the Occupation command itself. Mark Gayn was a journalist who covered the Japanese occupation for the American press. A shrewd observer of Occupation politics, he arrived in Japan in December 1945. He maintained a meticulous diary, which reveals the mixture of hope, confusion and disillusionment that accompanied early Occupation policies. Here he reports on a critical discussion he heard about the office of the Supreme Commander of the Allied Powers, General Douglas MacArthur. This entry is dated 20 December 1945.

While the outsiders, they said, get an impression of a coordinated and knowledgeable effort, the fact is that General MacArthur and his aides are confounded by the immensity of the problems before them. General MacArthur's views depend on whom he has seen at lunch, or on what the American press has said that morning in praise or condemnation of his actions. The various sections of his Headquarters are floundering on their own, with no guidance from above. Frequently, the only measuring stick of an important move is the publicity it might bring. Many of the measures for which General MacArthur has claimed credit have actually originated elsewhere. Thus the action to pick up the war criminals was initiated by a non-American official. The directive on civil liberties was born in Washington.

Apart from all that, the critics said, a dramatic cleavage has developed within Headquarters, dividing all policy planners into two warring camps. One of these believes that Japan should be reshaped drastically. The other opposes fundamental changes, on the grounds that a conservative Japan is our best ally in the coming struggle with Russia, and that all that is needed in Japan is a light face-lifting....

Most of us thought the crop of reform directives that has come out since Japan's surrender has been good. August was a month of basic directives on Japan's disarmament. In October, came the orders on man's elemental liberties – the purge of the Thought Control Police, removal of the last restrictions on political and civil rights, a firmly worded reminder to the Japanese that we expected a strong labor movement, and the dramatic release of political prisoners. In November and December came the orders on such fundamental reforms as the redistribution of land, a broad relief program for the unemployed, separation of Shintoism from the State, and dissolution of the great family trusts, the *zaibatsu*. Speech and assembly were free and in Hibiya Park, cater-corner from General MacArthur's own office, thousands flocked to listen to hoarse and passionate speeches by Communist orators, and Tokyo newspapers voiced opinions running the gamut from the extreme left to rabid nationalism. Labor union organisers were busy around the clock, and the labor movement was growing so fast that labor officers in Headquarters lagged weeks behind in their statistics. Even rural Japan, tradition bound and conservative, was waking up, and organizers were criss-crossing the countryside, bearing the news of the imminent land reform and arguing people into joining the Farmers' Union.

We agreed that these demonstrations of freedom were as yet scattered, and the broad masses of Japan remained lethargic. We agree that the great body of reform was still woven of words, as yet largely untranslated into action. But the words of the directives formed a thrilling pattern of a new democracy-in-the-making of which Americans could be proud.

Learned today that General MacArthur has decided to issue a directive postponing the elections, and defining the minimum standards which the government must observe if the election is not to be a gigantic fraud. ... The order is admittedly a direct intervention in Japanese politics – something which General MacArthur has been reluctant to do. However, the need for such a move has been evident for weeks. But for such intervention, there was every sign that the next "democratic" Diet would be dominated again by unrepentant nationalists. Such a Diet could effectively wreck General MacArthur's entire program for a reborn Japan.

Victors Writing History: The Tokyo War Crimes Trial Indictment

The indictment of the A-level War Crimes Trials shows in retrospect how clearly convenient, but also how deeply flawed, the prosecution's understanding of recent history had been. The notions that there had been a coherent plan in Japan's foreign policies, that there was a specific and limited group of individuals who could be held accountable or that, indeed, the Japanese population had been just passive receptacles that could easily be brainwashed one way or another were questioned at the time, and have been dismissed since. The Trials had been a clearly orchestrated attempt to apportion blame, to rid Japan of the disease of militarism and to let it face its future blame- and debt-free. But they began, rather than ended, many of the post-war debates.

In the years hereinafter referred to in this Indictment the internal and foreign policies of Japan were dominated and directed by a criminal militaristic clique, and such policies were the cause of serious world troubles, aggressive war, and great damage to the interests of peace-loving peoples, as well as the interests of the Japanese people themselves.

The mind of the Japanese people was systematically poisoned with harmful ideas of the alleged racial superiority of Japan over other peoples of Asia and even the whole world. Such parliamentary institutions as existed in Japan were used as implements for widespread aggressions, and a system similar to those then established by Hitler and the Nazi party in Germany and by the Fascist party in Italy were introduced. The economic and financial resources of Japan were to a large extent mobilized for war aims, to the detriment of the welfare of the Japanese people.

A conspiracy between the defendants, joined in by the rulers of other aggressive countries, namely, Nazi Germany and Fascist Italy, was entered into. The main objects of this conspiracy was to secure the domination and exploitation by the aggressive States of the rest of the world, and to this end commit, or encourage the commission of crimes against peace, war crimes, and crimes against humanity as defined in the Charter of this Tribunal, thus threatening and injuring the basic principles of liberty and respect for the human personality....

War Fiction and Beyond: T. A. G. Hungerford

After the Pacific War many service personnel sought to use the written word make sense of their experiences. Memoirs were popular choices, but other veterans used fiction to explore their recent past. In the United States, some, such as future novelist James Jones, took advantage of the post-war 'GI Bill' to attend university and learn their craft. Many others simply took up pen and paper, and wrote. Whether fiction or non-fiction, many audiences believed a veteran's words imbued their works with great authenticity. Indeed some publishers considered some manuscripts too authentic in both their language and the horrors of war they were representing. Many novels in Australia in the early post-war period were rejected on these grounds. But many readers craved the gritty realism and naturalistic style of much of this fiction. That the style made them accessible to a general audience, and provided insights into the reality of war, increased the pedagogical power.[2]

In the United States, during the early post-war period, writers such as James Michener and Thomas Heggen gave American readers insights into the lived experience of the Pacific War. Some found wider audiences with theatrical or cinematic adaptations. Commenting on the stage adaptations of Heggen and Michener's work in 1956, a New York theatre critic asked: 'Will future generations think of World War II in terms of *Mister Roberts* and *South Pacific*?'[3]

One Australian who used fiction to explore his Pacific War experience was Tom Hungerford, a playwright, novelist and author, and a member of the British Commonwealth Occupation Forces. Regarding the act of writing, he 'was surprised by the ease with which' the war stories he was writing 'plunged' him 'back into a world which' he assumed he 'had forgotten'.[4] Hungerford's most successful novel, *The Ridge and the River*, chronicled his experiences in the military backwater that was the Southwest Pacific in the twilight months of the war. Another of his novels, *Sowers of the Wind: A Novel of the Occupation of Japan*, made an important contribution to a Pacific War literary sub-genre, which explored the Allied Occupation of Japan.[5] Although *Sowers of the Wind* is a work of fiction, it portrays vividly the tensions of the period. Indeed, the first meetings between Occupation soldiers and the Japanese population were fraught with mutual distrust and hatred.[6] That ill-feeling, according to Hungerford, led to a delay in the publication of his work, because Army authorities were concerned about the portrayal of soldiers and their often exploitative relationships with the Japanese. In this extract we follow two main characters on their first night in Japan.

Lane and Flannery, once they got away from the wharves, hitched a ride up to the centre of the city and walked along the ill-lit, ruinous main street, jostled by crowds of Japanese and American servicemen. Walking aimlessly, they found themselves half-way up a long, shallow incline, with the town spread below them.

The street was flanked by bombed-out buildings and vacant blocks, wells of utter, impenetrable blackness in the pale-gold glow shed by the rare street lamps. Passing a gaping doorway in a ruined shop, Flannery, who was walking on the inside of the footpath, felt a hand drop on to his arm. A voice said gently in his ear, "*Gozaimasu* – please. You chocoletto, cigarette? Biscuit-o?"

"Holy mackerel!" Flannery jumped aside. "He scared hell out of me, the bastard!" He peered into the shadows. "What d'you want, you flaming ape?"

The Japanese edged out, partly into the pale light, half bowing, with a greasy cloth cap held against his chest and his shaven head bobbing backwards and forwards like a mechanical toy on his narrow shoulders. A grimace that might have been of pain or of pleasure distorted his features, disclosing the great square teeth of the cartoon Jap; he bobbed and hissed, drawing his breath inward between his teeth, and repeated his request, "You, chocoletto, cigaretto?"

"What's he want?" Flannery peered in bewilderment at the Japanese, who had produced a tightly packed roll of dirty notes, and once again repeated his demand. "Look at the wad of dough he's got!"

"Wants to give it to us," Lance volunteered dryly. "Let's roll him and shoot through with his purse."

An American serviceman, who had been watching from the other side of the road, walked over to them, calling out as he came, "don' sell nothin' to that son of a bitch, Aussie – they don' pay nothin' like the real price. You come on up the hill with me if you got stuff to hock."

Flannery looked at Lane with a grin. "Come on, the game's on"

[As the American serviceman takes the two Australians up the road, they discuss the bomb-damage visible around them]

"Yeah, incendiaries. That's why all the damage down town is on one side of the road. Only that stopped the whole goddamn' joint from going up." The American paused reflectively. "Say, you should see Tokyo. This place ain't nothin'- apart from its docks it's just a brothel town. Even the Japs admit that. Tokyo's the place where the bomber boys really went to town. Yes, sir!"

"Yeah, I know," Mark [Flannery] said. 'I read it in the paper. But they plastered Tokyo for some time. They did all this in two raids."

"Well, wait until you see Hiroshima, then. That got flattened with one goddamn' bomb. Holy cow, you should see it! I bet them yellow-bellies hate our guts!"

"What, even now?" There was surprise in Lane's voice. "The war's over and they brought it on themselves, anyway."

The American stopped walking and regarded him in amazement. "Say, what Sunday supplement do you guys read? If they done it to you, what would you do – welcome the bastards? If your wife and kids was fried, or your old man was killed overseas somewheres, would you glad-hand them when they walked in? Like hell! I on'y been here a few months, but my bet is that unless we make a good job of it this time we'll have to slap them down again some day the yellow bastards."

He's right, too, by hell, Mark thought. And here we are, batting the breeze in amongst them! We could all be dominoed and chucked into a sewer, and nobody'd be any wiser! He peered down a lane that slanted from the corner they were passing, at the dim and formless figures that bobbed about in the shadows. For a moment, in the half-light and the strangeness, the old familiar crinkle corrugated his spine.

'How to' Endure the Peace

For the Japanese people under the Occupation, debates about Japan's democratic future were the kind of luxury one could indulge in to distract oneself from the immediate problems of food and housing shortages, spiralling black market prices and unemployment. These problems were exacerbated by the return home of civilians and soldiers from the former colonies and occupied territories.

For many families, however, loved ones did not come home. The following is the introduction to a 'Practical Handbook for Daily Life', a 230-page self-help publication for the families of people missing overseas since the war. It also listed practical information for those arriving back to Japan after many years overseas. Although most repatriations were completed by late 1948, there were still tens of thousands of people awaiting repatriation in 1950 when the book was published. Many families in Japan had little or no information on the fate of their loved ones. The book provided information on bureaucratic procedures, useful contacts, services for employment, health and housing and also on procedures for locating missing persons.

On the occasion of publication:

It is difficult to overstate the abyss of mental and physical pain of the families who are missing a relative and have been waiting already for nearly five years. For many of the 400,000 repatriates in this city alone, as well as those who were injured during the war, the economic woes and the chaos of our country have been a great shock, and there will be many obstacles to recovery.

Since its inception in 1947 as an organisation representing the families of those missing, this association has worked tirelessly in its aims of promoting the repatriation of those overseas, and providing welfare for those with missing relatives. The question of repatriation is one with many difficult international ramifications, and even today it is an undeniable fact that we, the poor families of the missing, cannot by ourselves accomplish our primary objectives. At the same time, the longer repatriations are delayed, the more difficult become the daily struggles of their families, who only live in the hope of the return of their loved one. This is not just a problem facing this association: it has to be understood as an important social issue and one related to our responsibility for the war.

It is in that spirit that we had initially prepared a written guide for daily life for the families of the missing, which would also be useful to others affected by the damage wrought by war: repatriates themselves, war disabled, even families of the war dead and war widows. As numerous requests for this guide came from all sides, we decided to publish it as a book. Although this book, from the perspective of our early aims, has many imperfections, we hope that it finds some use despite its deficiencies, as a little bit of sustenance for the heart of those who are still grieving because of the war.

1 December 1950
Kanzō Tokuyasu, Head of Committee, Tokyo Association of the Families of the Missing For the Progress of Repatriation of Compatriots Overseas

The End of War: The San Francisco Peace Treaty

Despite the Japanese surrender having been signed in September 1945, it took another six years before the state of war between Japan and the Allies was officially ended. Part of the reason for the delay related to the mounting tensions between the United States and the Soviet Union. The instrument used to end the conflict was the 1951 Treaty of San Francisco. The treaty set out the terms by which Japan could move forward as an independent, democratic and demilitarised nation. Many commentators saw the treaty with Japan as a 'soft peace' aimed at ensuring the Japanese could quickly become a bulwark to communism in East Asia. Consequently, the requests of nations such as Britain and France for reparation were set aside. Since the United States had dominated both the prosecution of the war and the Occupation, the treaty was signed on American terms. That same day Japan and the United States signed a security treaty that allowed the United States the long-term use of several bases on Japanese soil.

TREATY OF PEACE WITH JAPAN

WHEREAS the Allied Powers and Japan are resolved that henceforth their relations shall be those of nations which, as sovereign equals, cooperate in friendly association to promote their common welfare and to maintain international peace and security, and are therefore desirous of concluding a Treaty of Peace which will settle questions still outstanding as a result of the existence of a state of war between them;

WHEREAS Japan for its part declares its intention to apply for membership in the United Nations and in all circumstances to conform to the principles of the Charter of the United Nations; to strive to realize the objectives of the Universal Declaration of Human Rights; to seek to create within Japan conditions of stability and well-being as defined in Articles 55 and 56 of the Charter of the United Nations and already initiated by post-surrender Japanese legislation; and in public and private trade and commerce to conform to internationally accepted fair practices;...

Silences: The Trauma of Imprisonment

One of the most enduring public memories of the Pacific War in Australia concerns the poor treatment of Australian and Allied POWs at the hands of the Japanese. With some notable exceptions (such as Rohan Rivett and Russell Braddon who wrote popular accounts of their time as 'Guests of the Emperor') few Australian POWs were willing to share their experiences with their families, let alone the general public.[7] In Japan and the United States, Japanese POWs and those interned by the American government also fell silent although their motivations reflected different experiences of captivity.[8]

For all these prisoners of the Pacific War, life could never quite get back to normal, even years afterwards. Although former POWs were generally able to talk about their experiences with those who had shared it, it was only many years later that some were able to share their experiences with the wider public. In Australia, one of the catalysts for the unburdening of POW memories came with an Australian Broadcasting Corporation radio documentary aired in the early 1980s. In a book of oral recollections compiled for the programme, former POWs, men and women, revealed how their war experience was still engraved in their daily lives.

Silvia Muir: often people open my pantry and said, 'What are you going to do with all that?' But you must be prepared, see? And it's become a thing. Because you mightn't get food for a week. So my little pantry is always completely chock-a-block with tinned stuff and I'm prepared for anything.

Herb Trackson: You always seemed to be frightened of something. As far as my case goes, it could not bear to be on my own. I had to have someone with me or someone around me, even if it was strangers. To be in a room by myself was just impossible. I'd have to get out or make an excuse to go and see someone.

Joyce Braithwaite: There was this recurrent thing we had about lice in the bed. We would get up fairly regularly, strip everything off and examine the mattress minutely. He said to me, "I know you don't ever think there's vermin in the bed but look at my arms." And he literally had bite marks and raised lumps. I don't know, I suppose it's psychosomatic. One was filled with a great sadness that this should have happened and wondered how long this would have to last for him.

Geoff O'Connor: I gave my wife a start one night. She came in and I dreamt there was a jap outside the window and I thought, oh, I'll throw a hand grenade that'll fix him. But I grabbed the light on the bed and I let fly and nearly knocked her bloody head off. She wasn't real happy about that.

Roy Whitecross: Only twelve months ago, I was having a drink with three or four chaps and one of them came round to me and sort of whispered to me, 'Whitey, do you have nightmares? About, you know, the old days?' And I said, 'Of course, I do'. He said, 'How often?' I said, 'Oh, a really bad one, once every couple of months but, you know, might be one a week or every now and then I have them'. 'Oh,' he said, 'thank Christ for that. I have them too'. And I said, 'Yeah, and you thought you were going round the bend'. He said, 'Yeah, yeah, I did. It's been worrying me for a long time.' So I said to the others, 'Righto', I said, 'how many of you blokes don't have nightmares?' And they all looked at me as if I was crazy. And each one said, 'Yes, of course we do'.[9]

Still Fighting: For Recognition

Corban K. Alabado was a soldier of the Philippine Army, which was inducted under the United States Armed Forces in the Far East (USAFFE) in July 1941. After the war, the United States did not recognise the service of Filipino soldiers as 'active service', which denied these soldiers the kinds of benefits to which 'regular' soldiers had been entitled. Until his death in 1999, Alabado tried to publicise what he saw as a great injustice. This extract from an open letter to the US Congress was the Afterword to his 1995 memoir of the war in the Philippines.

Was it not in the active service that we went to Bataan and Corregidor and fought side by side with our American brothers? Were we not in the uniform of the USAFFE when the United States Military High Command gave us orders to surrender on April 9, 1942? Were we not taken prisoners of war and made to walk the many kilometres of the brutal Death March? We endured the harshness and cruelty of the conquerors in Capas O'Donnell concentration camp. We were released from the same camp, still as POW's, our whereabouts checked regularly by making us report to the Philippine constabulary once a month. As soon as we had recovered from malaria and dysentery, many of us joined the resistance underground movement. When the Americans returned to the Philippines, we returned to military control. Again, we served with them in mopping-up operations in Cebu, the Cordilleras, Baguio, Intramuros, Batangas, until we were honourably discharged.

What of the above services are not "active" as described by the Rescission Act?

The cruelty and incongruity of the said Act is even more bitterly felt by us when we remember our dead comrades, those who died in action. They were never fully accorded the status of US military casualties. Oh yes, an American flag was given to the next of kin to drape around the coffins of their fallen loved ones.

Nationals of sixty-six other countries who were similarly inducted into the United States Armed Forces received an altogether different treatment. They were granted equal rights and all privileges and benefits that the US servicemen were entitled to.

We note too another discriminatory and unjust act of the United States after the war: it took massive measures to rehabilitate, not the Philippines which was totally ravaged by the conflagration, but Japan, its former enemy; it paid each Japanese – American family interred in camps in the United States, twenty-thousand dollars.

What did the Philippines get? A paltry sum from the War Damage Act, and the Rescission Act of 1946.

Honorable members of Congress, we veterans are now in the twilight years of our lives. We are feeble and disabled. Our thoughts are happiest when we think that we had done our duty, but sad, that we have been discarded like an old useless rag. We still look forward though to the day when through your help and support the injustices brought about the Rescission Act are correct. Repeal the Act. Restore our dignity and respect.

Museums as Memories and Memories at War: The Enola Gay Controversy

As the distance between the present and the Pacific War lengthens, the ethical and historical outlook of society today raises new issues about the past or gives them new significance. Consequently, constructions of the past around forms of remembrance and commemoration become problematic. As well as monuments and memorials, museums play important and controversial roles in the public debate of the past. In 1994 the Smithsonian Institution was completing plans for an exhibition to commemorate the end of the Pacific War. The focal point of the exhibition would be the Enola Gay, the B-29 which had dropped the atomic bomb on Hiroshima. The way the exhibit's curators were representing the aircraft and the decision to use the bomb outraged many veterans groups and fuelled a national controversy. Competing voices of the Pacific War can thus be within nations rather than between combatants.

Washington Post, 26 September 1994

2 Views of History Collide Over Smithsonian A-Bomb Exhibit

Nearly 50 years after the United States brought World War II to an end by dropping two atomic bombs on Japan, a final skirmish is underway at the Smithsonian's National Air and Space Museum over how those bombs and their impact will be remembered: as an event that ended great suffering or as one that caused it. For the majority of Americans now alive, including curators of the divisive proposed exhibit of the Enola Gay, the B-29 that dropped the bomb on Hiroshima, World War II is old history [...]. For veterans like Grayford C. Payne, 74, of Annandale, who survived the Bataan death march in the war's earliest days plus "three years, five months and 20 days" of starvation and slave labor in five Japanese prison camps, it was something else. "In the latter part of June 1945," Payne remembers, "a note was posted in our camp" at Hanawa in northern Japan. "It was signed by [Japanese premier] Hideki Tojo. And it said, 'The moment the first American soldier sets foot on the Japanese mainland, all prisoners of war will be shot.' ...

   The atomic bomb, which killed between 80,000 and 140,000 in Hiroshima and about half that number in Nagasaki (the exact figures remain disputed), shocked the Japanese into surrendering without an invasion, Payne says. "That's why all of us who were prisoners in Japan – or were headed for it to probably die in the invasion – revere the Enola Gay. It saved our lives." For Michael Neufeld, the 43-year-old curator of the exhibit, the Enola Gay, which marked the end of a nightmare for Payne's generation, began a nightmare for his. The postwar generation, he says, "grew up cowering under the bedclothes expecting World War III to drop on us any minute, and thinking 'Oh, God, it's going to happen to us and be 50,000 times worse.'" ...

   The gulf separating the worldviews of Michael Neufeld and Grayford Payne is partly generational, partly ideological, partly one of experience. It also reflects what Neufeld describes as a "huge disjuncture" between the way mainstream America views American history and the way it's viewed in many academic circles today.

Collective Memories: Comfort Women

The issue of sexual slavery in Japanese military brothels is another notorious example of an ongoing debate about how the war should be remembered, war crimes atoned for and war legacies understood. The establishment of the Women's Tribunal in the year 2000 exemplified how understandings of war crimes have changed in the decades since the Tokyo War Crimes Trials. War does not just affect those combatants in uniform, nor does the fighting end with surrenders and peace treaties. Indeed, it takes novel ways, such as an informal trial, to bring victims of the war some form of justice. The following is taken from the website of a Japanese organisation that opposes violence against women in war, and that was one of the organisers of the Women's Tribunal.

What Is the Women's Tribunal?

"Our collective memory must be written indelibly in our history with our strongest condemnation." Aurora Javate de Dios, Prosecutor, the Philippines.

"The Women's International War Crimes Tribunal on Japan's Military Sexual Slavery" (the Women's Tribunal) was a people's tribunal organized by Asian women and human rights organizations and supported by international NGOs. It was set up to adjudicate Japan's military sexual violence, in particular the enslavement of "comfort women," to bring those responsible for it to justice, and to end the ongoing cycle of impunity for wartime sexual violence against women.

First proposed early in 1998, the Women's Tribunal (the Tokyo Tribunal) was held in Tokyo on 8-12 December 2000. Sixty-four survivors from nine countries and areas in the Asia-Pacific region took part. More than one thousand people from throughout the world, some from as far as Africa and South America, came to observe the Tribunal each day, along with more than three hundred media representatives. For the first three days, the Tribunal heard the testimonies of survivors, scholars in history, international law, and psychology, and two Japanese veterans. In addition, the court received the voluminous evidence submitted by the nine country prosecution teams and two chief prosecutors. On the fourth day, the Tribunal was in recess while the Judges deliberated, and a Public Hearing on Crimes against Women in Recent Wars and Conflicts was held in order to show how the failure to adjudicate past crimes has affected recent affairs. On the fifth day, 12 December 2000, the Tribunal issued its preliminary judgment, which found Emperor Hirohito guilty, and the State of Japan responsible, for the crimes of rape and sexual slavery as crimes against humanity.

It took a whole year for the Tribunal to render its Final Judgment. On 4 December 2001, the Final Judgment was issued in The Hague, the Netherlands, the "home of international law," to show the significance of the judgment to the whole world. More than 1,000 paragraphs and 200 pages long, the Judgment discusses in full detail the factual findings of the Tribunal, and law applicable to the case. It finds all ten of the defendants accused in the Common Indictment guilty, either as individuals or as superiors, of crimes against humanity. In a case of mass rape in a Filipino village, the Judgment does not find Emperor Hirohito guilty as an individual, but only as a superior. The Judgment also makes detailed recommendations, not only to the Government of Japan but also to the former Allied nations, and to the United Nations and its member states. A copy of the Judgment was handed by the Judges to each of the survivors who attended the session to take back to her own people. The Judgment's two last paragraphs read as follows:

> The Crimes committed against these survivors remain one of the greatest unacknowledged and un-remedied injustices of the Second World War. There are no museums, no graves for the unknown "comfort woman," no education of future generations, and there have been no judgment days for the victims of Japan's military sexual slavery and the rampant sexual violence and brutality that characterized its aggressive war.
>
> Accordingly, through this Judgment, this Tribunal intends to honor all the women victimized by Japan's military sexual slavery system. The Judges recognize the great fortitude and dignity of the survivors who have toiled to survive and reconstruct their shattered lives and who have faced down fear and shame to tell their stories to the world and testify before us. Many of the women who have come forward to fight for justice have died unsung heroes. While the names inscribed in history's page have been, at best, those of the men who commit the crimes or who prosecute them, rather than the women who suffer them, this Judgment bears the names of the survivors who took the stand to tell their stories, and thereby, for four days at least, put wrong on the scaffold and truth on the throne.[10]

END MATTER

PACIFIC WAR TIMELINE

Prelude
- 1854: Commodore Matthew Perry compels Japan to open some of its ports for trade
- 1868: Meiji Restoration in Japan
- 1894–1895: Sino–Japanese War
- 1898: Spanish–American War
- 1904–1905: Russo–Japanese War
- 1910: Japan annexes Korea
- 1914: Japan joins the Western Allies in World War I
- 1915: Japan presents its Twenty-One Demands to China
- 1917: The United States joins World War I
- 1918: Fighting ends in World War I
- 1919: Japanese-sponsored racial equality clause rejected at the Paris Peace Conference
- 1921–1922: Washington Conference
- 1924: American Immigration Act excludes Japanese immigration
- 1928: Kellog–Briand Pact seeks to outlaw war
- 1931: Mukden Incident precedes Japanese invasion of Manchuria
- 1932: Shanghai Incident
- 1933: Japan leaves the League of Nations
- 1937 (June): Japan withdraws from Washington Conference
- 1938: Japan relinquishes the hosting rights to the 1940 Summer Olympics
- 1939 (September): Germany invades Poland, launching World War II in Europe
- 1940 (July): Japan occupies Indochina

1941
- 12 August: Winston Churchill and Franklin Roosevelt sign the Atlantic Charter
- 17 September: Tripartite alliance between Germany, Italy and Japan
- 7 December: Japanese bomb Pearl Harbor, Hawaii, and attack other areas throughout the Asia-Pacific
- 8 December: The United States and Britain declare war on Japan. Japanese forces enter Thailand and land near Singapore
- 9 December: China declares war on Japan
- 10 December: Japanese sink the *Prince of Wales* and *Repulse*
- 10 December: Japan invades the Philippines and seizes Guam
- 11 December: Japan invades Burma
- 18 December: Japan invades Hong Kong
- 22 December: Japan invades Luzon in the Philippines. First US troops arrive in Australia
- 23 December: General Douglas MacArthur begins withdrawing from Manila to Bataan; Japanese take Wake Island

25 December: British surrender at Hong Kong

27 December: Japanese bomb Manila

1942

7 January: Japanese attack Bataan in the Philippines

11 January: Japanese invade Dutch East Indies and Dutch Borneo

18 January: German–Japanese–Italian military agreement signed in Berlin

23 January: Japanese forces take Rabaul on New Britain in the Solomon Islands and invade Bougainville

24 January: Japanese capture Rabaul

30–31 January: The British withdraw into Singapore and the siege of Singapore begins

1 February: US aircraft carriers *Yorktown* and *Enterprise* launch raids on Japanese bases in the Gilbert and Marshall Islands

2 February: Japanese invade Java in the Dutch East Indies

4 February: Australian garrison at Ambon surrenders

8–9 February: Japanese invade Singapore

15 February: British and Commonwealth forces surrender at Singapore

19 February: Japanese launch air raid against Darwin, Australia

21 February: Japanese invade Timor

22 February: President Franklin D. Roosevelt orders General MacArthur to leave the Philippines

23 February: Japanese submarine shells an oil refinery near Santa Barbara, California

7 March: British evacuate Rangoon, Burma; Japanese attack Salamaua and Lae on New Guinea. Japanese Army rejects Navy plan for invasion of Australia

9 March: Dutch and Allies surrender in Dutch East Indies

11 March: General MacArthur leaves the Philippines; flies to Australia

18 March: MacArthur appointed commander of the Southwest Pacific Theatre. War Relocation Authority established in the United States, with responsibility for interning Japanese-Americans

24 March: Admiral Chester Nimitz appointed as Commander in Chief of the Pacific Theatre

3 April: Japanese attack American and Filipino troops at Bataan

9 April: American forces on Bataan surrender unconditionally to the Japanese

10 April: Bataan Death March begins as 76,000 Allied POWs are forced to walk 100 kilometres. Thousands die en-route

18 April: 'Doolittle' air raid surprises the Japanese and boosts Allied morale

1 May: Japanese occupy Mandalay in Burma

3 May: Japanese take Tulagi in the Solomon Islands

6 May: Japanese conquer Corregidor

7–8 May: Japan suffers naval defeat at the Battle of the Coral Sea

10 May: US troops on Mindanao surrender

30 May: US troops arrive in New Zealand

31 May–1 June: Midget submarine raid on Sydney

3 June: Japanese invade Aleutian Islands. Japanese land on Guadalcanal

4–7 June: Major American naval victory in the Battle of Midway

21 July: Japanese troops land near Gona, New Guinea. Advance towards village of Kokoda

4 August: Japanese air attacks on Milne Bay

7 August: First American amphibious landing of the Pacific War as Marines attack Tulagi and Guadalcanal

8–9 August: American naval forces defeated off Savo Island, north of Guadalcanal. Americans capture Henderson Field

30 August: American troops invade Adak Island in the Aleutian Islands

3 September: Japanese withdraw from Milne Bay

5 September: Japanese forces push back Australian forces on the Kokoda Trail to within 80 kilometres of Port Moresby

9–10 September: Japanese aircraft drops incendiary bombs on forests in the state of Oregon

12–14 September: Battle of Bloody Ridge on Guadalcanal

27 September: British offensive in Burma

2 November: Australians recapture Kokoda

19 November: Australian and American forces launch attacks on Japanese beachheads at Gona and Buna

2 December: Enrico Fermi conducts the world's first nuclear chain reaction test at the University of Chicago

9 December: Allied victory of Gona, New Guinea

1943

2 January: Allies take Buna, New Guinea

14 January: Casablanca Conference

22 January: Allies defeat Japanese at Sanananda, New Guinea

1 February: Japanese begin evacuation of Guadalcanal

1–4 March: Allied aircraft destroy a Japanese reinforcement convoy in the Battle of Bismarck Sea

18 April: American fighter aircraft shoot down the plane carrying Japanese Admiral Yamamoto

21 April: President Roosevelt announces the Japanese have executed several airmen from the Doolittle Raid

22 April: Japan declares captured Allied pilots will be given 'one-way tickets to hell'

10 May: American troops invade Attu in the Aleutian Islands

14 May: Japanese submarine sinks the Australian hospital ship *Centaur*, killing 299

21 June: Allies advance to New Georgia, Solomon Islands

25 August: Allies complete occupation of New Georgia

4 September: Allies recapture Lae-Salamaua, New Guinea

30 September: Japanese adopt New Operations Policy

7 October: Japanese execute approximately 100 American POWs on Wake Island

26 October: Emperor Hirohito admits his country's situation is 'truly grave'

1 November: American Marines invade Bougainville in the Solomon Islands

20 November: American Troops invade Makin and Tarawa in the Gilbert Islands

15 December: American forces land on the Arawe Peninsula of New Britain in the Solomon Islands

26 December: Full-scale Allied assault on New Britain

1944

9 January: British and Indian troops recapture Maungdaw in Burma

1–7 February: American forces capture Kwajalein and Majura Atolls in the Marshall Islands

17–19 February: American carrier-based planes destroy the Japanese naval base at Truk in the Caroline Islands

20 February: American aircraft destroy the Japanese base at Rabaul

23 February: American planes attack the Mariana Islands

24 February: Merrill's Marauders commence ground campaign in northern Burma

5 March: General Wingate's forces begin operations behind Japanese lines in Burma

15 March: Japanese begin offensive toward Imphal and Kohima

17 April: Japanese launch their final offensive in China

22 April: Allies invade Aitape and Hollandia in New Guinea

5 June: First mission by B-29 Superfortress bombers when they attack Japanese facilities at Bangkok

15 June: American Marines invade Saipan in the Mariana Islands

15–16 June: B-29s based in Bengal, India, attack steel works at Yawata, Japan

18–21 June: The Battle of the Philippines Sea

19 June: The 'Marianas Turkey Shoot' as American aircraft shoot down 220 Japanese planes, for the loss of only 20 American planes

8 July: Japanese withdraw from Imphal

21 July: American Marines invade Guam. Japanese issue new defensive plan

24 July: American Marines invade Tinian

27 July: American forces liberate Guam

8 August: American forces complete the capture of the Mariana Islands

15 September: Allied troops attack Morotai and Palau Islands

11 October: American air raids against Okinawa

20 October: American Army forces attack Leyte in the Philippines

23–26 October: Battle of Leyte Gulf ends in a decisive American naval victory

25 October: First Kamikaze attacks against American warships

15 December: American troops attack Mindoro in the Philippines

17 December: United States Army Air Force begins preparations for dropping the atomic weapons by establishing the 509th Composite Group

1945

3 January: MacArthur is given command of all American ground forces and Nimitz command of all naval forces as assaults are planned against Iwo Jima, Okinawa and Japan

4 January: British forces occupy Akyab, Burma

9 January: American Sixth Army invades Lingayen Gulf on Luzon in the Philippines

28 January:	Burma road is reopened
3 February:	US Army attacks Japanese in Manila
16 February:	American forces recapture Bataan
19 February:	American Marines invade Iwo Jima
2 March:	American airborne troops recapture Corregidor in the Philippines
3 March:	American and Filipino troops liberate Manila
9–10 March:	270 B-29s firebomb Tokyo
20 March:	British forces liberate Mandalay, Burma
1 April:	United States Tenth Army invades Okinawa
12 April:	President Roosevelt dies, succeeded by Harry S Truman
1 May:	Australian troops invade Tarakan (Dutch Borneo)
8 May:	Victory in Europe Day
20 May:	Japanese forces begin withdrawing from China
25 May:	US Joint Chiefs of Staff approve 'Operation Olympic', the planned invasion of Japan, scheduled for November 1
9 June:	Japanese Premier Suzuki announces Japan will continue fighting to the very end
10 June:	Australian forces invade Borneo
18 June:	Japanese resistance ends on Mindanao in the Philippines
22 June:	US forces complete the capture of Okinawa
28 June:	Japanese resistance in the Philippines ends
5 July:	Declaration of the liberation of the Philippines
10 July:	1,000 bomber raids against Japan commence
14 July:	First American naval bombardment of Japanese home islands
16 July:	Atomic bomb is successfully tested in the United States
26 July:	Components of the 'Little Boy' atomic bomb are unloaded at Tinian Island in the South Pacific
26 July:	US President Truman, British Prime Minister Churchill and Chinese President Chiang Kai-shek issue the Potsdam Declaration, declaring that Japan would face 'utter devastation' if it did not surrender
29 July:	Japanese submarine sinks the *Indianapolis*
6 August:	Atomic bomb dropped on Hiroshima
8 August:	Soviet Union declares war on Japan, then invades Manchuria
9 August:	Second atomic bomb is dropped on Nagasaki. Emperor Hirohito and Japanese Prime Minister Suzuki decide to seek an immediate peace with the Allies
14 August:	Japanese accept unconditional surrender. MacArthur appointed to head the occupation forces in Japan
29 August:	Soviets shoot down a B-29 dropping supplies to POWs in Korea. American forces land near Tokyo to begin the occupation of Japan
30 August:	British reoccupy Hong Kong
2 September:	Formal Japanese surrender ceremony. President Truman declares VJ Day
3 September:	General Yamashita, Japanese commander in the Philippines, surrenders to General Wainwright

4 September: Japanese forces on Wake Island surrender

5 September: British land in Singapore

8 September: MacArthur enters Tokyo

9 September: Japanese in Korea and Dutch East Indies surrender

13 September: Japanese in Burma surrender

24 October: United Nations is born

THE LIMIT OF JAPANESE ADVANCE

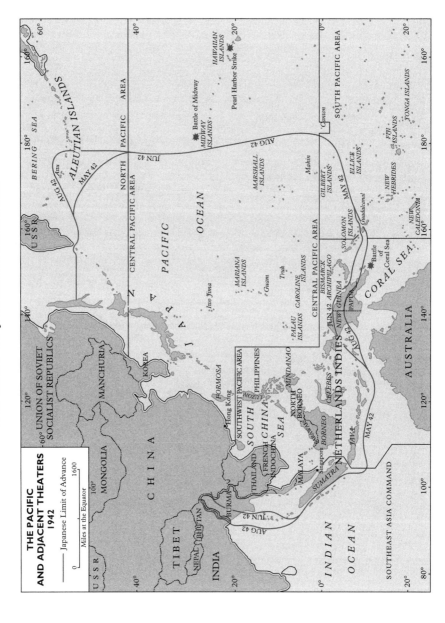

THE PACIFIC
AND ADJACENT THEATERS
1942

— Japanese Limit of Advance

Miles at the Equator
0   1600

USSR

TIBET
NEPAL BHUTAN
BURMA
INDIA

CHINA

MONGOLIA

MANCHURIA

KOREA

FORMOSA

Hong Kong

THAILAND
FRENCH
INDOCHINA

MALAYA
Singapore

SUMATRA

JAVA

MAY 42

JUN 42
AUG 42

INDIAN
OCEAN

SOUTHEAST ASIA COMMAND

AUSTRALIA

NETHERLANDS INDIES

BORNEO
NORTH
BORNEO
CELEBES

PHILIPPINES
MINDANAO

SOUTHWEST PACIFIC AREA

SOUTH
CHINA
SEA

PALAU
ISLANDS

CAROLINE
ISLANDS

MARIANA
ISLANDS

Guam

Iwo Jima

Truk

CENTRAL PACIFIC AREA

NEW GUINEA
PAPUA

BISMARCK
ARCHIPELAGO

SOLOMON
ISLANDS

Guadalcanal

Battle
of
Coral Sea

CORAL SEA

MAY 42

JUN 42

AUG 42

NEW
HEBRIDES

NEW
CALEDONIA

GILBERT
ISLANDS

ELLICE
ISLANDS

Makin

MARSHALL
ISLANDS

FIJI
ISLANDS

TONGA ISLANDS

SOUTH PACIFIC AREA

Canton

MAY 42

JAPAN

PACIFIC

OCEAN

NORTH
PACIFIC
AREA

CENTRAL PACIFIC AREA

NORTH PACIFIC AREA

BERING SEA

ALEUTIAN ISLANDS

Attu

MAY 42
AUG 42

JUN 42
AUG 42

USSR

UNION OF SOVIET
SOCIALIST REPUBLICS

MIDWAY
ISLANDS

Battle of Midway

Pearl Harbor Strike

HAWAIIAN
ISLANDS

60°
180°
160°
160°
140°
120°
100°
80°
40°
20°
0°
20°
40°
60°
140°
120°
100°
60°
160°
180°
160°
140°
120°
100°
80°

THE ALLIED COUNTER-OFFENSIVE

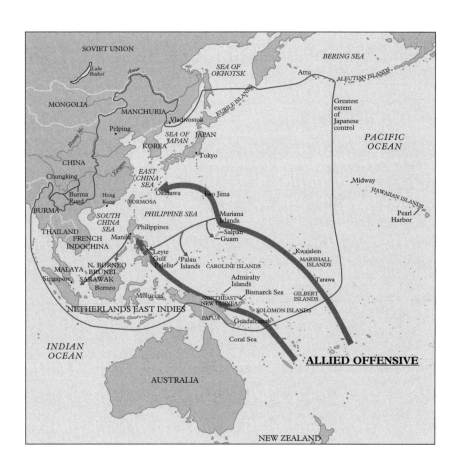

SOURCES AND COPYRIGHT HOLDERS

Extracts have been reprinted with permission. Every reasonable effort has been made to trace the owners of copyright materials in this book, but in some instances this has proven impossible. The authors and publishers will be glad to receive information leading to more complete acknowledgements in subsequent printings of the book and in the mean time extend their apologies for any omissions.

Chapter One: The Path to War

1. **A Japanese Newspaper Denounces America's Restrictive Immigration Legislation of 1924.** This source selection is from 'The Senate's Declaration of War', *Japan Times and Mail*, 19 April 1924, 4. http://historymatters.gmu.edu/d/5077.

2. **The United States Neutrality Act of 1935.** This source selection is from US Department of State, Publication 1983, *Peace and War: United States Foreign Policy, 1931–1941* (Washington, DC: US Government Printing Office, 1943), 265–271.

3. **Konoye Funimaro's Plans for a 'New Order' in Asia (1938).** This source selection is from Dennis Merrill and Thomas G. Paterson, eds., *Major Problems in American Foreign Relations. Volume II: Since 1914. Documents and Essays*, 6th ed. (Boston: Houghton Mifflin, 2005), 121–122, reprinted from US Department of State, *Papers Relating to the Foreign Relations of the United States, Japan: 1931–1941* (Washington, DC: Government Printing Office, 1943), I, 477–478.

4. **Franklin D. Roosevelt's 'Quarantine Speech', 5 October 1937.** This source selection is from http://www.vlib.us/amdocs/texts/fdrquarn.html.

5. **Stanley K. Hornbeck Discusses American Options to Curtail Japanese Aggression (1938).** This source selection is from Thomas G. Paterson & Dennis Merrill, eds., *Major Problems in American Foreign Relations. Volume II: Since 1914. Documents and Essays*, 4th ed. (Lexington, Mass.: D. C. Heath & Co., 1995), 133–134.

6. **Japanese and American Newspapers Report on the Fall of Nanjing.** These source selections are from eyewitness report: the last day of Nanking 'The scariest thing was the artillery', as reported by a New York Times journalist. By Special Correspondent Nakamura in Nanking. Source: The Asahi Shimbun, 16 December 1937. Translated by Beatrice Trefalt. Reprinted with permission and F. Tillman Durdin, 'All Captives Slain'; Civilians Also Killed as the Japanese Spread Terror in Nanking from *The New York Times*, 18 December 1937, 1.

7. *The New York Times* **Discusses Japanese Attitudes and Intentions, 1940.** This source selection is from Hugh Byas, 'Japan Undeterred by US. Embargo; Even Stronger Action by This Country Is Expected, Possibly Ban on Silk Purchases HELP TO REICH IS HINTED Reprisals Are Mapped by High Japanese in Shanghai – Would Bar Imports From Indies', from *The New York Times*, 27 September 1940.

8. **American Journalist and Essayist Otto Tolischus Writes from Tokyo, February 1941.** This source selection is from Otto D. Tolischus, *Tokyo Record* (London: H. Hamilton, 1943), 13–14.

ChapterTwo: Pearl Harbor

1. **Prime MinisterTōjō Hideki Sums Up Japanese Sentiments, 1 December 1941.**
This source selection is from Akira Iriye, ed., *Pearl Harbor and the Coming of the Pacific War: A Brief History with Documents and Essays* (Boston: Bedford/St. Martin's, 1999), 90–91.

2. **Franklin D. Roosevelt Appeals to Japanese Emperor Hirohito, 6 December 1941.** This source selection is taken from US Department of State Bulletin, Vol. V, No. 129, 13 December 1941, http://www.international.ucla.edu/eas/documents/us-jpn411206.htm.

3. **Recalling the Attack on Pearl Harbor: A Japanese Memoir.** This source selection is from 'Attack at Pearl Harbor, 1941, – the Japanese View', EyeWitness to History, http://www.eyewitnesstohistory.com/pfpearl2.htm. Ibis Communications, Inc. Reprinted with permission.

4. **Recalling the Attack on Pearl Harbor: An American Eyewitness.** This source selection is taken from Wallin, Homer N. Pearl Harbor: *Why, How, Fleet Salvage and Final Appraisal.* (Washington DC: Government Printing Office, 1968): 297–327. Accessed: http://www.history.navy.mil/docs/wwii/pearl/survivors2.htm.

5. **Remembering Pearl Harbor: A Nurse's Perspective.** This selection is from Oral History of LT Ruth Erickson, NC (Nurse Corps), USN. Source: 'Oral history provided courtesy of the office of the Historian, Bureau of Medicine and Surgery'. Accessed: http://www.history.navy.mil/faqs/faq66-3b.htm.

6. **President Franklin D. Roosevelt Labels 7 December 1941 as a 'Date which Will Live in Infamy'.** This source selection is from http://historymatters.gmu.edu/d/5166/.

7. **The Japanese Population IsTold of the Attack.** This source selection is from Editorial, 'taibeiei no sensen', *Asahi shinbun*, 9 December 1941.Source: The Asahi Shimbun, 9 December 1941. Translated by Beatrice Trefalt. Reprinted with permission.

8. **British Prime Minister Winston Churchill Reacts to the Japanese Attack at Pearl Harbor.** This source selection is from Churchill, Winston, *The Second World War. Volume III: The Grand Alliance*, London: Cassell and Co., 1950: 537–540. Reproduced with permission of Curtis Brown Ltd, London on behalf of The Estate of Winston Churchill. Copyright © Winston S. Churchill.

9. **A Case of Mistaken Identity: Reporting Casualties.** This source selection is from http://my.execpc.com/~dschaaf/hamlin.html#memorial.

10. **Rebuilding after Pearl Harbor.** This source selection is from 'To The NewYork Times, NewYork via *The NewYork Times* Washington Bureau, From Robert Trumbull. Confidential and not Released. Pearl Harbor, 13 December (passed by naval censor) . . .' Box 11, William Rea Furlong Papers, Naval Historical Foundation Collection, Manuscript Division, Library of Congress, Washington, D.C. Reproduced from the Collections of the Manuscript Division, Library of Congress.

ChapterThree: The Japanese Advance, 1941–1942

1. **The Personal Letters of Gordon Bennett.** This source selection is from Personal Letter of H. Gordon Bennett to Stanley Ricketson, 08 November 1941, Papers of Ferdinand Henry Wright, National Library of Australia, MS 8119, Series 6/1. By permission of the National Library of Australia.

2. **Canadian Newspaper Reports on the Allied Garrison at Hong Kong.** These source selections are from *Globe and Mail*, 10 December 1941 and Staff Writer, 'Garrison of 6,000 Troops, including Canadians, Capitulates to Japanese', *Hamilton Spectator*, 26 December 1941. Reprinted courtesy of The Hamilton Spectator.

3. **Alec Hodgson's Diary.** This source selection is from Dawson, Kate, Obey, Pray and Hope : the P.O.W. diary of Sgt. Alec Hodgson 2/6 Field Park Co. R.A.E. Changi and the Burma-Thailand Railway, 1942–1945, transcribed by Kate Dawson (Perth, W.A.: K. Dawson, © 1990). Reprinted with permission.

4. **An Australian Newspaper and the Fall of Singapore.** This source selection is from *Sydney Morning Herald*, 12 February 1942.

5. **Shimada Housaku's Recollections.** This source selection is from Shimada Hōsaku, *Mare senshatai* (Tokyo: Kawade Shobō, 1967), 266–267. Translated by Beatrice Trefalt.

6. **Alec Hodgson's Diary and Defeat.** This source selection is from Dawson, Kate, Obey, Pray and Hope : the P.O.W. diary of Sgt. Alec Hodgson 2/6 Field Park Co. R.A.E. Changi and the Burma-Thailand Railway, 1942–1945, transcribed by Kate Dawson (Perth, W.A. : K. Dawson, © 1990). Reprinted with permission.

7. **Shimada Housaku's Memoir and Victory.** This source selection is from Shimada Hōsaku, *Mare senshatai* (Tokyo: Kawade Shobō, 1967), 272–273. Translated by Beatrice Trefalt.

Chapter Four: The War at Sea: Coral Sea, Midway and Beyond

1. **Air Power Ascendant: The Sinking of the *Prince of Wales* and the *Repulse*.** These source selections are taken from 'The Sinking of the Prince of Wales and the Repulse', Ralph Robinson, 'The Sinkings: Ralph Story: Life in the British Navy', http://www.ralphrobson.co.uk/ralph5.htm. Reprinted with permission.

2. **Striking at the Japanese Homeland: The Doolittle Raid.** These sources are taken from *Sensō: The Japanese Remember the Pacific War* ed. Frank Gibney (Armonk, New York: M. E. Sharpe, 1995), 203, and *Fading Victory: The Diary of Matome Ugaki, 1941–1945*, trans. Masataka Chihaya (Pittsburgh: University of Pittsburgh Press, 1991), 112–113.

3. **The Battle of the Coral Sea: A Crewman Aboard the *Lexington* Describes a Japanese Attack.** This source selection is taken from p.118 *Action Stations Coral Sea: The Australian Commander's Story* by Chris Coulthard-Clark, (Allen and Unwin, 1991 © C. D. Coulthard-Clark.1991), Reprinted with permission of Allen & Unwin Book Publishers.

4. **The Battle of the Coral Sea: A Japanese Pilot Describes the Perils of an Attack.** This source selection is taken from p.119 *Action Stations Coral Sea: The Australian Commander's Story* by Chris Coulthard-Clark, (Allen and Unwin, 1991 © C. D. Coulthard-Clark.1991), Reprinted with permission of Allen & Unwin Book Publishers.

5. **Australian Prime Minister John Curtin Describes the Significance of the Battle of the Coral Sea.** This source selection is taken from Prime Minister John Curtin's speech to the House of Representatives, *Commonwealth Parliamentary Debates (House of Representatives)*, 170, 8 May 1942, 1060–1061.

6. **A Japanese Pilot Describes an American Attack During the Battle of Midway.** This source selection is taken from http://www.nps.gov/history/nr/twhp/wwwlps/lessons/90midway/90facts3.htm.

7. **On the Wires: The Associated Press and the Battle of Midway.** This source is from Midway Victory May Turn Tide in Battle of Pacific: *'Jap Attacks Seen As Answer to Raids on Tokyo'*, by DeWitt Mackenzie, Wide World War Analyst, Winona Republican Herald, 8 June 1942.

8. **An American Ensign Uses V-Mail to Tell His Family of the Victory at the Battle of Midway.** This source selection is taken from Letter of Arthur T. Burke (letter from Midway). Reprinted with kind permission of Craig Burke. http://www.centuryinter.net/midway/veterans/arthurburke.html.

9. **Submarine Warfare in the Pacific.** This source selection is taken from Diary: Rear Admiral Corwin Mendenhall USN (RET) with an introduction by Admiral I J Galantin USN (RET), Algonquin Books of Chapel Hill, 1991. @ 1991 by Corwin Mendenhall.

10. **Torpedoed: The Sinking of the *USS Indianapolis*, July 1945.** These source selections are taken from Statement of Rear Admiral John D. Hutson, JAGC, USN, Judge Advocate General of the Navy before the Senate Armed Services Committee on the USS Indianapolis, 14 September 1999, p. 5, http://armed-services.senate. gov/statemnt/1999/990914jh.pdf, and A Survivor's Story: In Woody's Words, http://www.ussindianapolis.org/woody.htm.

11. **Japan's 'Special Attack' Weapons.** This source selection is from Yokota Yutaka, 'Volunteer', in *Japan at War: An Oral History*, ed. Haruko Taya Cook and Theodore F. Cook (New York: The New Press, 1992), 306–312.

Chapter Five: Turning the Tide on Land, 1942–1943

1. **War Diary, 39th Battalion, Australian Military Forces.** This source selection is from 39th Battalion War Diary, AWM52, Item 8/3/78, Australian War Memorial. Available online at: http://www.awm.gov.au/diaries/ww2/folder.asp?folder=537. Reprinted with permission.

2. **Doc Vernon's War Diary.** This source selection is from 'War diary of field services on the Owen Stanley-Buna campaign, 1942', PR00787, Australian War Memorial.

3. **Watanabe Toshio's Diary.** This source selection is from wartime translations of seized Japanese documents: ATIS reports, 1942–1946 (Bethesda: Congressional Information Service, 1988), 10-SR, 12, 13, 15.

4. **General Horii's Message to the Troops.** This source selection is from wartime translations of seized Japanese documents: ATIS reports, 1942–1946 (Bethesda: Congressional Information Service, 1988), 10-SR, 12, 13, 15.

5. **Ralph Honner's Speech at Menari.** This source selection is from Peter Fitzsimons, *Kokoda* (Sydney: Hodder Headline, 2004), 362–363.

6. **Japanese Diary from Milne Bay.** This source selection is from wartime translations of seized Japanese documents: ATIS reports, 1942–1946 (Bethesda: Congressional Information Service, 1988), 10-CT-4

7. **'My Guadalcanal': Inui Genjuru's Diary.** This source selection is from 'My Guadalcanal': Inui Genjuru's diary, a selection from *A Marine Diary: My Experiences on Guadalcanal*. Web site owned by James R. 'Rube' Garrett http://www.gnt.net/~jrube/Genjirou/genjiru3.htm. Reprinted with permission.

8. **Imamura's Recollections of Rabaul.** This source selection is from Imamura Hitoshi, 'Extracts from the Tenor of My Life', Pacific Manuscripts Bureau, Australian National University, Canberra. Source: The Netherlands Institute for War Documentation (NIOD). Reprinted with permission.

9. **Yoshida Kashichi's Poem.** This source selection is from Saburō Ienaga, *The Pacific War* (New York: Pantheon Books, 1978), 44.

10. **American Poets and Guadalcanal.** These source selections are from 'Life in Guadalcanal', by Jim Epperson. Epperson Folder, Infantry-Americal Division Papers, US Army Military History Institute, Carlisle, Barracks, PA and 'Somewhere in Guadalcanal', anonymous poem. Isom J. Terry Papers, 90th Field Artillery Battalion, 25th Infantry Division, World War II Veterans Survey Collection, US Army Military History Institute, Carlisle, Barracks, PA.

11. **The Pacific War as a Race War.** This source selection is from Ralph Noonan Papers, Military History Unit, US Army Heritage & Education Center, Carlisle, PA.

12. **Private Descriptions of the Brutalities of War.** This source selection is from Ralph Noonan Papers, Military History Unit, US Army Heritage & Education Center, Carlisle, PA.

13. **'Fuzzy Wuzzy Angels'.** This source selection is from Beros, Sapper H 'Bert', 'The Fuzzy Wuzzy Angels', *The Fuzzy Wuzzy Angels and Other Verses*, (Sydney: H. Johnston, 1944). NX 6925, 7th Div., RAE, AIF. Source website: http://www.anzacday.org.au/anzacservices/poetry/fuzzywuzzy.htm.

14. **A Feature Writer's Perspective of the War on Land.** This source selection is from 'The Sinking of the Wasp', *Time*, Monday, 02 November 1942.

15. **A Feature Writer's Perspective on the War at Sea.** This source selection is from 'War in the Papuan Jungles', *Time*, Monday, 14 December 1942.

Chapter Six: The Allied Counter-Offensive, 1943–1945

1. **Fighting Words in the Sky: 22 SQN RAAF's Operations Record Book.** This source is from Unit History Sheet 22 Squadron, RAAF. RAAF Unit History Sheets (Form A50) and A51, Number 22, City of Sydney Squadron, A9186, 45. Courtesy of the Royal Australian Air Force.

2. **Words of Commendation: Bravery Award Citations.** This source selection is from *London Gazette*, 19 October 1943.

3. *The New York Times* **Reports on the Battle of Saipan.** This source selection is from George F. Horne, 'Japanese Lose 300 Planes in Saipan Battle, Biggest Since Midway; Island Airfield Taken. Fleet Is Attacked', *The New York Times*, 20 June 1944.

4. **Kawaguchi Taro's Diary from Saipan.** This source selection is from http://www.bdblodgett.com/Saipan/Kawaguchi%20Diary.htm

5. **A Pilot's Fighting Words: Marshall Chester's Diary.** This source selection is from Marshall Chester 'First B-29 raid on Tokyo', *Flight Journal*, April 1999. Section from Marshall Chester's diary.

6. **Japanese Combat Propaganda.** This source selection is from the author's collection.

7. **Allied Combat Propaganda.** This source selection is from American Office of War Information Leaflet 101 and OWI Leaflet 1049, cited at http://www.psywarrior.com/OWI60YrsLater2.html.

8. **Radio Propaganda.** These source selections are from the Sound Division of the National Archives and Record Administration.

9. *Kamikaze* **Writings.** These source selections are from Rikihei Inoguchi and Tadashi Nakajima with Roger Pineau. *The Divine Wind: Japan's Kamikaze Force in World War II* (Annapolis: Naval Institute Press, 1958), 183–184; Midori Yamanouchi, Joseph L. Quinn, *Listen to the Voices from The Sea* (Scranton: Scranton University Press, 2005) and Captain Ryoji Uehara 'My Thoughts. Midori Yamanouchi, Joseph L. Quinn', Listen to the Voices from *The Sea* (Scranton: Scranton University Press, 2005).

10. **An Allied Perspective on the *Kamikaze*.** This source selection is from Wallace, Irving, 'Japan's Last Hope', *Liberty*, 5 May 1945.

11. **A Japanese Account from Iwo Jima.** This source selection is from the 'Diary of First Lieutenant Sugihara Kinryu', 1945. Originally translated by the US Army in 1946. Diary later reproduced in Stephen J. Loftgren, 'Diary of First Lieutenant Sugihara Kinryu: Iwo Jima, January to February, 1945', *Journal of Military History*, 59 (1995), 97–133.

12. **An American Account from Iwo Jima.** This source selection is from 'Letters from Iwo Jima', Mary Beth Kennedy Voda, *Military Officer Magazine*, February 2005, http://www.moaa.org/magazine/February2005/f_letters.asp.

13. **Photo as Text.** This source selection is from 'Story of a Picture', *Time*, Monday, 26 March 1945.
14. **Women's War: Nursing the Wounded.** These source selections are from Alice Aurora Goudreau, 'Nursing at an Advance Naval Base Hospital: During the Iwo Jima Campaign', *The American Journal of Nursing*, 45 (1945), 884–886. Reprinted with permission and Olivine B. St. Peter, 'The Marianas', *The American Journal of Nursing*, 45 (1945), 1012–1013. Reprinted with permission.
15. **The Air War: Over Tokyo.** This source selection is from Lieutenant F. H. 'Pete' Reed, The 'Fourteenth', April 1945 letter to his parents, *The Breeze*, 2 (1945) 9–11. Re-published on the NOAA History web site by NOAA Central Library at: http://www.history.noaa.gov/stories_tales/b29.html. Source: NOAA Central Library.

Chapter Seven: Occupation Experiences

1. **H. J. Heijnen's Account of the Last Days of Dutch Colonial Rule in 1942.** This source selection is from Ministerie van Kolonien te Londen 1940–1945, National Archives of the Netherlands, 2 October 1945, 812.
2. **Lieutenant Nievera's Open Letter.** This source selection is from Soriano, Rafaelita Hilario, 'Japanese Occupation of the Philippines, with Special Reference to Japanese Propaganda, 1941–1945', PhD Thesis, University of Michigan, 1948.
3. **Wanatabe Wataru's Directives for the Occupation of Southeast Asia.** This source is from Akashi Yōji (ed.), *Watanabe Wataru Shosho gunsei* (Tokyo: Ryūkei shosha, 1998), 213–214. Translated by Beatrice Trefalt.
4. **Japanese Propaganda and Filipino Civilians.** This source selection is from *Shin Seiki/New Era*, No 8, May 2603 (1943).
5. **The Singing Imamura Hitoshi.** This source selection is from Imamura Hitoshi 'Extracts from the Tenor of My Life', Pacific Manuscripts Bureau, Australian National University, Canberra.
6. **Southeast Asian Memories.** This source selection is from Phaik, Lim Kwee, *The Phoenix Transcends* (Sydney: Self-published, 2001) 171–175.
7. **Speaking Allegiance.** These source selections are from Soriano, Rafaelita Hilario, 'Japanese Occupation of the Philippines, with Special Reference to Japanese propaganda, 1941–1945', PhD Thesis, University of Michigan, 1948; Simon Makalinaw, 'The Fence Sitter's Hour of Decision', *Philippine Review*, 11, No. 10, (December 1944), and *Pramoedya Ananta Toer, Perburuan: tjerita jang dimahkotai hadiah I Balai* (Djakarta: Perpustakaan Perguruan Kem. P.P. & K., 1955).
8. **Remembering the Black Market.** This source selection is from Mamoru Syonan Shinozaki, *My Story: The Japanese Occupation of Singapore* (Singapore: Asia Pacific Press, 1975).
9. **Words of Resistance.** This source selection is from. Sybil Kathigasu, *No Dram of Mercy* (Singapore: Oxford University Press, 1982).
10. **Islander Oral History.** This source selection is from Lin Poyer, Laurence Marshall Carucci and Susanne Falgout, *The Typhoon of War: Micronesian Experiences of the Pacific War* (Honolulu: University of Hawai'i Press, 2001), 224 and 226.
11. **Declaring Independence.** This source selection is from Ho Chi Minh, *Selected Works*, Vol. 3 (Hanoi: Foreign Languages Publishing House, 1960–1962), 17–21.

Chapter Eight: Home-Front Experiences

1. **Civil Liberties in Wartime: Interning Japanese-Americans.** This source is from *The Kikuchi Dairy: Chronicle from an American Concentration Camp; The Tanforan*

Journals of Charles Kikuchi. Copyright 1973 by the Board of Trustees of the University of Illinois. Used with permission of the University of Illinois Press.

2. **Civil Liberties in Wartime: The Japanese Home Front.** This source selection is from 'Informed Upon and Mistreated by Military Police', in Frank Gibney, ed., *Sensō: The Japanese Remember the Pacific War. Letters to the Editor of Asahi Shim* trans. Beth Cary (Armonk, New York: M. E. Sharpe, 1995), 177–178. Pacific Basin Institute. Reprinted with permission.

3. **Race Relations in Wartime: African-Americans at War.** These source selections are from *Major Problems in American History, 1920–1945*, ed., Colin Gordon, (Boston: Houghton Mifflin, 1999): 406–408. Originally published as Charles F. Wilson to Franklin Roosevelt (9 May 1944), Philip McGuire (ed.), and *Taps For a Jim Crow Army: Letters from Black Soldiers in World War II* (Santa-Barbara: ABC-Clio, 1983), 134–139.

4. **Women's Domestic Labours Assist the War Effort.** This source selection is from Prime Minister's Wife. Gives Lead to the Nation, Mrs. John Curtin, *The Australian Women's Weekly*, 19 September 1942. Currently available at: http://john.curtin.edu. au/curtinhouse/house5/house5j.html. Reprinted with permission.

5. **Women at Work in American Industry.** These sources are from Donovan, Katherine, 'Bay State Victory Girls Meet the Challenge of War', *Boston Sunday Advertiser*, 13 December 1942. Source: Scrapbooks, 1942–1943, Watertown Arsenal (Watertown, Massachusetts), Public Information Office, Records of the Chief of Ordnance, Record Group 156, NARA-Northeast Region (Boston) and De Leuw, Carl, 'Girls Man Huge Cranes: 30 per cent of Arsenal Workers are Women', *Boston Traveler*, 30 April 1943. Source: Scrapbooks, 1942–43, Watertown Arsenal (Watertown, Massachusetts), Public Information Office, Records of the Chief of Ordnance, Record Group 156, NARA-Northeast Region (Boston).

6. **Encountering the Home Front: Americans in Australia and New Zealand.** These source selections are taken from Mack Morriss, *South Pacific Diary, 1942–1943*, 101–102. Reprinted in *The Faraway War*, ed. Richard J. Aldrich, (Lexington, KY: University Press of Kentucky, 1995): 281.

7. **The War Comes Home: Sydney Under Attack.** This source selection is taken from Gunfire Shakes Sydney: Graphic Stories of the Raid, *The Age*, 2 June 1942. Reprinted with kind permission from *The Age*.

8. **Children's War.** This source selection is taken from Satō Hideo, 'Playing at War', in *Japan at War: An Oral History*, ed. Haruko Tay Cook and Theodore F. Cook (New York: New Press, 1992), 233–39.

9. **Life under the Bombs: Japanese Experiences.** These source selections are from Kogawa Shigenori, ed., *Ano hi o wasurenai: kakareta Tōkyō daikūshū* (Tokyo: Hakushobō, 2005), 135. Translated by Beatrice Trefalt.

10. **Sustaining Love: Advice on How to Write to Servicemen.** This source is from Ethel Gorham, *So Your Husband's Gone to War!* (New York: Doubleday, 1942), 185–192.

Chapter Nine: Prisoner-of-War Experiences

1. **An Allied Prisoner in Singapore.** This source is from Hugh Clarke, *Last Stop Nagasaki* (London, Allen and Unwin, 1984), 13.

2. **The Ordeal of the Bataan Death March.** This source is from Gene S. Jacobsen, *We Refused to Die: My Time as a Prisoner of War in Bataan and Japan, 1942–1945* (Salt Lake City: University of Utah Press, 2004), 89–90. Reprinted with Permission.

3. **Surviving the Horrors of Sandakan.** This source is from Christopher Dawson, *To Sandakan: the Diaries of Charlie Johnstone, Prisoner of War 1942–1945* (Sydney, Allen and Unwin, 1995), 80–81.

4. **Transportation to Japan: One Prisoner's Experience.** This source is from *Captured on Corregidor: Diary of an American P.O.W. in World War II* © 1988 John M. Wright, Jr. by permission of McFarland & Company, Inc., Box 611, Jefferson NC 28640. www.mcfarlandpub.com.

5. **Indian Prisoners of War Recall their Incarceration by the Japanese.** These source selection are from John Baptist Crasta, *Eaten by the Japanese* (Bangalore: Invisible Man Publishers, 1999), 21–22 and 'Letter from Jemedar Chint Singh (Indian Officer), ex-POW of Japanese at Wewak', Australian War Memorial, Series number AWM 54 779/1/20.

6. **Life and Death on the Burma-Thailand Railway.** This source is an excerpt from Tom Fagan's diary, in Leslie Hall, *The Blue Haze: POWs on the Burma Railway* (Kenthurst, N.S.W: Kangaroo Press, 1996), 227–228.

7. **A Japanese Perspective.** This source is from Kazuo Tamayama, *Railwaymen in the War: Tales by Japanese Railway Soldiers in Burma and Thailand, 1941–1947* (London: Palgrave McMillan, 2005), 141–143.

8. **Prisoners of War in Japan.** This source is from Herbert Zincke (with Scott A. Mills), *Mitsui Madhouse: Memoir of a U.S. Army Air Corps POW in World War II* (Jefferson, North Carolina: McFarland and Co, 2003), 128.

9. **The Execution of Flight Lieutenant Bill Newton VC.** This source is from 'The execution of Flight Lieutenant Bill Newton VC', *Allied Translator and Interpretor* Section, General Headquarters, South West Pacific Area, Information Bulletin No 10, Australian Archives Series A4311/5 Item 747/6

10. **Japanese Prisoners' Perspectives.** This source is a record of the Allied Translator and Interpreter Section South West Pacific Area, M report, 30 April 1943, Australian War Memorial, AWM 55 [9/1].

11. **Japanese Prisoners Contemplate Defeat.** This source is from Ōoka Shōhei, *Taken Captive: A Japanese POW's Story* (translated by Wayne P. Lammers) (New York: John Wiley and Sons, 1996), 245–246. Reprinted with permission from John Wiley and Sons, Inc.

Chapter Ten: Hiroshima and the Defeat of Japan

1. **Scientists Protest the Use of Atomic Power.** This source is on record in the US National Archives, Record Group 77, Records of the Chief of Engineers, Manhattan Engineer District, Harrison-Bundy File, folder #76.

2. **Extract from Harry Truman's Diary (Potsdam, 25 July 1945).** This source is from President Harry S. Truman's diary, 25 July 1945. Source: The Harry S. Truman Library and Museum, administered by the National Archives and Records Administration.http://www.trumanlibrary.org/whistlestop/study_collections/bomb/large/documents/fulltext.php?fulltextid=15.and Robert Ferrell, ed., *Off the record: the Private Papers of Harry S. Truman* (New York: Harper and Row, 1980), 55–56.

3. **Truman's Announcement of the Atomic Bombing of Hiroshima.** This source is from White House press release, 'Statement by the President of the United States', ca. 6 August 1945. Source: The Harry S. Truman Library and Museum, administered by the National Archives and Records Administration. http://www.trumanlibrary.org/whistlestop/study_collections/bomb/small/mb10.htm.

4. **A Japanese Newspaper Describes the Atomic Attack on Hiroshima.** This source is from 'New type of enemy bomb on Hiroshima' Source: *The Asahi Shinbun*, 8 August 1945. Translated by Beatrice Trefalt. Reprinted with permission.

5. **An Australian Newspaper Reports the Attack on Hiroshima.** This source is from 'Triumph and Menace', *The Age*, 8 August 1945.

6. **A Survivor's Description of the Attack on Hiroshima.** This source is from Park Sunam, ed., *Mō hitotsu no Hiroshima: Chōsenjin Kankokujin hibakusha no shōgen* (Tokyo: Hatsubaimoto koseisha, 1983), 216–218. Translated by Beatrice Trefalt.

7. **Japanese Memories of the Nuclear Attacks.** This source is from poems by Ayako Etsuchi, Sadako Ishii, Tokuzaburō Imai, and Poem by Asao Izumi from Jiro Nakano, ed. and trans., *Outcry from the Inferno: Atomic Bomb Tanka Ideology* (Hawai'i: Bamboo Ridge Press, 1995), 2, 20, 23, 28.
8. **Prisoners of War under the Bomb.** This source is from Eric Hooper, quoted in Hugh Clarke, *Last Stop Nagasaki!* (Sydney: George Allen and Unwin, 1984): 97, 99.
9. **Living with the Scars.** This source is from Horikawa Keiko, Ogasawara Nobuyuki, *Chinchin densha to jogakusei: 1945-nen 8-gatsu 6-nichi: Hiroshima* (Tokyo: Hyōronsha, 2005), 214–215. Translated by Beatrice Trefalt.

Chapter Eleven: Surrender

1. **President Truman Addresses the Japanese People.** This Source is from Amerika gasshukoku daitoryou hari Esu Tsuruman yori issho wo teisu/A message from the President of the US to the People of Japan. National Diet Library of Japan. Copyright © 2003–2004. Reprinted with permission from the National Diet Library of Japan.
2. **The Allies Demand Unconditional Surrender from Japan.** This source is reprinted at http://www.ndl.go.jp/constitution/e/etc/c06.html.
3. **Emperor Hirohito Announces Japan's Surrender.** This source is from David John Lu, ed., *Sources of Japanese History*, Vol. 2 (New York: Oxford University Press, 1974), 176–177.
4. **The Experiences of a Japanese Factory Manager Based in China.** This source is from Kawagoe Sōichi, *Waga jinsei*, unpublished manuscript, translated by Watanabe Yoshimi.
5. **Japanese Reactions to the Surrender.** These sources are from Awaya Kentarō, ed., Shiryō: nihongendaishi. Haisen chokugo no seiji to shakai (Tokyo: Otsuki shoten, 1980), 52–53. Translated by Beatrice Trefalt.
6. **Demobilizing the Japanese Military: Experiences and Tensions.** This source is from Awaya Kentarō, ed., Shiryō: nihongendaishi. Haisen chokugo no seiji to shakai (Tokyo: Otsuki shoten, 1980), 184–185. Translated by Beatrice Trefalt.
7. **An American Pilot's Exhilaration and Pride at the End of the War.** This http://www.history.noaa.gov/stories_tales/b29.html source was a letter from Pete Reed originally published in *The Breeze*, 2, No. 8, 1–3.
8. **Return Anxiety: Welcoming Returned Servicemen Back to Their Pre-War Lives.** This source selection is from *The Doins*, August 1945, published by the Bondi Surf Bathers Lifesaving Club.
9. **An Australian Reflects on His Wartime Experiences and Contemplates the Future.** This source is from the unpublished diary of Basil Archer.
10. **Loss, Grief and Mourning.** These source selections are taken from http://www.arlingtoncemetery.net/wagalllagher.htm and Nellie Simpson to Tom Simpson [?] August, 1945, reprinted in Margaret Reeson, *A Very Long War: The Families who Waited* (Melbourne: Melbourne University Press, 2000), 48.
11. **A Wife Waits: Searching for the Unaccounted.** This source is from Royal Australian Air Force, Government file LYON, John (Flight Sergeant); Service Number 401706; File type Casualty Repatriation; Aircraft Boston 11A A28-3; Place Salamaua, Papua New Guinea; Date 18 March 1943. File number A705 166/25/26.

Chapter Twelve: Legacies

1. **An American Journalist's Diary of the Occupation Period.** This source is from Mark Gayn, *Japan Diary* (Tokyo: Tuttle, 1981), 43–45.
2. **Victors Writing History: The Tokyo War Crimes Trial Indictment.** This source is from 'International Military Tribunal for the Far East', in *The Tokyo War Crimes Trial* (New York: Garland, 1981).

3. **War Fiction and Beyond: T. A. G. Hungerford.** This source is from T.A.G. Hungerford, *Sowers of the Wind: A Novel of the Occupation of Japan* (Sydney: Angus and Robertson, 1954), 25–27.

4. **How to' Endure the Peace.** This source is from Tokyo-to zaigai douhou kikan sokushin rusukazoku dōmei, *Hikiagesha/rusukazoku no tame no seikatsu dokuhon* (Tokyo, self-published, 1950), Translated by Beatrice Trefalt.

5. **The End of War: The San Francisco Peace Treaty.** This source is taken from 'Treaty of Peace with Japan', in the United Nations Treaty Series, 136, No. 1832, 1952, 46–47.

6. **Silences: The Trauma of Imprisonment.** This source is from Hank Nelson, *P.O. W.: Prisoners of War: Australians under Nippon* (Sydney: ABC Enterprises, 1985), 213–214.

7. **Still Fighting: For Recognition.** This source is from Corban K. Alabado, *Bataan, Death March, Capas: A Tale of Japanese Cruelty and American Injustice* (San Francisco: Sulu books, 1995), 114–115.

8. **Museums as Memories and Memories at War: The Enola Gay Controversy.** This source is from Ken Ringle, 'At ground zero: 2 views of history collide over Smithsonian A-bomb exhibit', *The Washington Post*, 26 September 1994.

9. **Collective Memories: Comfort Women.** This source is from 'The Women's International War Crimes Tribunal' webpage.http://www1.jca.apc.org/vaww-net-japan/english/womenstribunal2000/whatstribunal.html.

NOTES

Introduction

1. John W. Dower, *War without Mercy: Race and Power in the Pacific War* (New York: Pantheon Books, 1986).
2. David Barton, Mary Hamilton and Roz Ivanic, eds., *Situated Literacies: Reading and Writing in Context* (New York: Routledge, 2000), 1.
3. David Barton and Mary Hamilton, 'Literacy Practices', in Barton, Hamilton and Ivanic *Situated Literacies*, 7.
4. Brian V. Street, ed., *Cross-cultural Approaches to Literacy* (New York: Cambridge University Press, 1993), 2.
5. Paul S. Dull, *A Battle History of the Imperial Japanese Navy*, 1941-1945 (Annapolis: Naval Institute Press, 1978), xiv.
6. Steven Roger Fischer, *A History of Reading* (London: Reaktion, 2003), 123.
7. Such documents have sometimes been labelled 'life writings', or, as the Dutch historian Jacques Presser put it, 'ego documents'. See Rudolph Dekker, 'Jacques Presser's Heritage: Ego documents in the Study of History', *Memoria y Civilizacion: Anuario de Historia de la Universidad de Navarra*, 5 (2002), 13–37.
8. Lindemann, cited in Rudolf Dekker, 'Introduction', *Ego-Documents and History: Autobiographical Writing in Its Social Context since the Middle Ages*, ed. Rudolph Dekker (Hilversum: Verloren Publishers, 2002), 9; Peter Burke, 'Representations of the Self from Petarch to Descartes', in *Rewriting the Self: Histories from the Renaissance to the Present*, ed. Roy Porter (New York: Routledge, 1997), 21.
9. Martha Howell and Walter Prevenier, *From Reliable Sources: An Introduction to Historical Methods* (Ithaca, NY: Cornell University Press, 2001), 21.
10. José van Dijck, *Mediated Memories in the Digital Age* (Stanford, CA: Stanford University Press, 2007), 10.
11. See Thomas Söderqvist, ed., *The History and Poetics of Scientific Biography* (Burlington, VT: Ashgate, 2007), 62; Howell and Prevenier, *From Reliable Sources*, 21.
12. Jeremy D. Popkin, *History, Historians, and Autobiography* (Chicago: University of Chicago Press, 2005), 71.
13. Alan Forrest, *Napoleon's Men: The Soldiers of the Revolution and Empire* (New York: Hambledon and London, 2002), xvii.
14. Christopher Seeley, *A History of Writing in Japan* (Honolulu: University of Hawaii Press, 2000), 150.
15. Margo DeMello, *Bodies of Inscription: A Cultural History of the Modern Tattoo Community* (Durham, NC: Duke University Press, 2000); Douglas Emerson Blandy, Doug Blandy and Kristin G. Congdon, *Pluralistic Approaches to Art Criticism* (Bowling Green, OH: Bowling Green State University Popular Press, 1991), 85.
16. See Sean Brawley and Chris Dixon, 'The Hollywood Native: Hollywood's Construction of the South Seas & Wartime Encounters with the South Pacific', *Sites: A Journal for South Pacific Cultural Studies*, 27 (1994), 15–29 and Sean Brawley and Chris Dixon, 'War and Sex in the South Pacific, 1941–1945', *Australasian Journal of American Studies*, 18 (1999), 3–18.
17. Addressing the South African Parliament in February 1960, British Prime Minister Harold Macmillan declared, 'The wind of change is blowing through this continent. Whether we like it or not, this growth of national consciousness is a political fact'. Macmillan's reference to the anti-colonial struggles throughout Africa was equally applicable to the struggles for national liberation raging throughout much of the Asia-Pacific region.

Chapter One: The Path to War

1. Jonathon Marshall's *To Have and Have Not: Southeast Asian Raw Materials and the Origins of the Pacific War* (Berkeley: University of California Press, 1995) problematises this notion, by suggesting that America also had some significant resource needs in Southeast Asia, notably rubber.

2. Alexis Dudden, *Japan's Colonisation of Korea: Discourse and Power* (Honolulu: University of Hawaii Press, 2005).

3. Marilyn Lake and Henry Reynolds, *Drawing the Global Colour Line: White Men's Countries and the International Challenge of Racial Equality* (Cambridge: Cambridge University Press, 2008), 263–283.

4. Sean Brawley, *The White Peril: Foreign Relations and Asian Immigration to Australasia and North America 1919-1978* (Sydney: University of New South Wales Press, 1995), 11–35; Lake and Reynolds, *Drawing the Global Colour Line*, 284–309.

5. Brawley, *White Peril*, 36–47.

6. Regarding the ongoing debate surrounding the extent to which the war in the Asia-Pacific was part of an eight-year war, or a fifteen-year war, see Sandra Wilson, 'Rethinking the 1930s and the "15-year War" in Japan', *Japanese Studies*, 21 (2001), 155–164.

7. Brawley, *White Peril*, 114–137.

8. On US foreign policy during the 1930s, see Robert Dallek, *Franklin D. Roosevelt and American Foreign Policy, 1932-1945* (New York: Oxford University Press, 1979).

9. On the United States and China, see Warren I. Cohen, *America's Response to China: A History of Sino-American Relations*, 4th ed. (New York: Columbia University Press, 2000).

10. There is continuing disagreement regarding the number of Chinese victims in Nanjing. See Joshua A. Fogel, *The Nanking Massacre in History and Historiography* (Berkeley: University of California Press, 2000).

11. Antony Best, *Britain, Japan and Pearl Harbor: Avoiding War in East Asia, 1936-41* (New York: Routledge, 1995).

12. For a revisionist account of the oil embargo and its consequences, see Keiichiro Komatsu, *Origins of the Pacific War and the Importance of Magic* (New York: St. Martin's Press, 1999).

13. Cited in Marc Trachtenberg, *The Craft of International History: A Guide to Method* (Princeton, NJ: Princeton University Press, 2006), 112.

14. Mary Kimoto Tomita, *Dear Miye: Letters Home from Japan, 1939-1946* (Stanford, CA: Stanford University Press, 1995), 106.

15. Shizhang Hu, *Stanley K. Hornbeck and the Open Door Policy, 1919-1937* (Westport, CT: Greenwood Press, 1995), 1.

16. Masahiro Yamamoto, *Nanking: Anatomy of an Atrocity* (Westport, CT: Praeger, 2000).

17. Curt Reiss, ed., *They Were There: The Story of World War II and How It Came About* (New York: Putnam, 1944), 654.

Chapter Two: Pearl Harbor

1. On Japanese-American relations in the period preceding Pearl Harbor, see Akira Iriye, *The Origins of the Second World War in Asia and the Pacific* (New York: Longman, 1987).

2. For a discussion of these issues consult Peter Michael Wetzler, *Hirohito and War: Imperial Tradition and Military Decision Making in Prewar Japan* (Honolulu: University of Hawaii Press, 1998), 40–60.

3. Roosevelt, cited in Robert Dallek, *Franklin D. Roosevelt and American Foreign Policy, 1932–1945* (New York: Oxford University Press, 1979), 310.

4. See, for example, Robert Alfred Theobald, *The Final Secret of Pearl Harbor: The Washington Contribution to the Japanese Attack* (New York: Devin-Adair, 1954), and Robert Stinnett, *Day of Deceit: The Truth about FDR and Pearl Harbor* (New York: Free Press, 2000).
5. On the lead up to, and the historiographical debates surrounding the Japanese attack at Pearl Harbor, see Hilary Conroy and Harry Wray, eds., *Pearl Harbor Reexamined: Prologue to the Pacific War* (Honolulu: University of Hawaii Press, 1990). See also Akira Iriye, ed., *Pearl Harbor and the Coming of the Pacific War: A Brief History with Documents and Essays* (Boston: Bedford/St. Martin's, 1999).
6. See Stephen S. Large, ed., *Showa Japan: Political, Economic and Social History, 1926-1989* (New York: Routledge, 1998), 6; M. J. Thurman and Christine Sherman, *War Crimes: Japan's World War II Atrocities* (Paducah, KY: Turner Pub., 2001), 154.
7. Nobutaka Ike, 'Japanese Memoirs-Reflections of the Recent Past', *Pacific Affairs*, 24 (1951), 185.
8. Stefanie Schüler-Springorum, 'Flying and Killing: Military Masculinity in German Pilot Literature, 1914-1949', in *Home/front: The Military, War and Gender in Twentieth-Century Germany*, ed. Karen Hagemann and Stefanie Schüler-Springorum (New York: Berg, 2002), 232.
9. Brenda Dyer and Lee Friedrich, 'The Personal Narrative as Cultural Artefact: Teaching Autobiography in Japan', *Written Communication*, 19 (2002), 265.
10. Jan Vansina, *Oral Tradition as History* (Madison: University of Wisconsin Press, 1985), 4.
11. Eric Hobsbawm, *On History* (London: Weidenfeld and Nicolson, 1997), 206.
12. Michael Frisch, *A Shared Authority: Essays on the Craft and Meaning of Oral and Public History* (Albany: State University of New York Press, 1990).
13. For an examination of this issue, see Trevor Lummis, *Listening to History: The Authenticity of Oral Evidence* (Totowa, NJ: Barnes & Noble Books, 1988) and Sherna Berger Gluck and Daphne Patai, eds., *Women's Words: The Feminist Practice of Oral History* (New York: Routledge, 1991).
14. Emily S. Rosenberg, *A Date Which Will Live: Pearl Harbor in American Memory* (Durham: Duke University Press, 2003), 11.
15. Sandra Silberstein, *War of Words: Language, Politics, and 9/11* (New York: Routledge, 2002), 15.
16. See Simon Partner, *Toshié: A Story of Village Life in Twentieth-century Japan* (Berkeley: University of California Press, 2004), 97.

Chapter Three: The Japanese Advance, 1941–1942

1. On Wavell and his leadership, see Brian P. Farrell, 'The Dice Were Heavily Loaded: Wavell and the Fall of Singapore', in *Leadership and Responsibility in the Second World War: Essays in Honor of Robert Vogel*, ed. Brian P. Farrell (Montreal: McGill-Queens Press, 2004), 182-234.
2. On the problems of joint command, see John R. Kennedy, *Command in Joint and Combined Operations: The Campaign for the Netherlands East Indies* (Fort Leavenworth: Army Command and General Staff School of Advanced Military Studies, 1990).
3. Mark Peattie, 'Japanese Strategy and Campaigns in the Pacific War, 1941-1945', in *World War II in Asia and the Pacific and the War's Aftermath, with General Themes*, ed. Lloyd E. Lee (Westport, CT: Greenwood Press, 1998), 60.
4. Allen R. Millett, 'Assault from the Sea: The Development of Amphibious Warfare between the Wars. The American, British and Japanese Experiences', in *Military Innovation in the Interwar Period*, ed. Williamson R. Murray and Allan R. Millett (New York: Cambridge University Press, 1998), 50.

5. See Kyoichi Tachikawa, 'General Yamashita and His Style of Leadership: The Malaya/Singapore Campaign', in *British and Japanese Military Leadership in the Far Eastern War, 1941-1945*, ed. Brian Bond and Kyoichi Tachikawa (London: Frank Cass, 2001), 55–87.
6. Louis Morton, 'Pacific Command: A Study of Inter-service Relations', in *The Harmon Memorial Lectures in Military History, 1959–1987*, ed. Harry R. Borowski (Washington, DC: Office of the Air Force, 1988), 129–132.
7. T. R. Moremon, *The Jungle, the Japanese and the British Commonwealth Armies at War, 1941-45: Fighting Methods, Doctrine and Training for Jungle Warfare* (London: Routledge, 2005), 5.
8. Raymond A. Callahan, *The Worst Disaster: The Fall of Singapore* (Newark, NJ: University of Delaware Press, 1977), 200; Henry Gordon Bennett, *Why Singapore Fell* (Bombay: Thacker, 1945), 179.
9. New Zealand Government to Pacific War Council, London, 17 February 1942, Ministerie van Kolonian to London 1940-49, 2 October 1945, General State Archives, The Hague, Netherlands.
10. See Roger Bell, Sean Brawley and Chris Dixon, *Conflict in the Pacific, 1937-1951* (Melbourne: Cambridge University Press, 2005), 81.
11. See Deborah Montgomerie, *Love in Time of War: Letter Writing in the Second World War* (Auckland: Auckland University Press, 2005).
12. David Halberstam, *The Powers That Be* (Champagne-Urbana: University of Illinois Press, 2000), 161.
13. Timothy Woods, *Strategy and Tactics: Infantry Warfare* (Osceola, WI: Zenith Press, 2002), 72.
14. Anonymous, 'World War II, 1941-1945', *Military History: Special Edition: Eyewitness to War* (2002), 42.
15. Chris Tiffen, 'Private Letters and the Fortunate Voyeur', *Voices*, 7 (1997), 7–14.
16. Earl Miner, 'The Traditions and Forms of the Japanese Poetic Diary', *Pacific Coast Philology*, 3 (1968), 38.
17. See, for example, *Censorship and Security in New Guinea: An Explanatory Booklet*, New Guinea Force, 1944, in the private papers of John Land, MSS 631, Mitchell Library, State Library of New South Wales.
18. Aaron Moore, 'The Peril of Self-Discipline: Chinese Nationalist, Japanese and American Servicemen Record the Rise and Fall of the Japanese Empire, 1937-1945', PhD Thesis, Princeton University, 2006, 10.
19. Henry Frei has offered a useful correction to this perception with *Guns of February: Ordinary Japanese Soldiers' View of the Malayan Campaign and the Fall of Singapore, 1941-42* (Singapore: Singapore University Press, 2004).
20. Kathleen Dehler, 'Diaries: Where Women Reveal Themselves', *The English Journal*, 78 (1989), 53–54.

Chapter Four: The War at Sea: Coral Sea, Midway and Beyond

1. For a discussion of naval development and innovation, and the consequences of naval arms limitation during the interwar years, see John Costello, *The Pacific War* (London: Pan Books, 1984), 36–53, 87–89.
2. On the Japanese Navy during World War II, see Paul S. Dull, *Battle History of the Imperial Japanese Navy, 1941-1945* (Annapolis: US Naval Institute Press, 1978).
3. David Lawrence Hanley, 'Kokubokan: Japanese Aircraft Carrier Development, 1922-1945', MA Thesis, San Jose State University, 2000.
4. For an overview of the rise of Japanese sea power, and the clash with the United States, see Sadao Asada, *From Mahan to Pearl Harbor: The Imperial Japanese Navy and the United States* (Annapolis: Naval Institute Press, 2006).

5. On the role of air power in the Pacific War, see Eric M. Bergerud, *Fire in the Sky: The Air War in the South Pacific* (Boulder, CO: Westview Press, 2000).

6. On the Battle of Midway, see, for example, Jonathon B. Parshall and Anthony P. Tully, *Shattered Sword: The Untold Story of the Battle of Midway* (Washington, DC: Potomac Books, 2005). Samuel Eliot Morison's fifteen-volume *History of United States Naval Operations in World War II* was originally published between 1947 and 1962, but remains a useful source for any student interested in the war at sea. For students of the Pacific War, Volumes 3, 4, 5, 6, 7, 8, 12, 13 and 14 are most relevant. See Morrison, *History of United States Naval Operations in World War II* (Urbana: University of Illinois Press, 2001–2002).

7. Yamamoto's statement that the Japanese attack at Pearl Harbor had served to 'awaken a sleeping giant and fill him with a terrible resolve' has become part of the accepted folklore of the Pacific War. However, there is no documentary evidence that Yamamoto ever said, or wrote, those words. The phrase was used to dramatic effect at the conclusion of the 1970 film *Tora! Tora! Tora!*, and, subsequently, in the 2001 film *Pearl Harbor*. The producer of *Tora! Tora! Tora!*, Elmo Williams, reportedly found the phrase in Yamamoto's diary, and Williams himself claimed that the film's screenwriter, Harry Forrester, found the quote from Yamamoto in a 1943 letter from Yamamoto to the Japanese Admiralty. But Yamamoto did not keep a diary, and Forrester has been unable to produce the letter. See 'Isoroku Yamamoto/sleepinggiantquote', http://www.knowledgerush.com/kr/encyclopedia/Isoroku_Yamamoto/sleeping_giant_quote/

8. Douglas Vaughn Smith, *Carrier Battles: Command Decision in Harm's Way By* (Annapolis, MD: Naval Institute Press, 2006), 77.

9. See David C. Evans and Mark R. Peattie, *Kaigun: Strategy, Tactics and Technology in the Imperial Japanese Navy, 1887-1941* (Annapolis, MD: Naval Institute Press, 1997).

10. 'The Training of Recruits in the Imperial Japanese Navy', *Shin Seiki*, No. 8, May (1943), 12; and Andrew Fishkin, 'Seventy Years: Japanese Naval Development from the 1870s to the 1940s', MA Thesis, California State University, Long Beach, 2000, 134.

11. See John Dower, *War without Mercy: Race and Power in the Pacific War* (New York: Pantheon Books, 1986).

12. Stephen Howarth, *The Fighting Ships of the Rising Sun: The Drama of the Imperial Japanese Navy, 1895-1945* (New York: Atheneum, 1983), 115; Frances Margaret Cheadle McGuire, *The Royal Australian Navy: Its Origin, Development and Organization* (Melbourne: Oxford University Press, 1948); William P. Mack and Royal W. Connell, *Naval Ceremonies, Customs, and Traditions* (Annapolis, MD: Naval Institute Press, 2004).

13. http://www.hazegray.org/navhist/denver/logaug43.htm

14. Robert G. Albion, 'The Navy's War History', *Military Affairs*, 7 (1943), 245.

15. See, for example, *War Diary, USS Alabama, 1942-1944*, privately published, 1944; *USS Ticonderoga War Log, 8 May 1944 to 5 October 1945* (Baton Rouge: Army and Navy Publishing Company, 1946).

16. *USS Ticonderoga War Log* (no page numbers).

17. Joan Beaumont, 'Australian Memory and the US Wartime Alliance: The Australian-American Memorial and the Battle of the Coral Sea', *War and Society*, 22 (2004), 69–87.

18. Rod Kemp, *Speaking for Australia: Parliamentary Speeches That Shaped the Nation* (Sydney: Allen and Unwin, 2004), 99.

19. Reporters of the Associated Press, *Breaking News: How the Associated Press Has Covered War, Peace, and Everything Else* (New York: Princeton Architectural Press, 2007), 222.

20. For a discussion on Comint and Midway, see Edwin T. Layton, Roger Pineau and John Costello, *And I Was There: Pearl Harbor and Midway—Breaking the Secrets* (Annapolis: Naval Institute Press, 2006).

21. See Dashiell Hammett to Lillian Hellman, 13 September 1944, in *Selected Letters of Dashiell Hammett: 1921-1960*, ed. Richard Layman and Julie M. Rivett (Washington, DC: Counterpoint, 2001), 373.
22. William Claire Menninger, *Psychiatry in a Troubled World: Yesterday's War and Today's Challenge* (New York: Macmillan, 1948), 67.
23. Richard Cartwright Austin, ed., *Letters from the Pacific: A Combat Chaplain in World War II* (Columbia: University of Missouri Press, 2000), 7.
24. Patrick Morley, '*This Is the American Forces Network': The Anglo-American Battle of the Air Waves in World War II* (Westport, CT: Praeger, 2001), 44.
25. Lisle Abbott Rose has suggested that the 'samurai spirit' which infused Japanese submariner culture did not regard civilian merchant shipping as a worthy adversary and so the fleet concentrated its efforts on destroying Allied warships. See Rose, *Power at Sea* (Columbia: University of Missouri Press, 2007), 385.
26. See Steven Trent Smith, *Wolf Pack: The American Submarine Strategy that Helped Defeat Japan* (New York: Wiley, 2003).
27. Brent G. Filbert and Alan G. Kaufman, *Naval Law: Justice and Procedure in the Sea Services* (Annapolis, MD: Naval Institute Press, 1998), 6–7.
28. See Doug Stanton, *In Harm's Way: The Sinking of the USS Indianapolis and the Extraordinary Story of its Survivors* (New York: H. Holt Publishers, 2001).

Chapter Five: Turning the Tide on Land, 1942–1943

1. An engaging study of the Kokoda battles is Peter Fitzsimons, *Kokoda* (Sydney: Hodder, 2005).
2. For an examination of the Battle of Milne Bay and the wider Papuan Campaign, see Peter Brune, *A Bastard of a Place: The Australians in Papua* (Sydney: Allen and Unwin, 2005).
3. William Slim, *Defeat into Victory* (London: Cassell, 1956), 188.
4. For an examination of the battle, see Henry I. Shaw, *First Offensive: The Marine Campaign for Guadalcanal* (Darby, PA: DIANE Publishing, 1992).
5. See Samuel Eliot Morison, *History of United States Naval Operations in World War II*, Vol. 5, *The Struggle for Guadalcanal, August 1942-February 1943* (Champagne-Urbana: University of Illinois Press, 2002).
6. Charles W. Koburger, *Pacific Turning Point: The Solomons Campaign, 1942-1943* (Westport, CT: Praeger, 1995), ii.
7. See Aaron Moore, 'The Peril of Self-Discipline: Chinese Nationalist, Japanese and American Servicemen Record the Rise and Fall of the Japanese Empire, 1937-1945', PhD Thesis, Princeton University, 2006, 13.
8. Moore, 'The Peril of Self-Discipline', 8.
9. Earl Miner, 'The Traditions and Forms of the Japanese Poetic Diary', *Pacific Coast Philology*, 3 (1968), 38.
10. John F. Kries, 'Assessing the Watchers: The Allied View of Japanese Air Intelligence', in *Piercing the Fog: Intelligence and Army Air Forces Operations in World War II*, ed. John F. Kries (Honolulu: University Press of the Pacific, 2004), 291.
11. Moore, 'The Peril of Self-Discipline', iv.
12. Owen Connelly, *On War and Leadership: The Words of Combat Commanders from Frederick the Great to Norman Schwarzkopf* (Princeton: Princeton University Press, 2002), 1–2.
13. For a discussion of this idea and its application see, Thomas P. Rohlen, *Teaching and Learning in Japan* (Cambridge: Cambridge University Press, 1999), 69–70.
14. Connelly, *On War and Leadership*, 1.
15. Peter Brune, *We Band of Brothers: A Biography of Ralph Honner, Soldier and Statesmen* (Sydney: Allen and Unwin, 2000), 136–137.

16. John W. Dower, *War without Mercy: Race and Power in the Pacific War* (New York: Pantheon, 1986), 10.

17. Beatrice Trefalt, 'The Japanese Imperial Army and Fanaticism in the Second World War', in *Fanaticism and Conflict in the Modern Age*, ed. Matthew Hughes and Gaynor Johnson (London: Frank Cass, 2005), 33–47.

18. Jay Winter, *Sites of Memory, Sites of Mourning: The Great War in European Cultural History* (Cambridge: Cambridge University Press, 1995), 2.

19. See Carolyn Forche, *Against Forgetting, Twentieth Century Poetry of Witness* (New York: Norton, 1993).

20. See Dower, *War without Mercy*; Mark Johnstone, *Fighting the Enemy: Australian Soldiers and Their Adversaries in World War II* (Melbourne: Cambridge University Press, 2000); Peter Schrijvers, *The GI War Against Japan: American Soldiers in Asia and the Pacific during World War II* (New York: New York University Press, 2002), esp. 143–156; and Gerald Horne, *Race War!: White Supremacy and the Japanese Attack on the British Empire* (New York: New York University Press, 2005).

Chapter Six: The Allied Counter-Offensive, 1943–1945

1. For an excellent analysis of the campaign in the Southwest Pacific Theatre that provides a nuanced examination of Douglas MacArthur's leadership, see Stephen R. Taafe, *MacArthur's Jungle War: The 1944 New Guinea Campaign* (Lawrence: University of Kansas Press, 1998). See also Charles W. Koburger, *Pacific Turning Point: The Solomons Campaign, 1942-1943* (Westport, CT: Praeger, 1995).

2. See Edwin P. Hoyt, *Japan's War* (New York: McGraw-Hill, 1986) and John Toland, *The Rising Sun: The Decline and Fall of the Japanese Empire, 1936-1945* (New York: Random House, 1970).

3. For a study of the amphibious warfare that characterised war in the Central Pacific, see Donald L. Miller, *D-Days in the Pacific* (New York: Simon and Schuster, 2005).

4. For a discussion of ULTRA's use in the Southwest Pacific Theatre, see Edward J. Drea, *MacArthur's ULTRA: Codebreaking and the War against Japan, 1942-1945* (Lawrence: University of Kansas Press, 1992). See also John Winton, *ULTRA in the Pacific: How Breaking Japanese Codes and Ciphers Affected Naval Operations against Japan* (Annapolis: Naval Institute Press, 1993).

5. For an examination of this battle, see Bill Sloan, *Brotherhood of Heroes: The Marines at Peleliu, 1944 – The Bloodiest Battle of the Pacific War* (New York: Simon and Schuster, 2006).

6. See Albert Axell and Hideaki Kase, *Kamikaze: Japan's Suicide Gods* (Harlow: Longman, 2002).

7. Despite its desire to be part of the proposed invasions of the Philippines and Japan, the Australian Army was left to 'mop-up' in the Solomons and New Guinea and secure strategic locations in the Netherlands East Indies. See Peter Charlton, *Unnecessary War: the Island Campaigns of the Southwest Pacific, 1944-45* (Melbourne: Macmillan, 1983).

8. See Michael Sherry, *The Rise of American Air Power: The Creation of Armageddon* (New Haven: Yale University Press, 1987).

9. See Robert S. Burrell, *The Ghosts of Iwo Jima* (College Station: Texas A&M University Press, 2006).

10. See Robert Leckie, *Okinawa: The Last Battle of World War II* (New York: Viking, 1996).

11. See Peter Dennis and Jeffrey Grey, eds., *The Foundations of Victory: The Pacific War 1943–1944, The 2003 Chief of Army's Military History Conference* (Canberra: Army History Unit, 2004).

12. See James F. Dunnigan, *Victory at Sea: World War II in the Pacific* (New York: Harper, 1996), esp. 320–343; and Anthony W. Gray, 'Joint Logistics in the Pacific Theatre', in

The Big "L": American Logistics in World War II, ed. Alan Gropman (Darby: Diane Publishing, 1997), 293–338.

13. See Edward J. Drea, *In the Service of the Emperor: Essays on the Imperial Japanese Army* (Lincoln: University of Nebraska Press, 1998), esp. 26–42 and 60–74.

14. For a discussion of 'victory disease', see Andrew Fishkin, 'Seventy Years: Japanese Naval Development from the 1870s to the 1940s', MA Thesis, California State University, Long Beach, 2000, 34–39.

15. See Richard J. Samuels, *'Rich Nation, Strong Army': National Security and the Technological Transformation of Japan* (Ithaca: Cornell University Press, 1994).

16. Edward J. Drea, *In the Service of the Emperor: Essays on the Imperial Japanese Army* (Lincoln: University of Nebraska Press, 2003), 60.

17. 'Naval Air Fighters', *Shin Seiki*, No. 8 (May 1943), 10. On the role of Bushido in the creation and maintenance of the Imperial Japanese Army, see Meirion Harries and Susie Harries, *Soldiers of the Sun: The Rise and Fall of the Imperial Japanese Army* (New York: Random House, 1992).

18. See Sherry, *The Rise of American Air Power*. See also Craig M. Cameron, *American Samurai, Myth, Imagination and the Conduct of Battle in the First Marine Division, 1941-1951* (Cambridge: Cambridge University Press, 1994) and Peter Schrijvers, *The GI War Against Japan* (New York: New York University Press, 2002), esp. 244–262. On the notion of the Pacific War as an American laboratory, see Roy McLeod, 'Introduction' to *Science and the Pacific War: Science and Survival in the Pacific, 1939-1945*, ed. Roy McLeod (Dordrecht: Kluwer, 1999), 2.

19. For a discussion of the origins of the Victoria Cross see Robert Macklin, *Bravest* (Sydney: Allen and Unwin, 2008), 7.

20. For a study of psychological warfare, see R. D. McLaurin, *Military Propaganda: Psychological Warfare and Operations* (New York: Praeger, 1982).

21. Hans Speier, 'The Future of Psychological Warfare', *The Public Opinion Quarterly*, 12 (1948), 5–18.

22. Richard Storry has taken this argument further and suggested that rather than being ineffective, Japanese propaganda was so poor it was counterproductive. See Richard Storry and Ian Nish, *Collected Writings of Richard Storry* (London: Routledge, 2002), 96.

23. Allison B. Gilmore, *You Can't Fight Tanks with Bayonets: Psychological Warfare Against the Japanese Army in the Southwest Pacific* (Lincoln: University of Nebraska Press, 1998).

24. See Russell Warden Howe, *The Hunt for Tokyo Rose* (New York: Madison Books, 1993) and Masayo Duus, *Tokyo Rose: Orphan of the Pacific* (Tokyo: Kodansha International, 1983).

25. Chiran Koujo Nadeshiko Kai, ed., *Gunjou: Chiran Tokkou Kichi Yori* (Kagoshima City: Takisyobou, 1979).

26. For discussions of Kamikaze and their writings, see Mako Sasaki, 'Who Became Kamikaze Pilots and How Did They Feel towards Their Suicide Mission?', *The Concord Review*, 7 (1996), 175–209; Emiko Ohnuki-Tierney, *Kamikaze Diaries: Reflections of Japanese Student Soldiers* (Chicago: University of Chicago Press, 2006) and Albert Axell and Hideaki Kase, *Kamikaze: Japan's Suicide Gods* (New York: Longman, 2002).

27. Caroline Brothers, *War and Photography: A Cultural History* (London: Routledge, 1997), 1.

28. Lamont Lindstrom and Geoffrey M. White, *Island Encounters: Black and White Memories of the Pacific War* (Washington, DC: Smithsonian Institute Press, 1990), 2.

29. Miles Orvell, *American Photography* (New York: Oxford University Press, 2003), 205.

30. See Robert E. Allen, *The First Battalion of the 28th Marines on Iwo Jima: A Day-By-Day History from Personal Accounts and Official Reports* (New York: McFarland, 1999), 1.

31. See Derrick White, *Iwo Jima, 1945: Pacific Theatre* (London: Osprey Publishing, 2001), 85; Eric M. Hammel, *Iwo Jima: Portrait of a Battle – United States Marines at War in the Pacific* (St. Paul, MN: Zenith Imprint, 2006), 122.

32. 'Story of a Picture', *Time*, Monday, 26 March 1945.
33. James Bradley, *Flags of Our Fathers* (New York: Bantam books, 2000), 4.
34. What the American Surgeon General called 'combat fatigue' became a major issue for the American military during the Pacific War. See Josephine Bresnahan, 'Dangers in Paradise: Battles against Combat Fatigue in the Pacific War', PhD Thesis, Harvard University, 1999.

Chapter Seven: Occupation Experiences

1. See A. J. Grajdanzev, 'Japan's Co-prosperity Sphere', in *Japan and South East Asia*, ed. Wolf Mendl (London: Routledge, 2001), 231–244.
2. Louis Leo Snyder, *Varieties of Nationalism: A Comparative Study* (Orlando: Dryden Press, 1976), 245.
3. Rana Mitter, 'An Uneasy Engagement: Chinese Ideas of Global Order and Justice in Historical Perspective', in *Order and Justice in International Relations*, ed. John Lewis Gaddis, Andrew Hurrel and Rosemary Foot (New York: Oxford University Press, 2003), 216.
4. For a discussion of this notion, see Mark R. Peattie, 'Japanese Attitudes to Colonialism, 1895-1945', in *The Japanese Colonial Empire, 1895–1945*, ed. Ramon Hawley Myers and Mark R. Peattie (Princeton: Princeton University Press, 1984), 123.
5. Francis Jones, *Japan's New Order in East Asia: Its Rise and Fall, 1937-45* (Oxford: Oxford University Press, 1954), 374.
6. Mitter, 'An Uneasy Engagement', 216. For use of the term after the Pacific War, see Sun Yat-sen, *The Vital Problem of China* (Taipei: China Cultural Service, 1953), 173.
7. Nicholas Tarling, *Nations and States in Southeast Asia* (Cambridge: Cambridge University Press, 1998), 84; Ken'ichi Goto, *Tensions of Empire: Japan and Southeast Asia in the Colonial and Postcolonial World* (Athens, Ohio: Ohio University Centre for International Studies, 2003).
8. See Adrian Vickers, *History of Modern Indonesia* (Cambridge: Cambridge University Press, 2005), 85.
9. See Nicholas Tarling, *A Sudden Rampage: The Japanese Occupation of Southeast Asia, 1941-1945* (Honolulu: University of Hawaii Press, 2001).
10. See Roger Bell, Sean Brawley and Chris Dixon, *Conflict in the Pacific, 1937-1951* (Melbourne: Cambridge University Press, 2005), 117.
11. See Hilary Conroy, 'Thoughts on Collaboration', *Peace and Change*, 1 (1972), 43–46.
12. For a discussion of passivity as a dominate response, see Poshek Fy, *Passivity, Resistance and Collaboration: Intellectual Choices in Occupied Shanghai, 1937-1945* (Stanford: Stanford University Press, 1993).
13. Paul H. Kratoska, *The Japanese Occupation of Malaya: A Socio-Economic History* (Honolulu: University of Hawaii, 1997), 2.
14. Boon Kheng Cheah, *Red Star over Malaya: Resistance and Social Conflict during and after the Japanese Occupation* (Singapore: Singapore University Press, 1987), 1.
15. Yoji Akashi, 'The Anti-Japanese Movement in Perak during the Japanese Occupation, 1941-45', in *Malaya and Singapore during the Japanese Occupation*, ed. Paul H. Kratoska (Singapore: Singapore University Press, 1995), 117.
16. Robin Ramcharan, *Forging a Singaporean Statehood 1965-1995: The Contribution of Japan* (New York: Kluwer Law International, 2002), 77–78. See also Yoji Akashi, 'The Japanese Occupation of Malaya: Interruption or Transformation?', in *Southeast Asia under Japanese Occupation*, ed. Alfred W. McCoy (New Haven: Yale University Southeast Asia Studies, 1980), 5–6.
17. Tarling, *Nations and States*, 84.
18. S. Javed Maswood, 'Japanese Foreign Policy and Regionalism', in *Japan and East Asian Regionalism*, ed. S. Javed Maswood (London: Routledge, 2001), 7. The quote is from

Wang Gungwu, 'Memories of War: World War II in Asia', in *War and Memory in Malaysia and Singapore*, ed. Patricia Pui Huen Lim and Diana Wong (Singapore: Institute of Southeast Asian Studies, University of Singapore, 2000), 17.

19. Historians of European colonialism have found 'mining court cases for historical data' most useful. See Richard Roberts, 'Text and Testimony in the Tribunal de Premiere Instance, Dakar, during the Early Twentieth Century', *The Journal of African History*, 31 (1990), 447–463.

20. See T. G. Ashplant, Graham Dawson and Michael Roper, 'The Politics of War Memory and Commemoration: Contexts, Structures and Dynamics', in *Politics of War Memory and Commemoration*, ed. T. G. Ashplant et al. (London: Routledge, 2001) and James M. Mayo, 'War Memorials as Political Memory', *Geographical Review*, 78 (1988), 62–75.

21. Wang Gungwu, 'Memories of War', 12–13.

22. Cheah Boon Kheng, 'Memory as History and Moral Judgement: Oral and Written Accounts of the Japanese Occupation of Malaya', in Lim and Wong, *War and Memory in Malaysia and Singapore*, 23–44.

23. Kratoska, *The Japanese Occupation of Malaya*, 1.

24. James Horne Morrison, Patricia Pui Huen Lim and Chong Guan Kwa, *Oral History in Southeast Asia: Theory and Method* (Singapore: Institute of Southeast Asian Studies, 1998), 1.

25. For a discussion of sources, see Antonio S. Tan, *The Chinese in the Philippines during the Japanese Occupation 1942-1945* (Manila: University of the Philippines Asian Center, 1981), 16.

26. For a discussion of this notion and the role of public speaking in modern British history, see Robert T. Oliver, *Public Speaking in the Reshaping of Britain* (Newark: University of Delaware Press, 1987).

27. Lin Poyer, Laurence Marshall Carucci and Susanne Falgout, *The Typhoon of War: Micronesian Experiences of the Pacific War* (Honolulu: University of Hawaii Press, 2001), 3.

28. Geoffrey M. White and Lamont Lindstrom, *The Pacific Theater: Island Representations of World War II* (Honolulu: University of Hawaii Press, 1989), 3.

29. Poyer, Carucci and Falgout, *Typhoon of War*, 13. See also Donald T. Fitzgerald, 'The Machine in the Pacific: The Diverse Legacy of Technology', in *Science and the Pacific War: Science and Survival in the Pacific, 1939-1945*, ed. Roy McLeod (Dordrecht: Kluwer, 1999), 71–82

30. Geoffrey M. White, *The Big Death: Solomon Islanders Remember World War II* (Suva: University of the South Pacific, Institute of Pacific Studies, 1988), 127. See also Bruce M. Petty, *Saipan: Oral Histories of the Pacific War* (New York: McFarland, 2001).

Chapter Eight: Home-Front Experiences

1. On the American home front, see John Morton Blum, *V was for Victory: Politics and American Culture during World War II* (New York: Harcourt Brace Jovanovich, 1976); Richard Polenberg, *War and Society: The United States, 1941-1945* (Philadelphia: Lippincott, 1972); Allan M. Winkler, *Home Front U.S.A.: America during World War II*, 2nd ed. (Wheeling, IL: Harlan Davidson, 2000). A useful survey of American democracy during World War II is Roger Daniels, 'Bad News from the Good War: Democracy at Home During World War II', in *The Home Front War: World War II and American Society*, ed. Kenneth Paul O'Brien and Lynn Hudson Parsons (Westport, CT: Greenwood Press, 1995), 157–172. For the impact on popular culture, see John Bush Jones, *The Songs that Fought the War: Popular Music and the Home Front*,

1939–1945 (Waltham, MA: Brandeis University Press, 2006). On the Japanese home front, see Saburō Ienaga, *The Pacific War, 1931–1945: A Critical Perspective on Japan's Role in World War II* (NewYork: Pantheon Books, 1978), 97–128, 192–202; Ben-Ami Shillony, *Politics and Culture in Wartime Japan* (Oxford: Oxford University Press, 1981). On the Australian home front, see Joan Beaumont, ed., *Australia's War, 1939-1945* (Sydney: Allen and Unwin, 1996) and Michael McKernan, *All In!: Fighting the War at Home* (Sydney: Allen and Unwin, 1995).

2. See Michael Weiner, 'The Mobilisation of Koreans during the Second World War', in *Shōwa Japan: Political, Economic and Social History 1926-1989*, ed. Stephen S. Large (London: Routledge, 1998), 250.

3. See Bowen C. Dees, *The Allied Occupation and Japan's Economic Miracle: Building the Foundations of Japanese Science and Technology 1945–52* (London: RoutledgeCurzon, 1997).

4. On Japanese internment, see Roger Daniels, *Concentration Camp, U.S.A.: Japanese Americans in World War II* (NewYork: Holt, Rinehart and Winston, 1971); Peter Irons, *Justice at War: The Story of the Japanese American Internment Cases* (NewYork: Oxford University Press, 1983).

5. Tetsuden Kashima, *Judgment without Trial: Japanese American Imprisonment During World War II* (Seattle: University of Washington Press, 2003), 97, 119.

6. Lawson Fusao Inada, ed., *Only What We Could Carry: The Japanese American Internment Experience* (Berkeley, CA: Heyday Books, 2000), 220.

7. On the 1943 Detroit riot, see Harvard Sitkoff, 'The Detroit Race Riot of 1943', *Michigan History*, 53 (1969), 183–206; Alan Clive, *State of War: Michigan in World War II* (Ann Arbor: University of Michigan Press, 1979), 130–170.

8. On the 1943 Harlem riot, refer to Dominic J. Capeci, Jr., *The Harlem Riot of 1943* (Philadelphia: Temple University Press, 1977).

9. Patsy Adam-Smith, *Australian Women at War* (Melbourne: Nelson, 1984).

10. On American women during World War II, see D'Anne Campbell, *Women at War with America: Private Lives in a Patriotic Era* (Cambridge, MA: Harvard University Press, 1984); Karen Anderson, *Wartime Women* (Westport, CT: Greenwood Press, 1981); Penny Colman, *Rosie the Riveter: Women Working on the Homefront in World War II* (New York: Crown Publishers, 1995); Maureen Honey, ed., *Bitter Fruit: African American Women in World War II* (Columbia: University of Missouri Press, 1999).

11. Anthony J. Barker and Lisa Jackson, *Fleeting Attraction: A Social History of American Servicemen in Western Australia during the Second World War* (Nedlands, WA: University of Western Australia Press, 1996).

12. For a discussion of the American presence in New Zealand, see Deborah Montgomerie, 'GI Joe Down Under: American Infantrymen in New Zealand during World War II', *New Zealand Journal of History*, 34 (2000), 262.

13. See Barrett McGurn, *Yank, The Army Weekly: Reporting the Greatest Generation* (Golden, CO: Fulcrum Pub., 2004), 11, 66.

14. John H. Moore, *Over-sexed, Over-paid and Over Here: Americans in Australia 1941-1945* (St. Lucia, Qld: University of Queensland Press, 1981).

15. Some relationships between American servicemen and Australian and New Zealand women ended in marriage. See, for example, Rosemary Campbell, *Heroes and Lovers: A Question of National Identity* (Sydney: Allen and Unwin, 1989).

16. See David Jenkins, *Battle Surface: Japan's Submarine War against Australia, 1942-44* (Milsons Point, New South Wales: Random House Australia, 1992).

17. Central Tokyo.

18. Margaretta Jolly, '"Dear Laughing Motorbyke": Gender and Genre in Women's Letters from the Second World War', in *The Uses of Autobiography*, ed. Julia Swindells (Oxford: Taylor and Francis, 2005), 45.

Chapter Nine: Prisoner-of-War Experiences

1. Michael McKernan, *This War Never Ends: The Pain of Separation and Return* (St. Lucia: University of Queensland Press, 2001), 7.
2. Van Waterford, *Prisoners of the Japanese in World War II* (Jefferson, NC: McFarland, 1994), 72.
3. Allied Translator and Interpreter Service (ATIS) Research Report No. 76.4 (7 February 1945), 16–17; Ruth Benedict, *The Chrysanthemum and the Sword: Patterns of Japanese Culture* (Boston: Houghton Mifflin, 1946), 38.
4. Ulrich Strauss, *The Anguish of Surrender: Japanese POWs of World War II* (Seattle: University of Washington Press, 2003), 48–49; Yamamoto Taketoshi, *Nihonhei horyo wa nani wo shabetta ka* (Tokyo: Bungeishunju, 2001), 18–19.
5. See Mark Weate, *Bill Newton VC: The Short Life of a RAAF Hero* (Loftus: Australian Military History Publications, 1999).

Chapter Ten: Hiroshima and the Defeat of Japan

1. See Osamu Tagaya, 'The Imperial Japanese Air Forces', in *Why Air Forces Fail: The Anatomy of Defeat*, ed. Robin Higham and Stephen Harris (Lexington: University of Kentucky Press, 2006), 177–202.
2. John Canaday, *The Nuclear Muse: Literature, Physics and the First Atomic Bombs* (Madison: University of Wisconsin Press, 2000), 223, quoted in J. Hughes, 'Deconstructing the Bomb: Recent Perspectives on Nuclear History', *The British Journal of the History of Science*, 37 (2004), 458.
3. Michael Kort, *The Columbia Guide to Hiroshima and the Bomb* (New York: Columbia University Press, 2007), Part II, 79–116.
4. John Whittier Treat, *Writing Ground Zero: Japanese Literature and the Atomic Bomb* (Chicago: The University of Chicago Press, 1995), xii.
5. See Uday Mohan, 'History and the News Media: The Smithsonian Controversy', in *Cultural Differences, Media, Memories: Anglo-American Images of Japan*, ed. Phil Hammond (London: Cassell, 1997), 175–200.
6. J. Samuel Walker, *Prompt and Utter Destruction: Truman and the Use of Atomic Bombs against Japan* (Chapel Hill: University of North Carolina Press, 2005).
7. D. M. Giangreco, 'Casualty Projections for the U.S. Invasions of Japan, 1945-1946: Planning and Policy Implications', *Journal of Military History*, 61 (1997), 569.
8. Brett A. Miller, Shannon E. Martin and David A. Copeland, *The Function of Newspapers in Society: A Global Perspective* (Westport, CT: Greenwood Press, 2003), 56.
9. Note from translator: It seems that Oh's notion that drinking water would bring death was based on medical understanding at the time (completely at odds with what is commonly understood today) that burns victims should not be given water.

Chapter Eleven: Surrender

1. Barton Bernstein, 'Introducing the Interpretive Problems of Japan's 1945 Surrender: A Historiographical Essay on Recent Literature in the West', in *the End of the Pacific War: Reappraisals*, ed. Tsuyoshi Hasegawa (Stanford: Stanford University Press, 2007).
2. Stephen Garton, 'War and Masculinity in Twentieth-century Australia', *Journal of Australian Studies*, 56 (1998), 92.
3. See Frank G. Clarke, *Australia in a Nutshell: A Narrative History* (Sydney: Angus and Robertson, 2003), 197–233.
4. See Sean Brawley, *The Bondi Lifesaver: A History of an Australian Icon* (Sydney: ABC Books, 2007).

5. Sgt. Archer's unit had been defending the Australian coastline against possible attack. By the beginning of 1945, the need to do this had passed.
6. See Beatrice Trefalt, *Japanese Army Stragglers and Memories of the War in Japan, 1950-1975* (London: RoutledgeCurzon, 2003).

Chapter Twelve: Legacies

1. See William F. Nimmo, *Behind a Curtain of Silence: Japanese in Soviet Custody, 1945-1956* (Westport, CT: Greenwood Press, 1988).
2. See M. Paul Holsinger, 'The "Western" Fiction of World War II', in *World War II in Asia and the Pacific and the War's Aftermath, with General Themes: A Handbook of Literature and Research*, ed. Lloyd E. Lee (Westport, CT: Greenwood Press, 1998), 272.
3. See Sean Brawley, 'Saving the South Seas: Thomas Heggen and *Mister Roberts*', *Inter-Cultural Studies*, 3 (2003), 19.
4. Megumi Kato, 'Representations of Japan and Japanese People in Australian Literature', PhD Thesis, University of New South Wales, 2005, 214.
5. Hungerford himself became an historical figure in the Occupation. For a discussion of his role see James Wood, *The Forgotten Force: The Australian Military Contribution to the Occupation of Japan, 1945-1952* (St. Leonards, NSW: Allen and Unwin, 1998). For a discussion of Occupation novels, see Kato, 'Representations of Japan and Japanese People in Australian Literature', 162–178.
6. T. A.G. Hungerford, *Sowers of the Wind: A Novel of the Occupation of Japan* (Sydney: Angus and Robertson, 1954).
7. See Rivett, *Behind Bamboo: An Inside Story* (London: Angus and Robertson, 1946); Braddon, *The Naked Island* (London: W. Laurie, 1952).
8. Ulrich Straus, *The Anguish of Surrender: Japanese POWs of World War II* (Seattle: University of Washington Press, 2005), 247.
9. Hank Nelson, *P.O. W.: Prisoners of War: Australians under Nippon* (Sydney: ABC Enterprises, 1985), 213–214.
10. 'What is the Women's Tribunal?', http://www1.jca.apc.org/vaww-net-japan/english/womenstribunal2000/whatstribunal.html (Accessed 30 June 2008).

BIBLIOGRAPHY

Adam-Smith, Patsy. 1984. *Australian Women at War*. Melbourne: Nelson.

Albion, Robert G. 1943. 'The Navy's War History', *Military Affairs*, 7, 245–247.

Allen, Robert E. 1999. *The First Battalion of the 28th Marines on Iwo Jima: A Day-by-Day History from Personal Account*. New York: McFarland.

Allied Translator and Interpreter Section South West Pacific Area, M report, 30 April 1943. Australian War Memorial, AWM 55 [9/1].

Anand Abbinav, R. P. 1981. *Cultural Factors in International Relations*. New Delhi: Abhinav Publications.

Anderson, Karen. 1981. *Wartime Women*. Westport, CT: Greenwood Press.

Anon. 1943. 'The Training of Recruits in the Imperial Japanese Navy', *Shin Seiki*, 8 May.

Anonymous. 2002. 'World War II, 1941-1945', *Military History: Special Edition: Eyewitness to War*, 42.

Asada, Sadao. 2006. *From Mahan to Pearl Harbor: The Imperial Japanese Navy and the United States*. Annapolis: Naval Institute Press.

Ashplant, T. G. et al. (eds.). 2001. *Politics of War Memory and Commemoration*. London: Routledge.

Austin, Richard Cartwright (ed.). 2000. *Letters from the Pacific: A Combat Chaplain in World War II*. Columbia: University of Missouri Press.

Awaya Kentarō, 1980. *Shiryō: Nihon gendai shi. Haisen chokugo no seiji to shakai*. Tokyo: Otsuki Shoten.

Axell, Albert and Hideaki Kase. 2002. *Kamikaze: Japan's Suicide Gods*. Harlow: Longman.

Barker, Anthony J. and Lisa Jackson. 1996. *Fleeting Attraction: A Social History of American Servicemen in Western Australia during the Second World War*. Nedlands, WA: University of Western Australia Press.

Barton, David, Mary Hamilton and Roz Ivanič (eds.). 2000. *Situated Literacies: Reading and Writing in Context*. New York: Routledge.

Beaumont, Joan (ed.). 1996. *Australia's War, 1939-1945*. Sydney: Allen and Unwin.

Beaumont, Joan. 2004. 'Australian Memory and the US Wartime Alliance: The Australian-American Memorial and the Battle of the Coral Sea', *War and Society*, 22, 69–87.

Bell, Roger, Sean Brawley and Chris Dixon. 2005. *Conflict in the Pacific, 1937-1951*. Melbourne: Cambridge University Press.

Benedict, Ruth. 1946. *The Chrysanthemum and the Sword: Patterns of Japanese Culture*. Boston: Houghton Mifflin.

Bennett, Henry Gordon. 1945. *Why Singapore Fell*. Bombay: Thacker.

Berger Gluck, Sherna and Daphne Patai (eds.). 1991. *Women's Words: The Feminist Practice of Oral History*. New York: Routledge.

Bergerud, Eric M. 2000. *Fire in the Sky: The Air War in the South Pacific*. Boulder, Colorado: Westview Press.

Blandy, Douglas Emerson, Doug Blandy and Kristin G. Congdon. 1991. *Pluralistic Approaches to Art Criticism*. Bowling Green, OH: Bowling Green State University Popular Press.

Blum, John Morton. 1976. *V Was for Victory: Politics and American Culture during World War II*. New York: Harcourt Brace Jovanovich.

Bond, Brian and Kyoichi Tachikawa (eds.). 2001. *British and Japanese Military Leadership in the Far Eastern War, 1941-1945*. London: Frank Cass.

Borowski, Harry R. (ed.). 1988. *The Harmon Memorial Lectures in Military History, 1959-1987*. Washington, DC: Office of the Air Force.

Braddon, Russell. 1952. *The Naked Island*. London: W. Laurie.

Brawley, Sean and Chris Dixon. 1994. 'The Hollywood Native: Hollywood's Construction of the South Seas & Wartime Encounters with the South Pacific', *Sites: A Journal for South Pacific Cultural Studies*, 27, 15–29.

———. 1999. 'War and Sex in the South Pacific, 1941-1945', *Australasian Journal of American Studies*, 18, 3–18.

Brawley, Sean. 1995. *The White Peril: Foreign Relations and Asian Immigration to Australasia and North America, 1919-1979*. Sydney: University of New South Wales Press.

———. 2003. 'Saving the South Seas: Thomas Heggen and *Mister Roberts*', *Inter-Cultural Studies*, 3, 17–24.

———. 2007. *The Bondi Lifesaver: A History of an Australian Icon*. Sydney: ABC Books.

Bresnahan, Josephine. 1999. 'Dangers in Paradise: Battles against Combat Fatigue in the Pacific War', PhD Thesis, Harvard University.

Brothers, Caroline. 1997. *War and Photography: A Cultural History*. London: Routledge.

Brune, Peter. 2000. *We Band of Brothers: A Biography of Ralph Honner, Soldier and Statesmen*. Sydney: Allen and Unwin.

———. 2005. *A Bastard of a Place: The Australians in Papua*. Sydney: Allen and Unwin.

Burrell, Robert S. 2006. *The Ghosts of Iwo Jima*. College Station: Texas A&M University Press.

Callahan, Raymond A. 1977. *The Worst Disaster: The Fall of Singapore*. Newark, NJ: University of Delaware Press.

Cameron, Craig M. 1994. *American Samurai, Myth, Imagination and the Conduct of Battle in the First Marine Division, 1941-1951*. Cambridge: Cambridge University Press.

Campbell, D'Anne. 1984. *Women at War with America: Private Lives in a Patriotic Era*. Cambridge, MA: Harvard University Press.

Campbell, Rosemary. 1989. *Heroes and Lovers: A Question of National Identity*. Sydney: Allen and Unwin.

Canaday, John. 2000. *The Nuclear Muse: Literature, Physics and the First Atomic Bombs* Madison: University of Wisconsin Press.

Capeci, Dominic J., Jr. 1977. *The Harlem Riot of 1943*. Philadelphia: Temple University Press.

Carter, Carolyne. 2002. 'Between War and Peace: The Experience of Occupation for Members of the British Commonwealth Occupation Force, 1945-1952', PhD Thesis, University of NSW.

Charlton, Peter. 1983. *Unnecessary War: The Island Campaigns of the Southwest Pacific, 1944-45*. Melbourne: Macmillan.

Cheah, Boon Kheng. 1987. *Red Star over Malaya: Resistance and Social Conflict during and after the Japanese Occupation*. Singapore: Singapore University Press.

Chiran Kōjo Nadeshiko Kai (eds.). 1979. *Gunjō: Chiran Tokkō Kichi Yori*. Kagoshima City: Takishobō.

Clarke, Frank G. 2003. *Australia in a Nutshell: A Narrative History*. Sydney: Angus and Robertson.

Clarke, Hugh. 1984. *Last Stop Nagasaki*. London: Allen and Unwin.

Clive, Alan. 1979. *State of War: Michigan in World War II*. Ann Arbor: University of Michigan Press.

Colman, Penny. 1995. *Rosie the Riveter: Women Working on the Homefront in World War II*. New York: Crown Publishers.

Connelly, Owen. 2002. *On War and Leadership: The Words of Combat Commanders from Frederick the Great to Norman Schwarzkopf*. Princeton: Princeton University Press.

Conroy, Hilary. 1972. 'Thoughts on Collaboration', *Peace and Change*, 1, 43–46.

Conroy, Hilary and Harry Wray (eds.). 1990. *Pearl Harbor Reexamined: Prologue to the Pacific War*. Honolulu: University of Hawaii Press.

Costello, John. 1984. *The Pacific War*. London: Pan Books.

Crasta, John Baptist. 1999. *Eaten by the Japanese*. Bangalore: Invisible Man Publishers.

Dallek, Robert. 1979. *Franklin D. Roosevelt and American Foreign Policy, 1932-1945*. New York: Oxford University Press.

Daniels, Roger. 1971. *Concentration Camp, U.S.A.: Japanese Americans in World War II*. New York: Holt, Rinehart and Winston.

Dawson, Christopher. 1995. *To Sandakan: The Diaries of Charlie Johnstone, Prisoner of War 1942-1945*. Sydney: Allen and Unwin.

de Matos, Christine. 2003. 'Imposing Peace and Prosperity: Australia, Social Justice and Labour Reform in Occupied Japan, 1945-1949', PhD Thesis, University of Western Sydney.

Dees, Bowen C. 1997. *The Allied Occupation and Japan's Economic Miracle: Building the Foundations of Japanese Science and Technology 1945-52*. London: Routledge Curzon.

Dehler, Kathleen. 1989. 'Diaries: Where Women Reveal Themselves', *The English Journal*, 78, 53–54.

Dekker, Rudolph. 2002. 'Jacques Presser's Heritage: Egodocuments in the Study of History', *Memoria y Civilizacion: Anuario de Historia de la Universidad de Navarra*, 5, 13–37.

——— (ed.). 2002. *Ego-Documents and History: Autobiographical Writing in Its Social Context since the Middle Age*. Hilversum: Verloren Publishers.

DeMello, Margo. 2000. *Bodies of Inscription: A Cultural History of the Modern Tattoo Community*. Durham, NC: Duke University Press.

Dennis, Peter and Jeffrey Grey (eds.). 2004. *The Foundations of Victory: The Pacific War 1943-1944, The 2003 Chief of Army's Military History Conference*. Canberra: Army History Unit.

Dijck, José van. 2007. *Mediated Memories in the Digital Age*. Stanford, CA: Stanford University Press.

Dower, John W. 1986. *War without Mercy: Race and Power in the Pacific War*. New York: Pantheon Books.

Drea, Edward J. 1998. *In the Service of the Emperor: Essays on the Imperial Japanese Army*. Lincoln: University of Nebraska Press.

Drea, Edward J. 1992. *MacArthur's ULTRA: Codebreaking and the War against Japan, 1942-1945*. Lawrence: University of Kansas Press.

Dull, Paul S. 1978. *A Battle History of the Imperial Japanese Navy, 1941-1945*. Annapolis: Naval Institute Press.

Dunnigan, James F. 1996. *Victory at Sea: World War II in the Pacific*. New York: Harper.

Duus, Masayo. 1983. *Tokyo Rose, Orphan of the Pacific*. Tokyo: Kodansha International.

Dyer, Brenda and Lee Friedrich. 2002. 'The Personal Narrative as Cultural Artefact: Teaching Autobiography in Japan', *Written Communication*, 19, 265–296.

Evans, David C. and Mark R. Peattie. 1997. *Kaigun: Strategy, Tactics and Technology in the Imperial Japanese Navy, 1887-1941*. Annapolis, MD: Naval Institute Press.

Evers, Leonard H. 1954. *Patterns of Conquest*. Sydney: Currawong.

Farrell, Brian P. (ed.). 2004. *Leadership and Responsibility in the Second World War: Essays in Honor of Robert Vogel*. Montreal: McGill-Queens Press.

Filbert, Brent G. and Alan G. Kaufman. 1998. *Naval Law: Justice and Procedure in the Sea Services*. Annapolis, MD: Naval Institute Press.

Fischer, Steven Roger. 2003. *A History of Reading*. London: Reaktion.

Fishkin, Andrew. 2000. 'Seventy Years: Japanese Naval Development from the 1870s to the 1940s', MA Thesis, California State University, Long Beach.

Fitzsimons, Peter. 2005. *Kokoda*. Sydney: Hodder.

Forche, Carolyn. 1993. *Against Forgetting, Twentieth Century Poetry of Witness*. New York: Norton.

Forrest, Alan. 2002. *Napoleon's Men: The Soldiers of the Revolution and Empire*. New York: Hambledon and London.

Frei, Henry. 2004. *Guns of February: Ordinary Japanese Soldiers' View of the Malayan Campaign and the Fall of Singapore, 1941-42*. Singapore: Singapore University Press.

Frisch, Michael. 1990. *A Shared Authority: Essays on the Craft and Meaning of Oral and Public History*. Albany: State University of New York Press.

Fy, Poshek. 1993. *Passivity, Resistance and Collaboration: Intellectual Choices in Occupied Shanghai, 1937-1945*, Stanford: Stanford University Press

Gaddis, John Lewis. 2003. *Order and Justice in International Relations*. Edited by Andrew Hurrel and Rosemary Foot, New York: Oxford University Press.

Garton, Stephen. 1998. 'War and Masculinity in Twentieth-Century Australia', *Journal of Australian Studies*, 56, 86–95.

Giangreco, D. M. 1997. 'Casualty Projections for the U.S. Invasions of Japan, 1945-1946: Planning and Policy Implications', *Journal of Military History*, 61, 521–582.

Gilmore, Allison B. 1998. *You Can't Fight Tanks with Bayonets: Psychological Warfare against the Japanese Army in the Southwest Pacific*. Lincoln: University of Nebraska Press.

Goto, Ken'ichi. 2003. *Tensions of Empire: Japan and Southeast Asia in the Colonial and Postcolonial World*. Athens, Ohio: Ohio University Centre for International Studies.

Gropman, Alan (ed.). 1997. *The Big "L": American Logistics in World War II*. Darby: Diane Publishing.

Hagemann, Karen and Stefanie Schüler-Springorum. 2002. *Home/front: The Military, War and Gender in Twentieth-Century Germany*. New York: Berg.

Halberstam, David. 2000. *The Powers That Be*. Champagne-Urbana: University of Illinois Press.

Hall, Leslie. 1996. *The Blue Haze: POWs on the Burma Railway*. Kenthurst, NSW: Kangaroo Press.

Hammel, Eric M. 2006. *Iwo Jima: Portrait of a Battle - United States Marines at War in the Pacific*. St. Paul, MN: Zenith Imprint.

Hammond, Phil. 1997. *Cultural Differences, Media, Memories: Anglo-American Images of Japan*. London: Cassell.

Hanley, David Lawrence. 2000. 'Kokubokan: Japanese Aircraft Carrier Development, 1922-1945', MA Thesis, San Jose State University.

Harries, Meirion and Susie Harries. 1992. *Soldiers of the Sun: The Rise and Fall of the Imperial Japanese Army*. New York: Random House.

Hasegawa, Tsuyoshi. 2007. *The End of the Pacific War: Reappraisals*. Stanford: Stanford University Press.

Haskel, Dennis, Megan McKinlay and Pamina Rich. 2006. *Beyond Good and Evil? Essays on the Literature and Culture of the Asia-Pacific Region*. Nedlands: University of Western Australia Press.

Higham, Robin and Stephen Harris (eds.). 2006. *Why Air Forces Fail: The Anatomy of Defeat*, Lexington: University of Kentucky Press.

Hobsbawm, Eric. 1997. *On History*. London: Weidenfeld and Nicolson.

Honey, Maureen (ed.). 1999. *Bitter Fruit: African American Women in World War II*. Columbia: University of Missouri Press.

Horne, Gerald. 2005. *Race War! White Supremacy and the Japanese Attack on the British Empire*. New York: New York University Press.

Howarth, Stephen. 1983. *The Fighting Ships of the Rising Sun: The Drama of the Imperial Japanese Navy, 1895-1945*. New York: Atheneum.

Howe, Russel Warden. 1993. *The Hunt for Tokyo Rose*. New York: Madison Books, New York.

Howell, Martha and Walter Prevenier. 2001. *From Reliable Sources: An Introduction to Historical Methods*. Ithaca, NY: Cornell University Press.

Hoyt, Edwin P. 1986. *Japan's War*. New York: McGraw-Hill.

Hughes, J. 2004. 'Deconstructing the Bomb: Recent Perspectives on Nuclear History', *The British Journal of the History of Science*, 37, 455–464.

Hungerford, T. A. G. 1954. *Sowers of the Wind: A Novel of the Occupation of Japan*. Sydney: Angus and Robertson.

Ienaga, Saburō. 1978. *The Pacific War, 1931-1945: A Critical Perspective on Japan's Role in World War II*. New York: Pantheon Books.

Ike, Nobutaka. 1951. 'Japanese Memoirs-Reflections of the Recent Past', *Pacific Affairs*, 24, 185–190.

Inada, Lawson Fusao (ed.). 2000. *Only What We Could Carry: The Japanese American Internment Experience*. Berkeley, CA: Heyday Books.

Iriye, Akira (ed.). 1999. *Pearl Harbor and the Coming of the Pacific War: A Brief History with Documents and Essays*. Boston: Bedford/St. Martin's.

Iriye, Akira. 1987. *The Origins of the Second World War in Asia and the Pacific*. New York: Longman.

Irons, Peter. 1983. *Justice at War: The Story of the Japanese American Internment Cases*. New York: Oxford University Press.

'Isoroku Yamamoto/sleepinggiantquote', http://www.knowledgerush.com/kr/encyclopedia/ Isoroku_Yamamoto/sleeping_giant_quote/

Jacobsen, Gene S. 2004. *We Refused to Die: My Time as a Prisoner of War in Bataan and Japan, 1942-1945*. Salt Lake City: University of Utah Press.

Jenkins, David. 1992. *Battle Surface: Japan's Submarine War against Australia, 1942-44*. Milsons Point, New South Wales: Random House Australia.

Johnstone, Mark. 2000. *Fighting the Enemy: Australian Soldiers and Their Adversaries in World War II*. Melbourne: Cambridge University Press.

Jones, Francis. 1954. *Japan's New Order in East Asia: Its Rise and Fall, 1937-45*. Oxford: Oxford University Press.

Jones, John Bush. 2006. *The Songs That Fought the War: Popular Music and the Home Front, 1939-1945*. Waltham, MA: Brandeis University Press.

Kashima, Tetsuden. 2003. *Judgment without Trial: Japanese American Imprisonment during World War II*. Seattle: University of Washington Press.

Kato, Megumi. 2005. 'Representations of Japan and Japanese People in Australian Literature', PhD Thesis, University of New South Wales.

Kawazoe Soichi. *My Life* (Waga jinsei), unpublished manuscript, 2002.

Kelen, Stephen. 1965. *Goshu*. Sydney: Horwitz.

Kemp, Rod. 2004. *Speaking for Australia: Parliamentary Speeches That Shaped the Nation*. Sydney: Allen and Unwin.

Kennedy, John R. 1990. *Command in Joint and Combined Operations: The Campaign for the Netherlands East Indies*. Fort Leavenworth: Army Command and General Staff School of Advanced Military Studies.

Koburger, Charles W. 1995. *Pacific Turning Point: The Solomons Campaign, 1942-1943*. Westport, CT: Praeger.

Kort, Michael. 2007. *The Columbia Guide to Hiroshima and the Bomb*. New York: Columbia University Press.

Kratoska, Paul H. 1997. *The Japanese Occupation of Malaya: A Socio-Economic History*. Honolulu: University of Hawaii.

———. (ed.). 1995. *Malaya and Singapore during the Japanese Occupation*. Singapore: Singapore University Press.

Kries, John F. (ed.). 2004. *Piercing the Fog: Intelligence and Army Air Forces Operations in World War II*. Honolulu: University Press of the Pacific.

Large, Stephen S. (ed.). 1998. *Showa Japan: Political, Economic and Social History, 1926-1989*. New York: Routledge.

Layman, Richard and Julie M. Rivett (eds.). 2001. *Selected Letters of Dashiell Hammett: 1921-1960*. Washington, DC: Counterpoint.

Layton, Edwin T., Roger Pineau and John Costello. 2006. *And I Was There: Pearl Harbor and Midway – Breaking the Secrets*. Annapolis: Naval Institute Press.

Leckie, Robert. 1996. *Okinawa: The Last Battle of World War II*. New York: Viking.

Letter from Jemedar Chint Singh (Indian Officer) Ex-POW of Japanese at Wewak, Australian War Memorial, Series number AWM54 779/1/20.

Lim, Patricia Pui Huen and Diana Wong (eds.). 2000. *War and Memory in Malaysia and Singapore*. Singapore: Institute of Southeast Asian Studies, University of Singapore.

Lindstrom, Lamont and Geoffrey M. White. 1990. *Island Encounters: Black and White Memories of the Pacific War*. Washington, DC: Smithsonian Institute Press.

Lloyd E. (ed.). 1998. *World War II in Asia and the Pacific and the War's Aftermath, with General Themes*. Westport, CT: Greenwood Press.

Lummis, Trevor. 1988. *Listening to History: The Authenticity of Oral Evidence*. Totowa, NJ: Barnes & Noble Books.

Mack, William P. and Royal W. Connell. 2004. *Naval Ceremonies, Customs, and Traditions*. Annapolis, MD: Naval Institute Press.

Macklin, Robert. 2008. *Bravest*. Sydney: Allen and Unwin.

Maswood, S. Javed (ed.). 2001. *Japan and East Asian Regionalism*. London: Routledge.

Mayo, James M. 1988. 'War Memorials as Political Memory', *Geographical Review*, 78, 62–75.

McCoy, Alfred W. (ed.). 1980. *Southeast Asia under Japanese Occupation*. New Haven: Yale University Southeast Asia Studies.

McGuire, Frances Margaret Cheadle. 1948. *The Royal Australian Navy: Its Origin, Development and Organization*. Melbourne: Oxford University Press.

McGurn, Barrett. 2004. *Yank: The Army Weekly: Reporting the Greatest Generation*. Golden, CO: Fulcrum.

McKernan, Michael. 1995. *All In! Fighting the War at Home*. Sydney: Allen and Unwin.

———. 2001. *This War Never Ends: The Pain of Separation and Return*. St. Lucia: University of Queensland Press.

McLaurin, R.D. 1982. *Military Propaganda: Psychological Warfare and Operations*. New York: Praeger.

McLeod, Roy (ed.). 1999. *Science and the Pacific War: Science and Survival in the Pacific, 1939-1945*. Dordrecht: Kluwer.

Mendl, Wolf (ed.). 2001. *Japan and South East Asia*. London: Routledge.

Menninger, William Claire. 1948. *Psychiatry in a Troubled World: Yesterday's War and Today's Challenge*. New York: MacMillan.

Michener, James. 1954. *Sayonara*. New York: Fawcett Crest Books.

Miller, Brett A., Shannon E. Martin and David A. Copeland. 2003. *The Function of Newspapers in Society: A Global Perspective*. Westport, CT: Greenwood Press.

Miller, Donald L. 2005. *D-Days in the Pacific*. New York: Simon and Schuster.

Miner, Earl. 1968. 'The Traditions and Forms of the Japanese Poetic Diary', *Pacific Coast Philology*, 3, 38–48.

Montgomerie, Deborah. 2000. 'GI Joe Down Under: American Infantrymen in New Zealand during World War II', *New Zealand Journal of History*, 34, 262–276.

———. 2005. *Love in Time of War: Letter Writing in the Second World War*. Auckland: Auckland University Press.

Moore, Aaron. 2006. 'The Peril of Self-Discipline: Chinese Nationalist, Japanese and American Servicemen Record the Rise and Fall of the Japanese Empire, 1937-1945', PhD Thesis, Princeton University.

Moore, John H. 1981. *Over-Sexed, Over-Paid and Over Here: Americans in Australia 1941-1945*. St. Lucia, Qld: University of Queensland Press.

Moremon, T. R. 2005. *The Jungle, the Japanese and the British Commonwealth Armies at War, 1941-45: Fighting Methods, Doctrine and Training for Jungle Warfare*. London: Routledge.

Morison, Samuel Eliot. 2001–2002. *History of United States Naval Operations in World War II. 1947-62*; reprinted. Urbana: University of Illinois Press.

Morley, Patrick. 2001. *'This is the American Forces Network': The Anglo-American Battle of the Air Waves in World War II*. Westport, CT: Praeger.

Morrison, James Horne Patricia, Pui Huen Lim and Chong Guan Kwa. 1998. *Oral History in Southeast Asia: Theory and Method*. Singapore: Institute of Southeast Asian Studies.

Murray, Williamson R. and Allan R. Millett (eds.). 1998. *Military Innovation in the Interwar Period*. New York: Cambridge University Press.

Myers, Ramon Hawley and Mark R. Peattie (eds.). 1984. *The Japanese Colonial Empire, 1895-1945*. Princeton, NJ: Princeton University Press.

'Naval Air Fighters', *Shin Seiki*, 8 (May 1943), 10.

Nelson, Hank. 1985. *P.O.W.: Prisoners of War: Australians under Nippon*. Sydney: ABC Enterprises.

New Guinea Force, Australian Army. 1944. *Censorship and Security in New Guinea: An Explanatory Booklet*, in the private papers of John Land, MSS 631, Mitchell Library, State Library of New South Wales.

New Zealand Government to Pacific War Council, London, 17 February 1942, Ministerie van Kolonian to London 1940-49, 2 October 1945, General State Archives, The Hague, Netherlands.

Nimmo, William F. 1988. *Behind a Curtain of Silence: Japanese in Soviet Custody, 1945-1956*. Westport, CT: Greenwood Press.

O'Brien, Kenneth Paul and Lynn Hudson Parsons (eds.). 1995. *The Home Front War: World War II and American Society*. Westport, CT: Greenwood Press.

Ohnuki-Tierney, Emiko. 2006. *Kamikaze Diaries: Reflections of Japanese Student Soldiers*. Chicago: University of Chicago Press.

Oliver, Robert T. 1987. *Public Speaking in the Reshaping of Britain*. Newark, NJ: University of Delaware Press.

Ōoka, Shōhei. 1996. *Taken Captive: A Japanese POW's Story*, trans. Wayne P. Lammers. New York: John Wiley and Sons.

Orvell, Miles. 2003. *American Photography*. New York: Oxford University Press.

Parshall, Jonathon B. and Anthony P. Tully. 2005. *Shattered Sword: The Untold Story of the Battle of Midway*. Washington, DC: Potomac Books.

Partner, Simon. 2004. *Toshie: A Story of Village Life in Twentieth-Century Japan*. Berkeley: University of California Press.

Petty, Bruce M. 2001. *Saipan: Oral Histories of the Pacific War*. New York: McFarland.

Polenberg, Richard. 1972. *War and Society: The United States, 1941-1945*. Philadelphia: Lippincott.

Popkin, Jeremy D. 2005. *History, Historians, and Autobiography*. Chicago: University of Chicago Press.

Porter, Roy. 1997. *Rewriting the Self: Histories from the Renaissance to the Present*. New York: Routledge.

Poyer, Lin, Laurence Marshall Carucci and Susanne Falgout. 2001. *The Typhoon of War: Micronesian Experiences of the Pacific War*. Honolulu: University of Hawaii Press.

Ramcharan, Robin. 2002. *Forging a Singaporean Statehood 1965-1995: The Contribution of Japan*. New York: Kluwer Law International.

Reporters of the Associated Press. 2007. *Breaking News: How the Associated Press Has Covered War, Peace, and Everything Else*. New York: Princeton Architectural Press.

Ritchie, Donald. 1955. *Where Are the Victors? A Novel of the Occupation of Japan*. Tokyo: Charles E. Tuttle Co.

Rivett, Rohan. 1946. *Behind Bamboo: An Inside Story*. London: Angus and Robertson.

Roberts, Richard. 1990. 'Text and Testimony in the Tribunal de Premiere Instance, Dakar, during the Early Twentieth Century', *The Journal of African History*, 31, 447–463.

Rohlen, Thomas P. 1999. *Teaching and Learning in Japan*. Cambridge: Cambridge University Press.

Rohrer, Scott R. 2006. 'From Demons to Dependents: American Japanese Social Relations during the Occupation', PhD Thesis, Northwestern University.

Rose, Lisle Abbott. 2007. *Power at Sea*. Columbia: University of Missouri Press.

Rosenberg, Emily S. 2003. *A Date Which Will Live: Pearl Harbor in American Memory*. Durham: Duke University Press.

Samuels, Richard J. 1994. *'Rich Nation, Strong Army': National Security and the Technological Transformation of Japan*. Ithaca: Cornell University Press.

Sasaki, Mako. 1996. 'Who Became Kamikaze Pilots and How Did They Feel towards Their Suicide Mission?' *The Concord Review*, 7, 175–209.

Schrijvers, Peter. 2002. *The GI War against Japan: American Soldiers in Asia and the Pacific during World War II*. New York: New York University Press.

Seeley, Christopher. 2000. *A History of Writing in Japan*. Honolulu: University of Hawaii Press.

Shaw, Henry I. 1992. First *Offensive: The Marine Campaign for Guadalcanal*. Darby: DIANE Publishing.

Sherry, Michael. 1987. *The Rise of American Air Power. The Creation of Armageddon*. New Haven: Yale University Press.

Shillony, Ben-Ami. 1981. *Politics and Culture in Wartime Japan*. Oxford: Oxford University Press.

Silberstein, Sandra. 2002. *War of Words: Language, Politics, and 9/11*. New York: Routledge.

Sitkoff, Harvard. 1969. 'The Detroit Race Riot of 1943', *Michigan History*, 53, 183–206.

Slim, William. 1956. *Defeat into Victory*. London: Cassell.

Sloan, Bill. 2006. *Brotherhood of Heroes: The Marines at Peleliu, 1944—The Bloodiest Battle of the Pacific War*. New York: Simon and Schuster.

Smith, Douglas Vaughn. 2006. *Carrier Battles: Command Decision in Harm's Way*. Annapolis, MD: Naval Institute Press.

Smith, Steven Trent. 2003. *Wolf Pack: The American Submarine Strategy That Helped Defeat Japan*. New York: Wiley.

Snyder, Louis Leo. 1976. *Varieties of Nationalism: A Comparative Study*. Orlando: Dryden Press.

Söderqvist, Thomas (ed.). 2007. *The History and Poetics of Scientific Biography*. Burlington, VT: Ashgate.

Speier, Hans. 1948. 'The Future of Psychological Warfare', *The Public Opinion Quarterly*, 12, 5–18.

Stanton, Doug. 2001. *In Harm's Way: The Sinking of the USS Indianapolis and the Extraordinary Story of Its Survivors*. New York: H. Holt.

Stinnett, Robert. 2000. *Day of Deceit: The Truth about FDR and Pearl Harbor*. New York: Free Press.

Storry, Richard and Ian Nish. 2002. *Collected Writings of Richard Storry*. London: Routledge.

Strauss, Ulrich. 2003. *The Anguish of Surrender: Japanese POWs of World War II*. Seattle: University of Washington Press.

Street, Brian V. (ed.). 1993. *Cross-Cultural Approaches to Literacy*. New York: Cambridge University Press.

Sun Yat-sen. 1953. *The Vital Problem of China*. Taipei: China Cultural Service.

Swindells, Julia (ed.). 2005. *The Uses of Autobiography*. Oxford: Taylor and Francis.

Taafe, Stephen R. 1998. *MacArthur's Jungle War: The 1944 New Guinea Campaign*. Lawrence: University of Kansas Press.

Takezawa, Yasuko I. 1995. *Breaking the Silence: Redress and Japanese American Ethnicity*. Ithaca: Cornell University Press.

Tamayama, Kazuo. 2005. *Railwaymen in the War: Tales by Japanese Railway Soldiers in Burma and Thailand, 1941-1947*. London: Palgrave McMillan.

Tan, Antonio S. 1981. *The Chinese in the Philippines during the Japanese Occupation, 1942-1945*. Manila: University of the Philippines Asian Center.

Tarling, Nicholas. 1998. *Nations and States in Southeast Asia*. Cambridge: Cambridge University Press.

———. 2001. *A Sudden Rampage: The Japanese Occupation of Southeast Asia, 1941-1945*. Honolulu: University of Hawaii Press.

Theobald, Robert Alfred. 1954. *The Final Secret of Pearl Harbor: The Washington Contribution to the Japanese Attack*. New York: Devin-Adair.

Thurman, M. J. and Christine Sherma. 2001. *War Crimes: Japan's World War II Atrocities*. Paducah, KY: Turner Pub.

Tiffen, Chris. 1997. 'Private Letters and the Fortunate Voyeur', *Voices*, 7, 7–14.

Toland, John. 1970. *The Rising Sun: The Decline and Fall of the Japanese Empire, 1936-1945*. New York: Random House.

Treat, John Whittier. 1995. *Writing Ground Zero: Japanese Literature and the Atomic Bomb*. Chicago: University of Chicago Press.

Trefalt, Beatrice. 2003. *Japanese Army Stragglers and Memories of the War in Japan, 1950-1975*. London: Routledge Curzon.

———. 'The Japanese Imperial Army and Fanaticism in the Second World War', in *Fanaticism and Conflict in the Modern Age*. Edited by Matthew Hughes and Gaynor Johnson. London: Frank Cass, 33–47.

Twomey, Christina. 2007. *Australia's Forgotten Prisoners: Civilians Interned by the Japanese in World Two*. Melbourne: Cambridge University Press.

USS Alabama War Diary, 1942–1944. 1944. Privately published.

USS Ticonderoga War Log, 8 May 1944 to 5 October 1945. 1946. Baton Rouge: Army and Navy Publishing Company.

Vansina, Jan. 1985. *Oral Tradition as History*. Madison: University of Wisconsin Press.

Vickers, Adrian. 2005. *History of Modern Indonesia*. Cambridge: Cambridge University Press.

Walker, J. Samuel. 2005. *Prompt and Utter Destruction: Truman and the Use of Atomic Bombs against Japan*. Chapel Hill: University of North Carolina Press.

Waterford, Van. 1994. *Prisoners of the Japanese in World War II*. Jefferson, NC: McFarland.

Weate, Mark. 1999. *Bill Newton VC: The Short Life of a RAAF Hero*. Loftus: Australian Military History Publications.

Wetzler, Peter Michael. 1998. *Hirohito and War: Imperial Tradition and Military Decision Making in Prewar Japan*. Honolulu: University of Hawaii Press.

White, Derrick. 2001. *Iwo Jima, 1945: Pacific Theatre*. London: Osprey Publishing.

White, Geoffrey M. 1988. *The Big Death: Solomon Islanders Remember World War II*. Suva: University of the South Pacific, Institute of Pacific Studies.

White, Geoffrey M. and Lamont Lindstrom. 1989. *The Pacific Theater: Island Representations of World War II*. Honolulu: University of Hawaii Press.

Winkler, Allan M. 2000. *Home Front U.S.A.: America during World War II*, 2nd edn. Wheeling, IL: Harlan Davidson.

Winter, Jay. 1995. *Sites of Memory, Sites of Mourning: The Great War in European Cultural History*. Cambridge: Cambridge University Press.

Winton, John. 1993. *ULTRA in the Pacific: How Breaking Japanese Codes and Ciphers Affected Naval Operations against Japan*. Annapolis: Naval Institute Press.

Wood, James. 1998. *The Forgotten Force: The Australian Military Contribution to the Occupation of Japan, 1945-1952*. St. Leonards, NSW: Allen and Unwin.

Woods, Timothy. 2002. *Strategy and Tactics: Infantry Warfare*. Osceola: Zenith Press.

Wright Jr., John M. 1988. *Captured on Corregidor: Diary of an American P.O.W. in World War II*. Jefferson, NC: McFarland.

Yamamoto, Taketoshi. 2001. *Nihonhei horyo wa nani wo shabetta ka*. Tokyo: Bungeishunju.

Zincke, Herbert (with Scott A. Mills). 2003. *Mitsui Madhouse: Memoir of a U.S. Army Air Corps POW in World War II*. Jefferson, NC: McFarland.

INDEX

ABDACOM. *See* American-British-Dutch-Australian Command (ABDACOM)
African-Americans, racial injustice faced by 178–179
Age (newspaper)
    Hiroshima attack 223–224
    Japanese attack on Sydney 185–186
Akagi (carrier) 33, 71, 80
Alabado, Corban K. 269–270
Allied bombing 188, 207, 215
Allied 'Grand Strategy' 49
Allies
    combat propaganda 131–132
    counter-offensive against Japan 119–122
    demand for unconditional surrender from Japan 238–240
    military intelligence 72
    perspective on *Kamikaze* 135–138
    reasons for defeat of 50
    treatment of Japanese POWs 196–197
American-British-Dutch-Australian Command (ABDACOM) 49
American casualty reporting system 43–44
American Journal of Nursing 143
AP. *See* Associated Press (AP)
ARCADIA Conference 49
Archer, Basil, wartime experiences of 249–250
Ariyama Sachi 177
Arizona (ship) 34
Asahi shinbun (newspaper) 16, 17
    Hiroshima attack 222–223
    Pearl Harbor attack 40–41
Associated Press (AP) 18
    Battle of Midway and 82–83
    formation of 81
'Atlantic Charter' 8, 153
atomic bombs 215, 227, 233, 257
    debates regarding use of 216–217
    scientists protest against possible use of 218–219
A51 Unit History Sheet 123
Australia 50, 55, 174, 261
    Americans in 182–184
    assistance for British in defence of Singapore 51
    Bondi Surf Bathers Life Saving Club 248–249
    Casualty Section in 252
    'Cowra Breakout' in 197
    Japanese attack on Sydney 185–186
    POWs war experience 268–269
    telegrams 43
    war diary in 97
Axis 19, 41, 134

Bataan Death March 199–200
Bataan (film) xxii
39th Battalion war diary 97–98
Battle of 'Bloody Buna' 115
Battle of Midway 70–71
    Associated Press (AP) and 81–83
    Fuchida's description of the *Akagi* attack 80–81
Battle of Milne Bay 95
Battle of Saipan 125–126
Battle of the Coral Sea 69, 70
    anti-aircraft fire in 79
    Lexington attack (Johnson) 78
    significance of (Curtin) 79–80
Battle of the Leyte Gulf 120, 133
Battles for the Beachheads 96
BCOF. *See* British Commonwealth Occupation Forces (BCOF)
'Beat Hitler first' 49, 119
Bennett, Gordon H. 61
    personal letters of 51–53
Bernstein, Barton 234
black market 165–166
'Bloody Buna', Battle of 115
Bondi Surf Bathers Life Saving Club 248–249
Bradley, James 142–143
Bradley, John 142
bravery awards systems 124
Britain
    Axis powers and 41
    Royal Navy 73
    United States association with 8, 41
British Commonwealth Occupation Forces (BCOF) 257
Burma–Thailand Railway
    Japanese perspective of 206
    life and death on 205–206
    POWs in 195, 196
Bushidō 196

FIGHTING WORDS

Fighting Words is an innovative and accessible new military history series, each title juxtaposing the voices of opposing combatants in a major historical conflict. Presented side by side are the testimonies of fighting men and women, the reportage of nations at war, and the immediate public responses of belligerent war leaders. Together, they offer strikingly different perspectives on the same events.

The extracts are short and snappy, complemented by brief introductions which set the scene. They vividly recreate the conflicts as they were experienced. At the same time, they open up new perspectives and challenge accepted assumptions. Readers will question the nature of primary sources, the motivations of the authors, the agendas that influence media reports and the omissions inherent in all of the sources. Ultimately, readers will be left to ponder the question, whose history is this?

Competing Voices from the Crusades
Andrew Holt and James Muldoon

Competing Voices from the Pacific War
Sean Brawley, Chris Dixon and Beatrice Trefalt

Competing Voices from Native America
Dewi Ioan Ball and Joy Porter

Competing Voices from the Russian Revolution
Michael C. Hickey

Competing Voices from World War II in Europe
Harold J. Goldberg

Competing Voices from the Mexican Revolution
Chris Frazer

Competing Voices from Revolutionary Cuba
John M. Kirk and Peter McKenna